Cambridge Studies in Social and Cultural Anthropology

Editors: Jack Goody, Stephen Gudeman, Michael Herzfeld, Jonathan Parry

72

The Bedouin of Cyrenaica

A list of books in this series will be found at the end of the volume.

THE BEDOUIN
OF CYRENAICA

Studies in personal and corporate power

EMRYS L. PETERS
Edited by Jack Goody and Emanuel Marx

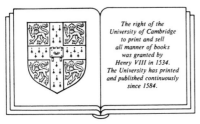

The right of the
University of Cambridge
to print and sell
all manner of books
was granted by
Henry VIII in 1534.
The University has printed
and published continuously
since 1584.

CAMBRIDGE UNIVERSITY PRESS
Cambridge
New York   Port Chester
Melbourne   Sydney

Published by the Press Syndicate of the University of Cambridge
The Pitt Building, Trumpington Street, Cambridge CB2 1RP
40 West 20th Street, New York, NY 10011, USA
10 Stamford Road, Oakleigh, Melbourne 3166, Australia

First published 1990

Printed in Great Britain by the Bath Press, Avon

British Library cataloguing in publication data
Peters, Emrys L., *d. 1987*
The Bedouin of Cyrenaica: studies in personal and
corporate power.
1. Libya. Cyrenaica. Bedouin. Cultural processes
I. Title II. Goody, Jack III. Marx, Emanuel
306'.0961'2

Library of Congress cataloguing in publication data
Peters, Emrys L., d. 1987.
The Bedouin of Cyrenaica: studies in personal and corporate power
/ Emrys L. Peters; edited by Jack Goody and Emanuel Marx.
    p.   cm.
Includes bibliographical references.
ISBN 0-521-38561-X
1. Bedouins—Libya—Barqah. 2. Barqah (Libya)—Social life and
customs. I. Goody, Jack. II. Marx, Emanuel. III. Title.
DT238.C8P47 1990
961.2—dc20 89-48036 CIP

ISBN 0 521 38561

*The author would have dedicated
the book to*

Stella

who shared so much in this work.

Contents

		page
List of illustrations		viii
Foreword by Jack Goody		ix
Preface		xii
Introduction by Emanuel Marx		1
1	The Sanusi order and the Bedouin	10
2	The Bedouin way of life	29
3	The tied and the free	40
4	Aspects of the feud	59
5	Proliferation of segments	84
6	The power of shaikhs	112
7	Debt relationships	138
8	Family and marriage	188
9	Bridewealth	214
10	The status of women	243
	Notes	278
	Bibliography	298
	Index	307

Illustrations

Plates (*between pages 150 and 151*)

1 A young freeborn Bedouin.
2 Women setting up a tent.
3 The colourful interior of a winter tent.
4 A polygynous household moving to a new camp site.
5 A bride is taken to the nuptial tent. She is hidden beneath the canopy.
6 The small daughter of a shaikh.
7 Measuring out the grain.
8 A married woman returning from the well.
9 Women spinning wool.
10 A holy man from one of the client tribes.
11 An old shaikh meditating on a verse from the Koran, painted on a board.
12 A legal case is being heard.
13 Shaikhs arrive at a camp for a peace meeting.
14 Portrait of the author, taken at the time of his fieldwork.

The photographs were taken by Stella and Emrys Peters.

Map
Cyrenaica in the 1950s.   *page* 12

Foreword

I met Emrys Peters in Cambridge when I returned there in 1946 and began to read anthropology. At that time Evans-Pritchard came across each week from Oxford where he was about to take up the chair in Social Anthropology previously held by Radcliffe-Brown. His lectures were a breath of fresh air, standing out head and shoulders above anything else on offer in the field. But quite apart from their intellectual qualities, his analyses of the internal and external struggles of the Nuer of the Sudan and the Sanusi of Libya were of deep interest to those of us who had spent much of our adult lives engaged in war or war-related activities. And this was especially true of those who had passed part of that time in North Africa.

Like myself, Peters was among the latter, having served in the desert in the Royal Air Force. His previous interest in human geography, which he had studied at Aberystwyth under Daryll Forde, at this time the very enterprising director of the International African Institute, combined with his wartime experiences gave him a deep interest in the Bedouin, which he shared with the rest of us. Indeed, then and later, that voice with the pronounced Welsh lilt engaged us in the evening hours with many a brilliantly recounted tale not only of Libya and the Near East, but of life in the R.A.F. and, more deeply felt, in the depression of the early thirties in the coalfields.

With this background, it was inevitable that, having finished his degree, he took the path, like many others including his close friend Godfrey Lienhardt, to join Evans-Pritchard in Oxford in order to undertake research among the Bedouin of Cyrenaica in the newly independent kingdom of Libya. I myself lost touch for awhile as I had taken up work of a different kind. But on returning to academia and to anthropology, I met him again in Cambridge in 1951 where he was a temporary lecturer in the department that had recently come under the headship of Meyer Fortes.

During his year there he was a great stimulus as a teacher but also in many a lengthy discussion about the feud, the lineage and kindred topics, each carefully and constructively dissected. I gained much from our friendship and it was sad for me when, in 1952, he went to the Department of Social Anthropology and Sociology recently set up by Max Gluckman at Manchester.

That city became his home from then on, and he devoted his energies to teaching as well as to academic life, not only in the University but on the national level in committees of the Social Science Research Council, the University Grants Commission as well as of professional bodies. In 1968 he followed Gluckman as Head of Department.

Emrys Peters retired from the chair in 1984, hoping to complete the writing up and publication of more of the extensive research he had carried out in Libya and in the Lebanon. His death in 1987 was both a personal loss and an academic one. He had presented his thesis in 1951 and some of us had hoped he would publish at that time. Emrys was of a different mind. He spent the next thirty years rethinking the material, and the result was a remarkable series of articles, some published, others not, which are presented in the present volume.

He did not get the opportunity to do further fieldwork among the Bedouin of Cyrenaica after 1950, but he continued to carry out research in Tripolitania as well as in the Lebanon for the rest of his life, and as a result his understanding of the Bedouin was enriched by the comparative material he brought to bear. This comparative work is represented in the chapter on the status of women, which first appeared in 1978, and he pursued the project in other papers that we have listed in his bibliography. But for his illness he would undoubtedly have gone on to expand this aspect of his work for he was totally dedicated to understanding the Arab communities of the Mediterranean world within a general framework of social theory. It was the intensity of this commitment, combined with the humour with which he would put up with new or difficult situations, that made this Welshman from Merthyr Tydfil so fine a fieldworker and so thorough an ethnographer.

For some years I had been hoping to include his essays in this present series. While the collection would obviously have been greatly improved had he been able to edit the material himself, I am pleased that we have been able to get together a volume of his work not simply as an act of homage but because of its high quality both theoretically and in terms of a sympathetic understanding of the Arab peoples. We decided to leave the published papers as they appeared in print since they have already made their mark on regional and theoretical studies and have been quoted extensively.

Three unpublished papers and one chapter of his thesis are included, and we are grateful to Ernest Gellner for working on the manuscript of chapter 1 on the Sanusi, and to Paul Baxter for doing the same with chapter 5 on the shaikhs. The major section on Bedouin ecology came from his thesis and has been edited by Emanuel Marx, who is largely responsible for getting the book together. But above all we have received great help and encouragement from Stella Peters, who shared in the fieldwork in Cyrenaica and herself produced a fascinating thesis on the Bedouin *bait* or tent (Oxford 1951). In addition I am sure the author would have wanted to thank profoundly the members of the communities with whom he worked.

Jack Goody

Preface

My field work among the Bedouin of Cyrenaica consisted of two periods. My first year's work in 1948 was made possible by a Studentship awarded me by the Emslie Horniman Anthropological Fund Trustees. In October 1949 I returned to Cyrenaica, and remained there until mid-December 1950. This second period of work was financed by the Treasury Committee for Studentships in Foreign Languages and Cultures. To the trustees of the Horniman Fund and the Treasury Committee I wish to make grateful acknowledgement.

During these two periods in Cyrenaica, I lived for two years among the Bedouin, and spent my time mainly among the Sdaidi of the 'Awaqir, the Jululat of the Zuwayya, the Shamakh of the Magharba, the Tamiya section of the Bara'asa and the Baraghla section of the Darsa tribes. I visited other sections of these tribes, but stayed with them for very short periods, and of the tribes I resided with for any length of time, my longest residence was with the Magharba and the Bara'asa. Of the semi-sedentary plateau tribes, I lived only among the Darsa' and my stay with them lasted only two months, but this was at the end of my second tour and was more profitable than if I had visited them earlier. I am however, aware that two months is a short period and have confined my remarks about the Darsa' to general statements. My work, in short, was confined almost exclusively to the more southern and mobile sections of the tribes.

During the first three weeks of field work in 1948, I was fortunate in having the services of Muhammad Kadiki, then an official of the British Military Administration, as an interpreter. We travelled together from camp to camp for these weeks, and after that I went to live with the 'Amarna folk of the 'Awaqir tribe, and spent three uninterrupted months with them learning their language.

Emrys Peters, Oxford

Introduction

Emanuel Marx

In his doctoral thesis Emrys Peters (1951) studied the Bedouin of Cyrenaica on the eve of national independence under Sanusi rule. His teacher, Sir E. E. Evans-Pritchard, had two years earlier published *The Sanusi of Cyrenaica* (1949), a historical account of the political ascent of the Sanusi sect, that relied mainly on books and documents. As an officer of the Military Administration of Cyrenaica, Evans-Pritchard had, of course, been in touch with the Bedouin population but, as he himself admitted, 'could not conduct any serious anthropological research' among them (Evans-Pritchard 1973: 21). His long-standing intention to study the Bedouin population of Cyrenaica was never to be realised. This task devolved on his student. Peters was well aware of the message of *The Sanusi of Cyrenaica*, that the so-called 'simple' societies, just like Western ones, are shaped by powerful historical forces and must therefore be studied in the widest political and economic context. Yet in his thesis the contextual analysis is incidental to the detailed description of Bedouin society. The thesis does not deal explicitly with the impact of Italian occupation and colonisation, the relations between the Bedouin and the British military administration, the growing influence of the Sanusi religious brotherhood which was just one year later to lead the new state of Libya, or with the market forces that were affecting pastoralism. It was devoted to another, though related, theoretical issue. It challenged the view that the Bedouin were a tribal society, an acephalous segmentary political system. Evans-Pritchard himself, of course, had given credence to this essentially non-contextual view of society in *The Nuer* (1940) and elsewhere and, quite inconsistently, adhered to it in his discussion of the Libyan Bedouin. In the Sanusi book he devoted just one chapter to the Bedouin (1949: chapter 2), in which he treated them as a distinct tribal population that was hardly affected by the policies and activities of its alien rulers, and could perhaps generate sufficient political power to resist the Italian rulers but not enough to run its own affairs. He believed that the Bedouin were incapable of establishing an orderly and regular government of their own, or that they could really be ruled by the Italian colonial administration. His position is subsumed in the statement that in this Bedouin society 'the fundamental principle of tribal structure is opposition between its segments, and in such segmentary systems there is no state and no government as we understand these institutions . . . [a chief's] social position is unformalized and . . . he must in no sense be regarded as a ruler or administrator' (1949: 59).

Peters argued for an altogether more complex picture of Bedouin society. He showed that Bedouin establish networks of relationships extending far beyond their corporate group and tribe, in order to safeguard their livelihood; that corporate groups congregate around leaders, who forge a variety of political links and alliances and generate a great deal of power; that membership of groups, though initially conferred as a birthright, is really voluntary and is retained as long as it serves members' interests, and therefore cannot derive from kinship ties; and that feuding between Bedouin groups is about the control of resources and cannot be explained by a mechanical model of fission and fusion. The concept of a segmentary political system could only develop in a functionalist paradigm, which viewed societies as homogeneous and stable closed systems almost impervious to external influences. For this reason the attack on the notion that the Bedouin were a segmentary society was eventually to lead Peters to question the validity of the functionalist paradigm and, in this roundabout manner, finally to return to Evans-Pritchard's book. He was no longer concerned with its treatment of Bedouin society, but rather with its major theme, the historical analysis of the Sanusi. While accepting his teacher's general approach, Peters reached independent conclusions which eventually led him to revise Evans-Pritchard's analysis of the Sanusi as the moral guides of the Bedouin and as mediators between their warring factions. Instead, he gave analytical preference to their control of long-distance trade which brought them wealth and influence over the Bedouin. Problems such as these engaged Peters' attention for many years, so that Libya remained his major research area through all that country's vicissitudes.

For more than thirty years Peters worked in and wrote about Libya, always concentrating on the Bedouin pastoralists and cultivators. During those years, he developed a contextualised analysis of the society. This volume includes most of the mature work of Emrys Peters on the Bedouin of Cyrenaica. Nearly all the themes can be traced back to his Oxford D. Phil. thesis. For the completion of the thesis marked the beginning of his lifelong efforts to understand human behaviour through his intimate knowledge of the Bedouin. He was dissatisfied with the theoretical conception underlying his analysis of the Cyrenaican Bedouin. His articles became a battleground on which he tried first to revise Evans-Pritchard's views on the Bedouin and then to overcome his own functionalist training. The latter was a continuous struggle, which never ended in a decisive victory. In this sense, he was a good representative of his generation. There were a number of social anthropologists who discussed the relevance of the functionalist paradigm for their day and age. Many of them realised that functionalism was outmoded; the literature abounds with statements to that effect. Thus Boissevain (1973: xi–xii) argues that 'What is badly needed is a real alternative to structural-functionalism. This last has been discredited, but it has not yet been displaced' (or see Kuper 1983: chapter 9). But many scholars continued to write in the functionalist manner, perhaps because they knew of no alternatives. Other scholars, in Britain and elsewhere, took up new modes of analysis, such as neo-Marxism, structuralism, symbolic interaction and so forth, thus enlarging the scope of the subject and adding to our understanding of human behaviour. One ought to add, though, that much of the work done in these modes of analysis kept well within the functionalist paradigm.

Some members of the circle that had formed around the Rhodes-Livingstone Institute in Livingstone (Zambia) and the Department of Social Anthropology in Manchester – sometimes referred to as the 'Manchester school' – sought to break out of the closed functionalist paradigm. Thus the Wilsons tried to understand conflict and change (Wilson and Wilson 1945), but failed because they looked at social process through functionalist eyes. And Gluckman (1958) attempted to show that the Zulu 'tribe' was part of South African society, by examining a situation in which both tribesmen and outsiders participated. While he succeeded in bringing the wider social context into the discussion of local affairs, he did not really escape from a functionalist perspective; he only enlarged the scope of the analysis from local community to state. These efforts were only partially successful because of the absence of an alternative analytical framework. But their cumulative effect was to point the way to new methods of fieldwork and analysis. The 'extended case' (Gluckman 1967) and 'situational analysis' (Van Velsen 1967) were harbingers of things to come. Peters was a senior member of the Manchester school and influenced by the work done in Central Africa. He knew the shortcomings of the functionalist paradigm and, like many others, he sought to revise it. For him, however, this became a major and long-term concern, second only to his unceasing efforts to make good theory out of his Bedouin material.

Peters set high standards for himself. He wanted theory to flow out of his field data, to explain the variance in his material, and to firmly marry data and their interpretation. So he set about rewriting his thesis, chapter by chapter, problem by problem and to preparing it for publication in a series of papers. These he planned to weld into a monograph on power relations among the Bedouin. He therefore constantly consulted the thesis and was loath to give students access to it. Progress was very slow, perhaps because he was a perfectionist: he needed time to move toward a progressively intricate interpretation of data. He would take up a problem, such as 'what are the genealogies for?' (as in chapter 5), or 'why do Bedouin think of killings as part of a series?' (chapter 4). When considering the full range of details, he would conclude that he was dealing with a series of interrelated problems and, accordingly, develop a complex and contextualised sociological model. The reader was allowed to follow the stages of growth of this model. He became a spectator who watched Peters battle with his problem, steadily gaining ground and finally obtaining hard-won new insights. He worked on persistently until, in the end, he had completely rethought and worked out most of the ideas in his thesis. Part of this work was published during his lifetime, and as each chapter appeared it was recognised as a major advance. Such are chapters 3, 4, 5, 8, 9 and 10 of the present volume. These papers address sociological problems, and provide ethnographic data only to the extent needed to prove his argument. Going by these papers only, the reader could never be aware of the quality and quantity of information Peters gathered in his long years of fieldwork.

Peters was an ethnographers' ethnographer. He had at his fingertips the countless details that go into the making of a paper. He could instantly recall a situation that happened perhaps twenty or thirty years earlier, in order to support an argument or to point out the weak points in an opponent's thesis. Many of these incidents were never used in his writings. The four chapters that are here published for the first time give some indication of the rich information that Peters collected and which, as his colleagues and students well knew, he had readily available. Two of these chapters (1 and 2) set out the political and ecological background of the Bedouin of Cyrenaica. The two others deal at length with two problems that occupied a central place in Peters' thinking: the nature of power, and the establishment and maintenance of relationships. The former is specifically discussed in the chapter on the Bedouin shaikh (chapter 6); the latter is illustrated by the chapter on debt relationships among the Bedouin (chapter 7). Like most of his other work, these essays developed over many years. They were, if possible, written at an even more leisurely pace. They were the result of long periods of reflection, followed by spurts of rapid and intensive writing. They show the breadth of Peters' scholarship, the intimate acquaintance with the ethnography and, to boot, many instances of his sharp wit. They too continue the reinterpretation of the Bedouin material, and seek to theorise it. While they are longer and more discursive than his earlier work, they are no less thoughtful and convincing.

Although he did several years of fieldwork in Lebanon, Peters wrote only two major articles that were specifically concerned with Lebanese society. He used some of the Lebanese material in comparative studies (as in chapter 10) or to underscore theoretical points in articles dealing chiefly with the Bedouin of Cyrenaica. The Lebanese material was thus often subordinated to his major regional and theoretical interests. The double focus on Libyan ethnography and on a small number of theoretical themes gave his professional career and his writing a consistency and purpose that, in retrospect, almost looks like a life plan.

His numerous graduate students derived the full benefit of this deep immersion in a clearly demarcated set of problems and in one culture region. They were trained to study situations within their social context, to examine the intricacies of power relations, to view ritual as an aspect of all social intercourse, to look primarily at the praxis of social life and to view ideologies, norms and values as emerging out of it. In short, they were given the benefit of Peters' thinking and at the same time encouraged to pursue their own line of interest. Their writings are no longer concerned with the paradigmatic issues that exercised his mind; they explore a variety of sociological problems, often without realising what effort was required to pave the way for them. Thus Abner Cohen begins his study of *Arab Border-Villages in Israel* by examining the impact on local society of changes in the national economy and of the shift from indirect absolute rule by a military government to direct administration by numerous agencies of the state (1965: 2). This allows him to explain the revival of the patronymic descent group (*hamula*) as a response to new conditions, and not as a reversion to tradition. Another student notes that Peters inspired him to view nomadism among the Hima of Uganda as an expression of conflict between the nomads and their rulers, and not as a purely ecological adaptation (Elam 1979: 157). Again, when I began to analyse my material on the Bedouin of the Negev, the first point Peters bade me to keep in mind was that these people were 'authentic Bedouin' pastoralists and cultivators largely because economic alternatives were closed to them by a restrictive military government (Marx 1967). From that point onward I treated the Bedouin as members of the Israeli polity and economy. Consequently the structure of households, corporate groups, chiefship and the tribe, all began to make sociological sense. Even the annual migratory cycle of the pastoralists turned out to be affected as much by patterns of political control and of land ownership as by the pastures available at various seasons.

In place of functionalism, Peters provides a preview of a new, as yet incomplete, paradigm. He deals at length with three of its elements: relationships, and the techniques for establishing and maintaining them (chapter 7); the accumulation of resources and their transformation into power (chapter 6); and the nature of political organisation (chapters 4 and 5). Another element that he greatly emphasised was situations, and their largely negotiated order, though he never made a detailed theoretical statement about them.

All his life Peters sought to understand power. It became a central interest, pervading all his work. In his thinking, power results from the efforts made by individuals and groups to control their social environment and to improve their lives. These efforts are made continuously and thus are embedded in all human interaction. People are not so much concerned with gaining an advantage over an opponent, as with obtaining the best possible terms of interaction, while preserving their relationships and conserving their resources. Peters was aware that the desire for power is the mainspring of some of the noblest actions of human beings, but that it also inspires aggressive and manipulative behaviour.

As power is an integral part of every social relationship, it cannot be treated without taking account of other components of the relationship, such as the social environment in which it occurs and the relevant interests, ideologies and values of the participants. It is not simply the capacity to impose one's will on others, even against resistance, as Weber would have us believe. For Peters, power is always tempered by the need for social approval. A person's power thus depends on the support he or she can marshall, and that has to be built up carefully over a long period. In Peters' scheme there are no powerless people; every person has potential power in relation to his partners in interaction. And only in interaction can that power be realised. A person's power depends on his ability and willingness to use the resources available to him and is always relative to the power of the other participants in interaction. They may support him and augment his power, but they may also withhold their support or oppose him. The more resources they range against him, the weaker he becomes. Resources, of course, are used in a variety of situations and in different combinations. Therefore, they do not have a stable value; they obtain and change value in interaction. It follows that resources such as money, the command of men, or physical prowess have no intrinsic value. While they may be valuable in some situations, they may have little value in others or may even cause harm. Under the colonial regime, for instance, men who were thought to possess such resources were liable to be persecuted. In certain conditions, traits that are generally considered undesirable may have their uses. One only has to think of the widow and her daughter who moved from one camp to the next and were fed by their hosts *because* they were so poor (p. 146).

The Libyans of Peters' times shunned violence. They had had more than enough of it during the Italian occupation; a generation of men had been killed or exiled. Now the new generation, and those who remained of the older one, hoped to establish a peaceful existence, and employed wealth and manipulative skills, rather than violence, to achieve their ends. Thus they unwittingly helped Peters to develop a more than usually complex view about the nature of power.

Peters' Bedouin material led him to argue that some relationships, especially among kin, may be very strong and enduring, and yet fraught with conflict. The father-son relationship is a good case in point (see chapter 8): until his marriage a son is utterly dependent on his father, who controls the major means of production, land and herds, with the full support of the agnatic corporation. The father tries to delay the handing over of land and herds, in order to enjoy the fruits of the son's labour for as long as he can. No wonder that a son may long for his father's death which would set him free. Eventually the agnates urge him to allow the son to marry and thus attain manhood and join the ranks of fighters. At that point, the father is obliged not only to arrange and finance the son's wedding, but also to hand over to him land and herds. But while he tries to slow down the son's progress toward economic independence, the father seeks to promote the son's position in society. He does so not only because he wants to be proud of him, but also because as a respected member of the community the son comes under the stricter scrutiny of his fellows, who will see to it that he fulfils his social obligations. The father of such a son can expect to be treated well in his old age.

Evidently, Peters does not attach much importance to kinship as such. He views the father-son relationship as a field of complex and changing forces, in which both are caught up, much as he would treat any other intimate and multiplex relationship. But people are never held so tightly by their ties as to lose their freedom of manoeuvre. If they are clever enough to see where their advantage lies and to use their resources efficiently, they may gradually alter their position. Peters thus views society as structured, in response to relatively stable ecological and political conditions. Even in this relatively rigid framework an enterprising person can achieve a great deal, to the point of subjecting and bending the social environment to his will.

This heroic view of men as political entrepreneurs is very pronounced in the analysis of chiefship (chapter 6). Chiefs provide a core around which people congregate. They also articulate the political frameworks by their and their adherents' movements and by the manipulation of their often far-flung networks of relationships. Marriage links play a major role in these operations, and chiefs marry more wives than most other people, partly in order to extend the span of their networks of relationships. Chiefs, then, are 'big men', in the sense employed in recent anthropological studies of New Guinea Highland peoples (for instance, A. Strathern 1971). But Peters extends this view to all Bedouin men; everyone seeks to enhance his position in society and to become a chief, if only of a camp. A society where all men strive and compete for power and position develops a close-knit hierarchical network of leaders. In ordinary daily life these men alternately collaborate and compete with one another and frequently change allegiances. But once they perceive a compelling joint interest or, as was the case under Italian colonial rule, a challenge to their very existence, the leadership is capable of uniting and becoming a nucleus around which men may readily rally, and which may mount concerted activities for long periods. Such a viewpoint helps towards a better understanding of how a 'segmented' and presumably divided society was capable of waging a long and determined battle against the Italian colonial regime.

Finally, a few editorial notes. One of Emrys Peters' perennial theoretical interests was the interplay between corporate and individual power. We felt that by arranging the chapters in a way that would give these themes salience, the book would become a monograph and not simply a collection of articles. The chapters do not therefore follow a chronological order, and this arrangement somewhat obscures the development of Peters' views over the years.

Six out of the ten chapters have been previously published; they are widely known and used by social anthropologists and are reprinted with only minor revisions. The four previously unpublished items take up nearly half the book. They consist of an analysis of the Sanusi order and its relations with the Bedouin of Cyrenaica (chapter 1); sections from the first chapter of Peters' D. Phil. thesis dealing with the daily life of the Bedouin, with land and water, herding and cultivation, the annual round of migration and pilgrimage (chapter 2); the geographical background is treated only in passing, because it has been examined in great detail by Johnson (1973) and Behnke (1980), both of whom put Peters' work to good account; and analysis of the power of shaikhs (chapter 6); and a discussion of debt and other relationships (chapter 7). These chapters required a certain amount of editorial work: the author's handwritten notes and corrections in the manuscripts were incorporated in the text; some passages were edited, and a few were deleted in order to avoid repetition; and references, as well as transliterations from Arabic, completed and checked. Our aim has been to follow Peters' text and to retain the flavour of his vivid style. Those chapters which have previously appeared include the following:

Chapter 3 is from 'The Tied and the Free: An Account of a Type of Patron-Client Relationship Among the Bedouin Pastoralists of Cyrenaica.' In *Contributions to Mediterranean Sociology: Mediterranean Rural Communities and Social Change*, J.G. Peristiany, ed., Paris: Mouton, 1968, pp. 167–88.

Chapter 4 is from 'Some Structural Aspects of the Feud Among the Camel-Herding Bedouin of Cyrenaica.' *Africa* (Journal of the International African Institute) 37 (3), July 1967: 261–82.

Chapter 5 is from 'The Proliferation of Segments in the Lineage of the Bedouin in Cyrenaica.' *Journal of the Royal Anthropological Institute* 90 (1), 1960: 29–53. (Reproduced by permission of the Royal Anthropological Institute of Great Britain and Ireland.)

Chapter 8 is from 'Aspects of the Family Among the Bedouin of Cyrenaica.' In *Comparative Family Systems*, M.F. Nimkoff ed., Boston: Houghton Mifflin Company, 1965, pp. 121–46.

Chapter 9 is from 'Aspects of Bridewealth Among the Bedouin of Cyrenaica.' In *The Meaning of Marriage Payments*, J.L. Comaroff ed., London; Academic Press, 1980, pp. 125–60. Copyright © 1980 by Academic Press Limited.

Chapter 10 is from 'The Status of Women in Four Middle East Communities.' In *Women in the Muslim World.* L. Beck and N. Keddie, eds., Cambridge, Massachusetts: Harvard University Press, 1978, pp. 311–50. Copyright © 1978 by the President and Fellows of Harvard College.

Acknowledgments

Jack Goody and I thank Paul Baxter and Ernest Gellner for their advice and editorial assistance. We thank Wendy Guise for her efficient processing of the book, and Susan van de Ven for her sensitive editing. I gratefully acknowledge the comments of Paul Baxter, Dale Eickelman, Jack Goody, Bruce Kapferer, Stella and Brian Peters, Frank Stewart, and Richard Werbner on various drafts of the Introduction.

1

The Sanusi order and the Bedouin

'One of the few genuinely historical books written by an anthropologist *de carrière* is my own book *The Sanusi of Cyrenaica*' (Evans-Pritchard 1962: 184).[1] The purpose here is to examine the way in which one of our foremost social anthropologists, whose initial training, at Oxford, was as historian, attempted to write the developmental history of the transformation of a religious fraternity into a political organisation. Throughout the book a consistent argument is pursued which, as I understand it, is woven around nine main issues. In this chapter, these will be summarised; then the theoretical premises on which the argument rests will be discussed critically, and an alternative view will be put forward.

First, when the founder of the Sanusi Order, Sayyid Muhammad ibn 'Ali as-Sanusi (hereafter referred to as the Grand Sanusi, a title often given him), went to reside on the plateau area of Cyrenaica, near the classical site of Cyrene, driven there by the ill winds of circumstance, he found there already existed a tradition of veneration for holy men. The Marabtin bi'l-Baraka (clients with divine blessing), who, until now, live in small groups among the tribes, had long lived in the country. The Grand Sanusi and his disciples were, like them, Sunni Muslims, of Arabic speech, grown accustomed to Bedouin ways during their extensive travels across the deserts of North Africa,[2] and accredited with saintliness of sorts, by virtue of their descent from the Prophet (Evans-Pritchard 1944), their teachings and their habits. The concern of the Grand Sanusi was with the regeneration of the spirit, and to achieve this he advocated a return to primitive Islam, the society of the Prophet, and to his teachings, divested of the excrescences which had grown around them over the centuries. With these aims in mind, he forbade alcohol and snuff, decried smoking, and excluded music, dancing and singing.[3] He exhorted his followers to work hard at their agricultural tasks, and set an example in the erstwhile inhospitable and virtually uninhabited oasis of Jaghbub, which he transformed into a thriving community.[4] Quietist in behaviour, and preaching a religion which made few demands on its adherents, the Sanusiya made such rapid progress among the Bedouin, that, even within the lifetime of the Grand Sanusi, most, if not all, of the Cyrenaican Bedouin had been won over. Cultural familiarity, that is to say, was a factor of critical importance in determining the ease of entry of the Sanusi Order into a country whose people were to experience a transformation in some parts of their daily lives and, ultimately, to become embroiled in conflict with several major European powers (Evans-Pritchard 1949: 64–70).

As far as is known, there was no external factor, such as an increase or decrease in population, nor expansion or contraction of natural resources, to make 1843, the founding date of the first lodge in Cyrenaica (p. 14), a moment of ripeness for the introduction and elaboration of a Sufi order in Cyrenaica. What happened was that the Grand Sanusi incurred the hostility of the more orthodox religious authorities in the Hijaz and Egypt (p. 13), although he always protested that he was not an 'innovator', and with a mind to return to his native land of Algeria, he left Hijaz and reached Gabes in Tunisia, where the news of the French colonisation in Algeria led him to retrace his steps to Cyrenaica. He was now about fifty years of age. Some twenty years earlier he had left Algeria for Fez, in Morocco, and during the next twenty years he literally travelled the entire length of North Africa twice in both directions, using different routes on each occasion, proceeding to Mecca twice, south to the Yemen, north to Jordan, visiting several desert oases on his travels, making many local journeys in all these countries, but still finding the time to preach, found lodges, direct activities in some of them, write long letters, and author nine books (p. 19). Although local tradition has it that the Grand Sanusi was greatly enamoured of al-Baida, his sojourn there lasted only about three years. In 1846, footloose as ever, he set out again for Mecca. He stayed in the Hijaz for seven years, founded two lodges there, and returned to Cyrenaica in 1853. This time he took up residence in al-Azziyat (he had sent instructions for a lodge to be built there, before his return). He left in 1856 (before the completion of the lodge) for Jaghbub, the desert oasis he was to make into a seat of learning during the last three years of his life. His cultural familiarity to the Bedouin was, no doubt, specifically important; his cultural anchorage in Islam, and the familiarity with the geography of thousands of miles of its domain were, in a more general sense, assets of much greater importance. The vast 'theocratic empire' of the Sanusiya thus began with the historical accident of a particular individual deciding to build a few religious lodges in a backward and sparsely populated country.

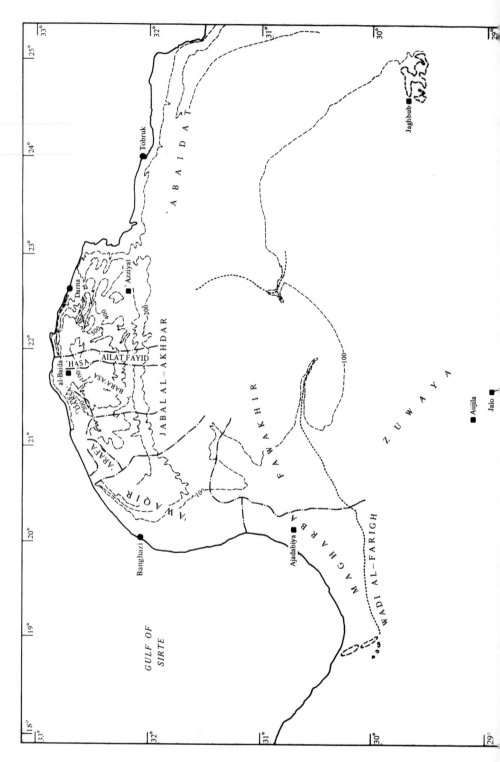

Map 1. Cyrenaica in the 1950s.

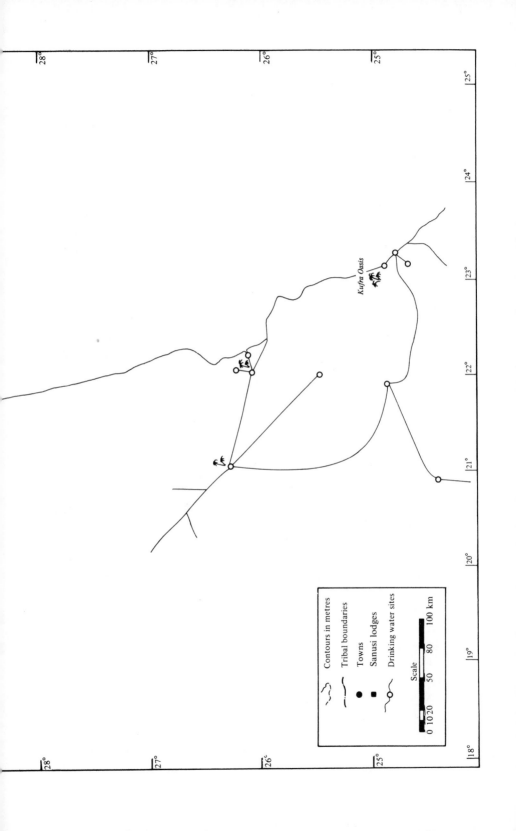

Kufra Oasis

Contours in metres
Tribal boundaries
Towns
Sanusi lodges
Drinking water sites

Scale

0 10 20   50   80   100 km

Second, although the Grand Sanusi and his disciples were culturally familiar to the people of Cyrenaica, they were not of Bedouin stock. Virtually all of them were foreigners, mainly from Algeria and Morocco (p. 18). Indeed, their claim to holiness was founded largely on this fact in the minds of the Bedouin, although for them their putative descent from the Prophet constituted the complete proof of their status. As foreigners, they could not be the owners of natural resources, but the religious services they were able to dispense gave them access to these, whether they were Sanusi or other sorts of holy men (p. 17); but the Sanusi could claim and were given these in greater measure, commensurate with their amplitude of *baraka*. The Sanusiya – that is, the family and the disciples – stood external to Bedouin society in an ethnic, jural and ritual sense, if not exclusively so in any of the three senses.

Evans-Pritchard insists on the considerable significance of their geographical externality as well. The Grand Sanusi established the first of his Cyrenaican lodges – inappropriately referred to as the Mother, Lodge by some writers, Evans-Pritchard included (p. 14) – on the high plateau among the tribes, or, more precisely, at a point where the territories of three important tribes converge. Shortly afterwards he moved his seat to al-Azziyat, but this was still in tribal territory. His third and last move was to Jaghbub oasis, well away from any of the tribal territories, about 170 miles as the crow flies from Tobruk, and well into the Sahara proper. Before he died, he had won over the Zuwaya tribe who have for long held the keys to the eastern part of the Sahara, as all the early travellers in the area testify. Their trading centre was, and still is, Kufra, from whence they travelled south into Chad, Wadai and Darfur, and to Kano in the other direction, and northwards to the coast through Aujila and Jalo. Kufra oasis is about 500 miles, as the crow flies, from Ajadabiya, the northern terminus of the Zuwaya traders. This inland base was of enough importance for him to establish a lodge there. His son and successor, Sayyid Muhammad al-Mahdi, moved the headquarters of the Order there in 1895, and four years later he moved it again, to Qiru in 1899 (p. 21). The third head of the Order, Sayyid Ahmad al-Sharif, under French pressure in northern Chad, moved the headquarters back to Kufra (p. 27).

Evans-Pritchard, like several other writers, gives as reasons for moving the headquarters, the desire for solitude on the part of the first two heads, their wish to keep away from the Turks and, in the case of the move to Kufra, to give the order a more central location. In his analysis, however, the prime significance was that 'The missionary organisation, the Sanusiya Order, was separate from the tribal system [of Cyrenaica] and, by centring it in the distant oasis of Jaghbub the Grand Sanusi prevented it from becoming identified with any one tribe or section of the country, as it might have become had it been centred in Cyrenaica proper' (p. 18). Additionally, 'This difficulty [the rivalries between tribes, and among their sections] was overcome by transferring the centre of the Order to desert oases, where it could not become identified with any particular tribe . . .' (p. 70). These are clear enough statements, and the same point is reiterated throughout the book. Perhaps the Grand Sanusi did yearn for the quiet life of contemplation, and perhaps his successor did seek solitude – although there is no evidence for the personal motives of either, save the guesses of writers. If these were their aims they certainly achieved them. The Sanusi are said to have despised the Turks (as well as the English, and Europeans in general), rather for what they regarded as dissolute living than for anything else. It is true that the Turks, like European powers, looked upon the prospering Order with hostile suspicion, and the Sanusi found them irritating, particularly when they courted their favour for political reasons around the turn of the century. While granting this, Evans-Pritchard nevertheless considers the southward moves of the headquarters as providing the Order with its essential externality.

Third, this dual externality of ethnic origin and territorial separation meant that the Order could now penetrate the tribes of Cyrenaica, freed of the disability of preferential attachment to any one of them. By the end of the nineteenth century, Sanusi lodges had been spread among all the nine tribes of the country. The distribution was not haphazard. There was order about it, and this order was consistent – indeed congruent – with the Bedouin social order. A quotation on this important matter is needed: 'This they [the Sanusi] were able to do [hold their Order together] by coordinating the lodges of the Order to the tribal structure' (Evans-Pritchard 1949: 11. See also pp. 69, 71, 78, 83, 84, 89, 91, 99, 166 and 228). Lest it should be thought that this sentence, taken in isolation, exaggerates the position, it must be clearly understood that it is the theme which holds the whole analysis together; it is the pith of his argument.

Evans-Pritchard's view is that the land of Cyrenaica is divided among nine structurally equal tribes, each with its own *watan* or homeland and natural resources. All tribes are divided into ordered and structurally equal segments, each segment possessing the same characteristics as the tribes themselves. His argument is that the organisation of the Sanusi Order was built on this tribal organisation, and, of course, if this is to be accepted, the two should match. One fact troubled him: the distribution of lodges showed unevenness. The number of lodges in any one tribe varied from one to fourteen. This variation cannot be accounted for by the differences in population among the tribes. Yet 'The tribal system and the Sanusiya organisation interpenetrated' (p. 71). How then to account for the seeming maldistribution of lodges? He does so with admirable ingenuity: 'So much was the Sanusiya organisation based on the tribal system that the distribution of lodges may be said to have reflected tribal segmentation, mirroring lines of cleavage between tribes and tribal sections' (Evans-Pritchard 1949: 71–72). Metaphors apart, what he meant was that the more cohesive the tribes, like those of the camel-herding Bedouin who inhabit the semi-desert plain areas to the west and south of the plateau, the fewer the lodges. On the plateau, a deeply fissured limestone block, where the almost sedentary cow herders lived, the tribal segments were cantonised and lodges were many. Thus the proliferation of lodges is an index of the degree of cohesion between the segments of the tribes, and what appears as a maldistribution is used, by Evans-Pritchard, to demonstrate the effectiveness with which the Sanusi organisation became clamped on to the tribes. 'It [the Order] seeded itself, as it were, in the crevices between the tribes, and its points of growth were thus also the points of convergence in tribal and lineage structure' (p. 73). This is a point which will be examined closely later.

Fourth, when the Sanusi arrived in Cyrenaica, the cult of saints was a common practice among the Bedouin. Although contrary to Sanusi sentiments, they nevertheless permitted pilgrimages to saints' tombs to continue. On the plateau, pilgrimages used to be held several times annually, often only so that a small group of people could meet to discuss business, after a sacrificial meal. In this area practically all the small tribal units had their own saint's tomb. When these units split, politically, new saints would come to be venerated. Thus, when I was residing with a tribal section in 1948, it split into two over the issue of its leadership and without further ado, the shaikh of the seceding group ordered a low wall to be built around some small stones on a nearby rise (where burials usually took place), and had the walls whitewashed, and gave the 'tomb' a name, vowing that he would never again make a pilgrimage to the saint of his erstwhile tribal section. On the plateau area these little whitewashed saints' tombs are to be seen everywhere, although it is necessary to add that some deceased saints, because they were thought to 'work fast' had greater renown than others, and these were the ones used for oath giving in deciding matters of import between tribes or sections. Among the camel herders, saints' tombs occur in fewer numbers, but they are all 'important'.

The significance of these saints' tombs is that they became incorporated – albeit loosely – into the organisation of the Sanusi Order (Evans-Pritchard 1949: 65–69). By the turn of the century, it is possible, following Evans-Pritchard's general lines of argument, to demonstrate considerable organisational elaboration, if both the distribution of the lodges and the saints' tombs are taken into consideration. The Order now had a headquarters, lodges of superior status staffed by the better known and more authoritative persons recruited from the Sanusi family or the more distinguished of the early disciples, and smaller lodges staffed by men of less repute: in an agreement made with the Sanusiya in 1921, the Italians recognised this difference, and paid them accordingly (p. 150). This part of the Order's organisation was underpinned by the cult of saints, in which there were recognised to be more efficacious saints and those of more restricted influence. The organisational matching, the 'fit' of the Sanusi with the tribes, was this ordering and distribution of lodges and tombs in relation to the segmentary tribal system, brief details of which have already been given.

Fifth, in whatever manner the history of the Order is to be interpreted, there is no gainsaying that its success is astonishing, and that the marvellous simplicity of its organisation is bound to evoke wonder. Evans-Pritchard asks why this should have happened, why the Sanusi cause should have swept the arid wastes of the desert, bringing to its inhabitants a new breath of life. His answer is that the Bedouin felt the need for it. In the book, there are several allusions to the needs of people (pp. 14, 22, 70, 73, 83 and 88), which fall into two categories. The first concerns the emotional needs of people, the early Sanusi included. This can be dismissed summarily, on the grounds that it is quite impossible to know what the emotional needs of the Sanusi were, even though the founder wrote copiously, and the same is true for the Bedouin concerning whom information on the subject is wholly lacking. The second sense in which he speaks of a 'felt need' must be taken seriously. He puts it with crystal clarity in one sentence: 'Their need was for some authority lying outside their segmentary tribal system which could compose intertribal and intersectional disputes and bind the tribes and tribal sections together within an organisation and under a common symbol' (p. 88). I must confess I find this a quite extraordinary statement, especially since it is the fundamental importance of the assumption of this kind of structural need which led Evans-Pritchard to shape the whole argument of the book in the way he did. It is doubly intriguing because, presently, it will be suggested that it is an assumption on which many anthropological analyses of religion rest.

Sixth, during its period of incubation and early development, it was of consequence to the Sanusi that the Turks occupied the country, albeit only the few towns and villages near the coast, in any effective manner. The characteristic of the Turkish presence in Cyrenaica was not merely that it lacked either the will or the physical force (or both) to nip the Order in the bud, but that it provided enough smouldering hostility in the background for the Order to stand out against it in relief. The Turks were emblematic of town living and all that was distasteful in it for the Bedouin. Based in the towns, the Turkish administration was never able to capture the tribal organisation. The Sanusi prospered because they eschewed the towns and penetrated the tribes. Eight other Muslim orders, centred on the towns, were, like the Turks, trapped in them; and they never grew to positions of political consequence, because the rudimentary organisations they possessed were not related to the distribution of political authority in the country (p. 87). The effect of these other orders, in the present context, was to sharpen the outline of the relief of the Sanusiya at those points where the effect of the Turks left it blurred. It would appear, therefore, that if a religious order is to progress to political significance there needs to be some kind of passive opposition available at an early stage in its development, to coddle it, so to speak, into a firm unity.

Seventh, by the turn of the century, stronger opposition seems to have been required for the Order to remain a coherent organisation. For what had been happening over sixty years, was that the diverse tribes had come to be identified with particular lodges, and this particularism gained momentum with the growth in the number of lodges. At the same time the Sanusi family was growing in numbers, and the more important lodges came to be taken over by some of them. During the first decade of the twentieth century cleavages were already present in the Sanusi family itself and among the families of its disciples, the Ikhwan (lit. brothers). These cleavages were deepened because the Bedouin came to give their allegiance, more and more, to their local lodge and its Sanusi or Ikhwan head, and the headquarters, by this time, had in any case been removed to the remote south. In other words, there comes a stage in the development of a religious organisation when it is threatened by disintegration because it lacks the power of political centralisation (pp. 64, 104). Until this time the head of the Order had shown no inclination to appropriate any political functions, and conspicuously shunned the attempts of others to cajole him into doing so.

Eighth, military opposition to the Sanusiya began in the far south, and it came from the French. The Order was forced to retract one of its tentacles, when, in 1902, Sayyid Ahmad al-Sharif moved the headquarters from Qiru in Chad to its earlier home in Kufra, some 300 miles to the north, as security from French attacks. Many of the lodges in Chad were destroyed. As far as Cyrenaica is concerned, the great threat came from Italy. If the Sanusi Order had been showing signs of disintegrative decay at the turn of the century, the Italian invasion of September 1911 stopped the rot (pp. 23–26).

Under the pressure of foreign colonialism the Bedouin fought first alongside the Turks. Little more than a year later Turkey signed a peace treaty with Italy. The Sanusi now accepted formal leadership of the war, first under the command of that romantic figure, Sayyid Ahmad al-Sharif, a larger-than-life charismatic leader, said to be equally at home in the saddle and in the library, who fought three major European powers on different fronts simultaneously. He left Cyrenaica by submarine in 1918. The headship of the Order passed, now, to his rightful heir, Sayyid Muhammad al-Idris, who was a minor when his father Sayyid al-Mahdi, the second head of the Order, died. Family rivalries among the Sanusi and the disciples, and the tendency towards particularistic loyalties they encouraged, went by the board. More and more they and their Bedouin followers came to give precedence to the single emblem of common membership of a religious order (pp. 88, 91, 99, 110, 115, 162). Restoration of unity within the Order was the consequence of dire external opposition.

Ninth, the Italian attack did more than revive the flagging fortunes of a religious order, the Sanusiya. Its role was transformed. The Italians were soon to discover that it was virtually impossible to deal with a tribal system containing multiple points of power. But the Italians knew they had to deal with someone, and the only person who could answer for the Bedouin was the head of the Order, Sayyid Idris. The war had dragged on. It had become a drain on Italian resources, and they were thoroughly fed up with it all. Therefore, they entered into negotiations with him, but in order to do so they also had to give him formal political recognition: someone had to put his signature to peace or surrender terms. In Sayyid Idris they met a tough negotiator. In an agreement he made with the Italians in 1920 he prized the title of Sanusi Amir out of them, and although he knew it was being given him so that he would renounce it later, he made the Italians look silly. Evans-Pritchard describes the arrangement as 'fantastic' for it not only gave a title to Sayyid Idris but it also provided for a Sanusi government, a second government wholly opposed to their own (pp. 148–152). Sayyid Idris did not achieve any distinction as commander of Bedouin forces, but it must be said of him that he laboured with some energy, considerable skill, and phenomenal patience in most trying negotiations, and it is to his credit that he made them even more trying for the Italians. The result of his endeavours was that the Italians turned his Order into a state (pp. 99, 105, 150). Hence the ninth point in the series: a state can only deal with a like system. An acephalous system must be given a head in confrontation with a centralised system.

Finally, to round off the historical account, Sayyid Idris fled the country, in December 1922, for Egypt. Resistance to the Italians continued under the leadership of one 'Umar al-Mukhtar, of the Ikhwan, who was born a client tribesman in the 'Abaidat tribe, in eastern Cyrenaica. With his capture and subsequent public hanging on 16 September 1931, almost exactly twenty years after the first Italian attack, resistance collapsed. During this second period of the war from 1922 to 1931, although 'Umar al-Mukhtar exercised a loose overall command, leadership was effectively in the hands of Bedouin tribal shaikhs; it must be noted here, since the issue of tribal leadership is to be raised presently, that the latter receive no mention from Evans-Pritchard, until this stage in the history. It looked now as if the Sanusiya was finished for good, the family dispersed, the members of the Ikhwan dead or gone elsewhere, and the mass of Bedouin followers, after years of privation, torture, concentration camps and death, finally cowed and beaten down to the ground. But after Italy entered World War II, the tribal shaikhs of Cyrenaica and Tripolitania met Sayyid Idris in Cairo, in August 1940, when they decided to form what came to be known as the Libyan Arab Force. Sayyid Idris returned in triumph to Cyrenaica in 1943. Subsequent events fall outside the period of Evans-Pritchard's history, but it is appropriate to add that Sayyid Idris was proclaimed Amir in 1949, and that on 7 October 1951, the National Assembly confirmed the King–designate as King of the new Libya, incorporating Cyrenaica, Tripolitania, and Fezzan into a federal state, whose boundaries were almost coterminous with those of the Sanusiya during its period of maximum expansion in the nineteenth century.

Thus far I have adhered closely to Evans-Pritchard's views, as I understand them, and the facts are nearly all those he used. In what follows, most of the facts to be used he would have known, for this is not intended as an attempt to rewrite the history of chronological events: the intent is to dispute the thesis he puts forward, as to the relation of the Sanusiya organisation to the tribal structure. In ascribing such priority to this relationship it was inevitable that he should see the history of the Sanusiya as contained within the relatively very small northern bulge of Cyrenaica, occupied by the Bedouin, and to neglect or underestimate developments taking place elsewhere. The area inhabited by Cyrenaican Bedouin, to give some sense or perspective to this statement, is about 300 miles or so from east to west; it is about 25 to 30 miles deep in the southwest; it stretches to about 75 miles southwards from the coast in the centre and narrows again towards the Egyptian border (it is quite adequately represented on the map as a section of the coastal corridor from Egypt to Tunisia, along which lodges were placed). In area, this represents only a very small fraction of the territorial spread of the Order. Only 32 of the lodges were located there. Over three times that number (115) were built outside the area. Moreover, the number of Cyrenaican Bedouin adherents far outnumbered by those living further afield. It can be argued, nevertheless, that it is legitimate to take one particular area of the Sanusi's activities, and treat it as a local adaptation to one of the many kinds of social organisations it spanned in its spread. Assuming the history to attempt only this, then the first task is to evaluate it in relation to the Cyrenaican context, and to this I now turn.

When Evans-Pritchard arrived in Cyrenaica in late 1942 as political officer in the British military administration, he became involved in the discussions concerning the future role of Sayyid Idris, who was still, nominally at least, the head of the Sanusi Order. In this sense he was, in a small way to be sure, part of the king-making process. With the historical tendency for the priest to become king, he was familiar from the writings of Sir James Frazer. Indeed, he had played a superb variation on the theme in his Frazer lecture on divine kingship (Evans-Pritchard 1962: 192–212), written at the same time as his Sanusi history. He was not concerned to establish that this kind of development occurred – Frazer had done that, and had scoured the literature with the aim of compiling instances. Evans-Pritchard's aim was to ascertain, by analysis, the necessary conditions which permit this kind of development to occur. For this purpose, he took his problem from the contemporary scene of 1943 and, thereafter, he evoked history as an aid to solving this contemporary problem. This, supposedly, is what he meant when he said, in a lecture: 'Historians write history, as it were, forwards and we [social anthropologists] would tend to write it backwards' (1962: 186). In fact, he wrote only three pages on the World War II years, the period he knew best at first hand (he spent two years in the country between 1942 and 1945, and travelled widely), largely, in my view, because the sort of theoretical framework in which he cast his history could not comprehend the developments of that period. His first task was to fashion a structural model of Bedouin society, very much akin to that which he used in an earlier study of the Nuer of the Sudan (Evans-Pritchard 1940 and 1951). Beginning in this way he makes it clear at the outset that his was not to be a historian's history, for the model was the first priority, and the general statements that refer to the conditions of the development are history only in the sense that they happened all to have a time context. Analytically, when the events occurred which provided the evidence for making these statements is irrelevant: the nine generalities were all encapsulated in the problem he posed, and most of them could have been extracted without recourse to history. Historical facts were used largely to corroborate ideas derived from contemporary observation.

The model of a segmentary structure, spanning the entire Bedouin population as a unified system of homologous parts, was an equilibrium model. Nothing can happen when this is employed, save to conform, to buttress or in some other way to fit what exists already. Hence Evans-Pritchard's history stops when the holy man assumes formal political power. It had to stop there because the system had now become a different system. Prior to then it had possessed utility because the underlying assumption is that for the previous century – or, indeed, for a much longer period – nothing had happened. This assumption is made explicitly, in another context, when he states: 'Indeed, I would say that a term like "structure" can only be meaningful when used as an historical expression to denote a set of relations known to have endured over a considerable period of time' (Evans-Pritchard 1962: 181).

Evans-Pritchard's first task, as he saw it, was to map out the structure of Bedouin society – a segmentary lineage system. His next step was to add complications arising out of the Bedouin 'need' for some external authority, which would unite the tribes under a common symbol. The result was that the divisions of the genealogy into tribes, primary sections and so on were matched exactly by the lodges and saints' tombs which came under the order. The congruency between the two organisational forms was virtually perfect, according to Evans-Pritchard. The Order penetrated the tribes and in doing so took them over. This picture looks all too familiar, for it represents an amplified documentation of ideas contained in works on religion throughout the nineteenth and into the twentieth century. What is implicit in most works on religion in our subject is the quite fundamental assumption that society cannot stand on its own. It must be buttressed by a system of values which explain, validate, and give its unity regular confirmation. Thus Victor Turner (1957: xxi) says that 'the instability of the secular social structure can be palliated but not controlled by secular means . . . But ritual . . . acts to keep the common values of Ndembu society constantly before the roving individualists of which it is composed'. In short, social relations must be enveloped in the ritual wrapping of society. I must now state it as a fact that when I worked among Bedouin, ritual did not gather together groups which were ever larger than the small corporate groups, numbering a few hundred people assembled around summer watering points and, from what Bedouin told me, they did not gather in larger numbers earlier on.

Cyrenaican society was defined for Evans-Pritchard by the limits of the genealogy, which anyone locally would provide. What he does not stress is that these genealogies, unlike those he collected among the Nuer, converge in a single ancestress. The latter, that is to say, is not only a point of definition of the society, but is a symbol of the unity of the Cyrenaican tribes, as Bedouin never tire of telling you. Why add another symbol? Did it in any way add to the common values of Bedouin society? The answer must be in the negative since the Order was not limited to Cyrenaica nor was its main anchorage there, as I will argue in a moment. What were these common values, anyway? Language? Religion? Mode of life? Descent? Economy? This is what seems to be meant by common values, but if this is so they are common to the whole of that semi-desert area from the Atlantic into Iraq.

The segmentary lineage system in Cyrenaica, while it is spread throughout the country, encompasses different types of relations in the northern part of the country compared with the more semi-desert areas. This difference is critical in looking at the point Evans-Pritchard makes with regard to the seeding of lodges in the crevices of tribes. As the argument goes, it is among the tribes inhabiting the plateau area, where the land is sharply divided, that the number of lodges there is greater and reflects a lack of cohesion. The facts are, unfortunately, that of the three tribes whose territories lie wholly on the plateau, two had only one lodge each. The argument about the degree of fractionisation fails to stand on another count: it cannot be said that the camel-herding tribes, where lodges are few, were any the less fractionised. The plateau and the camel-herding economies of Cyrenaica are wholly disparate; so are the nature of their groupings. On the plateau, the crop is regular every year and the animals remain in the vicinity of camps. In the camel-herding areas the economy is chronically unstable, whimsically veering from superabundance to shortage. What the distribution of lodges demonstrates, it seems to me, is that the stabler plateau economy produces multiple points of power, whereas the instability of the camel herding area permits power at a relatively few concentrated points. The area where the lodges were thickest on the ground was the area where Turkish control was most effective; it was the area the Italians wanted most; it was the area which, in the late 1930s, became dotted with Italian settler farms; it is the area of greatest population concentration and is now the area of agricultural schemes. The Sanusi, primarily, wanted people with stable resources in order to maintain their lodges. This is what the plateau offered them. The camel-herding economy was too unreliable to maintain many lodges. Only where resources couldbe concentrated permanently did lodges appear in the camel-herding area. And the number there was four out of a total of forty-five for Cyrenaica. Moreover, the view that I am now pressing explains the distribution of lodges outside the Cyrenaican bulge, whereas the argument concerning cohesion, even were it acceptable, would be restricted to one area only.

In suggesting that the distribution of lodges and the distribution of power, if not congruent, were at least closely consistent, the fit between tribal organisation and the distribution of lodges was rejected implicitly, for the view I am pressing is that power does not follow the lines of genealogical segmentation. If it is true that the Sanusi would not be able to get very far by seeking to know the tribes and their orders of divisions, how did they decide to establish a lodge here or there? It is necessary to bear in mind that labour needed to be available to build a lodge in the first place, and that had to be voluntary. The lodge had to include a mosque, a school room, guest rooms, private rooms for the head and his family, classrooms, rooms for the brothers of the Order and servants. A community had to be built, in short; and to support it productive land, water, food and transport all had to be available. Not all Bedouin groups possessed a regular surplus in any of these things, although, on the plateau, they were all more readily available, albeit on a small scale, commensurate with a span of power enjoyed by the shaikhs there. Availability of resources was not enough, however. The lodge had to acquire them. The way the Sanusi identified surpluses was to wait until two or more groups supplicated for a lodge in their territories, when an arrangement would be made for important members of the Sanusi family to visit the groups to hear their cases. These visits were the occasions for large jamborees and massive entertainment. When the Sanusi accepted these displays of hospitality they not only thereby spotted the areas of surplus wealth, but also an organisation to bring it together. The organisation to which I refer was the microstructure power commanded by the Bedouin shaikh. It was he, as leader, who negotiated a consensus among his followers on the use of resources for attracting a lodge.

It is my firm view that the distribution of lodges had nothing to do with bifurcations in a lineage system, but were highly consistent with the distribution of power as seen in the persons of shaikhs. Yet it is not until page 168 that Evans-Pritchard sees fit to refer to them as some of the 'best known names of the resistance'. What I wish to argue is that they had been of prime importance to the Sanusi Order throughout its history. As it was beginning to spread, in the middle of the nineteenth century, in Cyrenaica, there was one larger-than-life shaikh who was a virtual king of the central area of the country, and who was visited by an English traveller – who, incidentally, is not mentioned by Evans-Pritchard. The position of this shaikh had nothing to do with his tribe's lineage, but was due to the fact that the territory of his corporate group stretched from the highest reaches of the plateau to the desert proper, enclosing the full variety of ecological zones in between. No other corporate group had this highly advantageous spread of territory, and it is not surprising that the Sanusi sought out this shaikh very early on, for to have him on their side meant control of the central area of the country. I might add here that there is a fair amount of information from the middle of the nineteenth century onwards about shaikhs in the country, which Evans-Pritchard did not use. To my mind, this is a crucial omission, for it was on the shaikhs, as leaders, and their ability to rally tribesmen behind them, that the resistance to the Italians was based. In support of this, it should be remembered that the entire Sanusi family left Cyrenaica in the mid-1920s, and it was after this date that the serious resistance began.

Another important aspect of the development that I wish to stress but which Evans-Pritchard neglects, is that there had been a major switch in trans-Saharan trade, from 1840 onwards. But before examining the effects of this switch there is one point which needs to be made, namely that lodges had already been established in Saudi Arabia and in Egypt. When the Grand Sanusi fell sick in Cyrenaica in 1842, he was, in fact, on the return journey to Morocco. The French, it is important to note, had already entered Algeria, so his route to the west was cut off. Much more importantly, however, the flourishing trans-Saharan trade in the western half of the desert was severely hit from two directions at about the same time. First the Turks were pressed to discontinue their encouragement of the trans-Saharan slave trade. At this period, there was a British Consul in a place called Marzuk, some several hundred miles south of Tripoli, who could monitor some of these activities. Simultaneously, the steamship appeared, and much of the trade in West African goods became coastwise, increasingly from this time onwards. The oases and trade routes of the Eastern Sahara, by comparison, were still neglected and travel in that region, by all accounts, was hazardous to say the least. The Grand Sanusi saw his opportunity to clean up these oases and reduce the brigandage to which caravans had been so constantly exposed. It was for this reason that, during the thirteen years of his life that remained after he had set up his first Cyrenaican lodge, he saw to it that lodges were planted in many of the Cyrenaican tribal oases, as far distant as Kufra (some 700 miles south into the desert). It is clear from the letters which the Grand Sanusi sent to the heads of lodges, when they were being established, that his prime concern was that oases should be made into safe trading posts. His sentiments were quite clearly and simply expressed on this matter: do not engage in robbery, but give hospitality to travellers.

Following on this, I wish now to refer to the stress Evans-Pritchard gave to the matter of externality of the seat of the head of the Order in relation to Bedouin tribes. You will recall that during the first fifty years or so, what Evans-Pritchard refers to as the headquarters of the Order were shifted five times. The significance that Evans-Pritchard derives from this was the drive for externality. If this was so, the so-called headquarters need not have moved at all, since, when the first lodge was built, neutrality inhered in the *baraka*, the divine blessing, that the headquarters possessed. Otherwise, how could various lodges have functioned among the tribes and their divisions at all; for lodges, I must stress, were not placed on borders but in the territories of corporate groups. When the Grand Sanusi went careering off into the desert, quite clearly he had his sights fixed on something other than externality. The Order came to control all the points of departure across the eastern half of the Sahara, including places in Chad, Niger, Nigeria, the Sudan, and all the oases in eastern Sahara; and, for good measure, the Order erected a continuous line of lodges along the Mediterranean coast from Alexandria in Egypt to the Tunisian border. The Grand Sanusi was not worried about externality in relation to the Cyrenaican tribes; he had an empire to build. Hence his haste in moving off into the desert: for, tucked away in the small bulge of Cyrenaica he had no room to manoeuvre. Yet, Evans-Pritchard argues that the Sanusiya comprised a symbol to which the Bedouin clung and which enabled them to withstand twenty years of privation, near-starvation and death, during the resistance to the Italians. As evidence of this he cites nearby Tripolitania, where, on his own admission, the tribes are more fractionised than in Cyrenaica. On his own argument, since the proliferation of lodges is a function of the lack of tribal cohesion, then Tripolitania should be well and truly covered. It was not. In any event, what did happen there? The Italian advance to the interior was almost identical to the pattern of advance in Cyrenaica. Moreover, fighting continued there for as long as it did in Cyrenaica.

Further, and contrary to Evans-Pritchard's argument, the last thing that any of the Sanusi leaders wanted was that the Order should be irrevocably attached to any political structure. Indeed, the son of the Grand Sanusi explicitly eschewed titular political recognition, when twice he brusquely rejected the offer of the office of Khalifa proffered him by the Mahdi of the Sudan and, later, by another political figure in Darfur. For the sort of expansion that the Sanusi Order undertook, too close a consistency between its organisation and political structure would have restricted its movement very severely. As it was, unencumbered by such attachments, it was free to move cross-culturally and, more importantly perhaps, across political boundaries, at will. When, therefore, the Sanusi moved his seat from the plateau in Cyrenaica to a distant oasis, and when his successor moved on to Qiru in Chad, this had nothing to do with a desire for solitude, or for externality *vis-à-vis* the Cyrenaican tribes. The southward prongs in the movement of the Order represent a direction in the flow of trans-Saharan trade in the second half of the nineteenth century.

Although Evans-Pritchard sees the major threat to the Sanusi Order in the Italian invasion of Cyrenaica in 1911, the death knell of its expansion had certainly tolled some fifteen to twenty years before that. For in the early 1890s, the French had penetrated Chad, and had captured a string of Sanusi lodges on the south side of the Sahara – and it is this that the Bedouin, certainly those living in the south, stressed to me. This French capture of lodges was catastrophic, since the flow of goods across the Sahara and the profileration of lodges that went with this new prosperity, was brought to a summary end. The source of trade had been captured, and as it withered away, the Order not only ceased to expand as it had been doing for half a century, but was now forced to contract, and this many years before the Italian invasion.

Evans-Pritchard was, of course, well aware of the full extent of the spread of the Sanusi Order, and he was aware that the lines of expansion constituted a pattern. These matters he refers to as facts, *en passant*, without giving them analytic rating or allowing them to assume importance in his general argument. It may well have been that, arriving in Cyrenaica as he did, in the first flush of excitement over the return of the Amir Idris to his native country, he was misled into viewing the history of the Sanusi Order almost exclusively in terms of its local Cyrenaican peculiarities.

It is the spread of the Order which I find fascinating. What is true is that anywhere in the vast territory between the Atlantic and Iran the teachings of the Sanusi, the building of lodges, and the social and religious purposes of lodges, would be familiar to any Muslim. In a cultural sense there were no barriers to an Islamic order of this sort. But not all orders have spread in the way that the Sanusi Order has done. Indeed, I recently had occasion to read in detail an account of a religious order which has established itself south of Khartoum, and what is noticeable about this is how limited it is in its spread. The main reason for this, it seemed to me, was that its teaching is so culturally peculiar to that area, as indeed are the elaborate ritual practices which are attached to it. The genius of the Sanusi Order is that the teachings of the founder were so elementary, and that ritual was virtually none. Consequently, Sanusi adherence came to be found among highly sophisticated and simple-living people alike, in Morocco, Algeria, Mecca and Kufra, Egypt and Nigeria, in oases and coastal plains, and among tent and town dwellers. This very wide spread among highly differentiated peoples, both culturally and occupationally, I attribute to the message that the founder preached. To make a final point I think I must draw attention to the fact that the Order spread at a time when there was a great stir in the world, when religious sects were cropping up in Europe, as well as in Islam. Briefly, this also occurred during the seventh, eleventh, and sixteenth centuries, and again in the nineteenth century, at a time when both Europe and the Middle East were astir.

Evans-Pritchard's book is mainly concerned with the expansion of the Sanusi Order but, I repeat, there is almost no history relating to those sixty-five years. Instead, a stable structure is presumed. What history there is relates to the struggle with the Italians, and for this there is a great deal of material. Audrey Richards, when reviewing the book, wondered why there should have been so much of what she considers to be irrelevant detail, and I tend to agree. I think Evans-Pritchard saw himself as fighting the cause of the underdog – the Bedouin – and, in tune with most people's sentiments in this accounting after the war, he lambasts the Italians, to an unfair degree, as have more recent editors of books on Libya. What history there is could have been largely dispensed with. Otherwise there is virtually none – and perhaps the book is all the better for its absence – at least, we might not then have had the stimulus of the nine or ten points I have cited here.

2

The Bedouin way of life

It is possible to distinguish two major natural regions in that area of Cyrenaica inhabited by Bedouin, the Jabal in the north and the Barr to the south with the plateau foothills of the centre forming an intermediary but much less sharply defined zone. Each zone has its characteristic topography: high mountain ranges in the north, flat low-lying expanses in the south, with gently undulating country in between. Rainfall differences are equally well marked: heavy and regular falls in the north, with marked decreases in all directions away from the plateau, except for the coastal strip of the northwest. Vegetation differences reflect the varying rainfall, giving forests and continuous plant cover in the north throughout the year, and barrenness for the greater part of the year in the south except during seasons of good rainfall. The Bedouin way of life is adapted to these general environmental conditions.

Saying that the Jabal folk are semi-sedentary is almost synonymous with saying that they are cow-herders. 'The cow does not move, but the camel is always moving', the Bedouin say. Camels are an anachronism on the Jabal. They are large animals and are not at all suited to forests. They wander over considerable distances as they forage, and it would be difficult to keep control of them in amongst the trees. Camels belong to the south where the open spaces give them the freedom of movement they require. Cows are much more docile, and spend their time under trees in the vicinity of the camp. They rarely get lost, and it would be considered comic if a man was found to be travelling the country in search of his cow.

Where there are cows, there are few sheep. The Bedouin consider the Jabal a poor area for sheep-rearing because they so easily become entangled in the undergrowth and this spoils their wool. Sheep like warmth during the lambing period, and the south again is much more suitable in this respect. Those of the Jabal tribes who possess sheep usually send them to the southern slopes of the Jabal under the care of a shepherd, and rarely bring them into the forest area. There are a few sheep on the plateau, but the characteristic animal accompanying the cow is the much maligned goat. They are hardy animals, not as selective as sheep in their foragings, and gain most of their nourishment by nibbling at small trees and shoots. The claims are that the goat is rapidly denuding the Jabal of its forest covering, although if this is so, it is strange that there is anything of it left after the centuries the goat has been nibbling at it.

Conditions are different to the south and west of the Jabal. There is much greater mobility in these areas, some of the tribal sections being very mobile indeed. By mobility, it is not necessarily meant that there is marked and clear transhumance. Few tribal groups are consistently transhumant in the sense that they are always to be found in one particular area in winter and in another during the summer season. This kind of movement is perhaps best realised on the southern foothills of the plateau, in the Sirwal country. When rains falls there, the tendency is for camps to move southwards just before the sheep lamb, so that they may derive the benefit of the warmth which the south has to offer and the luscious pastures that grow there when there is sufficient moisture. In summer, some tribal sections leave the arid south for the less severe plateau foothills where the large wells are also located. When rainfalls permits, the 'Abd section of the Bara'asa tribe regularly make such movements. Transhumance is regularly practised again in the southwest, particularly by the Zuwayya tribe. They occupy a triangular area with its apex at Ajadabiya. In spring, they are to be found about thirty miles to the south of the village, the camps dispersed over a wide area, each camp separated by a distance of about two miles. In summer they all converge at the apex of the triangle. From April to November the camp of the Jululat section alone numbers over eighty tents, and a mile or so away there is usually another huge camp consisting of even more tents. Scattered among the dwellings on the outskirts of the village there are as a rule a number of other Zuwayya tents. Practically the whole of the two largest sections of this tribe, except those of their members who live in the distant oasis of Kufra or in the Sudan, pitch their tents within a radius of five miles of the village for the summer watering period. Other tribal sections living to the north of the village also practise the same kind of seasonal movements, moving west to the wells and ploughland in summer, and east to the pastures once ploughing has finished. Apart from these long seasonal moves, the camps are constantly moved during the summer months for reasons of cleanliness. The Zuwayya are particularly restless during the dry season, and when they are not actually moving, they are constantly talking about the next *haul al-qadam* (a move forward).

Many sections of tribes do not, however, move quite in this fashion. The famous Hadduth section of the Bara'asa tribe do not make these north-south movements. During the winter of 1949–1950, the rains failed, but they did not feel constrained to move the camps northwards either then or in summer. It appears that the main camps remain in the Sha'afa permanently, and that only detachments ever go up to the north for ploughing. The Jilghaf and al-Juwaifi sections of the same tribe also stick to one general area throughout the year. In spring the three sections mentioned are highly mobile, and if the rains have been poor they remain in one place only for a short time. During the winter of 1949 when the rains failed, they were on the move every ten or fifteen days. One of their members would return to camp after a journey with the news that he had seen pasture fifteen or twenty miles away; the following morning the camp might well be on its way to a new site. After ten days or so in this new home, the menfolk would begin to grumble that the flocks had exhausted the pastures in the area and another move would be made as soon as other pastures had been spotted. So they continued throughout the spring, until the onset of the watering season when man and beast would close in on the wells. Only the camels move much at this time of the year, and they still continue to wander very far afield.

The prime mover in Bedouin life is water. If water is available in adequate supply throughout the year in any given area, then the Bedouin might well stay there. The Hadduth section of the Bara'asa were able to stay in the Sha'afa because a large well (Bir Bil'amad) provided them with sufficient water. In 1950, their camels were sent north because there had been a drought during the previous winter, and the well was far from being full, but there was enough water for the sheep, so the camps stayed. Similarly, in the case of the Jilghaf section, the large well of Haqfat Jilghaf assured them a sufficient supply to satisfy the requirements of their animals. Most of the tribal sections of the Sirwal and Sha'afa each has its large well, which permits some if not all of the members to reside in these areas permanently.

While it is easy to appreciate the control that water supply has on Bedouin seasonal movements, this in itself is insufficient explanation of detailed movements. It is perfectly true that the section of the Magharba tribe which once lived twenty miles to the east of Ajadabiya and then moved to the south of the village and stayed there, had to have the assurance of water before they moved, but this is not the same as saying that they moved to their new homestead because considerations of water supply led them to make this move. Neither can the somewhat bewildering movements of the Madhkur section of the Magharba tribe be explained simply in terms of water supply. In both these instances, the wells which these sections used before they moved are still there, and have been amply filled with water since their departure. It is necessary therefore to seek another explanation.

Now the section of the Magharba (the name of the section was Haiba) which moved from the east to the south of Ajadabiya was not at the time occupying its own territory (*watan*). If asked why this was so, the explanation they would give would be in terms of pastoralism, which could carry with it a great deal of conviction. Against this argument was the fact that this section was hostile to other, larger sections of the tribe. Also, they set up their camp in the particular place they did – to the east of the village – because there had been an outbreak of hostilities between two rival claimants to the land and water on which the Haiba section settled. They went there as a neutral party in a dispute, and stayed there until a settlement had been reached. When they moved to the south, they did so because another Magharba section staked a claim to the homeland of their section. They were so angered by this rival claim that they decided to take their camp and pitch it on the disputed territory, thus challenging their rivals to a show of force. They had travelled about forty miles in the direction of their homeland when members of a closely related tribal group urged them to tarry and try conciliatory methods. Official pressure from the administrative authorities and the gratuitous advices of all and sundry were brought to bear, and they were finally prevailed upon to halt their journey south of Ajadabiya, where they remained for over a year, and where they were still when we left.

Similarly, the Madkhur section at one time had its camps well to the north of Wadi al-Farigh. Here they lived for several years, during which period they were almost continuously engaged in disputes with an old enemy. They placed their camps near the disputed territory so that if rain fell there, they could be the first to plough. At the end of 1948, this dispute was settled in their favour. Almost immediately they moved to Wadi al-Farigh, some thirty miles south, where they are now engaged in a dispute over a well.

It is our experience that movement in other parts of the country can be profitably viewed in this manner. The ultimate control that water supply exerts on Bedouin movements is accepted. This is factual and uninteresting. What is much more profitable is to see how these otherwise baffling movements become intelligible in terms of inter-sectional relationships. Water supply therefore is of significance, not so much in that it satisfies the basic needs of man and beast, but as a medium through which relationships between people are expressed. The importance of this will become clear when later, the details of feuds will be discussed.

Travel and visits to camps are a most important feature of life in the south. The excuse for these visits is sometimes lost sheep, but much more often, lost camels. It is difficult to imagine that such large beasts get lost, particularly since they are under the care of a shepherd. Bedouin never really worry about them, but occasions arise when they need them, and on these occasions they are almost invariably not to be found. Apart from the main herd, it is customary to keep a camel or two in the camp for whatever tasks might arise. A camel might be required to transport supplies to and from the market, for example. On his return, the owner unburdens his beast and then retires to his tent for the inevitable rounds of tea, while the other men of the camp gather round to hear the news. Periodically he orders someone to hobble the camel, but the orders are ignored, until in a rage, the owner compels his son to attend to the matter. By this time the camel has wandered off and is well out of sight. Nothing can be done, and no one knows which direction the camel has taken. Nothing might be done about the beast for weeks, until suddenly the owner decides that he must retrieve it. It is a safe guess that if a man is missing from a camp he has gone in search of a camel (*yidauru fi jamal*). Each and every day while we were with the southern Bara'asa strangers would appear in the camp, and whenever we enquired after their business, the reply came unfailingly – *yidauru fi jamal*. Now when a man sets off to find a camel, he usually has little idea of where he is going to find it. Except by accident, he will not go in the direction the camel took when it left the camp. We have often seen camels disappear northwards and then watched the owner begin his 'search' in a westerly direction. On foot, as a rule, he will set off and make for another camp, and enquire there whether anyone has seen the beast. For identification purposes he will give the details of the beast, its age, sex, colour, whatever peculiarities it might have, and in so doing might touch on various bridewealths or debts of other kinds, revealing the most interesting details of a variety of relationships. All this takes time. In any event, it would be insulting to leave a camp (*naja'*), once having entered it, without at least taking tea, a process which takes the best part of two hours. The searcher does not get very far in a day. Should he arrive in a camp towards mid-afternoon, when he prepares to leave, he will be pressed by his host to stay the night. Little persuasion is required and the camel is soon forgotten. Even if the camel is found, it might well be lost again overnight, and the search is begun again. While we were with the Jilghaf section of the Bara'asa, a man spent over a week in and out of our camp looking for his camel, finding it one afternoon and losing it again at night.

When the searcher goes off, he is always careful to choose his direction. The Hadduth men invariably went north or west, but never northeast. They always know where to 'descend', where they are likely to get a welcome, and where not. To the northeast, there lived groups with which they were hostile. To the north and west there was a series of camps with which they had connections of one kind or another, and searching for a camel was as good an excuse as any for a visit. While they were about it, they might also collect a few sheep or goats that were owing to them, or if they did not get either, they at least were fed for a few days. Happy go lucky as this business of *yidauru fi jamal* might appear, it is in fact one of the most important means of human intercourse in the south.

Second to searching for a camel is the business of asking for help (*talab*). Even if a man has a hundred sheep and requires only four for some purpose, it is our experience that he prefers to go round the camps asking for sheep from others rather than use his own. He seeks help, but as a rule is getting back part of a debt that is owing to him. Alternately, he might consider that certain relatives have 'eaten' some of his family's wealth in the past, and one way of recovering this lost wealth is to ask for help. While we were with the Hadduth folk, one man who came to *talab* stayed for several weeks. In this camp, there was a woman who had come to possess some wealth of her own. The visitor was her nearest male relative, but the year previous, during a serious illness, she had made it known to a *mi'ad* (a gathering of the men of the camp) that she wished her worldly belongings (*riziq al-dunya*) to be inherited by her stepson. The visitor apparently made a habit of visiting the camp for lengthy periods, thus assuring himself some of the wealth that he considered should have been his in any case. After he had been a fortnight in the camp, his hosts began to tire. As the days went by the signs of boredom became obvious, and many suggested that he was not in fact seeking help to marry a new wife as he had claimed, but that he had come to 'eat' the wealth which had been promised another. After twenty days, his hosts set him to work fetching water from the well, but still he showed no signs of haste. By this time, he had consumed almost the value of the sheep he had hoped to take away with him, even allowing for the use the camp folk had made of his donkey. Finally seizing the chance of a traveller who was going in the right direction, his hostess selected the worst goat she could find, gave it him, and was happily rid of a burden.

There are few activities which engage the Bedouin to the same extent as searching for camels and seeking help. Ploughing requires a great deal of effort, but this is seasonal. Until the rains fall, the men circulate among the camps. As soon as rain begins falling, they all make for home again, where they plough for about a month, showing a burst of energy which one would hardly credit. Each day, from morning to night, no matter what the weather is like, they are to be seen in the valleys behind their camels, pushing their ironshod wooden ploughs through the sodden earth. The better the rains, the harder they work, and all are content to tire themselves completely each day. Ploughing is their delight. It is the one thing they will not leave aside, no matter how pressing other matters might be. To young men, especially the poorer ones, ploughing is vital. 'I must plough as much as I can, because barley will bring me sheep, and sheep will bring me camels. With camels I can make a *bait* (a tent, i.e. a marriage) and then I will have lots of sons, and these sons will make a large tribe.' Ploughing is the beginning of a process the end of which is the life work of all Bedouin. Little wonder then that they show such enthusiasm over ploughing.

When ploughing is over, searching seriously begins anew, and continues until early summer, when the menfolk rouse themselves to another burst of effort with the harvest. After the grain has been stored away, except for the occasional wedding or funeral, there are few activities in the south until the rains begin again.

In between ploughing and the harvest, one of the few ceremonies in the life of the southern Bedouin takes place. There are no ceremonies before or after ploughing. Neither are there any ceremonies preceeding reaping nor is there any thanksgiving for the harvest. The ceremony of the year is sheep-shearing, and it is perhaps even more attractive than a marriage ceremony. It takes place at different times of the year in different places. In the far south, shearing begins towards the end of April, while further north, it is delayed until mid-May. Shearing a large flock might take up to ten days, and the help of a number of men is required. As a rule, some twenty-five to thirty men band together and shear the flocks in turn. These men are the members of the small tribal groups, and at least one able-bodied man from each family takes part. When the flocks of the Salah group of the Juwaifi section of the Bara'asa sheared their sheep in 1950, the young men of all the families of the group then living in the Sirwal banded together, and went from camp to camp shearing the various flocks. They went on their rounds dressed in women's garments, some rounding up the sheep, others shearing, a few making tea which is sipped the entire time, while others counted and stacked the fleeces. While all are busy with the various tasks, they sing as loudly as they can, the words of the songs relating to the increase of the flocks, but also having a double meaning. Normally, it is considered great *'aib* (shame) to sing anywhere near the camp, much less in the tent itself, and I have never heard this done, but during sheep shearing this *'aib* is dispensed with. When visitors approach the tents, instead of the usual greetings, they address the shearers with *'alaikum al-nur* (the light be upon you) to which they reply, *nur, wa la zulm al-iqbur* (light and not the darkness of the grave). Throughout the shearing, the men interrupt the singing with *qulu hoi ya jilama* (say hoi, oh shearers) repeating it twice on each occasion. As each sheep is finished, the shearer shouts out *ya raham* (oh group [literally womb]) and his fleece is then collected and stacked with the others. When a complete flock has been finished, the sheep go off again with the shepherd, looking rather odd with a little tuft of wool left on the back of each sheep 'so that they will grow their wool next year, because if it was all taken off it might not grow again'. The men then clean themselves for the sacrificial meal which brings to an end the shearing of each flock, no matter how big or small, and the sacrifice on this occasion must be a sheep, not a goat.

There are few events in the Bedouin calendar to compare with sheep shearing. It is one of the very few occasions when a number of men perform a task together. Camels are sheared by two or three men all working together, but there are no ceremonies associated with this activity. The same can be said of shearing goats, even though the herds might be very large in some cases, particularly on the Jabal. Sheep are considered by the Bedouin to be different from both camels and goats, and have a quality lacking in all other animals. 'When *baraka* was given from yonder, it was given in a hundred parts. Eighty-five parts were given to sheep, ten parts to grain, and five parts to the honest trader, but', as the Bedouin ruefully add, 'there are no honest traders, so these five parts are wasted'. It is not difficult to understand this importance attached to sheep, because they are such an asset in Bedouin life. They provide the choisest meat, and all who can afford it sacrifice a sheep at the annual *'aid al-lahm* (feast of the flesh). Most milk comes from the sheep. The roof which shelters the family is made of their wool. The grain bags are made of sheep's wool, as are the carpets which adorn the bridal camel on the wedding day, and the home of the bride later. Women at all times have the wool with them, spinning it, winding it or working at it on their looms. Debts are paid in wool and relationships are set up through it – a poor widow can always expect a few fleeces from the shearings of her camp, and the husband is proud to give some to his wife to weave another carpet or broaden the tent. After all this, there is usually a little left over for the market, where it is sold for cash, which in turn provides the luxury of new clothes and a little variety of food.

Searching for camels and seeking help in shearing sheep are two of the most important ways in which relationships are expressed and maintained in the south. Through these, connections are never lost or allowed to drop. Camels and sheep link up camps separated by long distances in the south and establish a sense of solidarity and community of feeling which is foreign in the north. People living far apart and with few excuses for inter-communication are thus brought together, and develop a strong sense of solidarity among themselves.

On the Jabal there is a marked absence of this freedom of movement and camaraderie. It is not at all unusual for a man to pass through the centre of a Jabal camp without anyone shouting a greeting. This would be quite unthinkable in the south. If a person passes near a camp without stopping to exchange greetings, there is great consternation, and the only conclusion to be drawn from such an act is that the traveller is of a hostile group. The custom in the south is to say *tafaddal* (do me the favour) to everyone, and it rarely happens that any traveller is allowed to leave the camp before, as they say, 'you have my water and salt in your belly'. If the visitor is a complete stranger a sacrifice is usually made, for this is part of the necessary procedure in meeting a stranger. Until he had partaken of meat, his host is obliged not to enquire about his identification, and it is not usual for a stranger to offer this information until the meat has been taken.

On the Jabal a stranger is not treated in this fashion, and is not encouraged to stay. Neither do the folk themselves spend much time when they visit other camps. Here there is a greater density of population. Visiting on the scale practised in the south would make living intolerable in the north, for there are many more camps in a smaller area. On a ten mile journey, one is likely to pass four or five camps. In the Sha'afa, the distance between camps is anything from five to fifty miles. The atmosphere on the Jabal is much more of going about one's own business. Even a closely related agnate living some distance away and whose visits are infrequent, will return to his camp rather than spend the night in another. These folk go at least once a week to the market, so there is little excuse for visiting. The southerners say of them, 'They put their camps in such places that you cannot find them. They keep away from all paths so that they will not have to entertain'. Whether this may be true or not, one certainly has the feeling that on the Jabal the folk prefer to be without visitors. Both those of the Jabal and the Barr are pastoralists and it was on the Jabal that I first heard the saying *hail al-bwadi al-haiwanat* (the strength of the Bedouin is their animals). Yet the pastoralism of the two areas is quite different, and has important consequences for us. The free-wandering Bedouin of the south show a greater degree of cohesion than do the more sedentary folk of the north. Tribal solidarity is striking in the south and extends to include larger groups. Tensions occur at all levels, from the elementary family to the largest tribal group in both areas, but the check on the spread of these hostilities operates within larger groups in the south, so that the feud is found fully developed at a higher structural level.

The Jabal is dotted with little white tombs, some of which have a cupola, others just four low walls containing the tomb of the *marbut* (holy man), with an entrance to the tomb at one end, and little else. Annually, tribal sections make a pilgrimage to these saints' tombs (or *haul al-marbut*: the move to the holy man, as they are referred to locally), each family taking with it its sacrifice of a sheep or goat, sometimes killed beforehand but usually alive to be slaughtered at the scene of the gathering. After arrival at the tomb, all, including the womenfolk, go to the saint's tomb to pray, kiss the tomb itself and perhaps place a little flag or a piece of garment on the wall surrounding the tomb or on the tomb itself. But the main event of the pilgrimage is the sacrificial meal. When the women, tucked away in the bushes, have finished cooking their meat, there begins a general clamour with the men shouting that the meat be brought out into the open. A young man of each family collects the bowl of meat from his womenfolk and, holding the bowls high above their heads, they come rushing to the spot chosen for the meal. While they do this, the other men fire their rifles as rapidly as they can, and the women set up their high-pitched trillings (*zagharit*). Under the shade of the spreading carob (*kharub*) tree, if there is one available, the men divide into groups for the meal. They do not eat in family groups on this occasion, but in groups of the same age, as far as possible, or at least so mixed up that all the sons of one family, for example, will not be seated around the same bowl. After the meal is over, and hundreds of glasses of tea have been passed around, it is customary, before those gathered disperse, to indulge in horse-riding displays. During the time the tribal section is thus gathered, there should be no quarrels or talk that might lead to quarrels. This is meant to be an occasion when all those who have gathered are one. Nevertheless, most of the elders retire to form small groups and argue furiously until sunset, when they begin to make their way home again.

Some tribal sections make the pilgrimage more than once a year. Individuals often go to their *marbut* for private purposes, but I am referring here to the communal gatherings when at least one of every family of the section goes to the tomb on a chosen day. Some sections of the Darsa' appear to make the pilgrimage frequently, sometimes four or five times a year. This is certainly true of the sections that inhabit the Lusaita country, who perhaps are more cantonised than any others.

We regard the number of saints' tombs in a tribal territory and the number of visits made to these tombs, as a good index of tribal cohesion. Where it is weak, there are a greater number of tombs, and the more urgent is the need for frequent restatement of solidarity.

Compared with the Jabal, the south has few saints' tombs. Neither is it customary there to make a pilgrimage to those that do exist. Individuals might visit a tomb, but they do so as individuals, with private reasons for doing so. Groups do not make a pilgrimage. Neither do the various tribal sections regard a particular tomb as belonging primarily to them. Of the two tribes whose southern sections I know well – the Bara'asa and the Magharba – I never saw any of these sections go off as groups to a tomb, and from what they tell me they do not feel obliged to do so. They might visit the tombs as groups for the purpose of oath-giving, but not on a pilgrimage at regular intervals. The contacts between the folk in these areas are sufficiently frequent, and there is no need to meet at regular intervals to keep the feeling of community alive. The ordinary course of events is sufficient among them to serve this end.

In making this comparison between the Jabal and the south with regard to the degree of cohesion, we note the fact that this is at its highest in the south where the flat open spaces permit easy movement, where the plant cover is such as to induce high mobility, where conditions of pastoralism are such as to necessitate a great deal of inter-camp and inter-section intercourse, where hospitality is one of the most binding obligations of all; where, in short, intercourse between people is much more intense and tribal cohesion is high. By comparison, the terrain of the Jabal induces cantonisation, which implies more difficult communication, less frequent intercourse in the normal run of daily life, and therefore a greater sense of separateness between tribal groups. In short, on the Jabal there is greater fractionisation and less cohesion.

3

The tied and the free

Several types of formal status relationships occur among the Bedouin, and some aspects of the relationships are common to all.[1] Part of the purpose of this discussion is to characterise one of these types, so that it can be identified and distinguished from the others; it is found between tribesmen who are known as the Marabtin (literally, 'the tied') and those who are referred to as the Hurr (literally, 'the free or noble'). Inevitably, in a reconnaissance of a wide field of relationships of this sort, a crop of problems appears, for, although a statement of the rules excluding the tied or clients from noble or patron status is simple enough, their relationships are not confined to a few specific sets of social situations, but enter into many, and significantly affect problems related to them. The relationships between patron and client do not constitute a single problem; they are cultural terms in which a bundle of various relationships are packaged, the separate parts of which are significant or unimportant not in isolation but in the context of particular problems. Since this is intended as a general account, only some of the problems involved can be raised. The choice of problems is admittedly somewhat arbitrary, and it is guided mainly by the desire to give the relationship distinctiveness, as well as by a personal interest in Bedouin power politics.

The terms Hurr and Marabtin are heard throughout the country, but the general social context differs so markedly between the sheep and camel herders of the more southern and western areas and the almost sedentary cow and goat herders of the north central plateau area that it would be quite erroneous to treat them together. Unless stated otherwise, reference is to the sheep and camel herders. In addition to this difference, Marabtin tribesmen are divided into two main classes. Marabtin bi'l Baraka are granted the use of land and water by their nobles in return for the spiritual services they give the Bedouin, and they are able to administer in this way by virtue of the fact that they are accredited with divine goodness (*baraka*).[2] They succour the sick, they write amulets for a number of purposes, they circumcise the young boys, and they are always present at peace meetings. These clients of the goodness are found in small numbers,[3] dispersed among the tribal sections. While in some aspects their status resembles that of other client groups to be referred to presently, their relationships with the noble tribesmen, and the functions they serve, differ so significantly in others that they are excluded from further consideration.

The Marabtin as-Sadgan (clients of the fee) constitute the other main class of clients. This class is said to have been one division of a type of client which included the Marabtin al-'Asa (clients of the stick) and the Marabtin az-Zibal (clients of the manure), but whatever importance these refinements might have had in the past, they are of little consequence any longer.[4] A further distinction is sometimes drawn between the clients of the red lands (the plateau area occupying the northern bulge of the country) and the clients of the white lands (the semi-desert areas),[5] but it is only used when the status of patrons living on the plateau to their clients is compared with this relationship among the people living in the semi-desert, and even then the reference may be expressed in other ways. Clients of the fee is the term usually used to designate any client who does not possess *baraka*. Many of these live on what is virtually their own land;[6] noble tribesmen claim that they can demand land from them whenever they wish, and these clients admit this as a possibility, although I have no record of it happening. They form tribes which are segmented into sections on the pattern of the noble tribes, and the internal relations of the sections are also akin to those of the noble tribes.

These client tribes are to be found mainly on the borders of the noble tribes, and acting as buffers between them. While their members acknowledge that they are clients of the noble tribes, and that their various sections are tied to particular sections of the noble tribes, they would fight for their homeland, and they are numerically powerful enough to oppose even the major sections of the noble tribes.[7] In these and other respects they are unlike the small groups of clients of the fee, who are dispersed among the noble tribes.[8] Buffer client tribes have a large membership, and although they show considerable numerical variation in their population, some of them have upwards of 1,000 members,[9] whereas the dispersed clients live individually in the camps of their patrons or in small camps usually consisting of three to six tents attached to a patron tertiary tribal section of some thirty tents or more. This great disparity in numbers between the concentrated client tribes and the fragmented groups of dispersed clients would alone make for discrete sets of relationships with their respective patrons. They are also quite unlike in their internal organisation, for while the client tribes are genealogically segmented, the dispersed client groups are not genealogically articulated but are distributed among patron tribes as ethnically disparate clusters. Consequently, the latter cannot defend themselves against the overwhelming force of numbers of their patron groups; even where they occur as significant numbers in the total population of a patron tribe they lack a unitary symbol to rally them, and they do not possess the territory on which to assemble in force. Erroneous as it would be to deal with both clients of the goodness and clients of the fee as undifferentiated within the compass of patron-client relationships, it would be a more serious error to lump together the two sorts of clients the Bedouin refer to as fee paying. In the following discussion the problems reviewed relate to the relationships between the small groups of dispersed clients and their patrons only, because the relationship, in its true form, is present between them and not the other varieties of Marabtin which have now been excluded.

Noble status is conferred on a person by virtue of his birth. Anyone who can successfully claim descent from the founding ancestress of all Cyrenaican tribes, an eponymous female called Sa'ada, is referred to as a Sa'adi tribesman, and this is synonymous with use of the term Hurr, or freeborn. Clients are those people who cannot claim this nobility of descent. Several scholars have speculated about their origin.[10] Perhaps the most popular theory is that which related to the two early Arab invasions of Cyrenaica. The first occurred during the late seventh century. This is believed to have been no more than a kind of preliminary colonising effort, as a result of which small groups of the invaders, who were partly assimilated into the autochthonous population, remained in the country. In about 1050 a second invasion (known as the Hilalian invasion, after the Bani Hilal tribe which led it) took place, but this time the invading armies swarmed into the country like locusts, according to the Arab historian, Ibn Khaldun.[11] The modern Sa'adi tribesmen, it is argued, are the descendants of the settlers who entered Cyrenaica during the second invasion, and the Marabtin are the modern descendants of Arabs of the first invasion, with some Berber admixture, who were subjugated by the new invaders, and compelled to pay a tribute. The evidence on which this theory is based is scant, and open to doubt, but however the relationship came about, the modern Bedouin do not concern themselves with historical explanations, and regard the distinction as a matter of birth. Marabtin, as far as they are concerned, are people who in origin were strangers to the land, and thus not descendants of Sa'ada. Everyone entering into their midst is classed as Marabtin for the same reason, and since most immigrants come from somewhere to the west, the appellation 'westerners' is used as interchangeable with clients.[12] Freeborn tribesmen can offer an unbroken line of descent from their immediately deceased forebears to the founding ancestress of all noble tribes, Sa'ada, and use, in all, some twelve generations to span the gap. Clients are unable to do this. Many clusters of clients bear the same ethnic eponym, but the descent lines offered by the individuals of these clusters bear little consistency, and they are not genealogically tied up around a unique ancestor. If a client wishes to pass himself off as freeborn by falsely merging his line with a noble one, he runs the risk of humiliation at the hands of a noble tribesman, who may call his 'bluff'.[13] While the importance ascribed to descent will be diminished later in this chapter, it must be stressed that this is the way the Bedouin have of conceptualising the relationship, and that it is this fact which enables them to see themselves as a class against the clients; they can also use it to call on genealogically related groups for assistance against clients when they so desire, or at least use their genealogical relationships to forestall action on the part of other noble sections. Conceived of in this fashion, the genealogical exclusion from noble descent provides the Bedouin with the cause of the relationship, for if they are asked why men are designated clients, they answer, simply, that since they are not Sa'adi they must have been strangers in origin, and therefore there are certain rights which they cannot acquire.

Certain consequences derive from the stress on descent. Since an individual cannot deny his origin, then the statuses of patron and client are immutable.[14] Wherever a noble moves in Cyrenaica, he remains a Sa'adi tribesman, although he suffers disabilities if he takes up permanent residence outside his *watan*. Wherever a client moves his status is unchanged; a change of tribal residence leaves him with the same privileges he enjoyed and the same disabilities he suffered as in his natal home. But the differentiation is not merely one of proud or poor lineage. A Sa'adi tribesman has rights to the country's natural resources which a client cannot claim. Arising out of this disability, the client's freedom to increase his mobile wealth is limited at several points. Since they are restricted in this context, the political uses to which clients are able to put their wealth are hedged around by restrictions which do not hamper their patrons. Consequently, when the clients use the marriages their daughters contract with patrons for establishing links, the alliances thus created cannot be of the same kind as those created when nobles design a strategy of marital links. From these three general prescriptions stem a wide range of other consequences which affect the social relationships, not only of patrons to their clients, but of those between patrons themselves.

Emphasis has been given to the genealogical division which separates patrons from clients, because of its conceptual significance for the Bedouin, and for its derivative consequences. It does not follow however, simply because the Bedouin say so, that it is either the cause of the relationship or that the two statuses are permanently held in the genealogical mould. If this view is accepted it would be necessary to accept that the Bedouin view of their genealogies as accurate representations of their descent is valid; it would also mean the exclusion of any possibility of movement from one status to the other. But if the Bedouin view of their genealogies is invalid, and changes of status can be demonstrated, then clearly the genealogical basis of the distinction must be relegated to the position of a fact of Bedouin thinking about their relationships, shorn of the primacy they grant to it.

It would be too much of a diversion to explore the various arguments for rejecting the Bedouin view that the Bedouin genealogies accurately represent the details of their descent.[15] A brief reference to some of the arguments is sufficient for present purposes. As far as the Bedouin are concerned, their tribes began with Sa'ada. The number of generations recounted to arrive at this ancestress is about twelve, or, as a span of time, some 250 years. Historical evidence indicates, however, that the forebears of the modern Bedouin arrived in Cyrenaica half-way through the eleventh century; that is, about 900 years ago or some forty-five generations earlier.[16] There is therefore, an error in the genealogy of about 650 years, or roughly thirty-three generations; and for this error to occur, genealogical manipulations have been employed in the past, at least. It can be shown too that the named ancestors on the genealogy represent the dispositions of the tribal sections in a definite pattern, in much the same way as they are used among some other peoples in Africa, and the Middle East. Moreover, this genealogical framework of tribal sections and a map showing the territorial distribution of tribes and their sections match. The genealogy is, in other words, the model the Bedouin use for conceptualising their territorial relationships. Therefore, since genealogical names are emblems signifying blocks of land, these names are as fixed in their positions as are the land domains of tribal sections.[17] Ancestral names and the positionings of descent lines formed from them are of serious concern to the Bedouin because they document landed property relationships. If, in other words, a group of people come to own a strip of land by conquest or any other means, they necessarily appear as a group on the genealogy as descendants of Sa'ada. Further, as a derivative of this, certain areas of contemporary social relationships bear consistency with the divisions on the genealogy. For example, the institution of the feud – cited in this context because it is rooted in competition for land – is interpreted by the Bedouin in terms of the number of generations which separate the two groups directly concerned. The genealogy is a rationalisation of known social relationships. But since it has to comprehend property and other social relationships which are known to exist, then adjustments in these relationships must be matched by alterations in some areas of the genealogy. In short, genealogies are only peripherally important, as statements about descent, to the present argument.

Secondly, if it is said that true descent from Sa'ada is what confers patron status and consequently the possibility of mobility is to be discounted, the refutation of the first part of the statement makes the corollary untenable. Factual evidence can also be adduced to show that the movement from client to patron status, and vice versa, has occurred. Many groups which are acknowledged to be of client origin function as groups of free men. Indeed, the noblest lineage in the whole of the land is reputed to be of client origin, and the tribesmen of this lineage, after recounting the circumstances which permitted their client ancestor to appropriate noblemen's lands, boast their Sa'adi status. Less distinguished client groups have grown to outnumber their patron groups, and although the information about their origin is used to discredit them by their debilitated patron groups, they have ceased to be clients in any meaningful sense of the word. In 1948, for example, the aged leader of a small noble group complained bitterly about the number of clients living on his tribal territory, but he could not rid himself of them because without them, he and his agnates alone would not constitute a viable corporation; in 1950, these clients announced their intention to water their animals at their patron's well – one of the conventional modes of staking a claim to a piece of territory and the wells in it – and although the patron group threatened the direst opposition, the clients successfully seized the well and the adjacent land. In another tribe, a large group of clients gathered on a tribal territory, asserted their right to it and beat off an attack by their patrons with guns. 'Clients are like the sides of our tents, which we fasten around us or discard to suit the vagaries of the wind,' is a sentiment the patrons are fond of repeating; but sometimes the sides fasten so tightly that there is no escape.

Individuals as well as groups can successfully alter their status. The manner in which this comes about is observable in the contemporary scene. A client may seek shelter in a new camp. Poor, perhaps, he offers his services as a shepherd to pay for his keep. The rewards for this should provide a small annual surplus, but if the client finds the camp amenable, instead of demanding his payment at the end of a year he will allow a debt to accumulate. By the time he is owed a small flock of sheep, he may decide to compound his credit for a wife from his patron group. A statement of bridewealth will be made, but only a small token of wealth is passed to the patron. Bound by the bond of mutual debt, their relationship shifts again when the birth of a child to the client and his patron wife adds kinship to debt. Client soon becomes freeman, and his descendants inherit a genealogical position in a noble lineage. Once a client is accorded free status by a small corporation, his lineal status as a descendant of Sa'ada is *ipso facto* conferred upon him. For, while much is made of true descent by the Bedouin, they are in fact speaking of the validity of status connections not of patrilineal consanguinity. Hence there is no contradiction in admitting client origin and boasting Sa'adi status simultaneously,[18] although clients generally try to cloak their origin.

Changes of status can be achieved in other ways. The Bedouin characterise the relationship between patrons and their clients as payments of fees by the latter. If then, a group succeeds in coercing another to make payments on demand, a patron-client relationship is initiated. Thus, in certain circumstances, when blood money is accepted after a homicide, by the victim's group, the offender's group may be required to pay an additional small annual fee, known as *sana'*. If this condition is accepted it means, in effect, that the offender's group is insufficiently strong to maintain its free status and is faced with the possibility of relegation to client status.[19] Secondly, if hearsay evidence is accepted, powerful groups have been able to appropriate the lands of their weaker neighbours and coerce them into accepting client status. In one form of feuding, the offender's group deny responsibility for a homicide. This is not only a challenge, but an implied rejection of the nobility of the victim's group. The latter should avenge the death of a member and the insult added to the injury, but to achieve this double retribution, status may in fact be forfeited when the challenge is issued by a group powerful enough to overwhelm. Some groups have chosen a loss of pride rather than a surrender of status.

Deeper knowledge of genealogies leads to increased suspicions about the origins of groups or parts of them. When quarrels occur or major disputes break out, some new facts relating to people's origins almost invariably emerge – and I am confident that not one of the tribal sections I recorded genealogically was composed wholly of freeborn tribesmen. It would be surprising if they were, for, down the centuries, movements of tribes or their sections have taken place, and on a lesser scale manipulations of the genealogy at a certain level are common, so that even if some of the descendants of the early Arab invaders still inhabit the land, there is no way of determining who they are; they are most likely to be lost among peoples of different origins, and the present genealogical positions they occupy cannot be accurate.

Genealogical origin and descent are together a manner of speaking about patrons and clients. Since the importance the Bedouin attach to them has been rejected, it becomes necessary now to show that the basis of the relationship is something other than descent differentiation. The core of the distinction is in property rights.[20] Any freeman has an equal right, with his fellow agnates of his corporation, to the unhindered use of the two natural resources, land (ploughland and pastures) and water. He may not in fact, by reason of poverty or physical incapability be able to use them, but, while he cannot alienate his right, he can temporarily transfer it to one of his agnates and gain materially in return by doing so. He loses this right if he leaves his corporation, for, although he is not compelled to relinquish his claim to descent from Sa'ada, which in theory gives him rights to land in Cyrenaica, his genealogical position in a particular group gives him rights in a particular strip of territory, but not in all. He is a Sa'adi wherever he goes, but he does not have rights in any part of the Sa'ada benefice.

Clients cannot claim the use of land and water as a right: they are granted access to both by patrons and this privilege is renewed annually. Pressure on land for growing a crop of barley is never very great in Cyrenaica. Shortage of territory is not a problem, since the population density is very low. What is scarce is land which is sufficiently moistened by rain in any year, and scarcer still is well watered ploughland located in fairly close proximity to the summer watering point, for the convenience of reaping. Before ploughing begins the agnates of the small corporations meet to discuss the allocation of the land available for ploughing. Client claims are low on their list of users. A more impelling consideration is the amount of water available to supply the needs of the animal and human population during the long period of drought from the end of April to the end of November. Clients have to supplicate for the use of water points every year; they have to do this for ploughland as well, but, for various reasons, there is much less likelihood of them being turned away over this issue than over a water shortage, since the bumper barley crops of the good years can be safely stored for up to five years, and these surpluses tide them over the bad years. As the dry season approaches the Bedouin busy themselves with problems of water allocation, taking into account not the number of people so much as the number of animals.[21] Whether clients stay with their patrons for long periods depends largely on the size of their flocks and herds. Among the patron group there may be individual water surpluses because some of the men are poor in animals, but the client has no right to demand – or for that matter, supplicate – for the use of these individual surpluses. An agnate is qualified to assert priority to water surpluses, and after these demands are met matrilateral or affinal relatives of other groups, and a category of people called Laff (literally, gathered up; the term is used to denote people who have been assimilated to a patron group) are given priority over clients. Individual agnates urge the necessity to meet the needs of their respective matrilateral or affinal relatives if they have a disposable surplus from their own shares, and if either of these relatives happens to be an agnate as well – this is often the case, as a result of parallel cousin marriage – the transfer of a surplus can be effected without consulting the group. Where clients are concerned, such transfer between individuals is not possible in that clients unlike relatives are attached to corporations and not to its individual members. They therefore occupy the most disadvantageous position in the list of priorities of users of resources. In the event of inadequate water supplies in the territory of one group, clients must perforce move to another. Patron groups are hesitant to dismiss their clients, and they only do so when all efforts to meet a critical situation have failed. The result of this movement is a disruption or a cessation of linkages and a disorganisation of the power field of a patron group. The effect is, paradoxically, less serious for the clients. Basically their aim is to gain access to the use of natural resources, and if this cannot be made available by one group, another is likely to welcome them. Resources are not owned by them, but they are always able to use them, and in so doing they are able to increase their stock and accumulate wealth. Granted this, then it may seem that their inferior legal status in landed property rights denies them very little in practice. This is not true. The critical point about their legal status is not that they are unable to use land and water, but that they lack managerial control over them; they are not proprietors, as Fustel de Coulanges pointed out.[22] Use and control of landed property is not a mere legal distinction. Control equips a patron for political action of a kind which a man in client status can never enjoy. Rights to dispose the use of land create political potentialities for patrons in the sense that they can attract a following from nobles of other tribal sections, from kinsmen in these or their own section or from clients. Permission to use land confers political significance on clients, certainly, making them objects of competition for patrons, but they lack the power to attract others in their own right.

The importance of landed property compared with other forms of property is that it is a stable and durable commodity. Animal wealth is not, since it is subject to so many vicissitudes that it cannot create enduring relationships. Political power that rests on ephemeral consumable goods is quite unlike power founded on landed possessions, since it then becomes subject to the same whims of fortune that strike the commodities. In Cyrenaica mobile property consists mainly of animals, which, like all forms of this class of property, are not only inherently more easily transferable than land, but may be lost through disease or reduced in numbers by extended droughts. Moreover, the power built on animal wealth varies directly with the personal skills of the owner in securing advantages. Inalienable landed property, particularly when it is vested in a corporation, guarantees an irreducible minimum political advantage. Mobile property offers a skilful individual the opportunity to achieve tactical success in power politics, but there is no guarantee that it will endure. Tied property in land offers the opportunity to plan a strategy for the capture of power over decades. Anarchic individual power is associated with manipulative property; fixed property is the basis of class power. It follows from this that if ownership rights in land are removed from the agnatic corporations, or if it ceases to be tied and converted to individual ownership, patron-client relationships terminate. In the plateau and off plateau areas some wells have passed into individual hands and some others are now under municipal control. During Italian rule in Cyrenaica,[23] some individuals bought cisterns which they subsequently paid to have repaired and the openings ringed with cement and secured under locked metal lids. The Italians declared other cisterns, in the vicinity of villages, which they did not require for their own use, public, and allotted hours to herdsmen for watering their animals, without regard to the original ownership. After the war, protracted disputes raged over the problem of ownership, but the rota system is still practised and the time for watering animals is shared by Sa'adi and Marabtin tribesmen alike. Such alterations to property ownership have caused far-reaching changes in patron-client relationships among the people living in these areas, and it is partly for this reason that this analysis is confined to the people inhabiting the semi-desert areas. It would not be true to say that the status distinction between the Sa'adi and Marabtin has become wholly defunct on the plateau, but people of client origin now occupy territory as owners, they use the water resources without first seeking the permission of freemen, and they dispute claims to land by the freemen, just as the freemen dispute these issues among themselves in the semi-desert territories. Many of the contemporary leading lineages among the plateau tribes are of known client stock and some of the most powerful shaikhs have been recruited from them. In the light of these changes, there may be some point in making the distinction between Sa'adi and Marabtin, but it would be seriously misleading to equate the terms with patrons and clients.[24] These brief remarks on changes among the inhabitants of the plateau have been included to make the importance of inalienable landed property in patron-client relationships more pointed, and not with the intention of opening a comparative discussion. While land remains tied to the agnatic corporation the relationship persists; but when it is freed the relationship collapses.[25]

The landed property vested in a corporation, among the semi-desert peoples, enables patrons to alter the population position of groups. When a group is poised to expand its power field, it may be inhibited because of its relatively numerical weakness. Population increase by natural process is too slow for power purposes. Recruitment of clients accelerates normal growth. In 1948, a tertiary tribal section had recently won a repute for its wealth and political dominance over other groups in its vicinity. Partly, this had been achieved by the disproportionate number of young able-bodied men to non-productive elders.[26] It was their boast then that they were a pure patron group without clients working for them or living with them. At critical periods of the year, however, the labour force was overstrained, and there was insufficient slack in it to allow one or two men to remain in the camp at all times – necessary in the semi-desert where women are ritually prohibited from slaughtering an animal, which in turn meant that the arrival of guests caused a crisis because they could not be entertained properly. The two elders were sometimes absent on political business and the other men fully engaged, so that the group had difficulty in meeting the demands on its hospitality, a serious matter where the obligation to offer the appropriate entertainment to a guest is given such strong precedence.[27] The leader complained that his eldest son ought to be available to relieve him of some of the burdens of leadership, particularly to fulfil the role of remaining in the camp to deal with eventualities, but he could not be spared from other tasks. Two years later, these men who had proudly announced the noble homogeneity of their community, had gathered in a cluster of five client tents.

The gathering in of clients is not merely a matter of wanting clients and seducing them away from other groups. Clients have to fit the demographic structure of the receiving patron group. If it requires more able-bodied men to exploit its resources fully, a client cluster – consisting mainly of aged people – would be unwelcome. If a patron group has an ample labour force, it may be in its interests to absorb clients with many animals and a disproportionate number of older men. The patron group referred to in the previous paragraph was in the fortunate position of having resources to offer without also having to pay much heed to the ages of prospective clients; in the event, it accepted a group of clients of a range of ages together with their camels, sheep and goats. Sometimes a group can do no more than accept one male, required, perhaps, to solve an urgent problem of shepherding. At all times, patrons aim at capturing followers, but it is never a simple matter of inviting anyone who may wish to join. How many clients a group wishes to receive at any given time must necessarily be responsibly related to its own animal and human populations, otherwise pressures of various sorts soon mount and the relationship breaks. By the same token, clients are not free to move capriciously: before they leave one group they must feel confident that there is a home for them elsewhere. Moreover, the departure of persons from a group, regardless of their status, leaves it with a smear of opprobrium, unless they are exiled as punishment for serious offences; otherwise patrons make every endeavour to hold their clients. If a move is made, without a specific cause, to a group where the rewards appear to be more attractive, this can precipitate hostilities between the two patron groups concerned. Induction involves the peril of punitive retaliatory action. Powerful groups, better able to withstand the consequences, engage in such manoeuvres, and declining patron groups are the favoured places of piracy. But if, when circumstances permit, clients can be detached from a powerful tribal section by a powerful competitor, success can become a triumph.

Mobility, whether voluntary or enforced, is always present in client status. But their desire to move, and their patron's wish to despatch them, are both circumscribed by the harsher necessities of population in its relation to available resources. Contraction of resources means the shedding of clients. Expansion of resources through falling numbers or more available land, makes the retention or increase of clients a matter of urgency. Age is only one factor which constrains the free movement of clients from their patron group, if they see or hear of better prospects elsewhere; the number of clients is no less critical. The attachment of a single client is never very troublesome, his reception into a group resting largely on his compatibility after a trial period of perhaps a few months. His departure from his previous group occasions slight concern, the loss is small and it can be put down to individual idiosyncrasy. Clients arriving in numbers of twenty or more (including females) cause serious problems of accommodation, necessitating a careful reappraisal of water resources, the labour force, the composition of the existing population, the kind of help most needed in the realm of female as well as male activities, the price to be paid for the anticipated economic and political advantage and so on. Individual clients possess the greater potential mobility; their absorption is much easier, paradoxically their moves less frequent; the single client presents virtually no threat, and marriage to a patron's daughter secures an enduring interest in his patron's group, thus diverting his interest away from his class status. Clusters of clients are not as easily deflected away from the interests they have in altering their status as a group, which an increase in their strength threatens. Single clients beget children for the patron group, in practice; the children of a group of clients add to the number of that group, and strength of numbers makes the possibility of a bid to capture land a worthwhile venture. To dismiss them diminishes a patron group, at the same time offering a gratuitous bonus to competitors. Dealing with numbers of clients is a dilemma, for a small patron group, with the spectre of extinction on one of its horns and relative loss of power on the other.

The task of keeping a balance in numbers is complicated by the fact that clients have their own livestock. Those who have many camels and a large flock of sheep find it more difficult to move to another group than those who have a small number of animals. Conversely, the exit of wealthy clients produces a gap in the total resources of a patron group which cannot easily be filled. Wealthy clients find entry into a new group difficult and they are obstructed by the old. Their choices are to seize their patron's land, to remain and see their wealth skimmed away by their patrons, or to divide and disperse. It is not possible for them to stay and continue to increase their livestock and to use it for their own political advancement. This latter course is not possible because, although they are owners of animals, ownership of mobile property is not the same for them as it is for their patrons; they are fettered in its use by the shackle of status. A client is liable to more and different demands than a patron is required to accept. There are some things clients can do with their wealth for their own immediate benefit. They can use it to better their diet and to ameliorate their standard of living a little; they can use it to entertain, albeit within close social limits;[28] when they die, it does not pass to their patrons, but is inherited by their heirs. The demands of a patron must, however, be met. Thus when a blood money payment is due, the agnates of a corporation bear equal responsibility to pay, but they are not the first to be approached for contributions; clients are approached before agnates, and in one case which I recorded a noble shaikh claimed he collected more than enough for a blood money payment from his clients alone, retaining the excess himself in his role as tribal 'banker'. Freemen, particularly if they are old, demand grain from them; one old man I knew returned from a visit to his clients with the surety of a year's supply of grain for his wife and himself. Funerals and weddings are two other occasions when clients give to their patrons. When they shear sheep, those who have an abundance give fleeces not only to their poorer kinsfolk, but to the poor among their patrons as well. The amount of dates they bring back from the distant oases supplies some, at least, of their patrons, needs as well as their own. It is true that wealth does not pass one way only. Patrons give to their clients in similar circumstances of need, but with a difference: the client is obliged to give, whereas the patron does not do so under duress; and, in any event, the amounts that pass from client to patron greatly exceed those which pass in the reverse direction. Since demands can be made on his wealth, the ability of a client to amass wealth is checked, more wealth evoking greater demands. Clients, therefore, have to produce to satisfy their wants, plus an additional amount to be given to their patrons.

As a class, clients are compelled to produce more than their needs. But overproduction still leaves them debarred from political power. Attached clients are politically important to patrons, and their acceptance of clients is basically an attempt to expand politically.[29] Sa'adi tribesmen demonstrate their descent status only when they have attached clients to throw it into relief. Their clients need not be their co-residents; they can be members of a section of one of the client tribes, referred to earlier,[30] as long as the tie is acknowledged by them. Demarcation of patron status is not achieved by the presence of an individual client, for an individual, no matter into which of the various status categories he falls, is distinct as a social person from a group of the same category.[31] Doubt is cast on Sa'adi status if a patron group lacks clients, as in the case of the Subh section of the Magharba tribe, of whom it was said that they could not be Sa'adi tribesmen properly speaking 'because they do not have any clients', although this was, partly, a manner of speaking about the contemporary period of political disunity and consequent fractionisation through which the group was passing. While they confer patron status on Sa'adi tribesmen they cannot themselves progress to political maturity. A shaikh, who had recently admitted a number of clients, said that he would never rely on them because he could not be certain that they would stay. Since there is no reason for them to move as long as they are given adequate water supplies and ploughland, and find that they are able to live in amity with the members of the patron group, the reservations of the shaikh were about the carrying capacity of the local resources because, socially, the relationships of the two classes were prospering. His view was that only agnatic kinsmen are reliable, but again, what he meant by agnatic kinsmen were people who have proprietory rights in the land of his corporation;[32] they are reliable in the sense that they stay, because a move away from their natal group is a surrender of the rights they have in land. In short, it is the mobility of clients which robs them of political responsibility and allows them nothing more than a participative role. In a state of feud – to give a spectacular illustration of the status differentiation – a client may actually fire the bullet which kills an enemy tribesman, this fact may be widely known, yet the responsibility for the homicide rests with the patron group. In 1950, a client of the Sa'ait stock attached to the patron group Mansur shot a client of the noble Subh section. The Subh noble tribesmen charged the nobles of Mansur with responsibility for the offence, but they refused to accept it, arguing that the killer was a Sa'ait client. 'Who are the Sa'ait?', asked the

Subh shaikh, adding, 'I do not know them. I only know 'Ait [lineage segment] Mansur. We must kill you.' In other words, clients perform acts which contribute to the political liabilities of their patron group, and, as long as they act in accordance with the political aims of their patrons, they enjoy freedom from vengeance which is exacted on noble tribesmen, as the illustration makes clear. From this partial political exclusion, it follows that the assessment of a client's worth in blood money is lower than that of a nobleman, since one aspect of blood money is its compensatory value for a political loss. The rule stated by the Bedouin is that the blood money for a client is half that for a noble man – the same amount as that for a woman. I did not hear of any contemporary blood money payment being made for the life of a client, but I doubt whether this reduced payment would be accepted nowadays. Also, the rule would be applicable only in certain cases. If a client killed one of his patrons, I believe the Bedouin when they say that they would exact heavy vengeance; and, in any case, the client would be expelled immediately. On the other hand, when a noble tribesman kills a client of an enemy noble section, this is regarded as calculated insult added to homicide and demands a heavy vengeance, which is exacted on noblemen. In these circumstances the political value of a client is rated as high as a nobleman. Therefore, how the political worth of a client is rated depends largely on the particular sets of relationships evoked by the homicide. Nevertheless, it is true to say that the blood money for a client is less than for a nobleman when considering status of persons without adding situational complications, even if the government authorities insist on equality, for there is nothing to prevent clients acquiescing to additional demands if they take a noble's life or accepting a reduced amount if one of them is killed, once the formal negotiations have ended.

Wealth in the form of mobile property does not buy political maturity for clients. They use it to make marriage connections in the same way as their patrons, but the connections thus established are similar only in the kinship idiom used to express them. Clients marry among themselves, they marry into other client groups, they give their daughters to their patrons and they marry the daughters of noble tribesmen: the general pattern of their marriage linkages and that of their patrons show much similarity in design. But it is the quality of linkages, not their pattern, which matters. Each link is described as patrilateral, matrilateral or affinal as suits the particular case, for both patrons and clients, the language they both use is the same, but the similarity in the words used to designate relationships established through marriage conceals the critical differences in the relationships themselves. A client who marries the daughter of his client agnate does not thereby alter his rights to land and water, but a nobleman who marries his parallel cousin has the chance of capturing his affine's water surplus, permitting him to increase his flock and herd. Agnation, if taken to mean the consanguineous relation of males of common patrilineal origin, cannot mean the same thing for clients as it does for nobles; its two forms are embedded in wholly different matrixes. Similarly, a patron marries his mother's brother's daughter and as a result has reason to anticipate advantageous access to water resources, possibly to his mother's brother's animal wealth also, if the latter has no male issue; but a client who marries his freeborn mother's brother's daughter does not gain water resources, because his father-in-law is not free to dispose of his surplus unilaterally to a client, and he is prohibited from passing his animal wealth on to a client son-in-law in any circumstances.[33] If a noble tribesman marries his parallel cousin his status is unaltered, yet if a client marries the daughter of a patron, his status shifts immediately, and there is a chance that it may be transferred to noble status ultimately. A noble tribesman's interest in an affinal alliance is the potential increase in power it offers, and any affinal alliance holds this promise; the significance of affinity for a client is determined by the status of the affines, whether they are of his cluster, or of another client cluster, and only if there are patrons does he begin to hope for a change of status. The particular marriage link a client wishes to make is impeded or facilitated by the amount of wealth he has at his disposal; however rich he is in animals he is precluded by his status from most of the benefits wealth brings to his patrons.

It would be erroneous to conclude from what has been said that clients suffer the servile indignities of a poor and oppressed class. In the ordinary run of daily life, it is impossible to distinguish between patrons and clients. When a guest arrives in a camp, the welcome given is the same for the noble and the client, and the latter is as exacting on his host as a noble: if a guest is heard to order his host to fetch him some water immediately and then complains that it is unpleasantly warm, or grumbles after an ample repast that the meat was underdone, or that the tea was not sweet enough, it would be impossible to tell from this whether the guest was a patron or a client. There is no difference of dress. Save for the tents of recent Tripolitanian immigrants, those of the freemen and clients are indistinguishable. There are rich and poor in both statuses, and the prime symbol of wealth, the horse, is to be seen tethered in front of the wealthy client's tent, as well as the wealthy nobleman's tent. This general sameness is not surprising, because the economy is marginal and differences of the kind that appear where rank occurs are insupportable. By and large, their camp life is indistinguishable, clients and patrons intermingling freely, exchanging gossip and so on. For all this, when quarrels break out among the agnatic patrikin, the division appears. Agnatic concentration is unusually high in Cyrenaican camps. Quarrels are endemic to them, arising out of the fact that men with the greatest identity of interests, whose behaviour is rigidly governed by strict rules and who are bound by impelling rights and duties, are co-residents. The disruptive effects of continuous quarrels among agnates would reduce life to chaos. Yet it is inherent in their relationships that precipitating occasions are ever present. Quarrels and even severe disputes do occur among agnates, but, significantly, the immediate cause is not attributed to agnatic relations. Clients, women and children (particularly the first two) are the cause of all quarrels between agnates, so it is said. In the sense that particular quarrels can be related to trivialities involving them, the statement is true, but the important fact is that some agnates are ranged against others in all quarrels. The allocation of blame to clients and women achieves the double purpose of giving each quarrel a uniqueness, thus preventing them becoming cumulative and rapidly reaching breaking point. Agnates quarrel, and if their relationships degenerate, the source of quarrels, as they see it, can be removed. Clients are compelled to move; others are brought in when necessary; the agnatic storm blows itself out and the lineage, wherein lies the core of conflict, is left to function unimpaired. When patrons attribute quarrels among agnates to their clients, what they do is deflect attention away from the institution of agnation, which fails to comprehend it, on to one, seemingly weaker in kind, which is able to deal with it. Clientage is able to serve in this way because clients, denied political control, participate in the tribal policy as the dictates of their patrons demand. To say that they are external to the lineage and intrusively participate in its affairs is to miss the essential fact that they coexist; and coexist they must if either is to survive. It would be wrong, also, to see them as minors along with women and children. Male children are minors, but in adulthood they reach full political majority; the political status of clients *vis-à-vis* their patrons remains unchanged. The position of women, on the other hand, is best discussed in the context of problems of sex roles. The three, however, have this in common: they are not permitted to interfere in the political proprietorship of adult agnates, so that its conflicts can be harmlessly sloughed off on to them.

A variety of issues, affecting many sets of social relationships, has been discussed. At the root of all these problems lies the relation of people to property in land, to the production and distribution of wealth. But why should this take the form of a patron-client relationship? Other ways of handling the problem are available; indeed wealth is distributed among Cyrenaican tribes, without recourse to status differentiation, for some purposes, gift exchanges for example. Why is this not extended? The

Bedouin answer is that descent gives land ownership to some but not to others. The explanation was rejected at the outset[34] as cultural. The sociological crux of the matter is that one class of people command the movements of another. This raises the question, why should a part of the population be pushed to move from one place to the next?[35] The immediate cause of this kind of population reshuffle is that the number of people using natural resources exceeds their carrying capacity. Mobility implies that the relationship itself is unstable. Instability is brought about in a number of ways. If the animal or human population increases, some displacement of population becomes necessary to restore the equilibrium. The resources themselves are subject to expansion and contraction, and this in turn affects population growth and decline. The resources are directly affected by the natural elements. In Cyrenaica, the vagaries of the climate are such that a surplus or deficiency is brought about almost whimsically. Of the climatic elements, the most important is rainfall. Water, in areas marginal to the deserts, is always the prime mover. The variability away from the mean rises to several hundred per cent. Admittedly the aggregate fall in any year is small and the fluctuations are of only a few inches, but small amounts make big differences in these areas. Some rainfall at any time of the year may suffice for human needs; some rainfall at specific times of the year may provide enough water for some or all of the animals; cereal growing is dependent not so much on the annual aggregate rainfall, but the time and frequency of its fall. Each year brings anxiety, and by about March the Bedouin must take stock of their supplies to assess their capabilities and dispose their groups. It is now that they must make the decision to welcome anyone who cares to join the camp, or to keep to their existing numbers, or to move some people away. If the decision is to send some people away no agnate will leave under compulsion. Agnate cannot shift agnate; they are equals as far as their rights to the natural resources are concerned, and to demand their departure would be tantamount to expulsion. But, where the climate is so marginal that it produces superabundance or nothing, where the extremes may alternate for a few years, or where near drought conditions may occur over a number of years, agricultural production fluctuates markedly and animal husbandry varies between success and failure. To meet this, and in order to exploit the environment to its maximum, there clearly must be the means for shifting people and their animals from place to place so that pressure can be relieved here and a surplus mopped up there. The pressure on resources cannot be met by protracted argument about who should leave. Decisive action must be taken, and therefore the power to command movement must be vested in part of the population to the exclusion of the remainder. Clients can be told to go; and although all the client clusters do not have to move annually – on the contrary, particular groups stay attached to the same patrons for long periods – a certain number move each year. The percentage of clients who move annually is an index of the general instability in the economy; the percentage of clients in the total population is an index of the way in which the general instability afflicts selected areas in specific years.

At the beginning of this discussion I found it necessary to exclude some categories of Marabtin. I have also omitted a number of other classes for similar reasons. The Laff do not supplicate annually for access to resources but they are not patrons either, since they are not yet fully assimilated; they stand out in disputes over land and water when nobles challenge their claims by referring to their status. Khut, agnates, is one of those elastic words which can be expanded in meaning to include patrilineal kin, Laff and Marabtin, contracting again to the narrow range of consanguineous brothers only. The Jar (neighbour) is a temporary resident, unless he stays to move into another relationship; he is given protection while a co-resident. The Nazil (from the root *nazala*, meaning 'to descend' or 'dismount') is a person seeking sanctuary; he is afforded protection in general and against his pursuer in particular. Finally, the Daif (guest) is a person whose sojourn may last from a few hours to a few days; he is given over, as the Bedouin say, to his host so that he can be given fitting hospitality and protection. I will readily admit that the various statuses have common forms of relationships. Dependence is one form they have in common, and protection another. But dependence of one sort or another occurs in practically all sets of social relationships, and therefore lacks all discriminatory usefulness;[36] the same remark applies to protection. To place many disparate statuses in one category leads to confusion and misses the sociologial significance in them all.

4

Aspects of the feud

When a Bedouin kills another in Cyrenaica, one of a number of consequences ensues.[1] According to the Bedouin, the particular consequence is determined by the genealogical positions of the persons or groups concerned. In the first part of this chapter an analysis of the disturbances in social relationships precipitated by homicide is made, using a lineage model as a framework. In this part of the discussion the arrangement of the information corresponds closely to the view the Bedouin give of their relationships. Additional information is then presented to show that this lineage model neither covers several important areas of social relationships nor enables an accurate prediction of events to be made. This raises the issue: can the comprehensive power of the model be increased by complicating it, or does complexity destroy its utility? The argument advanced is that the lineage model is not a sociological one, but that it is a frame of reference used by a particular people to give them a common-sense kind of understanding of their social relationships. For sociological purposes this means that the lineage model, with its supporting theoretical presuppositions, must perforce be abandoned. In the latter part of the chapter some of the implications of adopting this position are discussed. Particular stress is given to the feud, for this is one of the few societies in which it occurs.[2] What is meant here by a state of feud is a set of relationships between two tribal groups which are characterised by hostility whenever two or more of their members meet. These hostilities are of a sort which cannot be terminated; feud is not a matter of a group indulging in hostilities here at one moment and there the next, but a sequence of hostilities which, as far as the contemporary Bedouin are concerned at least, know no beginning and are insoluble. Feud and the other forms of relationships to be discussed presently are to be understood, in part, by reference to the ordered divisions of the tribes. It is necessary at the outset, therefore, to give a brief statement about the tribal organisation; other details will be included as they become relevant.

There are nine noble tribes in Cyrenaica whose members are referred to as freemen. These tribes see themselves as divided into three genealogical orders of sections: primary, secondary, and tertiary. The tertiary tribal sections correspond to the camps which cluster around the larger watering points during the drought season, May to November. Such camps consist of clusters of smaller camps in which the concentration of agnatically related males is over 80 per cent. Within the latter kinship links are known, so that these agnates are consanguinely related as well as politically united. The populations of most tertiary groups vary from about 200 to 700 or so, but a group ceases to be viable if the number of male adults drops much below fifty. Political division is absent from these tertiary groups, regardless of their precise size, for, whatever may be the condition of developing local lineages, the acceptance of a common name carries with it full political responsibility incumbent equally on all their members. Each of these tertiary sections, moreover, has its own watering point, ploughland, and pastures; each has its own *watan* or homeland. This statement is true of all tribal sections of whatever order of segmentation. In other words, the tribes and their sections correspond to an ordered division of the territory.

Names of tribal sections are the same as those given in the genealogies. Both tribe and lineage are identically ordered. Lineages develop and split at the tertiary order of segmentation,[3] and, *a fortiori*, the process is the same for the tertiary tribal sections. Split, in other words, occurs where relationships are most intense.

The summer community which constitutes a tertiary section breaks up once the rains begin in November or December. At this time of the year water is readily available in the numerous small cisterns, pasture is plentiful, and the animals are giving milk. These combined reasons lead the larger summer camp to divide into smaller camps of some five to ten tents. The latter are separated one from the other by short distances – a mile or so – but together they form a cluster in that they are territorially distinguishable from a neighbouring and similar group of camps. Tertiary sections are discrete also in the sense that all the major necessities of daily living are available within their several territories. Each controls its own natural resources, and these resources are the same for all the camel-herding groups – in any given year one may have more of a particular commodity than another, but the difference is in degree and is ephemeral, so that the opportunity for the development of trade relations is absent.[4] Save for straying animals, a section has no urgent need to seek relationships with others, as long as the rainfall is sufficient to permit exploitation of local resources.

The tertiary section is also regarded as the corporate group *par excellence*, in which 'the one word does for all'. Corporate identity is conceptualised as 'one bone' or 'one body'. An offence against one of its members is held to be an offence against all; if one of its members is killed 'we all lose blood'. When one of its members commits homicide the responsibility falls on all equally. Blood money, when received, is shared by all save for a special portion reserved for the 'owner of the blood', the nearest agnate of the victim. In opposite circumstances, all adult males accept the responsibility of contributing an equal share to the blood money. Rules of membership, simple in their brevity, express graphically this corporate identity: 'You must strike with us and be struck with us; you must pay with us and receive with us.' The group also bears a name, and there is never any doubt about the affiliation of any tribesman. That group of men – known as the *'amara dam* – who are agreed on the obligation to exact vengeance, to pay blood money when necessary, to engage in common defence, and to accept the possibility of death in vengeance, is a fixed and clear-cut group, not one whose membership has to be calculated by reference to degrees of kinship in regard to a specific situation, as appears to be the case among other peoples.

Homicide within the *'amara dam* brings about an impasse in relationships. A blood-money payment is out of the question since the acceptance of blood money by one part of a tertiary section from another of its parts is tantamount to a statement of split. Only in conditions where relationships within the lineage have developed to the point of political severance is it anticipated that a blood-money payment may be demanded; but this problem is not the same as that at present under discussion. Bedouin say that blood money cannot pass within the *'amara dam*, for those making the payment would be the persons receiving it. This is spurious reasoning, since the 'owner of the blood' is awarded more than any other members of the group as it is, and arrangements could obviously be made to pay him separately. Blood money is out of the question because it distinguishes relationships between people as belonging to two distinct political communities, and not because of any difficulty of distribution. In Bedouin thinking, an injury to 'the one body' is an injury to all its parts. Blood-money payments by members of a corporation to one or more of its members is a contradiction in terms. In the same way, vengeance is also excluded, for this merely doubles the original loss. A reprisal exacted in hot blood is always a possibility, but this is not referred to as *thar*, vengeance. Even if, at a later date, the closest kinsman of the victim should slay the offender, the act would not be referred to as *thar* and any connection with earlier homicides would be denied.

Stultified in the field of political action, there is little else that can be done. Expulsion is a possible course of action – and expulsion has occurred. Records show, however, that exile is almost invariably voluntary.[5] Moreover, exile is terminated as a rule by the return of the offender to his camp after the lapse of a number of years. For instance, a man who had already killed six people killed a seventh, his first paternal cousin. He and his brothers fled the tribe; he died in exile and it was not until some thirty years later that his brother and nephew returned. Another man, who had killed his first paternal cousin, used my entry into a camp as the occasion for his re-entry, pitching his tent rope on rope with mine, and mine in turn was rope on rope with the tent of the camp's shaikh.[6]

An effort is always made to hush up the matter when a homicide occurs within a tertiary section. It is for this reason that the name of the victim is not perpetuated. Normally it is an obligation to perpetuate the names of the deceased, especially when they have been killed in homicide, but in the circumstances now being discussed the name is suppressed. As one man expressed the general sentiments, stretching out his toga in front of him: 'Look at the hole in my toga; it would be better without it, but what can I do? Make it bigger? It is better to cover it up'. Any penal action taken against the offender could only enlarge the wound he had already opened. The notion of corporate identity is so strong that it eliminates the use of penal action against one of its members for the greatest offence of all. While overtly every effort is made to expunge the memory of a homicide of the sort described above, the Bedouin are most articulate in their views about the offender. He is referred to as one who 'defecates in the tent', thus likening him to an animal, for no human being would do this. Other expletives used in reference to him are: one who 'destroys the lineage', who 'corrupts the family'; he is one who 'brings confusion', who 'provokes God' and causes 'the evil of leprosy to eat into relationships'. Their feelings about the offender, who 'commits robbery internally', are summed up in the word *fitna*. This, in its Cyrenaican use, corresponds closely to the notion of sin as it is used in the Old Testament; in the sense, that is to say, of an act which causes an impasse in relationships, which creates chaos among a small group of related people, and produces internal calamity. And this is indeed the situation brought about by such homicide among the Bedouin. Flowing blood, they are wont to say, can only be staunched by blood (i.e. a vengeance killing), but if a man kills within a close agnatic range the corporate body continues to bleed. Nothing can be done. The group is left helpless, and this is sin.

The first step in this exposition, therefore, is to attach to homicide within a tertiary section the notion of its being *fitna*, carrying with it voluntary and temporary expulsion.

A homicide which involves two collateral tertiary sections is a different matter altogether, for now the parties constitute two discrete political groups. Political machinery can be set in motion to deal with the breach in relationships, and consequently a homicide of this sort does not pose the dilemma which is created when it occurs within a politically undivided group. Not only do agnates of two collateral tertiary sections behave towards each other as two groups of people, but the nature of their relationships is fundamentally different from those obtaining between members of an undivided group. It is erroneous to suppose that because the different orders of sections are homologous in their structural aspects they do not differ; they do, because the interests associated with the various orders are different.[7]

Collateral tertiary segments are associated with different tracts of territory. Each has its own watering rights as a group, and although groups may share a grain store, it is divided on group lines. Members of these different groups do not gather together in summer to form a single community, though at some of the very big watering points they are near each other. Social relationships between them are, however, intense. Visits are frequent. They meet to exchange news, or to inquire after the sick. They exchange greetings during the major festivals, and members of one group attend the funerals and weddings of the others, taking gifts. They also meet at the grain stores. Herdsmen, as they pursue straying animals, wander freely in their neighbours' territory. Relationships of this sort, some of them vital for survival, do not permit the feuding relationships to be described presently. Permanent hostility which characterises the feud would seriously disrupt everyday economic activities, limit the pastoral movements of the Bedouin beyond endurance, and sever lines of communication which they always strive to keep open.

A homicide, when it involves two collateral tertiary groups must, therefore, be resolved quickly. This can be effected in two ways. Vengeance may be exacted immediately. This is always referred to as a vengeance killing or *thar*, and is to be distinguished from a superficially similar act within a tertiary group, since *thar* carries with it the implication that it is premeditated. A *thar* between two tertiary sections is considered to be the best way of settling the affair and, after an appropriate lapse of time, a peace meeting is held at which it is accepted that the killings have cancelled each other out. The deliberations at this meeting are followed by a meal at which all present 'eat around the one bowl'; the meal over, they all pray together. A life had been taken for a life and the way is now open for the restoration of normal peaceful relationships. Vengeance needs to be distinguished from feud, for while retaliatory killings provide the propulsive force, in the feud a vengeance killing may be the means whereby a settlement of hostilities is made possible.

An end to hostilities may also be brought about by a promise to pay blood money or *diya*, and its acceptance by the victim's group. Arrangements for blood-money discussions are made by a category of persons known as Marabtin bi'l Baraka, or 'clients of the goodness', men who, by virtue of descent and origin, stand outside the descent lines of the noble tribes, and who are accredited with divine goodness. They tend the sick, write amulets, and are always present at a peace meeting to give it the weight of their *baraka*. Soon after the homicide has occurred they act as intermediaries to bring the hostile groups together at a peace meeting.[8] Ostensibly, the first part of the proceedings at these meetings is to settle the amount of the blood money, and how and when it is to be paid. Agreement on these counts will have been reached, however, before the large peace gathering is assembled, for there is a generally recognised amount of blood money to compensate a homicide. The wrangling that goes on at the meeting is of a conventional kind, and it is known in advance that several distinguished guests present will supplicate for a reduction of the amount demanded by the victim's group, until the amount generally accepted as appropriate is reached. Such haggling makes it possible for the victim's surviving agnates to maintain the fiction that they yielded only under the strongest pressure from the desert leaders and holy men. The main importance of the meeting is that the two hostile groups are brought together again for the first time, that the cleavage between them has been narrowed sufficiently to permit them to eat round one bowl, and that, by virtue of this commensal meal, the way is now open for the restoration of normal relationships. Subsequently there may be another killing, which, in the mind of the perpetrator, is connected with the earlier death of a kinsman, but it is not publicly recognised as one in a series of killings, or even as a vengeance killing; it is regarded as unique, and the method of dealing with it is on the basis of this fiction. Feud is not permitted between two collateral tertiary sections, for although the pattern of homicide may be similar to that of a feud, the two are never equated. There is good reason for this, since, whatever the similarity in pattern, the social relationships between the groups involved are radically different; each homicide involving tertiary sections is regarded as a unique event, and the relationship between times are friendly, whereas in the feud relationships are permanently hostile and need not be otherwise for social, economic, or religious purposes.

Blood money, when it brings peace, brings it because payment is made only in part. It is never regarded as a payment for the life of a man, to be dissipated wantonly. 'The owner of the blood' should marry a wife with it to beget children (one son to be named after the victim) or to buy camels to provide for a future marriage, or to buy a horse to be used to ride in bringing vengeance. Sufficient amount is paid to cover either of the first two alternatives; as far as my records go the third alternative is romanticism. At the peace meeting the offender's group does not promise to pay the total amount in one sum. An initial instalment is promised after the next lambing season or barley harvest. When the time comes it can be argued that the sheep dropped a disappointingly small number of lambs, or that the barley harvest did not fulfil expectations. If there is room for negotiation over the initial payment, the permitted manoeuvring over subsequent payments is much greater. Promises made at the peace meeting relating to these subsequent payments do not specify the exact amount of each; the statement is no more definite than that the remainder should be paid over the following three to five years. Consequently when the second payment falls due, the offender's group can argue more cogently that their circumstances do not permit even a reduced payment, for the payment of the previous year was substantial and they have not yet recovered from this outlay. 'The owner of the blood' is pressed to consider this, and to accept only a fraction of the wealth he had come to collect. The argument is cumulative, and can be used to excuse the rapidly decreasing payments of each successive year, until there comes a time when attempts to collect payments are discontinued. The arguments about the payments bear no relationship to the wealth possessed by a group. During the annual hagglings, and while members of the offender's group are declaring their straitened circumstances as an excuse for the small amount offered, the 'owner of the blood' knows full well that two or three hundred of their sheep are grazing in the neighbourhood. This is beside the point. What is important is that the offender's group is showing a desire to remain on friendly terms, and members of the victim's group are doing likewise by accepting reduced amounts. Compared with what the payments should be, after four years they are trivial and soon cease altogether. Blood money, if it is to achieve the purpose of restoring peaceful relationships, must work in this way among the Bedouin, for, as they view the matter, a single payment of the full amount would only terminate relationships. There would be no further obligations to hold them together. The payment of a debt in full means only one thing – hostility. 'Where there is no debt, there are no relationships.' Debt must be allowed to run between groups, for it is this which creates obligations and perpetuates social relationships.[9] As the debt of blood money mounts, the social relationships between the groups improve. The cessation of payments and the absence of further demands are final earnest that the relationships are again normal.

The second step in this exposition, therefore, is to attach to homicide between tertiary sections the penalty of vengeance or the payment of blood money, both achieving the same end of bringing about a restoration of peaceful relationships.

Between secondary sections, relationships are again different. Ecologically, the areas are distinct. The topography may be dissimilar – sand dunes in one area and low valleys in another; secondly, the soils may differ – sandy soil here and firm valley bottom soil there; thirdly, while the climatic regime of the two areas may be broadly similar, since there is marked variability in the aggregate annual rainfall which is coupled with a high variability from place to place, each secondary section has its own micro-climate, sufficiently well defined for one area to be well watered in any given year while a neighbouring area suffers partial drought. These differences affect productive activities. Seasonal movements are also affected: some secondary sections move annually over considerable distances and in fixed directions, while members of a collateral section may move only a few miles and these short moves may vary in direction from year to year. It is true that minor ecological differences exist between collateral tertiary sections, but these do not affect the economy and the way of life in the manner described for secondary sections. Partly because of their territorial extent, and partly because of the larger aggregate population, the secondary sections are more self-contained, not only ecologically and economically but also in terms of social relationships. More of the requirements of everyday living can be met within the territory and span of a secondary section than within those of a tertiary section. Secondary sections develop a kind of specialisation to the extent that in any year some of them will have more usable natural resources than others, but because these differences are ephemeral they do not lead to the development of permanent trade relations. Add to all this the fact that agnates are concentrated in camps on the territory which belongs to their lineage, and the discretion of secondary sections is immediately apparent. Marriage rules make this discretion, potentially, at least, even more sharply defined, for unlike other 'lineage societies' where exogamy, coupled with other marriage regulations, compels the dispersion of kin links among lineage segments, the Bedouin are free to marry within as close a range as the first cousin on either side. Preferential marriage with the father's brother's daughter exists, not merely as a sentiment, but with the legal force of permitting a man this choice against all other men. Before a father arranges the marriage of his daughter he first must seek the permission of his brother's son. Moreover, if a first-parallel cousin is not available, a Bedouin is free to take as a wife any parallel cousin within the minimal lineage. Much weight has been given to the value of exogamy as a device for the definition of groups; parallel-cousin marriage is equally suitable for the purpose – indeed it is better for it has the effect of knitting the members of a local group together as cognates, thereby throwing the group into isolated relief.

Consequently, when a homicide occurs between two secondary sections, there is no urgent necessity to make peace, the relationship between them being of a kind that can be controlled and altered to suit the circumstances. It is between these groups that the argument – if the argument is taken up at all – centres on the circumstances of the killing, every effort being made to show that insult was deliberately added to homicide, that one homicide is to be distinguished from another because a man of great renown was singled out as the avenger's victim, or that in a vengeance killing there was a breach of taboo as well. A debt is always left over, and it is an impelling obligation for the Bedouin to redeem it. They frequently speak of vengeance in this context as 'redeeming the debt'. Again, any homicide between two secondary sections is regarded as one in a series, whether the details or even the name of the victim of the previous homicide is known or not. I recall discussing a double homicide with a close kinsman of the slayer, and the only way he could account for it was by telling me that his kinsman had to kill because his victims were of such and such a group. The feud knows no beginning, and it has no end. It is a form of behaviour associated with a specific structural order, and it is as persistent as the structural order itself; in this sense it is eternal. It was most difficult to get the Bedouin to give accounts of homicides other than those which had occurred over the past fifty years or so, but they invariably claimed that the origin was earlier than this, although they were wholly unaware of the identity of the earlier victims. In any event, their only historical frame of reference is the genealogy; and history, as a chronological sequence of events, has no meaning beyond the founding ancestor of a minimal segment. When they refer events to points on the genealogy superior to this, they are no longer thinking in terms of the temporal order of events, but in terms of what they know to be the contemporary relationships between groups, for the names on the genealogy are names of groups and do not bear a relation to a time scale in any sense. Put in another way, for them a homicide which involves two secondary sections must be a feud, because this is the nature of the relationships between the groups, and there must have been previous killings, otherwise the people involved would not belong to two separate secondary groups.

The relationships which are referred to as feud are of a kind which requires at least a show of hostility whenever the parties happen to meet. Even if they do not actually meet, but are in the vicinity, some sort of demonstration is likely. Thus, several shots were fired at a man riding some distance away from a camp, and although positive identification was difficult at this range, the men of the camp argued it must have been a member of a group with which they were at feud otherwise the passer-by would have dropped in on the camp. In another situation, two men entered a shop in a market-place; inside sat two men of a feuding group who, instead of retreating hastily, greeted those who had just entered, and the latter returned the greeting with blows on the head from the butts of their rifles. Markets in Cyrenaica are recognised to be places of peace. In their actions the two offenders not only injured two others but also broke a taboo in a public place. The victim's group now had to avenge not only the injury but the insult that the breach of taboo carried with it, as well. In most feud relationships this is characteristic. It is never a matter of a simple homicide, but of killing a man at the entrance to his tent, between the centre poles of his tent, or taking the life of a minor, or an elder too old to carry arms and so on. Each successive killing ensures that the hostile relationships will be perpetuated.

The third step in this exposition, therefore, is the association of a state of feud with the secondary order of segmentation.

When the relationships between the structurally superior primary tribal sections are examined, the arguments against the necessity for peace are stronger than in the case of secondary sections. Relationships between them are few and irregular. Only occasionally do members of these groups meet, and then often accidentally; very many men of collateral primary sections are complete strangers one to the other. If a homicide occurs between two primary sections it is unlikely that any attempt to open negotiations will be made. The offender's camp may be raided by a *ghazi* recruited from the victim's kinsmen. There would be no question of these primary sections going to war. On a raid firearms may be used, but the action is limited to a strike-and-run affair. If the issue is joined and members of both sides are ranged against each other they fight with sticks to avoid large-scale slaughter: warfare must not be allowed within the tribe. Wars belong to intertribal relationships. For one of these wars, apart from hearsay evidence, some records exist. These tell of a war which took place during the period 1860 to 1865, in which there were planned campaigns, the organisation of fighters into groups, and provisions for a labour force in the home territory, large enough to produce sufficient food to maintain an army in the field. During this war several hundred people were killed.

At this point, it is possible to summarise the stages in this exposition of the Bedouin view in diagrammatic form, in fig. 1. To complete this general statement, two further circumstances are cited by the Bedouin. If a man kills a related person who is not an agnate (it is expressed as killing the mother's brother) the breach in relationships must be healed as quickly as possible. The convention for dealing with this is that the offender, bound hand and foot, mounted on a horse, is sent to the camp of 'the owner of the blood', in the company of a holy man, there to make an offer of his life, saying: 'Here is my knife, my life is yours; here is my shroud, my life is yours.' No Bedouin would agree for a moment to undertake this journey if he thought the offer might be accepted. In Bedouin sentiments a life offered in this way cannot be taken. It is the convention which precedes a peace meeting and blood money. Any other way of dealing with the confusion, which spreads as a result of a homicide between cognates, is excluded.

Secondly, if a woman is killed, whatever the intersegmentary distance, the homicide is said to be accidental, because a man never 'intends' to kill a woman. Blood money arrangements are made as soon as possible, and the wealth – half that of a man – passes to the deceased's father, not to her husband, for a woman's 'bone' always belongs to her father. Obviously women cannot be allowed to enter into feud; since it is demographically compelling (apart from other reasons) for some of them to marry outside their natal groups, they might well find themselves residents in the enemy's camps, if they were to become involved in feuds.

This statement of the different means available for the regulation of homicide at the several orders of tribal segmentation is the view the Bedouin themselves hold of their relationships. An analysis of the facts presented thus far could bring out a number of interesting points with regard to the relativity of morals, the typification of acts by their social context, the significance of the orders of segmentation, and so on. Rather than proceed along these lines, however, it is more urgently necessary to reflect on the significance of the fact that the arrangement of the material in terms of what is usually called the lineage structure coincides with the Bedouin ordering of the same details. It is, of course, important to note that

Figure 1.

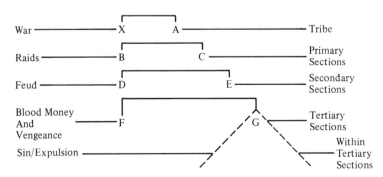

the account is not based on mere hearsay evidence. Each statement made can be documented from known homicides, and to this extent the model that has been used is consistent with reality. The model, nevertheless, can only be a representation of what a particular people, the Bedouin, conceive their social reality to be; it is a kind of ideology which enables them, without making absurd demands on their credulity, to understand their field of social relationships, and to give particular relationships their *raison d'être*. But, as will be shown, it would be a serious error to mistake such a folk model for sociological analysis. Such an error is difficult to avoid because the Bedouin, when defending their view, are able to cite enough bits and pieces of reality to make their argument convincing. The flaw in the reasoning is seen when it can be shown that its consequences are absurd. As an example of what is meant, the statement that feud is attached to groups at the secondary order of segmentation may be considered. If the statement were true, if each and every secondary section were at feud one with the other (and in a structural sense this ought to be so), then each tribe would be divided into small mutually hostile groups, which completely lacked any possibility of movement, even for pasturing purposes. Presented with this, the Bedouin would argue that this is not in fact so, because secondary and primary sections are interlinked in many ways. That is, they evoke what to them are contingencies to explain why they are at feud with one part of a secondary section but not with another. Once contingencies are permitted to enter in, the lineage model ceases to be of use, for what is implied is that at all times some parts of sections structurally situated for feuding do not in fact feud. Other facts can be adduced to show that the structural view is inadequate but, before proceeding to examine these, some general objections to the lineage theory need to be raised. In the first instance, the corner-stone in the theory of lineage systems is that they consist of parts which are in balanced opposition. It is no accident that the idiom generally used in discussing the segmentation of a lineage system is that segments bifurcate. Indeed bifurcation is necessary if lineage theory is to make sense, because if at any order there are more than two segments, then combinations can occur which are not comprehended by the theory. In the Cyrenaican lineage the number of segments at the tertiary order is haphazard, in some cases as few as two but in others as many as a dozen or so. Where there are many segments at this order it is rather pointless to speak in terms of balanced opposition. Moreover, at the secondary order of segmentation the number of segments is fairly consistent throughout the tribes, but they number more than two in all of them. It is also a fact that combinations occur and, moreover, these may be between the tertiary segments of two 'opposed' secondary segments.

Secondly, in lineage theory groups come together to constitute larger segments in opposition to like segments. Yet in lineage societies there is a lack of instituted authority, there are no chiefs distributed throughout the land as heads of segments of the hierarchical orders. This being so, then it is not possible for all the sections of, say, a secondary section to come together; there is no one to command the action. In fact, sections combine in Cyrenaica, but not in the way they should according to the lineage structure. In order to discuss this adequately, a lengthy diversion into an analysis of the distribution of power would be necessary. The matter must rest here with the admittedly somewhat dogmatic assertion that there are men who wield power over groups of varying populations, and that the extent of their domains cannot be understood by reference to orders in the lineage. Perhaps it is for this reason – because, that is to say, lineage theory effectively blocks the exercise – that relatively little has been written about the problem of leadership in these societies.

Thirdly, all segments should be fairly equal in numbers of people and economic resources, if the theory of lineage is to have substance in reality. In Cyrenaica the population of one tertiary segment may be three times or more that of another. Both may be structurally equal in the sense that they are named groups segmenting as a pair of brothers from a common father. As political groups, however, this equality has little meaning. Further, with regard to economic resources, some sections possess several wells and a territory of such extent that it straddles two or even more of what might be called micro-ecological areas. With marked preponderance in numbers and superiority of resources, some groups have grown into dominance, and the evidence points to the existence of this dominance in the past also. However alike sections may appear on a lineage chart, in political action there is conspicuous disparity. Each tribe possesses one tertiary section or more with a claim to be the owners of the 'Golden Stirrup'; these are large tertiary groups with relatively plentiful resources, with allies in other groups, and, in sum, with the power to terrorise other tribal groups.

These three objections to the lineage theory as a useful model for examining the consequences of homicide are serious enough in themselves, but another objection renders it still less satisfactory. This fourth objection relates to the implication that lineage theory cannot take account of women. Indeed, in some of the accounts of the political organisation of lineage societies, the impression is given that they are all-male societies: women belong only to the domestic and kinship realms. In terms of the theory, this must be so. Women, the marriage links they create, the forms of relationships that derive from marriage, the right of men to joke with others by virtue of a link through women, their rights to demand favours of men who are not their agnates, their right to expect contributions to bridewealth or blood money from maternal relatives – all these, and other forms of behaviour, have been dealt with as patterns of behaviour which interfere with or disturb agnation, or that cut across lineage affiliations. Such metaphors can only be justified if it is accepted that precedence must be given to agnation, to what people say they think their lineage relationships to be, and that there is some kind of primacy about what have frequently been called jural rules which constitute the structure, while behaviour which is not governed by these rules is to be relegated to the position of secondary forms having the effect of intruding only. But these secondary forms of behaviour are as impelling, as persisting, and are as much a part of social life as any of the so-called jural rules. It is possible to go further than this, and state that in societies where there is a high incidence of marriage among agnates of the local group, as occurs among the Bedouin, jural rules rarely appear in their 'pure' form in behaviour, since, in groups of this sort, each and every person constitutes a bundle of roles by virtue of the fact that he is one of a very complex cognatic group; a particular role, it is true, may take precedence in a particular situation, but all roles are present in each situation and affect behaviour. Precedence can only be given to specific forms of behaviour in relation to situations. There is no such thing as a general primacy with regard to any form. The concept of agnation as the centre of all political problems, disturbed or disrupted by, say, matrilaterality, is as inadequate as saying that the nucleus which pulls all other components into position is matrilaterality with agnation as a disturbing element. In reality there are numerous components present in all situations, which should not be lumped together under such categorising terms as agnation and matrilaterality, but which combine as separate components in a kaleidoscopic range of clusters.

Some of the components of behaviour subsumed under the notion of matrilaterality are briefly given here in order to appreciate more fully the consequence of inter-group marriage. Of paramount importance is the fact that, in Bedouin sentiment, to kill a relative is as sinful an act as the killing of a close agnate. When such a homicide did occur, during my period of residence among them, the Bedouin response was to assert that the offender was out of his mind – it was inconceivable that he could have committed the offence otherwise. Their attitude was reminiscent of the horror they display when a man kills his father or a full brother, and represents a much stronger reaction than is manifested when a man kills an agnate of, say, the third or fourth degree. They have every reason to be disturbed by the killing of a mother's brother, for, whatever personal affections may be involved, a crucial link is threatened. Their reasoning, however, is that relationships with the mother's brother are characteristically easy, that they are not demanding, that there is much joking in them, and that to kill within this range is, in terms of the general pattern of behaviour, stupid. What is of interest is that such killings do occur. I recorded three instances of men killing the mother's brother in the contemporary population, not to mention many others based on hearsay evidence only. Clearly, the relationship is more than a merely permissive one. The mother's brother may well be the only person who can help in certain crises, and if he withholds his assistance the sister's son is left in a dilemma. The form of behaviour in which demands are made is, as the Bedouin rightly say, that of asking a favour, but this does not mean that it is any the less urgent than a demand made against agnates. The range of favours is wide, and only a few can be detailed here. If a group has insufficient water to meet its needs a man first seeks help from his mother's brother. The request has a number of aspects to it: it is a test of the relationship itself; it is a matter of pride and status that a man can 'call' on another to help his group out of difficulties; it is an assurance that resources other than those jealously guarded by his agnates are available to him, and if a man is seeking to increase his power he must have available more than an agnate's share of local water resources to supply his flocks and herds. When a blood-money payment has to be made, the mother's brother is expected to come forward – it is his right to give without being asked. If a man wants a wife, he is not permitted to approach his father directly, but his mother's brother can put pressure on the father instead. If a man dies while his eldest son is still a minor, his brother may be required to act as guardian, and in this role he controls the son's property; disputes frequently break out as a result, with the son at a considerable disadvantage, for he cannot engage his father's brother in hostilities – but his mother's brother can do so for him. Whenever men come to possess animals before the demise of their fathers or when the father's brother is acting as guardian they mark them with the tribal and personal signs of their mothers' brothers. Men have the right to demand contributions for bridewealth from their agnates if they lack wealth; in practice it comes not from them, but from the mother's brother. Finally, in certain circumstances, if a man does not have male heirs, his sister's son might inherit all his wealth.

Affinity also carries with it a large number of rights. A poor man may take up residence in the camp of his father-in-law, and be kept by him. The latter may come to his son-in-law's aid in many of his dealings with his father. Like the mother's brother, the affine is a potential source of water-supply when rain has been insufficient on the homeland. He also helps with blood money and bridewealth, and he is expected to aid his daughter and her husband with gifts of food and wool.

The details given above by no means exhaust the list of rights a man possesses in his matrilateral and affinal relatives. Obviously, these are not the only forms of relationship either, and the other forms carry with them yet other claims of various sorts. Enough detail has been given, however, to make clear the point that local agnatic groups are so differentiated, and inter-group relationships are so important, that each aspect of homicide settlement previously described will require further examination, not in the sense that additional complications must be introduced, but with the question in mind, is not the structural presentation false? Before beginning this stage of the argument it is necessary to establish the fact that the links of affinity and matrilaterality which a group has with another are of a kind which necessitate their inclusion in an analysis of the arrangements for settling homicides.

Among the Bedouin, men are permitted to marry their father's brother's daughter and any other cousin of similar type within the local agnatic group. This means that most agnates will be related in other ways as well. Parallel-cousin marriage has the effect of diversifying the agnatic group, and creates small nuclei within it, each having its own characteristics and patterns of behaviour with others. Diversification of this kind leads to a differentiation between homicides within the tertiary group.

The Bedouin say that they always marry their parallel cousins, and do not give their daughters to others if they can help it. Census data does not support this view. Nearly as many men find wives outside their agnatic group as within it. Of importance in the present context is the direction taken by these external marriages. Perhaps the most striking feature is that the number of marriages with men of a collateral tertiary group is low, so low that they can be explained by special circumstances. Now collateral tertiary groups whose territories are adjacent experience intense day-to-day relationships. In the context of descent these are the most closely linked lineages – among older men there may be the recollection of the time when the two constituted a single community, and when they all lived together in the same summer camp. Common sentiment between them is very strong. The strips of territory they inhabit may be almost identical. Their discreteness lies almost entirely in the possession of separate natural resources, although in some cases pastures are shared. But their social boundaries are nevertheless sharply drawn, for the high incidence of parallel-cousin marriage within them, and the tendency for external links to leap-frog collateral segments, give them a definition which could not be bettered by exogamy. The basis of their discreteness lies, of course, in the competition that exists between them for natural resources; however much the Bedouin protest that their real enemies are the secondary or primary groups lying some thirty to fifty miles away, when they wish to enlarge their resources there is little point in attempting to capture a well a long distance away, which cannot be defended, and might be located alongside an enemy group. They do, it is true, engage in competitive hostilities over land and water situated some distance from their homeland, but when they engage in these activities they do so on behalf of a linked group, albeit with their own interests uppermost. The capture of natural resources for use by a tertiary group can only be achieved by an enlargement of its homeland, and this is only possible by expanding into a neighbour's territory.

Another feature of external marriages is that they are not spread among as many groups as in societies where there are exogamous clans, and where other rules of marriage appear to compel the maximum amount of dispersal. Instead, the external links created through marriage are highly selective, and are thrown out into ecologically differentiated areas, giving added economic security, or, in the case of date oases, an additional item to the diet at a time of the year when it is sorely needed. Once established these external links are perpetuated through cross-cousin marriages in successive generations. If the link is considered valuable, and relationships develop satisfactorily, other marriage connections will be woven around the first. Multiplicity gives added strength and durability, not in the mechanical sense of duplication, but of creating a more diverse kin structure, with its greater range of rights and claims, in which links can flourish. While the number of groups linked in marriage are few, the geographical spread is great. Marriage links exist with tertiary sections of collateral secondary sections, with collateral primary sections, and long distances away into other tribes. This spread can be interpreted as giving each tertiary group access to resources of wide ecological diversity. What is of interest in the present context is not the interpretation of the links but the effect they have on behaviour. Spread means that a group can call for help from a number of differently situated groups. Each one of these links not merely modifies the structural means for settling homicide, but converts the homicide into a sociologically quite different sort of act. It can, as the Bedouin like to think, be an act of merit for a man to kill another from a feuding secondary section, but there is no merit whatsoever in it if the tertiary section of that secondary section happens to contain affines or maternal relatives; this is a sinful act. The Bedouin themselves recognise this when they add to their structural explanation the rider that they do not feud with cognatic relatives. The difference between their position and a sociological one is that they see this as a contingency, not as a persistent necessity; they are able to maintain their position because they see their behaviour as explicable in terms of the simple ossified structure of their genealogical relationships. What they fail to appreciate is that these 'contingencies' are ecologically, economically, demographically, and politically essential. They are able to maintain their position also, because the model of a lineage structure they use, along with the two riders previously mentioned, affords them a kind of explanation for most occurrences. The argument is attractive both to Bedouin and to anthropologists because it is comprehensive and neat in its logicality. The next stage in the argument is to show that there is a far greater range of possible consequences to a homicide than those summarised in fig. 1 and that the additional consequences are related, not to the lineage structure, but to the linkages which have been discussed above.

I begin with a review of a homicide which involves two men of the same tertiary section. Bedouin classify all homicides within this range – as they do for any of the structural orders – as undifferentiated, but in each case, different sorts of relatives are concerned in the ensuing hostilities, and the consequences are, therefore, different also. Bedouin say that a man never kills his father or full brother. In the event of a man killing another man acknowledged to be his father, the act itself proves that he cannot possibly be his son. He is said to be illegitimate, thus making his mother an adultress and relieving the males of the agnatic line of the responsibility and the odium. If a maternal uncle of the agnatic group is killed, the offence is almost on a par with that of patricide or fratricide. When, however, the homicide is between two men who are agnatically distant, and not closely related cognatically either, but both are members of the same local agnatic group, what follows will depend largely on the size and stage of development of the group; if it is small, the homicide threatens to wreck it, but if it is large and on the verge of splitting the homicide may be the occasion for a split taking place and being recognised publicly by a demand for blood money. Threatened with wreckage, a small group meets a homicide by closing its ranks for self-preservation; a large group splits. The same event within the same kind of structural unit results in two quite dissimilar consequences. The reason is clear enough – the two groups are similar only in a general structural way, but sociologically they are not comparable.

When a homicide occurs between tertiary segments the solution, it was said earlier, is found in either a vengeance killing or a blood money agreement which later becomes caught up in a wider set of debt relationships. Records show that this is true in some cases, but in others the blood money is paid immediately and in one instalment. The recognition of a debt and its liquidation among the Bedouin is tantamount to a declaration of hostility, since without a debt the means for smooth-running relationships are lacking. Such a blood-money payment was made between two tertiary groups in the absence of the 'owner of the blood'; when he returned he sought out his brother's killer, and took two lives for one. Subsequently, there was a further blood-money settlement but there remained 'a man left over'. In other circumstances an annual payment, called *sana*, is demanded in addition to the prompt and full payment of the blood money. The attachment of the *sana* to a settlement is an invidious condition since it is regarded as a fee by those who have to pay it; it is said to lower the status of a group and 'one day, it must be repudiated'.[10] It may, circumstances permitting, serve to cast off all pretence of friendly relationships. It is more likely that it will lead to a further outbreak of hostilities. When I witnessed the payment of the *sana* the terms in which it was demanded were: 'You have a man on your backs. Are you going to repudiate this or are you going to give me *sana*? If you repudiate, we must seek vengeance.' The payment, one in a long series, was made on that occasion but there were loud grumblings among the men of the camp against their leader for his acquiescence and one suggested that they terminate the payments forthwith by shooting the claimant. Of the three forms of blood money cited, this latter is the extreme to which groups can go short of open feud. Its opposite is a blood-money payment which is mainly left as a debt, and which is accompanied by the 'gift' of a wife to the victim's group.[11] The wife is 'given' as an earnest that the offender's group wishes the full restoration of relationships ruptured by the homicide. There are, therefore, four forms of blood-money payment. The Bedouin view of these is that they are variants of what is, in principle, the same thing. Their view cannot be accepted. Each of the four payments points to diverse kinds of social relationships between groups, and their consequences are wholly disparate. These various kinds of relationships between the tertiary sections of the same secondary section exist because the relationships between all sections cannot possibly be the same if they are more than a pair in number. A secondary section which spans ten tertiary sections is not the same type of unit as one which spans only three. The greater the number of tertiary sections the greater the possible permutations in their relation-ships. What the Bedouin think of as variations in the form of blood money payment is related to the complexities that lie behind their simple lineage model. Bedouin can comprehend this complexity only by thinking in terms of a kind of average behaviour, regarding deviations from the average as fortuitous and explicable by the faulty reasoning that 'in this particular case, it just so happened' that this, that, and the other were part of the situation, failing to appreciate that apparent aberrations are constants to the extent that some sort of specifics occur in all cases. There is no reason why Bedouin reasoning should be followed in sociological analysis.

The consequences of homicides in which secondary groups are concerned present an even greater variety, for now the span has expanded to include many more groups, with a total population of several thousand people. Groups of this order are spread over a much wider territorial range; some structurally distant groups are neighbours by virtue of their propinquity, while some structurally proximate groups are far removed territorially. Some feuds lie dormant for long periods. Others erupt frequently. Some homicides between these groups are followed by the 'laying down of the denial' – the feud situation with most acrimony built into it, for one denial, followed by a vengeance killing, is met by a second denial and so on, excluding thereby any chance of a settlement. In other circumstances the offender's group boasts that it is responsible for a homicide, thus challenging the victim's group to a show of force. Only the more powerful tertiary groups would venture to do this, and it is only they who could meet a homicide against them with a spectacular show of force, compelling a weaker tertiary group (according to hearsay evidence) to break up and leave its homeland. The modes of killing in homicide differ in character. Some killings have been heinous and offensive in terms of general morality; their purpose is to sting the victim's kin to retaliate or to cause them to suffer general discredit and loss of status. While some parts of secondary segments are at feud, others are not. A homicide between affinally or matrilaterally linked groups, whether they are secondary or primary groups, is settled as quickly and as amicably as possible to prevent turmoil in their relationships. Feud concerns two tertiary sections, not the opposed secondary sections of which they are parts. Blood money and vengeance are not the responsibility of secondary sections, but of their respective tertiary sections.

At this point, a further statement concerning the external marriage links of tertiary segments throws further light on the feud. Previously it was stated that the competition between collateral tertiary groups for natural resources is indicated by a low rate of marriage between them. Their external marriage links reinforce the separation. One tertiary section, A, takes some of its spouses from section X of a collateral secondary section; A's collateral, B, takes some of its spouses from X's collateral, Y. A may be at feud with Y and B with X. The agnatic links between A and B, and X and Y do not mitigate the severity of the hostility in the two feuds, they exacerbate it. It would be erroneous to think of them as cross-cutting ties which promote peace. Stultified in the development of their hostilities by virtue of their territorial proximity and the sentiment associated with putatively close agnatic connection, A and B are able to express hostilities indirectly through their linked groups X and Y respectively. During discussions of disputes, homicides, or rival claims to water, whether the disputants meet in the camps or in administrative offices in the villages, men from the matrilateral and affinal groups of the parties directly concerned are also present to do most of the shouting. In some cases which I recorded a maternal relative was killed on behalf of an agnatic group to which he did not belong, although the latter accepted the responsibility. In the light of facts of this sort the lineage model obstructs analysis.

I now wish to make a few brief remarks about the relationships between collateral primary sections and paired tribes. Homicide, it was asserted earlier, results in raids and war between groups of these orders of segmentation respectively. Evidence can be adduced to show that both consequences have followed. The case usually cited to demonstrate that a single killing precipitates war between tribes is the celebrated war between the ʿAbaidat and the Baraʿasa tribes occupying a large part of central and eastern Cyrenaica. This war took place a hundred years ago, so that the evidence is mainly hearsay, but it is significant that when asked for details of the groups taking part the Bedouin make it clear that the entire tribes were not at war – some sections on both sides are said to have remained on friendly terms. Yet when wars are discussed in a general fashion, the Bedouin insist that tribes confront each other as such. If it is pointed out to them that men might be ranged against their maternal relatives the Bedouin mumble apologetically that they would not kill their maternal relatives – a lame argument since in the heat of battle men cannot make this kind of discrimination. Details of other wars also illustrate the point that only part of tribes face each other in strife, for though the stories of past events may be inaccurate there is genealogical evidence to substantiate their claims that certain groups were linked in the past, and in any case their statements assert that where these links exist they are not prepared to engage in hostilities. The several parts of each tribe, like the parts of primary and secondary sections, have as many different sorts of relationships as there are groups, and the general statement that tribes are warring units merely obscures the interest there is in their relationships. Tribes, further, lack the leadership to make war. I repeat that leadership does exist, but not even the greatest leaders, past or present, can rightly be described as leaders of their tribes, using the term in its structural connotation. Literature on the subject gives the impression that there are tribal leaders, because successive administrations have used the tribes and their divisions as a framework for attempting to rule the Bedouin, but the details of the power domains of individual leaders make it clear that they have little to do with the ordered divisions of tribes. A leader within part of one tribe may carry with him tertiary sections of another tribe, and if major hostilities break out between parts of these tribes, the sections of both which are joined as allies and related as kinsfolk will not fight against each other, for sections so linked enjoy stronger connections than the structurally linked tertiary sections of a very large secondary section. Consequently the statement that homicide results in tribal war when the offender and his victim are members of two separate tribes is not merely incomplete, not merely a simplification, it is wrong.

A point which has been implicit throughout the second part of this chapter needs now to be made quite explicit: groups do not come together in their respective structural genealogical orders. During my entire residence in Cyrenaica I did not see a group of agnates larger than a tertiary tribal section assemble for any purpose. It is true that the occasions when large groups are required to assemble are infrequent. It is also true that although the British Administration was serving a caretaker role only, it may have had an affect on the nature of tribal gatherings. Despite this qualification, there were several occasions when I expected tribal groups to assemble in lineage order if the fusion of sections in relation to like sections has any meaning in practice. Large groups of men did gather to dispute claims to wells, to argue about rights to ploughland, and to make peace. In every case that I recorded the agnatically closest groups of the main participants were absent, while members of genealogically more remote groups were present in strength. This statement applies to gatherings in the camps and in the administrative centres. One of the biggest gatherings I witnessed assembled in an administrative office in a village near the coast in the south-west of the country. Most members of the two tertiary groups directly concerned in the dispute were present. The agnates of the collaterally linked groups of the principals were unrepresented; indeed collaterals of one of the principals made it quite explicit that they were opposed to their genealogical allies and considered their pursual of the matter tiresome. The bulk of the crowd present was made up of men linked to the principals in a variety of different and non-agnatic ways, and it was they who provided most of the argument once the issue had been opened. It follows, therefore, that an analysis of political organisation and behaviour in Cyrenaica which is based on lineage theory leads to a gross misrepresentation. For, what I am arguing is not that the lineage model in its rarefied state is too simple, not that additional facts must be injected into it to complicate it, but that it does not provide an admissible basis for analysis.[12] The complication of something that is founded in error can only lead to complicated error, however many facts of real life are introduced in an attempt to give it substance. The Bedouin conception of their social relationships in terms of a genealogical ordering of groups is a fact of their social life, and in relation to some problems it is an important fact. My objection to the use which has been made of a people's ideology of their relationships is that it has been elevated from its status as a component of social life to such a position of universal dominance in all sets of social relationships that 'every sociological problem', as Fortes writes of the Tallensi, 'hinges on the lineage system'.[13]

If the ordering of groups within the frame of the Bedouin genealogy is abandoned as a basis for analysis, it does not follow that the only remaining view is that of small groups of people distributed throughout the country enjoying relationships merely as units. Regularity in relationships does exist, it is urgently necessary, and it persists; but this regularity is not consistent with a lineage model. Ultimately, feud is a violent form of hostility between corporations which has its source in the competition for proprietory rights in land and water. This competition makes it necessary for groups to combine to prevent the encroachments of others in similar combinations and also to expand their resources whenever the opportunity arises. The significant groups in a discussion of the feud are these power groups, and it is their composition, the shifting alliances within them, the growth and diminution in the power of tertiary sections constituting the combinations which makes the facts of feud intelligible. Furthermore, several different types of power structures exist which serve the different interests of the people composing them, and these are interlinked in combinations of superior span. But the formation of these structures and the modes in which they combine are quite unlike the articulations in a lineage system. Characteristically, the segments in a lineage system are conceived of as building up hierarchically to span what is spoken of as a total society, the apex of the system affording a spectacular and fixed definition of its boundaries. Had I been using this concept in this chapter the founding ancestress of the nine Cyrenaican tribes, Sa'ada as named by the Bedouin, would have served this purpose and would have been given inappropriate prominence. The views presented here have the consequences of retreating from a concept of a total society. The people to whom the facts given are related are the camel-herding tribes only. Some of them have relations of many kinds with the cow-herding folk who inhabit the northern plateau area, and these relations are also significant for the analysis of a wide range of problems. Genealogially both cow and camel herders are seen as part of a single structure, but the differences between them with regard to their economy, the size, composition, and distribution of their residential units, their political and ritual life is so great that to conceive of them as a single social structure is not useful. Moreover, the far western tribal sections have relationships of such urgency with their neighbours in Tripolitania (who are excluded from Cyrenaican genealogies) that to cut off these relationships as lying outside Cyrenaican society would be quite unwarranted. The same can be said of the relationships of the tribal sections in the eastern part of Cyrenaica with their genealogical cousins, the Aulad 'Ali of Egypt, who, although residing across a national border, are closely linked to some of the Cyrenaican Bedouin. Some tribes also have to rely on the people of the southern oases for an item of diet and an outlet for surplus wool, and the net of kinship is spread out to include them. In these cases they come into contact with other ethnic groups such as Berbers and Tibu, and through the oases they extend their lines of communication southwards to Wadai, Chad, and Bornu. As an indication of the effectiveness of these links, it is only necessary to add that people inhabiting Cyrenaica make periodic and regular visits to these far southern places, and that in 1948 a shaikh, living near Ajadabiya in southwestern Cyrenaica, collected blood money contributions from kinsmen in Wadai. A single structure cannot possibly include, for analytical purposes, these sorts of relationships.

Finally, it must be stressed that the facts given here refer to the period 1948 to 1950. Since then oil has been discovered in large quantities near the territory of a tribe where I spent most of my time while resident in the country, and where there was one tin shack in 1950 there is now a modern port with roads extending southwards from it into the wilderness. I see no reason to assume that social relations as I observed them are present today or that they were the same at any time in the past either. Before the advent of the Sanusi Order in the early 1840s, it is known that one lineage at least was dominantly powerful and that its leader tyrannised a large part of Central Cyrenaica.[14] His descendants constituted a powerful group in 1950, but his kind of tyranny was absent from the Cyrenaica of that period. From the mid-nineteenth century until the Italian invasion of 1911, the Sanusi Order established itself, spread its lodges throughout the tribes and in other more remote lands until it became what Evans-Pritchard speaks of as a theocratic empire.[15] The lodges served as areas of sanctuary and their staffs adjudicated disputes. Leaders of the Order had the power to coerce and the Bedouin obeyed. They obeyed out of personal regard for some of them in 1950, but the religious authority previously used by the leaders had given way to the political power they now exercised as functionaries in a state system. In the meantime, the country had been ravaged by the long Italo-Sanusi wars. Throughout the 1930s after suffering terrible privations and reduction in numbers through slaughter in war, death in concentration camps, and exile, the Bedouin were ruled by the Italians. During World War II the armies of three major contestants fought their battles where the Bedouin now tend their flocks and herds. After the war they were left to fend for themselves, with a minimum of administrative interference.

In the light of all this the conception of an equilibrium system is of little heuristic value, still less its derivative concept of a repetitive system. This does not mean, however, that an account of part of the social life of the Bedouin as it existed in 1950 must be nothing more than a disconnected piece of history, unrelated to a prior state of things and wholly useless for the understanding of the contemporary oil-producing cum mixed pastoral-agricultural economy. It would be little more than a piece of social historiography if the analysis was based on the concept of a total social structure of functionally interconnected parts, forming what Leach describes as 'a delicately balanced mechanism rather like the various parts of a wrist watch'.[16] Such a viewpoint would effectively exclude any possible comprehension of changes save those present as part of the dynamics of a system; its only answer to change is an account of a different system. If, instead, attention is focused on the analysis of a field of components arranged in a specific fashion to meet the interests of men at a particular time, it then becomes possible to see how a shift in their positions, the addition of new components, or the elimination of others produces this or that effect. It can make intelligible what has gone before, and if the future cannot be anticipated it can be demarcated within rough limits.

5

Proliferation of segments

In this chapter I do not propose to discuss the genealogies of the Cyrenaican Bedouin in full, but only such aspects of them as are strictly relevant to an understanding of their process of growth.[1] Many other aspects of these genealogies will be referred to, and indeed, some of the arguments put forward will presume an acceptance of views which cannot be developed adequately in this chapter.

The Bedouin of Cyrenaica claim that they are all descendants of a unique ancestress, Sa'ada. Writers in the past (e.g. Smith 1903) have considered the occurrence of female names in patrilineal genealogies as evidence of an earlier and matrilineal mode of descent. A more satisfactory explanation of the occurrence of female names is to be found in the combination of two facts; firstly descent in the patriline, whether or not male names are used, is assumed; and secondly the Bedouin are polygamous. If, then, half-brother differentiation or full sibling unity is to be shown genealogically, the obvious way in which this can be done is to use a maternal name in the genealogy. Thus, in the Cyrenaican genealogy, a number of tribal groups will be shown as sons of a particular father. If differentiation of these groups needs to be shown, this can be effected by clustering the groups round, say, two female names (the names of the respective mothers) thereby making the two clusters of groups stand in the relationship of paternal half brothers. The concept of the 'one womb', of maternal origin, is a critical one in the context of social cohesion, but it does not deny patriliny; on the contrary, it serves in a sense to reinforce it. Female names can be used to show a greater notion of cohesion than the mere use of male names, and the significance of a female name placed at the apex of the Cyrenaican genealogy is that it is the symbol of full brother unity at the highest political level.

The founding ancestress Sa'ada is credited with two sons, who in turn are considered to be the founding ancestors of the two largest groups of tribes in Cyrenaica. Each of these sons is said to have begotten two sons, as shown in fig. 2. The next generation shows a total of nine names, and these nine ancestors are considered to be the founding ancestors of the nine noble tribes of Cyrenaica.[2] Continuing the line of descent of one of these tribes – the Magharba – the same pattern of segmentation repeats itself: the tribe is divided into two primary sections having ar-Ra'aid and al-Shamakh as the respective founding ancestors. Al-Shamakh is said to have had four sons, and these are the founding ancestors of four secondary sections. These latter four are credited with a varying number of sons, as shown in the genealogy in fig. 2.

One feature of the Cyrenaican genealogy immediately stands out from this brief description: the uniformity in the number of segments at the various levels of segmentation. Along the line of descent from Sa'ada to Nasr, the number of sons shown in the first four descending generations is two. At the fifth level the number increases to four, and finally, at the sixth level there characteristically occurs a marked irregularity in the number of descendants forming the founding ancestors of the tertiary sections.

Another feature of the Cyrenaican genealogy is that its branches show an intimate relationship with ecological areas. Thus, the major division into two branches stemming from Sa'ada represents the eastern and western halves of the country with associated and clear differences in ecology. Continuing the line of descent, the Jibarna and Baraghith groups of tribes

Figure 2.

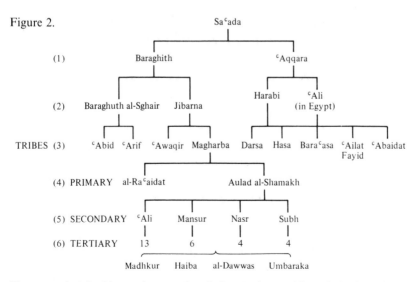

The names given in this genealogy are the tribal names in use. All are derivatives of personal names of ancestors, like all tribal names, except for some nicknames (e.g. Baragith means 'the fleas') and a few which refer to a general location (e.g. the Magharba means 'the Westerners').

occupy plain and mountain foot-hills respectively. The two Jibarna tribes in turn occupy two distinct kinds of plain. Following now the divisions of the Magharba tribe, its two primary sections are divided by a very conspicuous dry valley. The four secondary divisions of the Aulad al-Shamakh primary section likewise show a relation to ecological boundaries, albeit on a smaller scale than those previously referred to, but none the less important in this more local context. Finally the unevenly numbered tertiary sections which are derived from these four secondary sections, in their very unevenness, show a more sensitive relation to more detailed ecological differences.

At all levels of segmentation, therefore, a high degree of consistency between the ecological divisions of the country and the genealogical divisions can be shown. Indeed, the relationship is so close that it is tempting to consider the contemporary pattern of things as the only one possible. What historical evidence exists is against such a view. It is known that tribes have been displaced in the past, some of them or sections of them having been pushed out into Egypt, and others having altered their position. This being so, there obviously cannot be any finality about the present distribution of tribes in relation to the ecological divisions of the country. Rather, the existing pattern is one of a number of possible permutations. Again, as the relation between groups of people to their environment becomes progressively sensitive with the decrease in the size and order of the group, then the more unstable will be the relationship between the two. Conversely the greater the size and order of the group the more persistent will be its relationship to the ecology. In other words, the major ecological divisions are more fundamental in their effect on the way of life and the economy of people, whereas the more detailed ecological differences between, say, tertiary sections have a relatively minor effect. The ecological differences between the wooded plateau area with its cow and goat herding economy, and the arid semi-desert area with its camel and sheep herding economy has a much more profound effect on the general way of life, and is a more persistent division, than that which exists between two tertiary sections where the differences may only be in topographical details.

While therefore, the division of people into groups of various sorts is not permanently fixed in relation to ecological divisions, there is always an intimate relationship between the two which is progressively more enduring as the order of the structural segment increases. Yet even this statement of the relationship, guarded as it is, does not suffice, for the pattern and distribution of tribes and their sections at any given moment are not only a function of ecology, but they are also the result of a number of other complex factors which may be operating to reinforce or to complicate the more direct relationship of the distribution of groups of people to the ecology.[3]

The Cyrenaican genealogy, then, is a conceptualisation of a hierarchy[4] of ordered territorial segments. The groups stemming from the ancestor at the third order of segmentation are referred to as tribes, and each tribe is the apex of a three-tiered order of segments, which, following customary practice, are referred to as primary, secondary, and tertiary. The last, the tertiary segment, represents the group of people who, for a period of six to eight months, gather together and live in what, for all intents and purposes, is a single discrete residential group.[5] This tertiary group is also the smallest political group. It has its own homeland, with its water supplies, pastures, and ploughland. In this homeland live most of its members. It is a lineage segment, and most of the agnates of this segment live on their own homeland.[6] It is also the vengeance group, which means that any one of its members can be killed in vengeance for a homicide committed by any other, and that the obligation to exact vengeance falls on all members alike, regardless of relationship to the victim. Likewise, its members pay blood money as a group, and although when they receive it, a bigger portion goes to the nearest agnate of the victim, the remainder is distributed equally among all its members. The number of generations which supervene between the founding ancestor of a tertiary segment and the living is usually four or five, but there is little consistency in this number. Some tertiary segments show a lineage depth of three generations, while others show as many as six. No special importance is attached by the Bedouin to this number, although some writers claim that a depth of five generations is of particular significance among other Arab tribes.[7] Normally, in speaking of the vengeance group, the Bedouin refer to the name of the ancestor of a tertiary tribal section. Any one claiming membership of this group, regardless of his precise generational relation to the offender or the victim is immediately and equally involved with its other members. When speaking of the group as such, the Bedouin refer to it as 'those who have agreed on the blood', and use the phrase '*amara dam* to refer to it. Blood money does not pass between its members, and political division does not occur within it.

These small tertiary sections of tribes, then, are small residential groups. Their population varies from one group to another, but most of them have a total population of 150 to 200 souls. Successive generations – at least according to the Bedouin view – add to these numbers, and also increase progressively the number of generations in their genealogies. Substantial increases of population would, of course, constitute a pressure on local resources, on the water available in the particular well of a group, on the amount of land available for ploughing, and on the pastures for animals at the end of the rainy season. Again, if each generation is to be added to the existing genealogy, this would necessitate a realignment of structural relationships with each succeeding generation. The discussion that follows is an examination of the ways in which adjustments are made to maintain an equilibrium between the population of a group and the carrying capacity of the land on which its members live, and of the ways in which the genealogical structure is able to persist in the face of various contingencies which threaten it.

A beginning might be made by indicating the processes at work to keep the form of the genealogy fairly fixed when there is an absence of population pressure on resources. The first problem is the simple one of describing the mechanics of manipulation which enable the genealogy to remain constant in length and fixed in form despite its dynamic content.

One of the main processes at work in foreshortening genealogies is that referred to by Evans-Pritchard as telescoping.[8] This process is also a characteristic feature of the Cyrenaican genealogy, although its effects, to be discussed presently, differ conspicuously from those suggested in Evans-Pritchard's model. The way in which telescoping works in the Cyrenaican genealogy is that several male names come to be omitted in the genealogy below the name of the founding ancestor of the tertiary group. Usually, the form in which this occurs is that the name of a famous tribesman, and particularly his nickname if he has one, is retained along with the personal names of his lineal descendants in successive generations. The example given in fig. 3 is taken from the genealogy of the Haiba tertiary section of the Magharba tribe. The line shows five male names in all. The eldest surviving members of this time is Sa'aid who almost invariably is referred to, not by his personal name, but as Bu Shliby,[9] and on the infrequent occasions when his personal name is used it is followed by Bu Shliby and not by his father's name, which is the more common practice. Again, 'Abdul Qadar, when his

Figure 3.

father is not about, is called Bu Shliby, and when it is necessary to give him his personal name, then Bu Shliby is added, except among his more intimate family kindred, when only his personal name would be used. Likewise, his son Yunis carries Bu Shliby in addition to his personal name and is sometimes even referred to as Bu Shliby only. 'Abdul Qadar had never known his grandfather, was aware of his existence in the past, but did not feel it necessary to use his name, and whatever obligation he might have felt to keep the memory of his grandfather alive was fulfilled when he named his son after him. Many of the older members of the group are also aware of the lineal connections between Bu Shliby and Yunis, even though they use this knowledge in a genealogical context only, but many of the younger men of the group do not know these details. It is clear that when the boy Yunis grows to old age, three names in this line will have ceased to be used.

This practice of adding to a personal name the name of a deceased ancestor, making one the son of the other, is pushed to the extent of carrying forward through the generations a nickname which referred to some peculiar characteristic of the ancestor, but which has little relation to the present bearer. Thus the ancestor whose name has been retained might have been nicknamed 'The Lame One' or 'The Squint-Eyed One' because he suffered either of these personal defects; or he might have been nicknamed 'The Old One' because he lived to a ripe old age. Such nicknames might later be carried by men who are not lame, nor squint-eyed, nor old, while the names of the intervening ancestors are dropped in normal use.

Another process is at work, which needs to be distinguished from telescoping, for although the results in genealogical terms are similar, Bedouin view it in quite a different light. This is the process of fusing names. It is common practice among the Bedouin – and, for that matter, Arabs in other lands – to name a boy after a deceased relative. Rarely is a boy named after his father, unless the father's death occurs before the boy is born, in which circumstance, the new-born boy would certainly take his father's name. A much more common form of this practice is to name a boy after his grandfather, assuming the latter to be dead. The eldest son usually accepts this responsibility, but it by no means falls invariably to him. There are a number of reasons for this, but they need not concern us here, since they are of no relevance to the general argument. What is of concern at present is that one name in the genealogy might represent the fusion of several other similar names. When circumstances permit, an individual's line might run as follows: Muhammad – 'Ali – Muhammad – 'Ali – Muhammad. It is true that the man himself and those closely related to him might know full well that there are three men named Muhammad and two named 'Ali, but it would not be considered irregular if only one Muhammad and one 'Ali were given in the genealogy. One mature man, when giving his genealogy, omitted his father's name, Ibrahim. When asked about the omission, he insisted that he had given it, and when he was told that the name Ibrahim given by him was intended to refer to his young son, he impatiently dismissed the matter with the observation that having given the name Ibrahim once, it mattered little whether it had been put in the position of his son or father. Pointing to his son he added, 'There is my father, Ibrahim. He has taken my father's position, has he not?'

By the fusion of names, several persons drop out of the genealogy, and by and by, the line comes to be shortened. It also has the effect of giving a person's name a weighting which otherwise it would not possess. In a sense, a young son named after a father is not merely a son but a father and possibly a great-grandfather also. The young boy becomes the contemporary carrier of the personalities of those of similar name who have preceded him, while the behaviour of the living towards him is, in virtue of this, affected in a number of details. A man who had named his son in this way explained the matter thus: 'He is my son, but also my father because he has his name. I cannot beat him for it would be like beating my father. When he grows up and I grow old, he will look after me as if I were his son.'

Fusion of names appears in another context and for similar reasons. Not only are lineal descendants given the name of deceased ancestors, but a man may be given the name of any deceased agnate of his tertiary section. Usually, this is only done when a man passes on property to another who is not his direct heir. Commonly, this occurs when an agnate is also a mother's brother, as often happens as a result of parallel cousin marriage, and this mother's brother has no sons of his own. If he has a sister's son, who is also his paternal nephew, he is likely to pass on his wealth to this nephew. A father, the Bedouin insist, ought to perform three duties for his sons: attend to their circumcision, ensure their education in the Quran, and provide bridewealth when they marry. All fathers attend to the circumcision of all their sons; few provide for the Quranic education of any of their sons; most bear the burden of marrying off at least one of their sons. The performance of the last duty is what makes the continuance of the deceased's name an obligation, and whoever performs this duty must have his name perpetuated in one male offspring of the union which was brought about with his wealth. Wealth need not take the form of bridewealth; it can be a legacy willed by a father, maternal uncle of the kind described above, or any other agnate who has died without male issue. Conversely, if a man dies without leaving any property, even his sons might not perpetuate his name, and eventually it will drop out of the genealogy.[10] There are instances of men inheriting the wealth of a number of agnates, using each parcel of wealth to make a new marriage and naming the sons of the various unions after the several dead who had left wealth. The example given below is taken from the genealogy of the Dawwas section of the Magharba tribe. What happened here was that the two lines stemming from Faraj and Sha'aban, after proliferating normally, became extinct. As this happened, Ibrahim, the son of Miftah, began to inherit wealth to which he was not a direct heir; and as he did so, he entered into a plurality of marriages, begat sons, and replaced those men in the genealogy who had died without heirs. In the following generation the twin process of death and replacement continued. Death removed all the male descendants of Sha'aban and Faraj, and of Ibrahim Bu Miftah's many sons, only two, Sharif and 'Abdallah, were of age to marry at the time of my visits to their camp. Both had enjoyed a plurality of wives, although still young to have done so, and each marriage they contracted took place after the death of one of their kinsmen. The full and intricate details of this interesting genealogy are irrelevant here, since all the example is intended to show is how nine of eleven male names were perpetuated in the genealogy by repeating five of them twice and four of them three times, accounting in all for twenty-two names; and to do this, three men (one of them had died, but the other two were both under forty years of age) married a total of eight wives. All the names in the two lines which have died out have not yet been brought back into the genealogy, but 'Abdallah, the son of Ibrahim, who had already done extremely well in this respect, was confident that soon the obligations towards Musa, 'Abd al-Rahim, and Sa'ad would be redeemed.

Thus the fusion of names not only ensures that names threatened with extinction are perpetuated, but that one person, in the name he bears, can carry the genealogical burden of several other men of that name.

Figure 4.

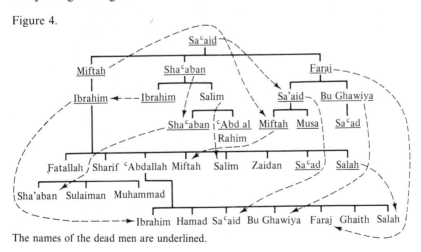

The names of the dead men are underlined.

Telescoping of names and fusion of names, taken together, can account for the fixity of the genealogy to a large extent. In addition, lines which showed every sign of normal development at one time, have petered out completely, even after they have sometimes assumed the status of tertiary segments. Conditions under which this is likely to happen are not difficult to envisage. If hearsay evidence is correct, disease, when it strikes in the desert, might rage in a camp like wild fire, bringing death to many, but not spreading to other camps, because the camps are so far apart. Even in springtime when men and beasts are together in the pastures, and the larger summer camp has split into four or five smaller ones, the distance between camps may still be a few miles. In summer, when camps are concentrated on the large watering points, the distances between them are considerably more. Disease, therefore, does not spread from camp to camp as rapidly as one might expect in such primitive conditions of living. In 1949 a number of men of a small camp died within a few days of each other. Bedouin opinion attributed these deaths to an allegedly false oath sworn by the deceased a year earlier. Medical opinion ascribed them to filth in a well which the deceased had been cleaning before their illness. In any event, a thriving line of a lineage was wiped off the genealogy. The portion of the Dawwas genealogy shown below indicates a similar process at work. Again, to give another example, the Nasr section of the Magharba tribe once included six tertiary sections, not four as are now given. Two of these six sections are now represented by only four men of whom two are too old and decrepit to produce heirs any longer, and are unmarried in any case; a third, whose wife has long passed child-bearing age, had two sons, but both died before the age of marriage; and the fourth, a very poor and old man, has only one daughter, and is a widower. Three of the four now live with their collateral tribal section, Madhkur, and count themselves members of this group. That they once belonged to two different groups might have passed unnoticed were it not that two elders of the Madhkur section insisted that they should be correctly placed and their entire genealogies be recorded. The younger men argued that although they were aware that the two groups named Farjiani and al-Khadhar at one time existed, it was pointless giving them separate status any longer; they were content to give the three men separate lines of a few generations, and then to tag them on to Madhkur, the founding ancestor of the segment.

Figure 5.

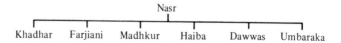

Nasr

Khadhar   Farjiani   Madhkur   Haiba   Dawwas   Umbaraka

Telescoping, fusion of names, and the extinction of lines are three ways in which the general fixed shape of the genealogy is retained. These three processes are only sufficient, however, in special circumstances, but before discussing these circumstances one further general condition relating to these processes must be made explicit. All three affect the genealogy within the tertiary segments only, and do not affect it at any of the more superior orders of segmentation. There is not a shred of evidence from contemporary Cyrenaican genealogies to show that telescoping or fusion occurs except within the tertiary segment, within that group; in other words, where precise genealogical links are known and can be specified, and within that small group which for most part of the year constitutes a single settlement. It is possible that groups of structurally superior levels to the tertiary have become extinct, in the way that tertiary lines have petered out. There is no definite evidence to support this, and from the analysis of Cyrenaican genealogies in general it seems that when any group is threatened with extinction – and this in turn means that fewer and fewer people will be using the same land and water facilities – there is a definite tendency for the lineage rump to fuse with a collateral lineage (and in so doing fuse their resources with those of the adopting lineage), or for a numerically more powerful lineage group to take it over by force. The number of tertiary segments spanned by a secondary segment, therefore, increases or decreases according to the circumstances; so that a secondary segment, numerically strong in its tertiary segments today, may become considerably weaker in future, and the numerically weak secondary section of today may proliferate its segments substantially in the future. Short of a significant decline in the total population of a tribe, then, the extinction of lines does not affect any order of segmentation superior to the tertiary. In this respect, the Cyrenaican genealogy differs fundamentally from those collected from the Nuer by Evans-Pritchard. In the quotation from his work on Nuer genealogies (1951), he asserts that telescoping occurs 'from the founder of the minimal lineage further up the line of ascent to the founder of the clan'. This major difference has serious implications for any discussion of lineage proliferation, but these must be left until the conditions under which proliferation is likely to occur have been analysed.

While it is true that the processes discussed are of importance in retaining the general shape of the genealogy, what is assumed so far is that the Cyrenaican population has been stable over long periods. Stability of population is not an unreasonable assumption to make for a people who live on the margin of subsistence in a country where extended periods of drought are not infrequent, though seldom leading, it is true, to actual famine conditions, but producing periodic and local food and water shortages. Disease, following quickly in the trail of shortage, it can be assumed, has kept the relationship of total population to the natural resources fairly constant. What evidence there is does not support even this very general assumption, since it is known that there have been large-scale tribal wars in the past, and a certain amount of movement of tribes, some being displaced and others pushed eastwards into Egypt. Unless these shifts were caused by increases in the aggregate population and the consequent pressure on land and water, it is difficult to account for them. This consideration of possible overall increases in population in the past poses interesting problems related to lineage structure which cannot be adequately treated here. For the moment it is proposed to neglect possible increases in the total population during past periods in the history of Cyrenaica. The historical depth of the view now to be discussed is about seventy years, and for this period I have no evidence of any large-scale increases in population. It is reasonable, therefore, to assume a general stability of population for this period. But the vagaries of the Cyrenaican climate are such that, in a given year, one area might be well drenched with rain, giving excellent pastures for animals and good crops, while a nearby territorial strip might suffer a partial drought giving insufficient pastures and poor crops. Good or bad crops, poor or abundant pasture, in turn mean a higher or lower milk yield from the animals and better or worse living conditions for human beings. Such factors as these may well, over a number of years, lead to unevenness in the distribution of population throughout the tertiary sections. Whatever the cause, the genealogies show that the population of the numerous tertiary sections is unequal. Some are numerically so weak that they have to join a collateral section. Others are numerically so strong that their natural resources are insufficient to meet the needs of all their members. It was these latter segments which were in the process of splitting, and which in some cases have already done so. The next task, then, is to demonstrate where, on the genealogy, proliferation is effected.

We have seen that in Nuer genealogies segments proliferate at all orders of segmentation. Here, the process is a continuous one, beginning at any point in time within the minimal lineage and progressing upwards to the apex of lineage bifurcation. As particular names become significant within the minimal segment, they are retained and become a permanent addition to the genealogy. In order to include these successively additional names, names of ascending ancestors are shunted further and further into the genealogical past, until presumably the effect is felt at the topmost limit of the genealogy, when the names here are pushed out of the genealogical framework altogether, and forgotten forever. More than this, the upward shift in names at each and every point in the genealogical line means also a consequent re-ordering of structural relationships, at all levels in the system. One vital difference between Nuer and Bedouin societies which may partly, at least, account for the different genealogical processes at work among them is that the Nuer, when they were studied by Evans-Pritchard, were expanding territorially, and that continuous proliferation of segments throughout the structure was the mode of dealing with a situation of expansion. The Bedouin, on the other hand, had suffered twenty years of terrible privation at the hands of the Italians, during which period thousands of them died in battle and in concentration camps, were shot up in their camps from the air, or died from want, before I went to live among them. Although I must confess that I now find it difficult to accept Evans-Pritchard's view of genealogical growth and development as stated for the Nuer, it was the view I originally held with regard to Bedouin genealogies. Indeed, thinking in genealogical terms only, it appears inevitable that the addition of successive generations can only mean the lengthening of the genealogy, or, if the length is to remain constant, extrusion of ancestral names must take place at the apex of the genealogy. If this view is to be accepted, several other conclusions must be accepted with it. The genealogy, as far as it goes at least, is an accurate record of descent – some names may have been lopped off at the top, but otherwise the genealogy represents a faithful statement of succession. Again, if successive generations are to be added to the genealogy, then its base must continually expand laterally. From what is known of contemporary Bedouin genealogies, there is no evidence which leads to the supposition that their base is progressively widening. With regard to the authenticity of the names in the genealogy, above the point of tertiary segmentation, I argue that names above the tertiary point of segmentation have remained fixed for very long periods of time, and that they bear slight relation to the passage of generations over the last century at least; moreover, it appears that what manipulation of the genealogy takes place does not affect more than about four or five ascending generations from the living.

Part of the difficulty in a study of this sort lies in the strong temptation to think of the genealogy *per se*, even though it is readily admitted that it has a value in itself for the Bedouin. Yet even in these terms the genealogy must always represent an ordered grouping of people, and these people live on strips of territory. The starting point of the analysis then ought to begin with the territorial ordering of groups of people. The relation of groups of people to land, moreover, is determined by the carrying capacity of that land, and it is this prerequisite which is the main variable in discussing genealogical manipulation, and not the other way around. The main landmarks of the Cyrenaican ecology are fixed points which cannot be manipulated to fit in with the genealogy; it is the genealogy which must be altered to comprehend the distribution of people in their ecological setting.

If, moreover, the view of a genealogy as a continually expanding line of descent is to be accepted, it must be accepted also that large structural units, even in conditions of population stability, are to experience a continuous re-ordering of their structural relationships. In practice, what this means is that in a tribe of say 20,000 souls, those individuals cease to be tribesmen of a named tribe and instead all become members of an almost identical group but with a different name. To take an example from the genealogy given in fig. 2: the Magharba tribe shown there has a total population of some 13,000 souls. If proliferation affected the topmost limits of this tribe, the apical name disappears and presumably the name of one of the primary sections is to be substituted. That is, half the tribe would have to take on the lineage name of their opposed section. The only alternative to the use of the name of a primary segment as a substitute for the abandoned tribal name is the acceptance by 13,000 people of a totally new name, which is most unlikely.

It is reasonable to assume therefore, that the genealogy, in its general form, is fixed for long periods of time at least. This still leaves the problem of how and where adjustments are made to face the contingencies of birth and death, of the succession of generations, and of the irregular increases and decreases of population among the tertiary segments. An important clue lies in the number of segments which appear at the various orders of segmentation. From Saʿada, the founding ancestress, in the line which runs to Nasr, each ancestor is shown as having a pair of sons for four orders of segmentation. At the fifth generation from Saʿada – this is now the secondary order of segmentation within the tribe – the number of sons increases to four. Not all tribes will show the same number of sons at each generation as the Magharba – some, for example, might show three instead of two at the primary order – but what is true of all tribes is that there is evident consistency in the number down to and including the fifth generation from Saʿada; if, that is to say, one of a tribe's primary segments is divided into three secondary sections, the other one or two, as the case may be, will be divided likewise. Throughout the tribes in Cyrenaica, then, segmentation of orders superior to the tertiary segments shows a pronounced consistency in their numbers.

At the next level of segmentation (this now being the tertiary order in any given tribe) the number of segments which appear is conspicuously irregular. For the Magharba tribe, the four secondary segments, ʿAli, Mansur, Subh and Nasr are divided into thirteen, six, four, and four segments respectively. Similar irregularity appears in other tribes.[11] The pattern of the genealogy is always one of regularity in the number of segments at all points in it except for the point of tertiary segmentation where conspicuous irregularity becomes immediately evident. Since these segments constitute the summer camps of the Bedouin, this is not surprising, for these small groups will show greater susceptibility to details of local water supplies, pasturing facilities, ploughland areas, and topographical features than would the numerically larger and structurally superior groups occupying larger areas of territories of greater ecological importance. If we follow the line from Sa'ada to Nasr again, the bifurcation at the first order of segmentation is consistent with the division of the country into the permanently green high altitudes of the plateau, and the extended low-lying plain area of the western half of the country. Between the territory of the Magharba tribe ('The White Plain') and that of its neighbour tribe, the 'Awaqir ('The Red Plain'), there is a major soil difference, which is such a conspicuous feature of the landscape, and so sharply defined, that one is almost aware when one has crossed the tribal boundary. Within the Magharba tribe, a prominent dry river valley cuts the territory in two, the landscape to the west of it being characteristically serrated, making travel in an east-west direction difficult, while to the east the landscape is much more docile and undulating. The four sections of the al-Shamakh branch again represent four quite distinct areas. The territory of one section is almost coterminous with the narrow belt of sand dunes along the coast; the territory of another is a block of rough and tumbled land in the west; the territory of a third, in the centre, is made up of a few low-lying shallow valleys; and the territory of the fourth, stretching across to the village of Ajadabiya in the east, topples in undulations away into the flat expanses of the desert to the south. At all these points of segmentation, the territories occupied by the various sections are large and roughly defined, and the population aggregates supported on these territories run from over a thousand at one end to tens of thousands at the upper limits. The tertiary sections are numerically much smaller, some of them numbering as few as a hundred souls in all, and the territories to which they are attached are correspondingly smaller. The relationship between the numbers in this order of section, and the precise amount of water available in the local wells is an intimate one. If the population of one of these groups increases, or if the number of animals rises, or if the springs show a decline in the volume of water they give forth, or if the winter rainfall has allowed the storage in wells of only a small quantity of water, a rearrangement of the group must be effected. A significant alteration of any one of these components must mean that the local group must split to enable a new adjustment to be made in the relationship of man and animals to water.

Whatever changes occur within groups of any size, since the genealogy embraces the entire population, must appear on the genealogy in some way or other. Now a genealogy is as rigid a framework, as fixed and final a pattern of grouping, as can be imagined. The impression that they are thus rigid and fixed, except for the addition of successive generations, is strengthened by the way in which the Bedouin use them. From their young boys to their old men, the Bedouin are expert genealogists, and the names of ancestors, for one reason or another, are never far from their lips. Names are kept alive by constant use, since all references to inter-group relationships must be in terms of these names. More than this, the Bedouin were proud to the point of boastfulness of their genealogical knowledge, and, wherever I travelled, the first request I had to comply with was to take down a large portion of a tribal genealogy. In recording their endless genealogies, one feature about them came to assume increasing interest; while there was remarkable unanimity with regard to most of the names given, there was one point of marked ambiguity – at the tertiary level of segmentation. I recorded genealogies in four tribes on an extensive scale, and in each tribe ambiguity surrounding the actual names and their correct position occurred at about the fifth ascending generation. Whenever this point was reached in the recordings, arguments would flare up over the names to be included or excluded and over the relation of these names to those above and below, with the result that for several people of the same segment there would be several versions of a genealogy which differed only at this one point. An example of this sort is given in fig. 6 from the

Figure 6.

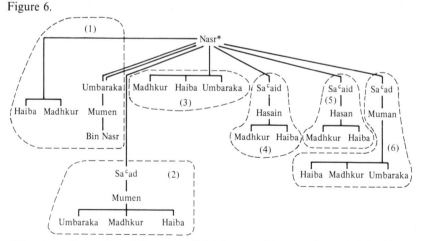

*There is another section, al-Dawwas, which belongs to this group, but to include this as well would greatly complicate the issue without giving any additional information.

genealogy of the Nasr section, which shows seven different versions of the arrangement of ancestors round about the fifth ascending generation from the living.

The confusion at and around the fifth ascending generation appeared with such regularity in the genealogies that I feel justified in referring to it as 'the area of ambiguity'. It seems likely, moreover, that in any society where the lineage structure is closely tied to the territorial disposition of groups, since the genealogy is so rigid, there needs to be in it somewhere an area of ambiguity if it is to be related to reality. Without this ambiguity, the form of the genealogy is too rigid to comprehend changes which occur. This point in the genealogy came to assume critical significance as the point where adjustments in it are made. Other kinds of evidence point to the same conclusion.

There are, in Cyrenaica, three major status groups among the tribes: the noble or freeborn tribesmen (the Hurr), those who have been adopted or grafted on to a tribe (the Laff), and the clients (Marabtin).

Those who claim to be freeborn also claim ownership of the natural resources. The Laff do not own these. They are people thought not to have originally been of the lineage of the tribe with which they are resident. They are found sometimes in ones and twos in the camps of the freeborn, but sometimes constituting tertiary groups themselves. Now when such people have resided with their freeborn hosts for several years and one of them has married one of the host's daughters, they are grafted to the genealogy at the point of tertiary segmentation, that is, where ambiguity occurs in the genealogy. Obviously, persons thus grafted to the lineage cannot be shown as descendants of one of the living or of the recently dead, remembered perhaps by some of the elders still living. It is equally true to say that they cannot be grafted to the lineage at a point superior to that of the tertiary segments, since this would involve recognition by a number of tertiary groups whose members may know little or nothing about them. When a person enters a new tribe, the only way in which he can do so is to go to live in a camp, and it is the concern of the people of that particular camp whether or not they accept him, since it is they who have to decide whether their resources are sufficient to support a newcomer. Once a man has been accepted as a full member of a tertiary section, membership of superior tribal sections is automatic, although to enter into tribal membership he requires the permission of members of a tertiary section only. To graft at a point superior to the tertiary would be the same as giving a man superior structural status, but without a camp in which to dwell. There is only one place for his incorporation, and that is where the ambiguity in the genealogy permits manipulation to include new lines. In this way the adoption of a person into a lineage does not offend the sense of kinship of the receiving group, since the point of inclusion is an ancestor about whom little or nothing is known and whose authenticity is frequently doubted by some. What has been referred to as an area of ambiguity is, moreover, something of a jumble of names, and it is not a difficult matter, if a new line has to be attached somewhere along the line, to attach it to one of these names. Bedouin welcome, as members of their camps, practically anyone who wishes to join, even, in the case of one group, an Italian. The limit to this acceptance of members is, of course, the number of people who can be supported by the local resources. If people are being admitted freely to membership of a particular camp, this means that there is a local surplus of land and water, so that the number of grafts being supported by any particular section is a useful index of the extent to which the resources are being used. Conversely, as sometimes happens when grafted elements become numerous, or when the water supply, for various reasons, dwindles, it may be necessary to detach a grafted group. Such action is always the occasion of a violent dispute, usually over watering rights, and not infrequently fights break out. Whether or not the grafted group wins, from then onwards it will be forced to exist as an independent group, and a new tertiary section will have been born. No matter which of the processes involving grafts is considered – incorporation or detachment – both are contained within the framework of the tertiary section, without an effect on the rest of the structure.

The position of the clients, in the context of this discussion, is not unlike that of the grafts. Briefly, clients are men who are considered to have originated from a country other than Cyrenaica, and who for this reason cannot claim rights to land and water – at least this is the theory, although in some circumstances they are able to do so successfully. They are of various kinds, but they are not included in the genealogies given by the freeborn. Clients are found grouped in two main ways. There are some large groups which constitute tribes in the sense that they display a genealogical and territorial organisation like those of the freeborn, and are usually to be found flanking the main tribes of the country on their borders. Some of these are powerful groups and enjoy considerable independence of action, but whatever their characteristics they none the less speak of themselves as 'for' or tied to the noble tribe whose territory includes theirs. Further, the sections of these client tribes have their special ties with tertiary sections of the noble tribes, which are not merely ties of sentiment, but which take the form of valuable mutual help in a number of situations. A whole client tribe, in the sense that it is occupying territory which cannot be said to belong to any particular section of their noble patron tribe, is tied to the patron tribe as such. Yet it is through the small tertiary segments that these ties are made effective. In this sense, a client tribe is a combination of small groups of people, each group having specific relationships with defined tertiary sections, and participating in the tribe of their patrons through these relationships.

Secondly, clients are found distributed in small groups, sometimes no more than one or two men, but often in clusters large enough to compose a small camp. Practically all tertiary sections of the noble tribes have some clients either living with them or sharing their resources. While clients continue to reside with a particular tertiary section, it is the members of the latter who are responsible for them and vice versa. If, for example, one of the clients commits a homicide, the gathering of blood money is the responsibility of the noble tertiary section to which he is attached, and vengeance can be exacted on any member of the noble section. In other circumstances, when the offender is a nobleman, then the clients of his group are the first to be approached for blood money. Tied in this way to a particular tertiary section, they are not, however, compelled to reside with its members permanently. On the contrary, they may be forced to move. If, for example, there is a pressure on local water supplies, the first to feel it are the clients. Annually, they supplicate for the use of water, and if their patrons decide that there is insufficient to meet all needs, the request is refused, albeit reluctantly. Clients constitute a socially mobile group; they are the pawns in the annual readjustment of men to their resources. Whenever they move, they pass on to another tertiary section, which may be a collateral section of the one they have left or structurally far removed from it, but as soon as they leave one, their duties and obligations cease and are taken up anew with another structurally like group. It is because their attachment is to a tertiary section, and not to one of superior order, that they can be as socially mobile as they are, which in turn facilitates a more efficient adjustment to the ecological situation from year to year.

Small groups of clients move frequently, groups of adopted people less frequently, and groups composed of the freeborn change their structural position only rarely. The latter change sometimes does, however, occur, and there is evidence to show that it does. For example, Agostini (1922–3, p. 323) in his tribal survey, records a section named Barsha as one of the groups stemming from Nasr.[12] In the genealogies I was given, the name did not appear, and even after some questioning, what information was known about it was concealed. Some time later the name cropped up accidentally in conversation, and I was then told that at one time it had been one of the Nasr groups, but that after a quarrel during a year of water shortage, the Barsha folk went to live with people with whom they had maternal connections, and in whose territory there was ample water that year, and never returned. The group, a tertiary one, was detached from the tertiary point of segmentation in the genealogies, and tied on to a tertiary group of another tribe in its new homeland.

To summarise briefly the argument thus far, the mechanical devices of telescoping, fusion of names, the ejection of those names which cease to be of any social significance, and the elision of names at or around the fifth ascending generation, taken together point to the importance of the tertiary order of segmentation in discussing the problem of maintaining the form of the genealogy constant in face of its natural tendency to alter; further, evidence of changes (adoption into a lineage, detachment from it, the inclusion and exclusion of clients) was presented, and this again led to the conclusion that the tertiary point of segmentation is critical in this respect. This being so, the manner in which change actually occurs still remains to be shown, and this is best done, perhaps, by discussing the mode of proliferation of tertiary segments. In order to do this adequately, it is necessary to say something briefly about certain features of Bedouin marriage.

Among the Bedouin there exists a preferential form of marriage between a man and his father's brother's daughter. Parallel cousin marriage of this sort carries with it the exclusive right of a man to this cousin. Without his consent no one else can marry her, and to attempt to do so would be to risk the marriage arrangements being nullified after negotiations had almost been concluded. I have been present on occasions when, after both parties have agreed to a marriage and the groom has collected most of the things necessary to present to the bride at the wedding celebrations, the girl's father's brother's son appears and demands the discontinuance of the arrangement. On one occasion, he did not appear until the actual day of the wedding, but was bought off with a cap, a cloak, and the promise of two sheep. The highest incidence for any form of marriage, moreover, is with the patrilineal parallel cousin, although not necessarily with the first cousin.

Parallel cousin marriage of this sort is not, however, the only form practised among the Bedouin. Much of the writing on Bedouin marriage leaves the impression that a solution to the problem of parallel cousin marriage (Murphy and Kasdan 1959) solves all the problems involved in their system of marriage. In addition to this form, there are a number of others; indeed there is another form of preferential marriage among them, which, although it does not have the compulsive character of parallel cousin marriage, is of major importance. I refer to cross-cousin marriage with the mother's brother's daughter. Such a cousin may be, of course, as a result of patrilineal parallel cousin marriage, a patrilineal parallel cousin as well. Such a cousin may be, on the other hand, a woman of another tribal section or of a different tribe altogether. A characteristic form of this marriage is that once it has been initiated, it is perpetuated in successive generations. Members of one line in a tertiary segment will, therefore, be building up kinship ties through marriage in one particular direction. At the same time, another line, by practising the same form of marriage, will be weaving ties in a quite different direction. One direction these marriages could take might be to a tertiary segment of a collateral secondary segment; another might be to a primary segment of the same tribe, and yet another to people living in a date oasis. Only occasionally do marriages occur between collateral tertiary segments, and then there is usually some specific reason. In other words, when men marry outside the limits of their own tertiary segment, they leap-frog adjacent segments and marry into structurally more remote groups.

The result of these two marriage patterns is that the people of any summer camp will have descent lines cross linked by the bonds of marriage with parallel cousins, and at the same time cleaved by the maternal links established by repetitive cross-cousin marriage to different groups outside the segment. Thus, in one of its aspects, marriage makes of an agnatic group a group of cognates as well. 'Marry your paternal cousins and both your paternal and maternal relatives will be one', to quote Bedouin sentiment on the matter. Within this agnatic group, nevertheless, other clusters of kin exist – those with maternal connections outside. In all, three areas of kinship can be defined,[13] although all the members of the segment will have the lineage bond of agnation in common. In normal circumstances, when split does not threaten the group, the bond of agnation, strengthened by parallel cousin marriage, takes precedence, although behaviour is significantly affected by maternal links at any time. There is, in the first instance, great jealousy between co-wives, which is passed on to their children. Each wife has her separate tent, and each is entitled to a strictly equal share of the husband's time. This applies similarly to favours he may grant his wives, and the distribution of his wealth among them. If, for example, the husband is the owner of a horse, he is required to tether it outside the tents of his wives in strict rotation; if he retires for the night with one wife, the following night he must favour the other; if he buys dress material for the one he must buy a length of identical material for the other; if he bestows favours on the children of one the children of the other must be given equal consideration. Many such details are meticulously observed; but while many are observed most of the time, it is difficult to observe them all, the whole time. Any breach of the rules is quickly taken up by the wives, and quarrels ensue, leading not only to bitterness among the co-wives, but between the offended wife and her husband, between the children of both wives, and between the children and their father. Often, when a man has co-wives, there is a marked discrepancy in age between them, for, when an elderly Bedouin marries a second wife he usually chooses a young girl of about twenty years. Children of the elder wife might be adult, therefore, when the children of the junior wife are infants. Great emphasis is placed on seniority, particularly among males, but strong emphasis is also placed on the equality of siblings and their equal legal status. Between brothers of widely differing ages, there is, then, this field of potential conflict. From an early date, competitive, if not hostile, relationships develop between the sons of co-wives. Competition between half-brothers results not only from their mothers being co-wives: one group might be the sons of a divorced wife. The latter situation is often much worse, for the sons born of the divorced wife are now being fostered by a woman who is not their mother. A similar condition of things is brought about when a widower with sons remarries. Yet again, when a wife grows old and her sons have reached maturity, her husband may not divorce her formally, but merely 'throw her off his back'; she will then go to live with her grown sons, while her husband, in turn, takes a new wife, usually taking up residence in another camp for a time at least. It would be too much of a digression here to discuss the inheritance disputes, and the disputes over marriage and bridewealth, which arise out of these various circumstances. Suffice it to note that such disputes are common and affect the alignment of people within a tertiary segment.

As half-brothers grow to maturity some of them will marry their maternal cross-cousins, and in succeeding generations some of their descendants will do likewise. In this way, a tertiary segment united by the bond of agnation will also have within it smaller groups of kin having different sets of cognative links. This group, as a residential unit, shows a very high concentration of agnates, and the Bedouin say with pride that members of the camps are always 'one' because of this agnatic bond, and indeed, the corporate identity of this group is strikingly displayed in many circumstances. It does not take precedence in all circumstances, for, built into agnation, with the heavy burden of duties which go with it, are serious stresses and strains which in some circumstances regularly come out into the open. In yet other circumstances cognatic kinship affiliations appear to be dominant, causing friction among agnates. A man, for example, may permit his maternal kinsmen to use the land and water facilities of his lineage; his agnates may give ready consent or bicker about it, but when it becomes necessary to clean a well, disputes are almost certain to break out in the camp between those who argue that their maternal relatives should not be expected to assist in its cleaning and those who insist they should as an acknowledgement of the use they have made of it. In these circumstances maternal links divide agnates. Conversely, if it becomes necessary for some of the same men to use the water and ploughland of their maternal kin, their agnates are only too pleased that they are able to do so, because the pressure on their own resources is relieved. In these circumstances, the maternal link strengthens the agnatic group. When, to give another instance, blood money has to be gathered, it is the duty of all agnates to contribute equally, and no member of the group, rich or poor, can contract out of this obligation without sacrificing his membership of the group. Payments of blood money are witness of the strength of the notion of 'oneness' among agnates, in one sense, but in so far as they are compulsory, they point also to the weakness in the relationship. Maternal kin are not directly concerned in this, but they can and do make contributions. In this context two aspects of agnation appear, and the value of the maternal link is emphasised. Again, maternal kinsmen are not directly concerned in inheritance disputes, but they are expected to intercede for their sister's sons, who often use their mother's brother's tribal brand on their own animals. During disputes of this kind, blame is thrown on to the maternal kinsmen for their interference in matters which, properly speaking, are not their business.

In marriage, however, events take quite a different turn. The responsibility for providing a man with a wife is first that of the father, and secondly of the members of the tertiary section; the father takes the initiative, and his agnates assist, not only in the negotiations, but also in defraying the heavy costs of the wedding festivities, the various gifts that precede it, and the bridewealth which follows. The mother's brother is also a key person in all these arrangements. He enters into the negotiations, assists with the entertainment on the wedding day, and makes a substantial contribution to the bridewealth. On the wedding day, there is no kinsman to compare with the mother's brother; a few weeks later, he is reviled for demanding a long overdue instalment of his daughter's bridewealth. He is the person who can be approached freely, to whom love tales can be told, from whom help can be expected, who gives support in disputes, and who also upbraids, who punishes, who withholds, who acts as a pull-away from the agnatic group. An agnate demands help, and also compels the fulfilment of obligations. An agnate is a man with whom relationships are formal, particularly if he is a senior. He is, too, the person who unfailingly, though perhaps grudgingly, gives help when it is most required; who, regardless of the merits of the case, defends one against external opposition; and who is always available at each life crisis. A kinship link is not to be defined by any one particular mode of behaviour. Each is a cluster of different sorts of behaviour, one form taking precedence in these circumstances, another in other circumstances, and so forth.

The little clusters of kindred can be defined clearly in any of the camps. It is customary among the Bedouin for those who are most closely linked as kindred to pitch their tents close to each other. For example, if a man has two recently married sons, their tents are pitched on either side of his, with the ropes of their tents crossing the ropes of their father's tent. More distantly related kin will be more distantly placed, and here and there, breaks in the continuity of the lines of tents are to be observed, corresponding as a rule to breaks in kinship. Each large camp in this way can be viewed as two or more nuclei of kindred. The camp as a whole is dominantly composed of agnates, but they are disposed in such a way as to show clusterings of varying kinship composition. Characteristically each cluster has a separate name, often a female name which refers to a common mother of the cluster, or of the head of the leading family in it. When these relatively large camps break up with the onset of the rains and disperse to form small camps of five to seven tents for winter pasturing, they will be seen to correspond almost identically with the kin clusters of the larger summer camp. Again, a tertiary segment may have two wells for its own use. In a particular year there may be sufficient water in one of them to meet the needs of the whole group, and its members then live together in one camp; the following year both wells may have to be used, and the camp of the previous summer will split up, roughly half going to one well, and the remainder to the other. It is usually an easy matter to predict, at least in a general fashion, how the group will divide, as long as the details of kinship are known; the camps will be composed of members of two sets of patri-lines in the tertiary segment, who will also represent two discrete clusters of cognatic kindred. If, therefore, a tertiary group increases in numbers to the point where a split in the lineage is inevitable, here then is the line of split, along a line, that is, of kinship cleavage and lineage differentiation. 'Men make the tribe; women divide it', is an oft-quoted saying among the Bedouin, but this, like most sayings, tells only part of the truth, as we shall see.

It is possible to show where on the genealogy change takes place, and it is possible to indicate the lines cleavages will follow, but the proliferation of a lineage does not occur merely because the possibility exists for it to do so. A group must, clearly, break up if the number of its members significantly exceeds that which can be supported by the available natural resources; water is the prime cause of the proliferation of lineages. Granting this, a group remains an undifferentiated corporation until occasion arises when its members, or some of them, can demonstrate unequivocally that they are no longer bound by its conditions of membership. There are a number of occasions when this can be done, some of which are discussed below.

The test, *par excellence*, of corporate affiliation is the acceptance of the responsibility to pay blood money. Refusal to accept this is the same as renouncing membership of the group. Individuals are sometimes excluded from membership in this way. There are occasions too when the payment of blood money involves renunciation by more than one or two individuals. If membership of a section has increased to the point of splitting, and should a homicide occur within it, one of the kin clusters within the group might demand blood money from the other. Nothing could make the statement of split clearer than this. The most impelling condition of membership of the tertiary group is that 'we pay as one and receive as one', a condition which, of course, excludes payment within the group. Any two groups between which the demand for blood money has been made are therefore, by definition, separate tertiary groups.

When a member of a group or his wife dies, there are specific days on which kin of various sorts should attend the mourning ceremonies, which extend over a period of a week. Allowance is made for those who may be away temporarily, although they are expected to hasten to the mourning camp as quickly as possible. Agnatic kin are expected not only to be present on the appropriate day, but are required to offer gifts consistent with their relationship to the bereaved; agnates of the tertiary segment are expected to offer a sheep, while some cognates ought to bring a goat and others a quantity of sugar and tea. At one funeral in a camp where I was resident, soon after the death occurred, the main concern of its inhabitants was whether or not certain men of their section would attend the mourning rites and bring appropriate gifts with them. These men lived at the time in another camp a few miles away, as they had been doing for several years past. They did not come when they were expected, and when they finally arrived at the end of the week they brought with them gifts of sugar and tea only – gifts which were totally inappropriate for agnates of the group. They were, in fact, now no longer members of it, and my neighbours were able to tell me, 'They have branched off from us. We will never live together again'. The lineage had proliferated and this was the first occasion for showing it.

Widespread in Cyrenaica is a cult of saints. The number of saints' tombs varies from tribe to tribe, there being fewer among the camel herders of the semi-desert than among the cow-herding, almost sedentary, folk of the plateau area. Whatever the number, the members of the group that venerates a particular saint make an annual pilgrimage to his tomb, and sometimes more frequent pilgrimages are made. In one area there were two men, accepted by their respective kin groups as leaders, who vied against each other for the leadership of their section. One of them had been a famous warrior during the Italian wars and, after being injured, fled to Egypt where he lived for seventeen years, until he returned to his homeland in 1947. The other had also fought against the Italians, failed to win renown, was a captive for a time, later released, and subsequently appointed leader of his section by the Italian authorities. The first, during his period of exile, had become impoverished. The second, during his years of freedom, had prospered. As far as their personalities were concerned, there was little doubt who was leader – the name of the former was known throughout the land. Now when the warrior returned from his Egyptian exile, his rival offered him a sheep as a gift. This act was wholly appropriate. Subsequently they continued to compete fiercely, but it soon became clear that the returned warrior was winning the greater support. In the face of this, the rival, in 1948, decided to break with tradition by staying away from the annual pilgrimage to the tomb of the local saint. Instead, he and his followers made their pilgrimage to a different tomb in the vicinity of their camp, and later built a low wall round the tomb, whitewashed it, and made it known that henceforward they would regularly use it for pilgrimages. The two kinship groups of a tertiary section now had their separate saint's tombs. Some months later, the rival decided to move with his small group to an area in which they had not previously resided. It is the custom among the Bedouin when they pitch their tents in a place for the first time, that the people of the neighbourhood should bring them gifts to mark the event. The returned warrior, who had now become a close neighbour of his rival was obliged, like others, to offer the latter a gift; he was also obliged to return the gift of a sheep that he had been given on rejoining his section in 1947. He brought a gift within a few hours of his rival's arrival, but it was a goat.[14] The rival and his followers were furious, and the argument that the warrior was too poor to give more was dismissed summarily. This was the final insult. The donor, in return, had been given less than he had presented. The reciprocity of gift exchanges had not only been arrested, it had been reversed. From then onwards the two groups made no attempt to conceal their hostility and went their separate ways.

Disputes stemming from circumstances such as these are the occasions which mark the proliferation of groups, although in all three cases cited, difficulties over water supplies had preceded the outbreaks of quarrelling.

In this discussion of the ways in which proliferation of segments takes place, the emphasis has been put on the tug of war between the interests of people in their agnatic connections and the interest they have in their maternal relatives. Stated thus sharply, this is a distortion of the process. To speak of the principle of agnation conflicting with the principle of cognation or maternal origin is nonsense, as the facts included in the discussion show. Agnation is not one thing, but many. Within its scope are included such aspects of social organisation as succession, status, inheritance, bridewealth, blood money, modes of domestic and political behaviour, and so forth; and each of these aspects, the closer we stick to reality, can be broken up into a number of components. The same can be said of cognation and maternal origin. All these principles, so-called, are clusters of numerous component parts, which combine, in reality, in a kaleidoscopic number of ways. In one situation a component of one combines with that of another to strengthen it; in a different situation the one component may repel the other; in a third situation, a number of the components in one will combine to exclude those of the other, and so on. If, therefore, an understanding of the way in which lineage proliferation occurs is sought, a view of the process as a conflict between the principle of agnation and the opposing pull of maternal origin is quite erroneous. It is of use in predicting the direction of cleavage to know that within a tertiary group there are also clusters of kin which are defined roughly by maternal links, and this knowledge serves as a rough and ready guide in predicting what the composition of groups, after they have split away from the parent group, will be. If a more precise picture of this composition is desired, other and more complex kinship links and the behaviour which accompanies them must be taken into account. If a still more accurate picture is desired, details of inheritance disputes, debts of bridewealth, the size of flocks and herds, and the like, must also be taken into consideration. If, finally, one has the opportunity to study groups after they have proliferated, the presence or absence of this or that man can often be explained only in terms of his eye for a pretty girl or a personal preference for neighbours.

The kind of change which has been discussed in this essay is not difficult to negotiate in genealogical terms. Earlier it was stressed that within the tertiary tribal sections, although they are always predominantly agnatic groups, clusters of cognatic kin also exist. Two ways of naming these clusters are adopted – all groups, whether they are elementary families, an odd assortment of kindred sharing a common tent for reasons of expediency, or tribal groups, have a name. Sometimes these clusters are named after a prominent living male, or a deceased kinsman of the same kind. Sometimes these little groups are named after a woman, perhaps the grandmother of the group.[15] Thus a small group of two or three tents will be distinguished from another similar cluster within the camp, and so on for a number of groups, depending on the size of the camp. Most camps, however many tents they contain, have names for progressively inclusive clusters of tents until a twofold named division is reached. Tertiary segments that are forced to split contain therefore two groups with names already attached to them. When a split occurs, the name of the tertiary segment is pushed into the area of ambiguity and the names of what were previously two clusters become the names of two new tertiary segments, with a minimum adjustment in usage and a minor reshuffle at the tertiary level of segmentation. Names cannot continue to be pushed into this area of the genealogy interminably, otherwise it would gradually expand into a vast pool of names. For a few generations the name dispensed with in this way becomes one of those ancestors about whom there is argument when genealogies are given. In the course of time, name after name is subjected to the process of elision and eventually will cease to be of concern to anyone.

I now summarise the main points of the discussion. The evidence that has been examined suggests that the mechanical devices of telescoping, fusion of names, and extinction of lines do not affect orders of segmentation superior to that of the tertiary order, and that in conditions of a completely stable population, these devices alone would suffice to retain the form of the genealogical structure. But, it was argued, conditions of complete stability cannot be assumed; the evidence of the present distribution of population among the numerous tertiary groups clearly points to marked fluctuations occurring within these small groups. This being so, proliferation of these groups in some areas at some times must follow, and conversely, while proliferation takes place here, combination will be taking place elsewhere as the population of groups decreases. The condition which compels proliferation is the alteration in the relationship of man and animals to the natural resources; and when this alteration builds up to an acute pressure on water and land, one group of a divided segment must move off to seek water elsewhere.

The next task was to demonstrate where this kind of change occurred on the genealogy. The sudden irregularity in the number of segments at the tertiary order, compared with the uniformity at others, provided a clue. Other evidence also pointed to this as a significant order in this context: there is ambiguity displayed with regard to the identity and positioning of ancestors here; members adopted into a lineage are grafted on to it here; clients are attached to tertiary sections; groups of noblemen, when they are detached and move off to another tribe, break away at this point. This is where change occurs, but, it was agreed, in understanding the way in which it takes place, certain forms of marriage have to be taken into account. Particular emphasis was placed on cross-cousin marriage with the mother's brother's daughter, and to women outside the tertiary segment, since the effect of these forms of marriage is to produce two or more clusters of cognatic kindred in camps largely composed of agnates, and to emphasise the line of cleavage in a lineage segment. So that when, therefore, a split occurs, the line it takes is predetermined. Proliferation, even when necessary, does not finally come about, however, until an occasion permits the separation of groups to be demonstrated by a violation of the conditions of membership of a group. Details of three such occasions were offered: the demand for blood money between agnates who previously had constituted a politically undivided section; behaviour contrary to the demands of agnatic kinship in attendance and gift-giving at funerals; and failure to participate in a pilgrimage to the saint's tomb of a particular section. But another query remained: how are the newly formed groups named? It was seen that names already in daily use by the small group of people concerned came to assume a new significance, while the name which had previously spanned them all is disregarded and pushed into the area of ambiguity whence later it is elided altogether. Change due to the normal and inevitable process of proliferation is thus managed within the structural limits of the tertiary section without disturbing any of the superior orders in the system. The latter remain fixed over long periods, but the tertiary sections of a particular secondary action may be reduced in number over a few generations while another secondary section may show a corresponding increase in the number of its segments.

By combining the various factors involved in change, it is possible to understand the details of lineage proliferation, or at least to travel along a well signposted road. In the light of this analysis, moreover, it is unnecessary to assume a stable population in each and every segment over long periods; the mechanisms of readjustment allow for substantial irregularities and fluctuations in population. It is possible that they are also sufficient to contain significant increases in the aggregate population. They could almost certainly control minor fluctuations, but it is seriously doubted whether a population increase sufficient to produce a country-wide and acute water shortage could be met merely by the proliferation of tertiary lineage segments. But to deal with this problem other aspects of the Bedouin genealogy and details of Cyrenaican history, which have necessarily been omitted from this discussion, would have to be taken into account, and this is best left for another occasion.

6

The power of shaikhs

The data in this discussion relates to the three years immediately preceding Libyan independence in 1951. Prior to the advent of the British, Cyrenaica had been under Italian colonial rule from the Italian invasion in 1911 until Italy entered World War II in 1940. For the first twenty years of this rule the Bedouin were at war with the Italians, until they were subdued by Graziani and the resistance brought to an end by the capture and hanging, on 16 September 1931, of the redoubtable but aged resistance leader, 'Umar al-Mukhtar. After the Italians had been expelled from Cyrenaica in 1943, the country was governed first by a British Military Administration, and then, from early 1948, by a Civil Administration. The main preoccupation of both administrations was to ensure that a minimum of order prevailed throughout the country, especially in the few small towns and villages, as they were then. The Civil Administration had the additional task of preparing for independence, and in 1948 a Four Power Commission arrived in the country to take evidence of political conditions, to be followed by a United Nations Council in 1950, led by Adrian Pelt, to plan the details of the move to self-government for Libya.

For centuries before the Italians occupied Cyrenaica, the country had been a Turkish colony. The Turks, like the Italians, gave Bedouin shaikhs official recognition; the Turks adopting a form of indirect rule on a modest scale by using the few more powerful shaikhs as administrators, mainly for the purpose of collecting taxes; the Italians attempting the more ambitious scheme of giving official recognition to nominated shaikhs of different orders of importance and paid accordingly. The British experimented unsuccessfully with the idea of representatives nominated by the people of the tribes and their sections themselves. These attempts to deal with the tribes all had their effect on Bedouin shaikhship – and further reference will be made to them presently – but during the period of fieldwork, titular recognition was not given to shaikhs. Consequently, power was being exercised unencumbered by the complexity of office, and if a study of Bedouin shaikhship has one thing above all else to offer, it is that power is to be seen virtually in its own right, as distinct from power as a component of authority.

In making a distinction between power and authority, it is not the intention to enter upon a philosophic discussion of the concept, but simply to use them as indicative of two general modes of behaviour and the consequences they entail.

Thus, in a south Lebanese village in which I worked, the population was divided until 1958 into three ranks; the Learned Families, as they were then called, occupying the upper stratum, the peasants the lower stratum, and petty traders the intermediate stratum. The economy was agriculturally rich, and people of the Learned Families (about 25 per cent of the population) were able to live a leisured style of life without working on the land. Some members of this group were acknowledged as religious experts, and for this reason their authority was accepted in matters of ritual practices, marriage rules, and general morality. So that, for example, it was they who proclaimed that the behaviour during 'Ashura (the first ten days of Muharram, the first month in the Muslim calendar) was to take this or that form, it was one of them who announced the end of Ramadan, it was only their public rebuke of a person's behaviour that would be tolerated, and it was only they who were accepted as competent to perform certain duties, for which payments were made, and which provided some of them with an additional and significant source of income.

A move upward on the part of a trader or a peasant meant the adoption of a different mode of living. It meant retreat from manual labour as a first step. In turn, this meant the loss of about half the products of his land. It also necessitated abandoning the mean clothes of the peasantry for the more costly garb appropriate to the new rank. A mud and timber house was no longer in keeping with the other trappings; a move to a more commodious stone or cement built house became urgent. And, as if to discourage idle thinking, onerous entertainment, sometimes involving relatively great expense, would have to be undertaken if only as a display of a man's new found puissance. A move upward where there is rank is a leap, not a progression. To make it successfully the surplus wealth would have to be very large.

In the village, not all men of high rank, it is true, were powerful; not all were rich. Once rank had been achieved and held confidently, it had its own momentum, acting as bulwark against dire economic and social threats, irrespective of the personal merits or failings of individuals: whatever the personality of a man of rank, his position secured him respect and provided the opportunity, not available to others, of additional income. A relatively poor man of rank could survive to enjoy easy living; a competitor needed to be wealthy to attain rank in the first place. For example, one peasant had plots of land whose value I estimated, in 1953, at £10,000. He also possessed a hoard of gold sovereigns of unknown value, as well as three pieces of property in the village, including a shop, all of which he let. He had spent a long and wearisome lifetime of patient accumulation, and, despite the pressures put on him by his community, he held his gains intact. He knew that to move out of the peasantry would be a move towards penury and a pauper's death. His son, however, was beginning to reap the benefits of his father's efforts in the form of an education in the city, thereby equipping himself with a lifeline in the event of loss of his father's land: he knew full well the history of peasants, over-eager to leap when their resources were insufficient, who lost all and who were relegated not to the comfort of prosperous peasants, but to the very lowest rungs of the hierarchy. Where rank is present, promotion is a task for at least a generation of endeavour. Where status rules, without the authority of rank or office, ambitions can be entertained on little, preferment is progressive and it can be rapid, but thwarted ambitions are not accompanied by the same harsh penalties. In ranked contexts, or in contexts where office is present, or where rank and office are both to be found, power is comparatively stable. The relative ease with which some degree of power can be won and lost without dramatic consequences, where it is not contained in rank or housed in office, gives it characteristic instability.

The distinction drawn here between power and authority is highly practical. The evidence adduced has been drawn mainly from a ranked community, deliberately so. Having highlighted some aspects of authority, it is permissible now to examine the problem of power among the Cyrenaican Bedouin, leaving the contrast with authority to emerge, as data relating to these particular people is brought forward. The concern now will be with Bedouin shaikhs exclusively.

An initial problem of the growth in power of Bedouin shaikhs can be stated quite simply. According to the labels of characterisation employed in social anthropology, Bedouin social relationships are to be fitted into the structure of a segmentary lineage system. In such a system, groups, as they segment into their various orders, stand in balanced opposition. Further, these groups, at any order of segmentation, constitute corporations based on agnatic affiliation. Agnatic corporate groups constituted of the descendants of putative ancestors of bifurcating patrilines, and formed on this basis only, lack the means to combine, since, descent being the sole criterion, the differentiation among men (which could provide the means) is absent. These two facts, balanced opposition between pairs of successively discrete corporations (without entering into an elaborate critique of lineage theory) eliminate the possibility of an analysis of power. For, if these facts are accepted then, firstly, leadership of or from any other corporate group is unacceptable. Were such leadership to be given analytic recognition, then the structural equivalence of like segments, the very core of lineage theory, is threatened. The spread of power is stultified at the very base of the system: the acceptance by corporate group A, in a state of fusion with its like group B, of the leadership of a shaikh from B would create a theoretically impermissible imbalance. Indeed, it is difficult to envisage the working, in practice, of fission and fusion (the other face of balanced opposition between like segments) unless there are leaders to bring pairs of groups together, and to fissure them into their separate groups when the necessity to combine has terminated. Moreover, although at first flush leadership within the elementary corporate group seems a possibility, the jural equality among its male members and the insistence on the equal rights of agnates to natural resources, debars the development of the differentiation on which perforce leadership rests.

Secondly, assuming that a man could rise to power within a minimal corporate group, expansion of this power across corporate groups is not possible either, because not only is a lineage system a scaled build-up of like corporate groups, but, in political relations, agnatic affiliation is given such overwhelming precedence that other kinds of relations are repudiated. For while it is readily admitted (by Evans-Pritchard, for example) that the sentiments, if not the claims, of kinship might inhibit a man from killing a mother's brother during hostilities between two corporate groups, this is viewed as a personal connection devoid of any significant effect on the structure of political relations.

This argument may be considered to be too theoretically rarified, but the absence of analyses of power in the works of authors using segmentary lineage theory is striking. Two of the foremost writers on lineage systems, Evans-Pritchard and Fortes, who, moreover, had a deep interest in political behaviour, have not written systematically about the development and distribution of power. The suggestion, therefore, is that this omission is not due to a lack of interest but to an inability to take cognisance of the problem when using a segmentary lineage model.

Others have attempted to approach the matter, but they have quickly retreated. Thus Barth states the compromise in his Southern Kurdistan book that 'Lineage segments which have become widely separated in terms of descent will continue as separate endogamous [*sic*] segments, and in such a situation it is difficult for one segment to accept the informal enforced authority of the leader of another segment' (Barth 1953: 70–71). Even those lineally separated segments might – as they often do – share borders, a 'situation' which, on Barth's own argument, requires leadership. Cunnison, in his Baggara book, states the problem of comprehending power within the limits of lineage theory with admirable clarity; having done so, he then passes on to discuss the Sudanese government's bureaucratic apparatus, informing the reader that the choice of tribal officials is made from the leaders of the various segments, but neglecting to analyse the pattern of relations which endow these government nominees with power in the first place (Cunnison 1966: ch. 12). Lewis also shows concern when he states that 'Somali society is constitutionally opposed to the bestowal of power in one person, particularly on a shaikh', but, 'there is always the possibility that under suitable conditions a man of religion of outstanding personality can marshal widespread public support and assume political leadership'. That is to say, given the coincidence of the right man and the ripe moment, political leadership can be assumed by one man. How this leadership 'can marshal widespread public support' is not explained; but there seems to be slight advantage to seeking it in other than agnatic terms from the statement that, 'Since the concern of this book is with politics, and not with marriage and kinship, we do not need to pay much attention to the affinal relationships created by marriage. Affinal ties are not normally a basis for political affiliation or cleavage' (Lewis 1961: 137, 138 and ch. 7).

Like many others, Lewis accepts the possibility of situational leadership. From the various statements made about this, it seems that a leader is thrown up in a situation of stress, when, presumably, concerted action becomes a matter of such urgency that concentration of the collective mind occurs, resulting in an instant acknowledgement of an individual as leader. Yet, if there is one moment when a consensus on leadership is intractably difficult, it is one of stress: stress itself causes enough problems without compounding it with a decision about leadership. Unless there is agreement on a leader prior to stress, then there is nothing to prevent the chaos of anyone and everyone gratuitously offering their services. Leadership is exercised in Cyrenaica when a camp is moved – every ten days or so in the rainy season – when decisions have to be made about ploughing, when the regular watering of animals is to begin, who is to use the water, how and where men are to gather for communal prayer on the morning of the Great Festival, and on a whole wide range of other mundane occasions. It is no accident that the men who lead in these activities are also the men who are out in front when moments of high drama are enacted or who direct activities from their bases. It was they who led guerrilla groups against the

Italians, and who, subsequently, were recognised as shaikhs guiding decisions concerning day-to-day activities. The idea of situational leadership derives from the failure to include within the purview of leadership the unspectacular events of daily living, such as the annually recurring moves to new pastures, the seasonal movements between pasture lands and watering points, decisions about marriage, and the like.

Alongside the idea of situational leadership the twin idea of charismatic leadership is often to be found. Rhetorical powers, argumentative skills, the ability to persuade, and physical characteristics are the kind of qualities which, singly or in combination, are cited to account for the leadership of particular shaikhs, and the Bedouin would concur with the view that such is the stuff of which their shaikhs are made – or of which they would prefer them to be made. While it is obviously true to say that a man's personality characterises the style with which he practises his power, personality is peripheral to the problem of leadership, neither endowing a man with it nor debarring him from it. On factual grounds alone, charisma must be rejected. One of the most powerful shaikhs in the Cyrenaican desert, his name known throughout the country, was a man of slouching gait, slovenly appearance, a cast in his eye, and inarticulate and disconcertingly drivelly. His followers were aware of the disabilities and lamented them; yet they gave him their devoted loyalty. Another man, one of the most charismatic Bedouin I knew, possessed all the personal trappings of greatness and such a command of language that when he spoke at gatherings he sent those present into deliriums of delight, but his wealth consisted of two camels only; he could count on a large number of admiring listeners, but virtually none followed him politically.

After arguing against situational or charismatic leadership, I shall now show how leadership is attained. Rejection of these suggestions does not mean the absence of leadership. The fact is that there are shaikhs of groups of people varying in size from small nuclei of some twenty-five followers to groupings of several thousands, recruited from a shaikh's own corporate group and allied corporate groups. The problem, therefore, requires an investigation of the differentiation that develops to allow the appearance of leaders of small nuclei, and then to account for its growth in span to comprise thousands of people. For, almost invariably, the stress is given to the egalitarianism that is said to exist among men of these local corporate groups, particularly with regard to political status.

In his history of the Sanusi Order, although Evans-Pritchard does not give the Bedouin shaikhs a role to play in the wars against the Italians until page 168 (in a book of 229 pages), he makes a number of statements about them in the second chapter dealing with Bedouin social organisation. The

Italian lawyer Savarese is quoted approvingly as saying: 'Each *bait* and each *'aila* has its shaikh, chosen for his age and wisdom or for his prowess, though the Shaikhship is generally hereditary in certain families.' (It should be noted that in Savarese's understanding, the concepts *bait* and *'aila* referred to very small groups and somewhat larger ones, whereas the Bedouin gave them various meanings, expanding them to refer to groups of several thousands, and contracting them to the limits of a small camp of some five tents.) Evans-Pritchard, expressing his own views, has many comments to make about shaikhs. He begins with the statement, 'Each section of a tribe, from the smallest to the largest, has its shaikh or shaikhs.' He ought to have known better, for while he was still in the British Military Administration, the process of appointing shaikhs to the largest sections had already begun. The Administration, if it was to penetrate the tribes at all, could only do so through appointed representatives; and a plausible starting point was to appoint a tribal adviser (*mustashar*) to each of the nine tribes. By 1948, only two such advisers had been recognised, one to a sedentary tribe occupying an area of the 'Green Mountain' in the north of the country, and the other to a powerful camel herding tribe – although his advisory role was severely curtailed because he dared not venture into much of this tribe's territory. A third adviser, a close confidant of the ex-king and a formidable resistance leader, was accorded his title by some sections of his large tribe but more generally thought of as a national figure engaged principally in the political life of Benghazi. There was so little agreement among the other tribes that it was pointless designating anyone as tribal adviser. This failure to make appointments is of special significance, because this was the period immediately succeeding the war and the expulsion of the Italians, when men who had distinguished themselves as warriors were available, and the memory of their valorous deeds had not yet faded. Failure to reach agreement among the majority of the tribes was clear indication that the wrong units had been chosen for representation. Therefore, it can be said that power does not reside in the apical points of the structures referred to as tribes.

Evans-Pritchard's statement about shaikhs in his work referred to earlier has another part to it: each of the smallest sections had its own shaikh. In 1950, the British Administration did not make any further attempts to make appointments at the top. Instead, it was decided to try the opposite. A nephew of the Emir (as the ex-King was then), with his weight of *baraka* (innate divine goodness) to buttress his regal presence, visited the tribal areas to listen to claims to shaikhship from members of small groups and, it was hoped, to make appointments. I attended one of these sittings, to use a euphemism. Many aspirants, with their followers, arrived to press their claims, and press them they did, until, after several hours of hearing claims and counter-claims shouted out in a babble of violent argument, the Emir's nephew felt constrained to leave by way of the window. The attempts to reach agreement on the appointment of shaikhs at this level was a failure. Therefore, it can be said that the smaller tribal sections (or lineage segments) are not units on which power is conferred.

Considering the results of these two experiments, and assuming that experiments concerned with making appointments to the middle range tribal sections would have been similarly unsuccessful, it can now be said that what the authorities regarded as the tribal structure with its ordered sections is not the meaningful framework for comprehending the distribution of power. Put another way, leaders exist but the tribal structure is not the instrument for identifying them: power is present and it has a distribution amenable to characterisation, but this distribution shows little consistency with points of division in the tribal structure. In this respect, foreign administrations (and, it is only fair to add, the Libyan administration at the time the country was given self-rule) ran into difficulties which were not encountered by the colonial powers in many others parts of Africa where the bureaucracies of native kingdoms and chiefdoms offered a ready means of governing: an administration was imposed on an existing apparatus. Among the Bedouin, the tribal structure did not provide a framework to which administrative positions could be attached. The problems of government in Cyrenaica were of the same nature as problems facing the government of the Sudan in its dealings with the tribes of the south, such as the Nuer.

Following his statement about the distribution of shaikhs among tribal segments from smallest to the largest, Evans-Pritchard then proceeds to the contradictory statement that because the tribal system 'is a system of balanced opposition between tribes and tribal sections from the largest to the smallest divisions, and there cannot therefore be any single authority in a tribe.' This is followed by a statement that leadership is situationally limited. Finally, he claims that 'the exact status of a shaikh can only be defined in terms of a complicated network of kinship ties and structural relations.' Despite the contradictions, Evans-Pritchard, unlike some others, showed awareness of the problem, he acknowledged that power existed, and his suggestion for its definition – taken along with brief and somewhat indefinite references to wealth, transmission of status, and gradings of shaikhs – gives a clue showing the direction in which investigation might proceed. I argue that men became leaders by astute accumulation of resources such as material goods (grain and animals), a following of men, networking of relationships and obligations, and their purposeful application throughout many years. As a preliminary to this, a few general remarks are necessary about the economy of camel herding Bedouin and the kind of possible status differentiation it permits.

The cash-cropping cum herding economy is very marginal, and each local area is subject to severe oscillations in its general environmental conditions, so that surpluses and shortages in annual subsistence requirements follow each other in erratic succession. As far as grain is concerned, it can be stored above ground in the desert and semi-desert for as long as five years – an advantage which must be stressed, since this has the effect of injecting an element of stability into an otherwise capricious economy, thereby affording men a foundation on which to build and retain their power, and to increase the span of that power. The significance of the long-term storage of a prime product can be seen in relief when compared with, say, those areas in the southern Sudan liable to widespread and prolonged annual floods, which make storage of agricultural products impossible, and also where aspirants to power, the 'bulls' of the Nuer, can only achieve leadership of a very small nucleus of kinsfolk. Storage of surplus grain reaped in years of abundance is, however, only one element in the local economic stability of the Bedouin, and as a single element it is insufficient to lift a man above his fellow men to become their leader. The quest for further economic stability is part of the process of power itself and the manner of its acquisition is a matter to which attention will be given presently.

The products in this economy are few: grain and animals, and the milk, wool and meat they yield. Every adult male has some of all these. The economic materials of power are available to all men, in different degrees it is true, and degrees of difference are of greater consequence to social relationships in this marginal economy than in rich economies. Despite the differentiation which exists, there also exists a strong egalitarian sentiment bred in the general uniformity of people's living. Men differ little in their outward dress. Their tents are very much the same, except that a shaikh's tent is bigger than the others in a camp – but only to give extra room for entertainment; many other men could enlarge their tents if the wool for weaving it were the only consideration. Inside the tents, what comforts exist are better for the shaikh. More meat is available in the shaikh's tent, but whenever he – or anyone else for that matter – slaughters an animal, all members of the camp partake of the meat. A shaikh has more animals than most of his followers, but insufficient in numbers to ossify differentiation into the permanence of rank. With the flocks and herds out of sight, a man of power and a nonentity are indistinguishable. Small wonder then that in these conditions men can realistically harbour thoughts of acceding to power: many do.

As soon as an aspirant to power has the means, he invests in a horse, the status symbol *par excellence*. All horses are not the same. The mount of a mature shaikh at the zenith of his power is likely to be a very fine animal indeed; a worn out or petty shaikh is more likely to own a matching old nag. Whatever its state, the horse has a utilitarian value, but apart from this, its ornamentation is elaborate and costly. The saddle, with its two high pommels, is woven through with silver thread, and the reins, bridle and body belts are similarly worked. Hanging from its neck is an amulet which, although inexpensive, is indicative of the place the horse holds in Bedouin sentiments. A horse's upkeep is expensive, for it is fed grain rather than pastured. Its care is exacting: not only has it to be taken to the well to be watered twice daily in the dry season, but during the intense heat of summer, it is sheltered in the tent for an hour or so during the hottest part of the day. Above all, it is costly to buy. Indeed, the cost of a horse and its trappings is equated with the bridewealth of a shaikh's son. When, under instruction to do so, I suggested to the shaikh that it was about time he married off his eldest son, he replied, seriously: 'I have bought him a horse, he cannot expect a wife now.'

The horse is given pride of place, tethered in front of its owner's tent. Its value is not in mere ostentation, nor in the prowess its owner shows at the horse-riding displays given on feast days. More than these marks of status, the horse gives mobility, used not for rounding up animals, but for carrying its owner speedily from place to place. There is little point in boasting about intentions to defend wells and ploughland if they cannot be reached in time. The shaikh has to be seen to be leading in the sense that he has the means to move quickly against intruders in any part of the territory. Further, if a shaikh is to grow in power, he must interfere in as many sets of relations over as wide a field as possible. Where dispute rages, there the shaikh must be also. Where settlement is being negotiated, he must be seen to participate. A tent-bound shaikh remains, at best, a strictly localised centre of power. Mobility provided by a horse does not create a field of power, but it enables a shaikh to exploit its full territorial extent. Shaikhs are given to keeping tallies of their appearances and triumphs; the greater his mobility, the more notches a shaikh can add to his tally. It is not for the sake of making conversation that the Bedouin are experts at assessing a horse's speed and staying powers, and the skill of a rider in handling it. For speed of movement not only allows a shaikh to be present at gatherings over a wide area and to participate in the affairs of people belonging to groups other than his own, but he thus enlarges his repute; it enables him to control his connections with people and to incur fewer obligations. When a man travels on foot, say, to market, it might take him several days. On the way he has to seek hospitality in the camps of kinsmen over nights, and make stops at other camps for refreshment. Travelling on a donkey makes little difference. Travelling by camel reduces the number of stops. Travelling by horse eliminates them all. Stops entail entertainment, and its acceptance incurs debts, to use Bedouin idiom. Pedestrian movement commits a man to onerous debts. A horse gives a man control over his obligations, and endows him with the capability, therefore, of configuring his relationships more consistently with his wishes.

The Land Rover, when it appeared in Cyrenaica, was an immediate attraction: it could be driven almost anywhere a horse could go, its speed was greater, it could be kept going for longer, visits could be made to more places in a day and their duration could be cut. As the Bedouin saw the difference, it could do anything a horse could do, but better. What was not apparent was its effect on the texture of social relationships. This has now been realised, and, seemingly incongruously in the days of massive oil wealth, some of the notable shaikhs whose followers continue to inhabit the semi-desert have reverted to the use of the horse, using mechanical transport only for long distance travel along metalled roads.

Identifying shaikhs in their camps, and grading them, presents little difficulty. Apart from the obvious emblems of power, the horse, the larger tent, the larger flock and herd, other less obvious differences become apparent. More grain is ground in the shaikh's tent, and there are more people to help. Clarified butter is more plentiful, and the women are freer with it. Carpets are greater in number, and there is always an unfinished strip of tent top or carpet on the loom. Tea is almost continuously available. Men and women call on this or that neighbour; they all amble along to the shaikh's tent sometime during the day on most days. Discussions are always held in his tent. Visitors either make for his tent or are ushered there. In the grain store there is a mound of grain for everyone; the shaikh will have more than most or all other people. The more detailed the description, the longer the list of things of which the shaikh has more. Material wealth alone does not, however, make a shaikh. The wealthiest Bedouin I knew had a herd of 500 camels, but I doubt whether he could count on 20 followers; a powerful shaikh had only about 20 camels, but he could count on the allegiance of over 500 followers. For a man to rise to power he needs to convert wealth into social relationships. To do this successfully he must be able to accumulate some wealth as a beginning. The next step lies in the answer to the question: how can differentiation in wealth be generated among a people who collectively own the natural resources, whose shares in well or spring water are allocated on the basis of strict equality among agnates, who are allocated a number of furrows for ploughing on the same basis, and whose inheritance of animals is equal for all male heirs? The question can be put in another way: how does an individual break through the barrier of even distribution to acquire a disposable surplus?

Inherent in power is competition among equals, at any of its levels. Thus, whether a man sees himself as a successor to great power, to corporate group leadership, to the shaikhship of a small camp, or as an aspirant only, he first has to contend with the most equal of all his contestants, his full brother.

Inter-fraternal tensions are endemic among Bedouin brothers, seeded in the rules of inheritance, which place brothers on an exactly equal footing, but which are modified in practice in a variety of ways. The precise pattern of inter-fraternal relationships varies with the number of brothers. Thus, if there are only two they will either combine or else oppose each other. In a family of three brothers, the eldest and youngest combine and the one in the middle attempts to achieve some sort of independence. The permutations, which increase with the number of brothers, are related to these two basic patterns. However complex they might become, initially at least, the eldest brother with or without support from a junior brother, stands in opposition to his middle brother with or without support of some of his other brothers. A middle brother of three, as a first challenge, might move away from his eldest brother's camp, he might serve as shepherd to a shaikh and hope to accumulate sufficient sheep to give him the economic start in challenging him – a long and wearisome task requiring great patience, and which few Bedouin undertake successfully.

Advantage lies with the eldest brother from the outset, for, on the death of a father, it is he who assumes his 'position', by which is meant that he acquires the father's status emblems (his toga, his seal and his horse, if he had one to leave). The father's authority over the domestic domain is transmitted to him, and his command has to be obeyed even though the disparity in age between the siblings may be very little. More importantly, perhaps, the eldest son becomes proprietor of his father's wealth until it is divided. His aim is to keep the inheritance, consisting almost entirely of animals, undivided. If he has yet to marry when his father dies, the bridewealth he gives for a wife is taken from the joint stock, as are the other many costs of marriage. He might delay the division of the inheritance until he has reared his family to adulthood, or division might be left as a problem for the succeeding generation. The eldest son, finally, inherits his father's 'debts', by which is meant that he becomes the keeper of the connections his father had forged during his lifetime, and he inherits the obligations which were incurred in bringing them about. Although, in a jural sense, the eldest is an equal heir along with his brothers, his seniority differentiates him from others inasmuch as it gives him preferential access to animal wealth, the labour of his siblings, command of a domestic unit and control of connections with other people.

Females are excluded as formal heirs, whether they be wives or daughters, but they nevertheless come to possess animal wealth by being given unpaid bridewealth and, if they wish, by selling their heavy silver armlets and anklets, and buying animals with the proceeds. There are other less common ways in which they acquire animals. Wealth thus gathered, they have the right to transmit to their sons preferentially, thereby significantly altering the distribution of inherited animals among sons. Sometimes the mother's preference goes to the eldest son, and it often falls to the lot of a middle son, however, in my records, a youngest son does not receive a preferential legacy of this sort. Women possess what might be legitimately conceived of as property, and of a kind which far exceeds in importance the camels or sheep they might come to own in later life. The connections which men seek are vested in women and they are as strong or as fragile as is the determination of women to maintain or sever them. Effective control over women, and the authority to choose a spouse for them, is a prize of high worth for any man to capture. The eldest son, with his deceased father's authority now in him, has the right to negotiate his sisters' marriages. What makes this authority even more telling is that, in this connection, women are not passive. Through marriage they come to possess, increasingly, claims on men – their husbands who have not paid all the bridewealth promised, their fathers or eldest surviving brothers who have received the part of the bridewealth handed over, on their fathers-in-law through their husbands, and on their own fathers on behalf of their husbands, not to speak of their claims on and influence over others of their sex. Women have in their hands a bundle of claims, and the man who can influence the use of these, whether directly through his own daughters or sisters, or through the fathers or brothers of other women, gains a wealth of social assets.

The domestic realm, in anthropological writings, has frequently been left isolated from the political realm as if the two realms were disparately autonomous. The image is of an overarching political structure underneath which domestic relations are to be inserted. In this context, women are seen as of little or no consequence to political relations, since the structure is made by the ordering of groups of men arranged on a framework of patrilineal descent. My analysis amounts to a complete rejection of this view: the aim is to establish that elements in what are isolated as kinship or domestic relations are as significant to a study of political relations as are any others, and that both sexes contribute to the process of configuring patterns of power. In amongst the relations between parents and children, between children themselves, between spouses and between affines, there exists a range of relationships of formidable complexity as the foregoing summary of the data is intended to indicate. Progress to power entails a specific patterning of these relationships to produce differentiation among the people in whom these relationships are parcelled; failure to achieve this pins a man down to the permanent status of a follower. The image offered here is not of a structural mould into which data are poured, but of individuals of power imposing an arrangement on an otherwise amorphous heap of relationships, as a magnet acts on a heap of iron filings by drawing them into a pattern.

The assets of power delimited by this field of relationships are only a fraction of the total available to the Bedouin. An apparent restriction on further differentiation is that corporate resources are owned by male members of a corporate group as a collectivity and, annually, shares in these resources are divided as equally as practicable among agnates. Thus, at the end of the rainy season, a rough estimation of the amount of well water available for animals is made, and this is divided into equal shares, each adult male receiving a share stated as so many skin buckets. For example, if it is estimated that the amount of water is sufficient to provide 500 skin bucketsful for the total need of all the animals each time they are taken to drink, and the number of agnates is 50, then, in disregard of the number of animals owned by them as individuals, each agnate is given 10 skin bucketsful as his share. In the division of land, once a decision has been taken that sufficient rain has fallen on a piece of the corporate territory, agnates gather in the shaikh's tent to estimate the number of furrows the well-watered plot will permit, and these will be divided equally among the agnates. Thus, if it is estimated that 500 furrows can be ploughed, each of the 50 agnates will receive a share of 10 furrows. Arguments, often violent, ensue, which relate to the exact location of each agnate's furrows on the plot to be cultivated, but the number of furrows to a share is never in dispute.

It must be stressed that agnatic rights in land and water are not negotiable. A man cannot transfer his shares, or any part of them, to another *qua* their status as agnates, whatever the consanguinity or closeness of social relationships between them. Yet if an individual is to be limited to an equal share of cultivable land and water, he is disabled, at the outset, in his aim to increase the number of his animals and to enlarge his stock of grain. Without these increases, disposable surpluses of wool, milk, clarified butter, grain and camels for transporting dates, would not be available for disposal to followers and in entertainment. Still less could offers of cultivable land and water be made to members of other corporate groups, even in years of abundance. The deadening effect of uniformity, as with inheritance, must be lifted, but agnation cannot serve as a lever. Other forms of relationship – affinity, matrilaterality, and their multiple compound forms – can, in the sense that they are accepted as valid grounds for supplication for use of resources or grants of products. If an individual is to gain preferential access to the corporate resources of his own group and to those of others, he must strive for differentiated connections with his agnates and differentiate his connections with other corporate groups in order to be able to redistribute property and products in a way that would attract followers.

Much has been written about parallel cousin marriage in works on peoples of the Middle East; indeed, the majority of authors write as if it is the only form of marriage practised among Arabs. The usual explanation is that everywhere, regardless of the circumstances, it adds to cohesion. I am quite certain that this is a mistaken view, in the sense that it wastefully adds a layer of cohesion where it is always said to be at its thickest anyway. Barth (1954) and Khuri (1970), both of whom subscribe to the notion of it contributing to cohesion, advocate that first parallel cousin marriage in particular is a way of gaining followers. Neither indicates how this comes about, whether it is by the wife drawing her husband into her father's or brother's net or whether it is the husband who does this. In either event, it is a high price to pay, among people whose assets are limited, to gain one or two followers only. Both authors also assume that closely related patrikin are fond enough of each other that the one will follow the other after the marriage has been made, and that it was desired in the first place on this basis.

The universal effect of parallel cousin marriage is to differentiate closely related patrilineal kin. In the case of the Bedouin, it differentiates among agnates of a corporate group who are conceived of in the idiom of patrikin. Parallel cousin marriage is usually treated as if the effects of its various forms are the same. This can never be true. Here, it is necessary to discriminate between first parallel cousin marriage, second parallel cousin marriage, and all other forms of parallel cousin marriage, more appropriately designated as marriage within the corporate group or agnatic marriage, since many agnates are not patrikin in a consanguineous sense but only in the sense of common group membership.

Earlier, certain limited aspects of inheritance were touched upon, with the main stress given to the elder brother's efforts to retain the whole inheritance intact. Whether his brother or brothers acquiesce willingly or reluctantly, the arrangement is fraught with a tension which grows as the succeeding generation matures to marriageable age to the point when division becomes inevitable. First parallel cousin marriage, since it lies within the range of individual inheritance of mobile property, is the instrument with which the tensions inherent in joint ownership are dealt with by the succeeding generation. It is recognised by Bedouin that a man has a pre-emptive right to his father's brother's daughter in marriage, and I have witnessed the assertion of this right: indeed, the father would be ill-advised not to seek the compliance of his brother's son before arranging his daughter's marriage, despite the fact that normally it would be disdainful for a senior to negotiate – much less supplicate – with a man of a junior generation. The proportion of first parallel cousin marriage in corporate groups is, however, only about 20 per cent, or less, of the total number of marriages. This means that such marriages, whatever expressed general sentiments indicate, are highly selective. A man who considers his father to have suffered materially from joint ownership seeks to redress the imbalance of unequal distribution of property in the following generation by claiming his right to his first cousin and deliberately defaulting on the bridewealth. Barth takes the simplistic and incorrect view that when a man gives away his daughter in first parallel cousin marriage, he unquestionably gains a follower. Taking Barth's view, it is difficult to see why an important marriage asset should be wasted to bring a nephew or first cousin (as the case may be) closer when the relationship has ample closeness in it without marriage. Tied to this is the equally simplistic, but opposite, view that to give a daughter in marriage thereafter makes the husband permanently subservient, a docile follower. For a husband, through his wife, can draw off wealth from her father, on whom she has claims which he must heed. Far from securing a follower, first parallel cousin marriage exacerbates the competition between two male first cousins, who, in the maturity of manhood, have become contenders for the shaikhship. A shaikh of some renown was forced to yield to the demand of his brother's son and give his daughter to him; retaliating, the shaikh arranged for his eldest son to make a similar demand, although earlier he had in mind to marry him to the daughter of an important shaikh of another corporate group. The first parallel cousin constitutes such a threat that the opportunity of an alliance between two groups was sacrificed in an attempt to nullify it. In another instance, a petty shaikh was forced to give a daughter to his brother's son, who subsequently made it known that he would reject a demand from any of the shaikh's sons for one of his sisters; but the shaikh vowed that he would insist his son took his first parallel cousin by force if necessary. The relationships between first cousins are made doubly difficult when a man dies prematurely and leaves young sons, who then fall under the guardianship of the deceased's eldest surviving brother. The most protracted and bitter relationships I witnessed among Bedouin related to the invidious practices involved in such guardianship.

At the stage in the development of relationships when first parallel cousin marriages are arranged, the key to its understanding is the competition between men who see themselves as equals. Later on, when affinity becomes transmuted into kinship, and the field of competition might have changed its shape, the effects might change dramatically to bring the children and grandchildren of contenders together in close co-operation.

Marriage between second parallel cousins is much less frequent. Division of inheritance, and the hostility it almost invariably evokes, has been done, leaving grandchildren separated yet consanguineously close through both parents, all simultaneously first cross cousins and second parallel cousins through their mothers and fathers. If this generation co-operates, it can be managed without recourse to marriage, so why waste an asset. Therefore, thus far in this delineation of marriage patterns, agnates who are patrilineally closest are converted to become affines and matrilateral relatives as well, although affinal interconnections tend to be omitted between second degree patrilineal cousins.

While marriages within the intensely close range discussed thus far have a marked effect on the distribution and re-distribution of animal wealth, they may have little or no effect on corporate wealth, land and water. For rights to the latter are not contingent upon the closeness of patrilineal consanguinity. Differential access to corporate resources is possible only if non-agnatic claims are available to give grounds for supplication. Therefore, when a man – an important shaikh no less, in some instances – arranges to marry his daughter to a poor fellow member of his corporate group, his immediate gain is all or a major portion of his son-in-law's share of land and water. Affinity is *par excellence* a bundle of reciprocal relationships. In return for granting the use of his agnatic resources, the son-in-law can expect liberal quantities of products. But what the man of power gives away in products is, for him, substantially less than the gain of being able to increase the number of his animals and his stock of grain, by acquiring more than his fair share of natural resources. Even shaikhs of stature use the affinity they are able to create with their children to throw out several lines of connections to men of their own group, in the hope that if one breaks or ceases to yield the anticipated advantages, others will continue to satisfy the paramount need of preferential access to resources. The task of maintaining a momentum of power is most complicated, but it is eased by the fact that in any corporate group there are always men with insufficient numbers of animals to use their rightful share of resources fully. It is these men who perforce attach themselves as firmly as possible to shaikhs, exchanging their rights for claims, if they are to enjoy a better diet, the comfort of a more commodious tent and the variety of other small advantages which alone make life tolerable in what is a very harsh environment indeed.

Thus far, three pattern areas have been depicted: a number of marriages within the closest permitted range of first parallel cousin; few marriages within the range of the second degree, and relatively intense marriages among other members of a corporate group without any regard to the precise degree of patrilineal relationship. These areas of the marriage pattern have been shown to be consistent with the acquisition of different forms of property, different in kind and in the proprietary control of them. But the territory of a corporate group, although potentially endowed with sufficient natural resources, does not provide them year in year out, given the nature of the ecology. Such instability, if power is to be permitted to grow and remain stable over a period of years, must be countered, and the only way of doing this is by gaining preferential access to the corporate resources of other groups. Unless a shaikh stabilises his economic position, and affords his followers some measure of protection against the vicissitudes of the ecology, his following will rapidly dwindle, since the demands on him to distribute goods in times of shortage is also the time when he will be faced with scarcity and, unable to meet their demands, he has no recourse but to let his followers drift away to another shaikh.

A shaikh, seeking the sort of connection with another corporate group which would allow him access to land or water when that group is experiencing abundance and he shortage, begins his overtures by inducing its shaikh, preferably, to visit him. Such a visit is intended as an occasion for relatively grand entertainment, the centre-piece of which is a sacrificial animal. It is beyond the scope of this discussion to go into the details of animal sacrifice. Suffice it to say that the recipient of this favour accepts impelling moral obligations towards his host. Foremost among these is the obligation to return the sacrificial gift, and to return it with increment on a suitable occasion. An initial gift of a sacrifice sets in motion a relationship of reciprocity and successive increments act to project it into the future, at the same time ensuring an increasing intensity. In certain circumstances, obligations can be arrested to secure a pause in relations, or they can be revoked to reverse relations by offering an inappropriate sacrifice, but if a shaikh wishes to probe for a relationship, he can offer a sacrifice for a guest confident that the response will be an acceptance of moral obligations. If these grow and prosper, they are likely to culminate in marriage; and if this is successful, it is likely to be followed by a spread of marriages between men and women of both groups until a kinship structure is created, having in it far greater durability than that contained in a single connection.

If connections with other groups are to be multiplied to give them durability and to virtually guarantee that their claims on each other's resources are granted, clearly external connections must be highly selective and not dispersed to the maximum extent. Were they dispersed widely, the possibility would arise of numerous groups making claims on one group in the same year, which would be bound to result in an intolerable run on its resources; relationships in such conditions would soon wither away and uncertainty would be introduced where it is urgently necessary for people to be sure that obligations could be discharged.

Needs for natural resources are of different kinds. Satisfying the need for water for human beings very rarely causes difficulties, since the quantity required is relatively little. Except during rare periods of famine, local sources of water can be relied upon to satisfy human consumption. Animals' needs are much more exacting because the quantity of water required is vastly greater. Local sources of water cannot regularly cope with these demands, but since any rain that falls at any time in winter or spring is water in the well for animals, the chances are that surplus water is available in the territories of nearby corporate groups. Very minor ecological differences in the territories of corporate groups are adequate guard against water shortage for animals, and while connections into what in segmentary terms are collateral groups would not assure a supply (ecologically neighbouring territories are for Bedouin purposes virtually identical), firm connections with two or three groups within walking distance are all that is required.

Conditions for growing a crop are such, in this marginal climate, that access to the ploughland of others over a relatively large area is essential. The amount of rainfall in a season is not the determining factor of a good crop. First, a heavy fall of rain must arrive before mid-December for ploughing to be undertaken. In January, a further heavy fall is necessary to assist growth. Finally, towards the end of February/beginning of March, the land should be deluged a third time. A crop needs a rainfall regime, not just a random series of heavy falls. A good year is one in which the regime is realised, and the returns then are abundant, sometimes, remarkably, over a hundred-fold. Few groups are thus blessed in the same year, and the likelihood of such conditions occurring in successive years is remote. The stored surpluses of good years tide many people over a run of poor years, but those who can afford it – mainly shaikhs – aim to grow some barley every year. So anxious are these men about the quantities of grain in store

that they sow a few furrows on the lands of two or three groups each year –
a sensible hedge against crop failure since suitable ploughing conditions do
not guarantee a good or even an indifferent crop. Connections to other
groups, in practice, are usually concentrated but, to give full security, they
should, ideally but unrealistically, be spread across the widest ecological
diversity.

The pattern which emerges from this analysis is shown in fig. 7, in
which the divisions of the territory are laid out as tribal sections
in their respective orders. The arrowed lines represent the marriages
controlled or influenced by the shaikh of group A. The chief feature
of this latter pattern is that it also represents the shaikh's pattern of
power, which shows that the pattern of structured tribal sections and that
of power bear little similarity. Taken as a map showing the territories of
corporate groups only, it is very revealing in the indications it gives of co-
operation and potential opposition. Conspicuously, external connections
leap-frog adjacent groups: since the ecological conditions are the same,
connections through marriage are redundant, and for general purposes, the
putative agnatic connection is enough rationalisation for the need to
observe a *modus vivendi*. Moreover, B's external connections, for example,
while displaying a similar pattern to A's, are with different groups.
Contiguous corporate groups are disconnected in two senses, one from the

Figure 7.

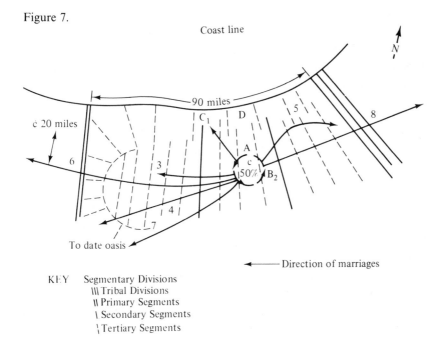

KEY   Segmentary Divisions
         ||| Tribal Divisions
         || Primary Segments
         \ Secondary Segments
         ⸜ Tertiary Segments

other, and in that their partners are disconnected also. A shaikh's connections not only define his field of power, they also delimit the boundary beyond which he is left free to compete with other corporate groups without being inhibited by the weight of cross-cutting ties, which apparently are designed to stultify hostile political action. The field of potential competition even within the territory shown on the map is extensive. This does not mean, however, that a shaikh wantonly engages all the corporate groups located there; but were it possible to show the patterns for all twenty-seven groups as shown for A then it would be relatively easy to read into the map the precise areas of competition. To state the facts briefly, A would compete against D, the partner group of B, and in so doing might well assist its own partner C against its contiguous group with which it has only a putative agnatic connection – and it would be consistent with the power interests of the shaikh of A were it to become feasible for him to usurp D's territory, since this would add a measure of ecological diversity to his territory.

Of a total of 77 extant marriages in the corporate group marked A, 16.8 per cent are to first parallel cousins, and a total of 48 per cent are within the group. One aspect of these marriages is that they indicate the paramount need to redistribute resources internally. Moreover, for a group of this sort, which was enjoying rapid political advancement after the Italian withdrawal, it is likely that this concentration would have been even higher were it not that many of its boys and young men – as well as young women – were killed during the Italian wars, leaving the group severely reduced in numbers. External connections fall into four different types: those marked 1, 2 and 3 are ecologically different from A, but situated near enough for some of A's animals to be placed among them when necessary. Those to which the arrows 4, 5 and 6 lead are further away, in such ecologically disparate areas that neither among themselves nor in relation to A will they be likely to experience the same or even similar ecological conditions in any given year. The likelihood is that the conditions in the territory of at least one of the groups will be sufficiently favourable for producing a good yield of barley. This being so, members of the more fortunate group in a particular year can allow its affinal partners of another group to grow a crop in their territory. As part of their significance, the affinal connections between these groups widen the ecological disparity to such an extent that they can grow at least a small amount of barley annually. The next arrow, marked 7, pointing in a southwest direction, indicates the affinity existing between members of group A and a distant oasis: to give an idea of its strength, suffice it to say that 10 of the extant marriages of men in group A are with women from this oasis. Here dates are grown, and this affinity gives group A access to a most valuable item of diet in later summer, at a time of year when the diet has been reduced to various cereal dishes with an occasional dash of clarified butter. It is a time of year when animal products, stored from the previous year, have been consumed, and when protein is at a premium. The arrow marked 8, pointing away to the northeast, allegedly connects A with a most powerful group in the centre of the country which, no doubt, was statistically inconsequential but of high political importance. Although the exact marriages were no longer known in either group (if, indeed, they ever existed), both insisted that the bond was still sufficiently strong to hold them united in the face of a serious attack on the territory of either.

The Bedouin recognise that there are different kinds of shaikhs. By far the most numerous and the most effete are the camp shaikhs, as they are called; their followers are the people of the small spring camps of five to ten tents with a total population of about twenty-five to fifty souls. Some of them are poor among the poor and are kept in their position by a more powerful shaikh, in order to retain their little following for him, and then only while they are successful in this task. Most of them are only marginally better off than their followers, capable perhaps of a little more generosity with their supplies of sugar and tea than the others. Their camps are usually in out of the way places. Wayfarers avoid their camps so that they are not embarrassed by onerous demands on their hospitality. Their relationship with their followers is often of a bickering kind, for they are accountable to them on a day-to-day basis. Enmeshed in the petty and detailed squabbles of camp life, they are unable to rise above their fellow men. Of the Middle Eastern communities in which I have lived, I have not known one in which as many men imagine themselves to be serious contenders for power as among the Bedouin, for their fancy can be fed on little. The camp shaikh is a position for which most men can bid at some time in their lives, and consequently there is much chopping and changing in it. Characteristically, the minimal power of the camp shaikh is unstable, lasting from a few months to at most a few years.

A second kind of camp shaikh holds sway in the bigger and wealthier of the small camps. He might be found in or near the camp of an important shaikh, acting as his deputy, taking on the burdens of hospitality, and acting independently in a manner which the resources of the shaikh of a small, poor camp could not bear. These are the men who have escaped from the treadmill existence of small camp shaikhs and are on the move. It was they, too, who were the backbone of the resistance to the Italians. The guerrilla movement was not led from a well organised centre; indeed, had it been, the task of the Italians would have been made very much easier; a successful strike at the centre could have collapsed the movement. Instead, they had to contend with attacks, usually by stealth, by half a dozen to a dozen or so men, here, there and everywhere, led by the more powerful camp shaikhs. The latter were always in touch and acted in concert with their superior shaikhs; shaikhs of corporate groups as they can be appropriately designated. Information about the deployment of Italian forces and the whereabouts of their arms and supplies was passed on wherever there were Bedouin able and willing to fight. But a hierarchical organisation culminating in a vulnerable centre or headquarters was absent. The power of the resistance lay with the camp and the corporate shaikhs to which the Head of the Sanusi Order gave the movement some sense of general purpose.

The largest politically undifferentiated group among the Bedouin is the corporate group, the one body. It speaks with one word as they are wont to say. Its men 'are struck together and strike together. We pay blood money together and receive it together.' If one of them kills, any one of them is liable to be killed in vengeance. The shaikh who captures the following of a corporate group has the power of this unity behind him. Difficult to achieve and hard to hold, the shaikh must pay dearly to remain only stationary. Indeed, it is a feature of power, as distinct from authority, that its possessor must dispense goods to followers on a relatively lavish scale, whereas a person in authority sucks in wealth as to a vortex. The flow of goods is away from power, but towards authority. Each outflow, however, is a new relationship made, an existing one strengthened and an old one renewed. The vitality of his relationships is the substance of the shaikh's power. A willingly devoted following provides him with a strong labour force which, in turn, means more animals and more grain. With assets of this kind, he is well placed to make more advantageous external connections: a bid for an important alliance is not taken seriously unless a corporate shaikh shows evidence that he will be able to sustain it. And just as the wives taken from a corporate group hold their men together in allegiance to their shaikh, so too do the women recruited from and given to other corporate groups provide the additional strength to complete his field of power and hold it firm.

Corporate shaikhship is more stable than either of the two previous forms. It might last the lifetime of the person who secures it. It might be sufficiently stable to be transmitted. The evidence indicates that it is not transmitted lineally for more than a generation. It is in the very nature of power that it must be earned continuously, and this alone militates against it becoming fixed. It is never inert. During the lifetime of a holder it fluctuates, and even if the general direction is upwards, the thrust takes him to a new position of even greater span. At the level of corporate shaikhship, a following numbers from about 200 to 700 people, a geometrical progressive increase compared with the followings of the two sorts of camp shaikhs. This is substantial power indeed: little wonder that such shaikhs are referred to as holders of the Golden Stirrup. They are not, however, all of a piece. The differences in numbers of followers, considered separately, discriminate among them, and reflect differences in resources held by them. Demographic differences are to be found among their followings. It does not mean, however, that a shaikh with a following of 200 people is necessarily weaker than one with a larger following. If the age of men and women of his corporate group is biased towards the able-bodied, the strength of his labour force is high compared to a larger group in which the age bias is towards older, less productive people. Further, while the value of external connections does not rest on their number, the greater their diversity, the wider the range of contingencies they are able to comprehend. A very large corporate following of some 600 or 700 people does, however, imply a vital labour force, secure access to economic resources on a permanent basis, and the right kind of diversity in its external connections. It is from this platform of power that a shaikh is able to soar to the position of command over a following of thousands of people and to become one of the national shaikhs.

A small number of shaikhs enjoyed national repute. When I was in the field, there were five of them. It was common to refer to them as shaikhs of tribes. This was mere administrative convenience. Not one of them commanded the allegiance of all the corporate groups in an area designated by a tribal name, whatever townspeople and administrators might say. The pattern of their power is not unlike that already mapped out for corporate shaikhs, although the texture of their connections and their corporate assets are decisively different.

The corporate territory of a national shaikh is to be distinguished by the fact that it straddles two or more disparate ecological areas. In the case of a shaikh of central Cyrenaica, his territory ran in a strip of about 100 miles long from the deep south to the highest point on the plateau in the north, enclosing a series of vegetational zones from the most marginal semi-desert through a range of intermediate areas to Mediterranean conditions. The great advantage of such ecological diversity is that it affords greater economic independence, since diversity is the basis of stability. Additionally, external connections can be perceived more in term of their political worth rather than as a response to urgent economic necessity. Finally, with substantial assets of this sort, the favours of the shaikh are eagerly sought, and consequently he can afford to be more discriminating in his choice of connections.

The position of a national shaikh is not attained only by judicious deployment of economic assets and social relationships. The ecological range within the territory of the national shaikh cited above is possible only for a small number of groups, since for them each to have this diversity would be a disastrous waste of land: indeed, to secure comparable ecological spread, it would be necessary for a territory to be coterminous with the limits set by the directional arrows of connections shown on the map. Ecological diversity implies that territorial aggrandisement has occurred. Where power has mounted to this scale, people claim that it has been preceded by expansion, and there is some factual evidence for supposing this to be true in the central Cyrenaican case. Whatever the truth about past events, people believe that expansion and contraction of corporate territories has been part of the process of their relations, and this belief motivates them contemporarily. I was present when an attempt was made by one group to seize the resources of another, which surely would have led to battle had not government forces intervened. There is substantial genealogical evidence that small nuclei within corporate groups are the rumps of previously existing groups which have either been expelled from their territories or decimated in battle; and there is evidence also that groups had moved their territories between the time the Italian ethnographer Agostini was at work in 1920, and my period of fieldwork.

On the views expressed above, the small number of national shaikhs is intelligible: the resources, both material and social, are so thinly spread that it would not be feasible for the number of shaikhs of this scale of power to be multiplied. There are five national shaikhs, and their domains, taken together, do not cover the whole country; neither is the territorial coverage achieved by them continuous – it is more a patchwork, with gaps appearing in various parts of its surface. It is interesting also that these five points of great power are not merged into a single point of supreme power. In saying this, I am not suggesting that the resources of the country determine, in crass fashion, that power cannot be focused into one point, that they are insufficient to support such an arrangement, that they are too whimsically available to permit the stability in the ascending rungs of power to lead to central power, or anything of this sort. The burden of this chapter has been to analyse the components of power, not its exercise, and the pursuit of this endeavour has been to show the modes of configuring patterns with these components. Components are arranged in pattern form by men with ideas about them, and how they choose to put components together in patterns determines the distribution of power and its variety of spans, not merely the environment or the economic resources it provides. On this view, there is a plurality of possibilities always available, of which the one discussed in this paper was employed by the Bedouin during the period 1948–50. The pattern must be right. The head of the Sanusi Order, which spread far and wide until the Italian invasion of 1911, is testimony of this; he virtually ruled the country.

7

Debt relationships

At the first camp in which my wife and I pitched our tent among the Bedouin, a sheep was brought in for slaughter shortly after our arrival.[1] This slaughter was to be both in recognition of our visit and that we were going to pitch our tent in the camp. Several hours passed before we, in company with all the adult males of the small camp, ate the meal. In the meantime carpets were laid out for us, on which to recline, and our host fussed about us, pushing cushions around us until he was satisfied that we were comfortable. All the people of the camp, women included, came to greet us. Thereafter, we exchanged the long sequence of conventional, but charming greetings with which we had come prepared; and after one round of exchanges had been completed with our constant host, he would begin again; until, after several repetitions, we were left to rest. The journey to the camp had lasted from dawn to sunset, and, tired as we were then, I thought it a very considerate courtesy to be left to rest. When the meal was brought to that part of the tent in which guests are entertained – the part also occupied by males, and which has the marital 'bed' (a straw mat) in it – we all sat around the bowl (the qas‘a) and ate without conversing, while the host urged us to eat more and more.

Following the meal, the utensils for brewing the treacle-like tea of the semi-desert were brought in. A heap of brushwood was set alight to provide glowing embers to boil water, and conversation leaped to life as suddenly as the flames from the fire. For some two hours, in the conviviality of ceremonial tea making and drinking, we were plied with questions about our origin, our families, our marriage, our history, our country and our travels; and the Bedouin freely gave similar details about themselves, showing an eagerness to do so, expounding some matters in detail, particularly their origin, their relation to other groups, and their wells, pastures and ploughland. The following day, another visitor appeared in camp, and while we were busied in meeting him, our host's son went to our tent and rummaged among our things until he found the spoons and forks he was seeking. When I showed some concern, he explained that the guest, coming from a village, was accustomed to spoons and forks, and he took our utensils because 'now we are exactly equal together' (*tawwan nahnu saua' saua' maba'dna*). This pattern of behaviour between hosts and guests was repeated in all the camps we visited, and it applied not only to us, but to all guests: first, the extended exchange of greetings, a period during which conversation was conspicuously absent, then the meal taken without any conversation but with the host urging his guests to eat, followed finally by the long drawn out tea drinking when conversation was intense and intimate and during which very many questions were asked and answered. This first experience of Bedouin hospitality had in it several of the elements of what, henceforward, will be referred to as debt (*dain*) relationships.

A cardinal feature of a debt relationship is that the initial exchange of gifts, at least, must show a difference between the original and return gifts. The Bedouin way of stating this is: 'The son of an *'anz* (a female goat which has had young) requires the son of a *na'ja* (a female sheep which has lambed)', and conversely; 'If you give me nothing, I will not even give you welcome'. Two points in the debt process arise from this. First, there must always be something left over in an exchange, otherwise the reciprocity on which debt relationships thrive would lose its momentum immediately, since an exactly equal return would precipitate a situation in which the impulse to continue the exchange would be lacking, and all impetus in the relationship would be lost. Stalemate of this kind could only result in casual gifting, since the parties, in these circumstances, would be left free to continue or discontinue the relationship, as they independently and capriciously felt fit. Reciprocity, however, is a process in relationships where there is mutual action between people; as such, it constitutes a regularity, enabling people to anticipate the behaviour of their fellow men. There is a significant difference, that is to say, between exchange (*tabdil*) and reciprocity, for which a number of words are used by the Bedouin, all expressing the idea of further social relationships of a predictable kind. Second, if each exchange is to show an increase in the quantity of the gift in strict accordance with the sentiment expressed in the saying about a goat requiring a sheep, then a debt relationship which persists for a few years soon reaches a stage where the quantity of the gift is an intolerable burden to either party. In fact, this stage is never reached. We were present at literally dozens of animal slaughters (*dhaba'ih*, sing. *dhabiha*) but nothing larger than a sheep was killed. On one occasion, a camel was slaughtered, and its owner – a poor man – made the best use he could of the meat to entertain as many as possible, but the camel was slaughtered only because it was thought to be near death, not because a debt relationship demanded it.

Many sheep or goats are slaughtered during funerals, weddings, pilgrimages to saints' tombs, and certain other occasions, but these are brought singly by individuals, and they are not to be regarded as a mammoth feast given by one man to create an instantaneous and wide network of debt relationships. The impediment to rapidly rising debt is raised on three of the main props to debt relationships. Bedouin distinguish with care and sophistication between types of goats and sheep, so that if the process starts with a small goat between two people, many exchanges (about ten, in my estimation) will have to take place before the most prized sheep are used; this means, of course, that the debt between the gift and its return is quantitatively very marginal, although as long as there is a difference, however fractional, it is sufficient to keep the mutual flow of recognised debt in motion. Nor is it possible to return the gift except when circumstances such as a funeral, marriage, a formal visit and so on, permit; for, although people in the camps, especially those of prominent shaikhs, boast of the amount of meat that is available and say with feigned surprise that 'there has been no slaughter now for three days,' in the vast majority of camps slaughters are infrequent, and in all camps animals are never killed simply for meat to eat: there must always be a stated purpose for an animal slaughter.

More important than both these considerations in preventing escalation of gift-giving to the absurd point of economic ruin, is that once a debt relationship has been solicited by an initial gift and this is appropriately acknowledged by a slightly greater return gift, then a regularised social relationship has begun, and in this new-found amity the fractional margin of debt incurred by either party at irregular and lengthy intervals in the future is lost in the welter of other social relationships which lie outside the strictly reciprocal area of relationships. Assuming that a gift is appropriately reciprocated, the formality of reciprocal gifting is soon replaced by the gift given for special occasions out of a sense of responsibility to chosen allies (*rubut*, sing. *rubat*), and by the general give and take of frequent informal social relationships, until the debt lying between people has grown into such a tangled mass that accounting becomes not only difficult but quite irrelevant: there is a point to the saying that a man's worst enemy is he who not only counts his debts but pays them. If gifting were allowed to escalate rapidly, a shaikh of any renown would have to slaughter a few camels or their equivalent in sheep and goats each week.

At one camp, of six tents, in which we resided for some two months, as many as twenty-three sheep and goats were slaughtered on that number of separate occasions. Six of the sheep were slaughtered (one for each tent) in recognition of our pitching a tent in their camp, and three were slaughtered for rather special non-recurring reasons. Of the remaining fourteen most were slaughtered by the shaikh as part of his debt relationships. The shaikh was wealthy and the camp was justly famed for its hospitality; but if this scale of generosity was allowed to escalate in accordance with the saying that a son of a female goat requires the son of an ewe, the shaikh would be reduced to paupery within a single season. It is necessary to note, further, that this generosity was witnessed in its full bounty because our residence in the camp coincided with the latter half of springtime when most of the animal slaughter for purposes of gift entertainment is done. During the summer and autumn months, when the flocks and herds are no longer at hand, and many or most of the male animals have either been slaughtered in the camps or sold in the markets for cash with which to buy sugar and tea and a few other oddments, the number of animal slaughters drops considerably, since it is accepted that this is not the time of the year to initiate or activate debt relationships, and what slaughters occur are confined to life crises ceremonies, the Islamic festival of the feast of the flesh (the day on which pilgrims to Mecca offer their sacrifices at Mina) and to one or two contingent circumstances. Allowing for the time of the year, however, the slaughter of twenty-three animals nevertheless constituted a heavy investment in social relationships, representing in monetary terms, at the time, between £80 and £90.

An initial gift is an invitation to another person (and indirectly to a corporation, as will be shown later) to enter into a certain form of social relationship. Before the return is made, there is a lapse of time, since the return must be made on an appropriate occasion only. It would be quite wrong to seem to be artificially creating an occasion to repay the gift by, say, virtually coercing the donor to pay a visit and slaughtering an animal for him. Such an act would stultify the purpose of the return gift. When the receiver[2] returns the gift, if it is not done in the context of one of the life crises, then it is given at a prearranged formal visit by the donor and perhaps his wife, or by the donor and a few kinsmen, and this will not take place for some time – a year or two, or even, in one case I know of, three years later. This time lapse between the two gifts is critical, because it is now that the social relationships sought by the donor are given a trial. During this period there are comings and goings between the two, often little more than trivial visits when only tea is taken, or one calls in on the other's camp as a friendly passer-by. During this period too, the receiver is susceptible to undefined claims by the donor. Claims are never specified because they cannot be given precision. They vary with every social relationship an individual or a corporation possesses, and the specific set of relationships in a debt bond is a matter of estimation between the two parties. Hence the importance of the time lapse between giving and receiving. The donor and the receiver are given a grace of time to judge how the behaviour of the other matches his expectations, and if they are mutually favourable a return gift then comes to have a propulsive force. The initial gift is a symbolic statement that a change in social relationships is desired. An appropriate return gift is the symbolic statement that this desire is mutual. Mutuality is also perpetuation. The fractional difference between the two gifts, small in a material measure, is symbolically great enough to keep the relationships in motion; for the equality or inequality in a gift lies not in fractional differences in the amount or kind of meat, but in the symbolic representation of social relationships contained in these differences.

Time is given between gifts for social relationship, tentative at this point, to be explored warily, and to be assessed. Time enters into debt in other than a temporal manner as soon as the giver and receiver come together after the first sacrificial meal between them has been taken. The hours of conversation between a guest and his hosts – and when an animal is slaughtered for a guest he would certainly stay the night, unless he had arrived early in the morning and has pressing business elsewhere – are not spent in idle chatter, but in conveying numerous details about themselves, one to the other. At the end of this first encounter, both have come to know a substantial amount about the affairs of the other, and they therefore move at once into the position of people who have known each other for some time. The hasty son of a host who borrowed my utensils without asking was indicating precisely this. After the meal, he behaved as if we had known each other for a long time. The marked reserve before the meal, and the equally spirited familiarity after it, are perhaps the single most conspicuous feature of the meeting between guest and host. If the kinds of social relationship generated by debt are to prosper, they can only do so with assumed familiarity at the outset. Normally, familiarity grows with time. Debt, by creating familiarity and providing for an accumulation of relationships, gives an immediate relationship a social time depth. The buoyancy and ebullience of conversation is not a frill to the sacrifice and the commensal meal, it is not just a matter of social conviviality. It makes up for time and social relationships lost in the past. The distilled concentrate of history that is pressed into this conversation charts the boundaries of the new field of relationships in which the participants expect to live together.

When the entertainment of a guest has lasted for many hours, if it is still several hours to sunset, it is polite that he shows signs of leaving. Sometimes a guest rises and moves a short distance away from the entrance of the tent.

He is followed by his hosts who cry out: 'Stay! Stay! It is night time. By God you must not go. On my wife be divorce if you go.' Whether the guest heeds these protests and submits, or goes his way, is also significant. It is a gesture showing he wishes to take the relationship further there and then, or that he wishes to assume control by retarding it for the time being. In either event there is now debt between guest and hosts, and the first phase in forging a new link has gone far enough to justify either in saying '*baainna fi dain*' (Between us there is debt). Debt is also nearness, and people in a debt link refer to each other as *qarib* (near), meaning by this that they engage in social relationships. The word also refers to spatial nearness in the sense of people being neighbours. Consequently, people living in relatively distant camps come to conceive of themselves as neighbours, as we learned to our cost and fatigue when walking for most of a day before reaching a 'near' camp; while a camp with which there are no links is described as *ba'id* (far) even though it is easily within vision – it is 'somewhere where we do not go, we do not know it'.

The twin features of giving a time depth to social relationships and of narrowing of social distance, that are at the core of debt relations, have the further interest that they are so unlike the concepts of structural time and distance. Time and territorial distance in their structural sense are derived from the divisions of a lineage system, so-called, so that the fewer the ancestors intervening between two individuals or groups (the less time, that is to say, that intervenes) the 'closer' they are said to be as related people, and the nearer they are said to be territorially. Close kinship and territorial propinquity are both a function of less time, whereas the social and territorial nearness of debt relationships rests on the assumption that there has been an accumulation of relationships over a long time: 'They are our friends from long ago'. A structurally distant and territorially far off corporation can be socially close and the distance 'does not make a kilometer'. The nearest structural corporation is its collateral lineage segment, but, interestingly, there is rarely debt between them; as in the marriage pattern of any particular corporation, the most conspicuous lacuna in the field of debt relationships is the very corporation with which, in structural terms, there is no gap. Moreover, the debt patterns of two structurally collateral corporations do not show an overlap. The lines of debt are thrown out hither and thither to make a configuration of great complexity. The articulations of the lineage structure present a well ordered pattern of successively enclosing groups with matching neatness in the corresponding ascending orders of territorial divisions. Debt destroys the lineage pattern and demolishes the order of its tiered segments. This is not to say that debt subsumes all relationships and the lineage none. It does mean that chosen social relations, whether in the camps or when travelling (a person invariably uses his debt partners' camps as stepping stones), when seeking water for animals or watered land to plough, when collecting blood money or gathering allies, are where debt is, and the hostile restriction of structural relations are pared down to the minimum. 'Debt', say the Bedouin, is 'the untying of the hobbling cord' (*talq al-'iqal*), and it leaves men the freedom to wander as they choose. Structural obligations shackle and restrict manoeuverability. The consequences of debt running through the camps to form a particular pattern, but, retracting and spreading to include different camps later in shifting configurations, obviously has profound effects on relations between corporations and their leaders; and the co-existence of debt relations alongside jural structural relations brings into being such fascinating interplay of choices and constraints as to merit a separate study. Aspects of some of the problems raised when men set the options of debt against the authority of structural duties, are more appropriately discussed when dealing with the shaikh's use of debt; before entering into this discussion, it is necessary to further the analysis of the process and forms of debt in order to understand something of the complex significance of its patterns.

The seemingly simple act of slaughtering a sheep or goat for the commensal meal which follows, immediately influences behaviour. Yet, in achieving this effect, the initiative appears to be entirely in the power of the giver. This impression is confirmed by behaviour itself, for while a guest is granted the freedom to ask for what he likes and is given attention which exceeds service to the point of becoming servility, responsibility for a guest lies with his host. Giving a sacrifice to a visitor, in some instances, can be seen as an attempt almost to abduct a guest, and the protestations that 'You are now one of us' or 'We are now exact equals' are an almost brazen trumpeting of the victory; I was indeed told, in some cases, that the purpose of giving the gift was to gain a lien. Moreover, a person can be captured unwittingly, since anyone passing within sight of a camp should call in, particularly if riding a horse, and if he shows no signs of doing so, he is hailed from the camp and invited to enter. If, after he is exhorted to do so, a passer-by does not enter the camp, his behaviour is seen as hostile, causing consternation at least. In one instance I recorded, two young men of a camp, after calling out to a rider on horseback, seeing that he was ignoring them, fired their rifles in his direction – but more in defiance than with either intention or any realistic hope of hitting their target. A man who does not give in is said to be base or ignoble (*fasal*) and I have heard Bedouin demand a due for such an insult (*haqq al-fusala*). It is as imperative to return a gift as it is to receive one: 'It is obligatory (*lazim*) to requite (*taddy*)'. By this, the Bedouin do not mean that an exact repayment should be given: 'If I give a gift exactly the same as you gave me, I have not given you a gift at all. There must be increment (*ziyada*). You must, you must give like this. If a man does not give in return, he is not a man. People will say of him he does not know how to return appropriately (*yrudd il-kafa'*).' There are many words relating to the concept of gift, most of them specific to kinds of gifts. At this point it is sufficient to quote the commonly used and general term *salaf*, which has the meaning of something given without conditions attaching to its return, but with the expectation both of a change in social relationships and a return at some unspecified time.

Without debt, the cultural pressure to offer hospitality and to accept it is very strong. As an example of this, the following incident is worth relating. Accompanied by a guide and a helper from the camp to which we were journeying, we passed a small camp, about a hundred yards before getting there. An old lady called out to us to go over to the camp. Already several hours late, we had no desire to tarry. We all answered the old lady with the Bedouin pleasantries which make it politely clear that an invitation is being declined; whereupon the old lady asserted: 'You will not walk through our homeland (*watan*) without our water and salt (*ma' wa milh*) in your stomachs'. Our companions stopped immediately, and told us we had to go over to the camp and accept hospitality (*diyafa*). Since this cultural pressure exists to press hospitality on a guest, and to provide appropriately when giving it, it follows that a guest expects and can demand hospitality befitting his status, not only in the sense of asserting his importance as a shaikh, but also in relation to the peculiarities of the circumstances. Thus one of the guides who travelled with us, at another time went on a journey alone which took him over a hundred miles away from his homeland. He 'descended on' (*nazala*) a distant camp where he was received with the customary courtesies, until the meal was ready. His host fetched water for him to wash his hands, and a meatless meal was laid out before him. This greatly angered him, and according to his evidence, he rose abruptly, refusing the meal and asking whether it was the custom of this tribe to wash the guest's hands only to present him with a meatless dish. This, he continued, 'is not the custom in my tribe, where a man of another tribe, whoever he is, is given a slaughtered animal', he went on to say that he would certainly make this meanness known on his way back, and he would tell all his tribesmen about them on his return. His lecture was effective, the meal was removed, he was later given meat and he stayed the night. Caught in this compulsion to give is the idea that to withhold appropriate hospitality is to court disgrace not merely in a status sense but in a moral sense also.

In a similar way, but in quite dissimilar circumstances, an aged widow made use of the sentiments about hospitality to eke out a tolerable existence. Her nearest male relatives, and in particular those who had held her bridewealth, had been killed during the Italo-Bedouin wars, and those of her agnates still alive had migrated to Benghazi. Her children had all died, and left to her was her orphaned daughter's daughter. With this teenage girl the old lady spent the winter and spring months travelling from camp to camp, her tent loaded on a donkey. Bedouin custom is that the arrival of 'a female guest requires an animal slaughter', unless the female is well known and a frequent visitor. It is also a custom that when a tent is pitched in a camp an animal must be slaughtered. The widow therefore had two strings on which she could pull. In some of the camps she visited she was well enough known not to occasion an animal slaughter, but, even in these camps she would stay sometimes a night, sometimes a week or so and thus became a neighbour (*jar*) living, however temporarily, in a separate tent of her own. At the camp she visited when we were resident, an animal was slaughtered for her and her tent, and when she left two days later she was given a few fleeces. During her stay with us she talked quite incessantly, and she saw to it that the conversation did not deviate for long from the discussion of the hospitality she had received in other camps, expressing herself without inhibition about the generosity or meanness of her erstwhile hosts, always adding, as if by way of threat, that she was sure she would have nothing but good to say about our camp. After she had gone, the people of the camp used the visit to stress their generosity, but it soon became explicit that they found her tiresome, and that they – like everyone else who knew her – thought of her as a professional scrounger. Nevertheless they did entertain her appropriately. This wretch of a woman, bereft of material means and human dignity, fared reasonably well for food and shelter without becoming an intolerable burden on the resources and patience of anyone.

In both these cases of the guests forcing the observance of cultural sentiments for their own immediate gain, it could be argued that the hosts profited from the repute the guests would spread abroad; but my guide spread disrepute, and the rasping praise and complaints the wizened old woman distributed among the camps, weighed very lightly in the Bedouin scales for measuring prestige, repute, and power, although they might have been of a little consequence in assessing honour and generosity when it suited people to use her reports for this purpose. Whatever benefits accrue to a host from the gift of animal slaughter, the promptings to give come from general cultural sentiments in the first place, since although the giver commands the situation in which he gives, cultural pressure sometimes coerces him to do so against his better judgement. If a Bedouin wishes to open a debt relationship which he thinks will profit him but has failed because he has been unable to manoeuvre a particular person into becoming his guest, he can instead pay him a formal visit himself, perhaps taking his wife and some other members of his camp along as well to make a big occasion of it: I have heard Bedouin mutter some choice expletives as an undesired guest and his entourage appear in sight, although when they enter the camp the apparent warmth and noisy spontaneity of the greetings accorded them completely conceal the host's *bouleversement*. The host is constrained to receive his guest, and must publicly concur in the opening of a debt relationship in which he is temporarily at a disadvantage – a heavy debt responsibility if the guest is accompanied by his wife and some other men.

Choice and control enter debt manoeuvres in another way. A host can delay the return gift by eschewing the camp and company of the man who earlier forced his hand by ceremoniously visiting him. He can, of course, be forced again to keep the relationship active if a life crisis occurs, for then he can be visited by the same man who this time comes bearing a gift of an animal. Nevertheless, although there is compulsion to give and to receive, a latitude of choice is left to both parties, at least to the degree they wish to accelerate or retard the relationship. Important men with large followings are very careful both in guarding against their vulnerability to gifting, and in controlling accessibility to them for this purpose. A man with deep Bedouin roots who spent much of his time among them, but who was also an administrative official, never accepted individual Bedouin hospitality. Instead, he always took his animal slaughter with him, entertaining his lesser officials to a meal in the open country away from the camps, sometimes sending for the shaikh of the camp to be visited, to join him. If he had accepted all the hospitality pressed on him, he would have surrendered his administrative powers, since the weight of accumulated debt, and the claims it implies, would have stultified his independence of action. Again, if one enters a camp it is possible to leave after taking tea only, though the host wishes to capture the guest; pressing reasons are acceptable as an apology for an early departure, and this applies to the stranger and the known person alike. Unravelling the complexity of debt relationships would be relatively simple if the element of choice were absent from it.

The process of establishing a debt relationship does not end with considerations involved in the obligation to give and to receive; nor do the ruses which have been discussed comprehend the whole range of possible manipulations. Attention has been directed to what is considered to be appropriate giving and receiving, but this is not the pattern always followed. There are circumstances when excessive gifting might take place, or when the gift is demonstrably inadequate, or when the receiver gives a return of exactly equal amount; all three modes of gifting have distinctly different consequences on behaviour, and any one of them can convert a debt relationship of one kind into one of a variety of others. Thus excessive gifting, in essence, is a statement of complete dominance (since to return excess with greater excess would be ruinous even for the richer Bedouin), or it is a bid for making claims against the receivers of an order which would be too onerous to be tolerable. As an instance of the former, the slaughter of twenty-three animals in two months in one small camp mentioned earlier, shows the kind of confident dominance which excessive gifting can achieve. One of the most numerically powerful corporations in its own right, taken together with its allies, it is probably the most powerful grouping in the whole country. Ecologically, it possesses the best spread of territory, and consequently its economy is more stable than those of most other corporations. With these two prize assets in its possession, it is easier for it to accumulate animal wealth than for the other corporations. There is little point in competing against this corporation, since it could easily out-gift any challenger without suffering privation. Some of the poor camps welcome a new neighbour with a single animal slaughter; the tradition in this powerful corporation is for all households to give an animal slaughter. In less wealthy camps visitors from other nearby corporations who are either kin or well-known, are not usually offered an animal slaughter; in the camps of this powerful corporation an animal would be slaughtered. In most camps a distinguished shaikh is given a big sheep as a slaughter; in the main camp of this powerful corporation two or three would be given. Since competition is futile, other corporations either opt out of all debt relationships with it, or remain 'under the victory' (*taht al-ghalba*) – that is, they accept its dominance and become its allies.

An instance of the second form of excessive gifting occurred when a shaikh wanted the assistance of a corporation, more powerful than his in manpower, to fight for a disputed well. His way of doing this was to put this corporation massively in his debt by inviting all its adult males to eat with all his followers at a single feast for which he slaughtered his entire herd of nine camels. I am always sceptical about figures whenever they are given in hearsay evidence, but it is safe to say, since many men I talked to witnessed the feast, that it was on a mammoth scale. Massive debt enabled the shaikh to make a massive political claim against his hosts (for the corporations were otherwise unconnected), and he succeeded in his immediate political aim. The harsh fact of the situation was that he did not have enough strength in numbers either in his own corporation or to attract stable alliances with other corporations. Hence, to meet the emergency, he had to expend a ruinous amount of his economic assets to create a major alliance forthwith. I knew his son well; a man who despite his possession of most of the personal appurtenances which are said to make a shaikh great, is shaikh of two small camps only. Over gifting, however, saved the son the ignominy in which his father's excess would certainly have left him, for after the father died, a section of one of those client tribes who occupy their own territory on the borders of the main tribes, wanted his assistance in a fight over one of their wells. Twenty women, it is said, were sent to plead with him for his assistance, and while they were in his camp he slaughtered his only camel for them and gave a promise of assistance. He and his followers moved across country, and formed part of the war camp (known as *halaqa* or ring, because the men take up defensive positions in the form of a ring, with the women occupying the middle space) with the clients. After the threat was beaten off, the clients rewarded the shaikh with a gift of twenty camels, one for each of the women who went on the supplicatory visit.

Excessive gifting is a card which has to be played with skill, for without the strength of resources to meet a counter-challenge the result could prove politically, economically and socially disastrous, since it could mean not only a diminution of power, not only a catastrophic diminution of material assets, but without the means to give and receive any longer, existing debt links would snap, and people would not be anxious to forge new ones. To deal in excessive gifting a man needs to be overwhelmingly dominant politically, and either possess, or have access to, strong economic resources. The sort of gifting that can be met in such cases is that given to the ex-King Idris when he returned from his Egyptian exile to his country and people after the Italians had been ejected during World War II. According to Bedouin accounts given three or four years after the events, the Emir, as he was then, visited the districts severally, and each visit was the scene of vast gatherings to which large numbers of Bedouin brought their sheep and goats as a thanks offering (*shukran*). The same kind of gifting occurred on a smaller scale when the shaikhs of corporations and small camps returned from exile. I have the precise details of animals given as gifts to a shaikh who, at that time, was the unchallenged leader of his corporation when he returned from a long exile in Egypt. He received a sheep from each adult male member of his corporation, and many more from his debt partners in other corporations, the total number of sheep amounting to a substantial flock. Gifts given to him, like those given to the Emir, were parts of debt relationships, it is true, but it is not a misjudgement for leaders to receive excessive gifts from those whose allegiance they command, for these gifts are given as pledges of continued support, and it is not expected that they will be appropriately repaid either in one excessive return or within a strictly limited period.

This discussion of excessive gifting has been included here since it is germane to the general analysis of the processes at work in debt relationships. Obviously, some of the matters raised in this section are highly relevant to problems of political leadership; but only brief reference has been made to this because this aspect of debt is better treated in a discussion of the shaikh. In the meantime it is necessary to return to the process of debt relationships and to discuss the consequences of under gifting.

When the receiver returns a gift inadequately, whatever his material circumstances happen to be, this act is considered as a calculated insult. This being so, then a return gift of lesser measure than the gift received is a symbolic statement that the initial attempt to steer social relationship into a favourable debt partnership is being rejected with the full knowledge that rejection stimulates hostile relationships. The details of such an exchange will make the involvement clear. One of the great Bedouin shaikhs, a man whose name was known throughout the land, returned from exile in the Sudan, in 1947, greatly reduced in material circumstances resulting mainly from the part he played in the wars against the Italians. During his absence, a man who had previously been politically inconsequential, rose in status to become a shaikh, and was formally confirmed in this status by the Italian administration, receiving a small annual payment from this source. One of the first people to visit the great shaikh was this upstart shaikh, taking with him the very appropriate – indeed generous – gift of a fine large female sheep. Their relationship during the ensuing months nevertheless continued to be uneasy. The great shaikh, at various gatherings of tribesmen, sent his listeners into ecstasy with the easy flow of rhetoric he carefully cultivated, captivating their hearts if not their minds, and usually succeeding in driving his listeners to a surge of enthusiasm; the upstart shaikh, by contrast, matched his small stature with a mean personality, speaking publicly in a cackle of sound as if permanently irate with the tangle of ethnographic minutiae in which he appeared always to be ensnared. The balance of debt, however, was in favour of the upstart, and he had the additional advantage of wealth over his rival. The struggle for position of leadership (*qalada*, from *qalada*, to entrust with power, or to follow another's opinion blindly, but used as a noun by the Bedouin to indicate strife in struggling for power) came to a head in 1948 when the upstart decided to leave the camps for a house in a village where administrative officials would be more accessible to him – and we went with him on this move.

Plate 1. A young freeborn Bedouin.

Plate 2. Women setting up a tent.

Plate 3. The colourful interior of a winter tent.

Plate 4. A polygynous household moving to a new camp site.

Plate 5. A bride is taken to the nuptial tent. She is hidden beneath the canopy.

Plate 6. The small daughter of a shaikh.

Plate 7. Measuring out the grain.

Plate 8. A married woman returning from the well.

Plate 9. Women spinning wool.

Plate 10. A holy man from one of the client tribes.

Plate 11. An old shaikh meditating on a verse from the Koran, painted on a board.

Plate 12. A legal case is being heard.

Plate 13. Shaikhs arrive at a camp for a peace meeting.

Plate 14. Portrait of the author, taken at the time of his fieldwork.

When a change of residence of this kind is made, it offers an excellent occasion for gifting. The shaikh, who, less than a year earlier had received the fine female sheep (*na'ja*) came to greet the upstart, bringing with him a big goat (*'anz*), wholly inappropriate as a gift, since the circumstances demanded the largest and best ram (*kabsh*). Only the upstart shaikh's wife was in the house when the gift was brought, but she, a senior woman of noble bearing and dominating authority within her husband's group, was well accustomed to receiving distinguished guests. As soon as she had accepted the goat with customary courtesy, she came to me in a state of evident distress, beseeching me to entertain the guest, for she could not possibly do so. She explained that the gift he had brought was quite insufficient, and when I explained that the shaikh was very poor, she dismissed the argument abruptly, saying: 'Has he not got a *bait*?' (meaning, in this context, a tribal section). None of the apologies I offered mollified her. 'We gave him a sheep, and he has now brought us a goat. What have we done? We must have done something to him for him to do this to us', was a view she kept muttering to herself, repeating 'a goat for a sheep' in stupefied surprise. The distinguished visitor, when I joined him, affected to be in blithe spirits, talking volubly, and producing choice turns of phrase with an arrogant ease, winking knowingly at me and pointing in the direction of the room in the house to which the lady had retired, making evident his enjoyment of the disturbance he had caused.

By and by the upstart shaikh returned to entertain his guest, and he went through the customary courtesies of greeting and thanks, but thereafter sat stolidly in a black mood of smouldering anger, while his guest continued to display his dazzling command of language. An appropriate return gift means that the receiver must acquiesce in the consequential claims that can be made on him, but however onerous this position might be, the relationship he initiated is kept in motion. The act of under-gifting with a goat was a clear sign that the relationship was to discontinue. The upstart had to receive the gift despite the pain it caused. He could and did make much of the great shaikh's meanness, but he knew, and all around him knew, that the return gift was deliberately given to cut the upstart down to size, since, fobbed off with a goat, he was being told that politically he was of such little consequence that the appropriate gift would be an over representation of his worth. Moreover, there was subtle calculation in the gift that was given: it was, after all, a large female goat, and this of itself is not meanness. For the charge of meanness to carry weight, the gift would have had to be of much lesser worth in gift exchange values. Caught in the cleft stick of being obliged to receive the gift, but also having to admit its inferiority, the upstart shaikh knew that he could not pass it off as the meanness of an impoverished rival, and was left to make his hostility overt as the only alternative.

This exchange of gifts was part of the political rivalry between two men. One had the advantage of a towering personality, wit, rhetoric, connection in high places and, then, a devoted following still revelling in his recent return, but very small personal material assets and a diseased wife. The other had material advantage, a wife of true nobility who dwarfed her husband physically and in general personality, but a wavering following most of which had gathered around him in the shifting sands of expediency during the Italian occupation. As these two men vied with each other, using gifts as the instrument of competition, they were also pitching the strength of their followings one against the other, for did not the upstart's wife brush aside the plea of the great man's poverty with the significant remark that he had a tribal section? The gift of the goat was a declaration that the majority of men in the corporation were henceforward committed to following the man who dared humiliate his rival in this way. Thereafter, the upstart shaikh and his rump of a following ceased to join the rest of the members of the corporation on its annual pilgrimage to their saint's tomb; instead, the upstart built a square of low walls around some stones on the rise near his camp where people were buried, whitewashed them, gave the 'saint' he claimed was buried there a name, and henceforward his faction made their pilgrimage to their own saint's tomb.

The interest in excessive and under gifting is that they transform relationships and perpetuate them in whichever direction the gift exchanges guide them. Excessive gifting serves as a dramatic act of domination in which the vanquished perforce publicly acquiesce, or it serves as public attestation of loyalty to a leader; it always contains a component of domination, imposed or voluntary, enduring or temporary. A gift of lesser measure than is appropriate converts a relationship into hostility, and if the hostility has been latent previously, draws it out into public view by making it explicit and gives a new twist to the future form of hostility. The third course is to return a gift in exact equal measure, and the effect of this is to suspend relationships, to call a halt to their progress, whether they are deteriorating or prospering. A pause in the seriously deteriorating relationships between two corporations, A and B, was brought about by equal gifting after a series of homicides between them. The territories of both groups are situated on a broad elevated stretch of land on one side of a dry valley. Group A occupied the southern part, and although passage to the high plateau area in the north of the country is possible at all times of the year via the dry valley, it is much easier and more convenient to use the direct route. Moreover, A's firm allies, inhabiting territory both to the south and north, use the direct route through B's territory and they are not actively engaged in hostilities with B themselves. Within living memory, A and B have always been at loggerheads, and every now and again contention flared into serious hostility resulting in homicide. The most recent outbreak occurred when a man of B tried to interfere with A's shepherd, threatening to take several of his flock. The latter shot and killed him. A blood money agreement was concluded. The transfer of wealth involved was to take five years. Payments were made annually for four years, but during this fourth year a man from B attempted to kill a man of A mounted on horseback. His shot missed the man but killed the horse. An agreement was drawn up at a peace meeting which followed soon afterwards, whereby the debt of blood money outstanding was to be paid immediately by A, and B had to give A a horse exactly like the one killed. These arrangements were accepted as making relationships between the two groups equal. The person recounting these events added: 'And now, if we go to them they kill a sheep for us, and if they come to us we kill the same kind of sheep for them. There is no debt between us, because there is no *sghara* (meaning, literally, juveniles, but used by the Bedouin, in such contexts, to refer to ties created by children)'.

Similar relationships were brought about between two other corporations after a succession of homicides: 'They went on killing until there were eight on either side, *taufa* (a word with a complexity of meaning, referring to a state where redemption is made perfect, or where payment of debt is complete, or fulfilment, or a number of other related meanings some of which refer to death, but to be translated, in this context, as they equalised in the number of vengeance killings). There is no proper peace between them. But they do not kill each other now.' Exchanges recognised as equalising relationships occur in circumstances other than those involving homicide. Among agnates much of the gifting is of this sort, and in any gifting relationship successive marginal increases can be brought to a halt by an equal exchange. The commonness of such behaviour among agnates and among other kin will be discussed presently. Here, it is necessary to note the consequences of equal exchanges. Without any increment (*ziyada*) between gifts, there is no debt. Recognition that debts are equally balanced achieves the effect of bringing a particular set of relationships to a halt, or at least effecting a pause. Real peace was not brought about by the exchange of blood money and a horse, although equal gifts were exchanged between the two corporations. Explicitly recognised equality in exchanges is a recognition that relationships are desired, but at the same time these relationships are pegged down to formality, and remain in this state until an increment is added to the exchanges and appropriately returned. Living conditions had become intolerable, and men could not go about their pastoral activities free of immediate threat. Equal exchanges recognised the need for a *modus vivendi*, nothing more. Without debt there can be no *ribat*, or bond. In a technical sense, there was debt between them, an oscillation of debt moving regularly from one to the other depending on who was the last to give a sacrifice. This is not how the Bedouin saw the matter. In their view hostility had always existed and still continues. Sacrifices did not serve to stimulate debt relationships, they served only to keep the peace, to ward off the temptation to allow relationships to deteriorate into disastrous strife. Sentiments of a similar kind brought the series of killings cited in the second case to an end. Out of the exhaustion produced by a surfeit of homicides, the participants found refuge in the formality of accepted equality, a tit-for-tat exchange sufficient to contain hostilities, but inhibiting, with each successive gift, the swell of intensity in relationships which establishes the public amity characteristic of debt. Animal slaughter for guests does not necessarily generate a free flow of sociability; unless each successive exchange shows an increment, gifts have not been given.

Before examining the various categories of relationship to which debt is attached, it might clarify matters to take stock, briefly, of the points of significance in the process of making debt relationships. At the outset, it must be stressed that, whether the gift is excessive, equal or deficient, meanness in the sense of cheese-paring or miserliness does not enter the process. If a man does not wish to give he pitches his tent in a camp situated well away from the main routes and tucked away in a little blind valley or small depression. A mean-spirited person is well enough known in his district, and none is likely to seek his tent. Anyone happening on his tent is not welcomed with an animal slaughter, for, in cases of this kind, it is said: 'The honour is broken' (*kasir al-sharaf*), and by this phrase the Bedouin mean that a man reneagues on one of their most important cultural values. Poverty is not the point; however poor a man is, an animal can be provided by one of his fellows. Therefore, if a man declines to give his guest the due gift, he does injury to his guest and brings disgrace (*ma'arra*) on them too.[3] He is best left out of sight, tied to his fellow men by agnatic rights, duties and obligations only. Relieved of the costly business of gift giving, a man might gather together substantial numbers of animals over the years, but when he then emerges from obscurity he finds the road that leads back to full participation in gift relationships littered with impediments. The richest Bedouin I met was a man who had spent most of his life gathering, not giving. It was said of him: 'He is like a shepherd and only sheep will go with him'.

Compared with other means of establishing social relationships, debt is the easiest and quickest way to make a start. Negotiations for marriage take a long time. Marriage also requires a heavy commitment of resources, and it implies a permanency and order of relationships much too onerous for the purpose of simply inaugurating relationships; it is the culmination of a process, not the opening of a way. Incorporation is a move of great gravity; it is irrevocable, and, once the choice has been made, choice is surrendered in favour of prescribed demands and duties. Debt makes an instant relationship, costs little, and the commitments it carries do not clamp a man in a strait jacket. Debt can be terminated as summarily as it was begun; it can be accelerated to give a fillip to prosperously developing relationships, it can retard them when difficulties are encountered; and when they turn sour, it can convert them into public hostility. Debt does not figure in the stalemate of mere exchange; this *per se* is a series of frustrated initiatives. Whether it be the motion of increasing intimacy, or the motion of burrowing enmity; the element of perpetuity is always present in debt. It adds to the range of choices among a people where differentiation is relatively undeveloped. Pride of place among its characteristics must, however, be given to its potential as an instrument with which to explore social relationships. Reactions can be tested, people can be prodded to behave differently, men can measure each other socially by it, and, if its probings are unsatisfactory, its tentacles can be rapidly withdrawn.

But the strength of debt is its weakness. The relationships it appropriates from the general fund of social relationships are tenuous. Unspecified claims, of a wide variety because they are ambiguous, are made against debt; but they cannot be forced as rights. They fall into the category which the Bedouin designate 'as a favour' (*bi'l fadl*), and they can be requested, granted, or withheld without necessarily jeopardising the whole relationship. By contrast, agnatic relationships are placed in the *bi'l qasm* category, those relationships apportioned among men, which because they are apportioned are known and shared, and which, because they are of this kind, are also compulsory, covering most rights, duties, obligations. Debt permits a person to solicit (*talaba*); it does not give him the right (*haqq*) to demand. The limitation of a debt relationship is the frailty of favours and it remains vulnerable until it becomes embedded in a matrix of other kinds of relationships. But the stamina of this frailty is its indispensability in social life. For while it usually occurs as a part of a structure of relationships, some relationships are held together by debt alone. Whatever its weakness and limitations, it possesses a separate integrity as a link. Hence, Bedouin are able to distinguish it verbally as a *ribat* (plural, *arbita*). Synonymous with the word *ribat*, used for people tied by debt, are two other words, which, although they express different sentiments are only used where debt connexions exist. One is *rab'*, meaning home, and is used to refer to territorial propinquity, as in being reared together. Several camps in an area might satisfy this territorial qualification, but only selected camps are assigned the status of territorial partners, although in some instances the nearest camps do not fall within this category, while more distant ones are included: it is a matter of social distance. The other is *bu maqrun*, meaning literally, 'linked sons,'[4] but which is more in keeping with Bedouin idiom when translated as, 'sons of similar circumstances'. The word *qarn*, in its derivative *maqrun*, means animal horn, and the Bedouin made it clear by their gestures that in their use of *bu maqrun* they were thinking of two separable persons or groups held together in common relationships. Each of these three expressions refers to a form of alliance, but the nature of the alliance gains its social anthropological significance not from the use of a cultural term to conceptualise what are similar sets of social relationships, but from the relationships which surround debt, or from the absence of these supporting relationships.

Kinship, in its many varieties, consists of an assortment of bundles of relationships, and when most of these bundles are unravelled debt is found to be one of the strands in them. It is not present in all kin relationships, and it would be dangerous to lose sight of this simple but fundamental fact, otherwise debt becomes so confused with other relationships that any and every relationship becomes a debt relationship. As this analysis proceeds, part of its purpose will be to clarify the specificity of the debt relationship and, by doing so, to detach it from other kinds. Thus, it would be quite erroneous to conceive of the relationships between a father and son as debt relationship. These are governed almost exclusively by jural rules. A father who feeds his son, and a son who gives his labour are not held together by reciprocal debts. Food is not a gift which a father gives or withholds at will; from the moment of birth a son has the right to food, clothing and shelter, and when he matures he has the right to a wife. A son cannot withhold or give his labour as he feels fit: his father has the right to command it. While his father is still alive, whether able-bodied or sunk in the senility of advanced old age, the son cannot gift his father: he lacks the wherewithal to do so, and his father remains proprietor of the stock until death. Nor can a father gift one of his sons[5] only, since Bedouin law is explicitly opposed to discrimination, at least while a father is still alive. Jurally circumscribed in this way, debt does not enter into their relationships until the father dies, when it is recognised in an annual sacrifice offered by the son who has benefited preferentially (usually the eldest) from inheritance. If the father dies leaving nothing, the sacrifice is not offered. In short, the jural relations which govern the behaviour of father and son are so dominant and pervading that debt between them is excluded. Between a mother and son, jural considerations control much of the total of their relationships, but in disposing of whatever property she possesses, a mother is not bound by the same restrictions as a father, nor does disposal affect her status adversely in the way it would threaten the proprietory status of a father. I was present at a gathering of men when a woman chose to give to one of her three sons the gift of a female camel in recognition of his devotion to her, and I witnessed her wish, at her insistence, along with the other men. After the ceremony, the mother had the beast branded with her brother's individual animal sign, as a double precaution to ensure that her son's agnates would not interfere with her wish.

Death, however, sees the pattern of relationships, between a father and a mother to their heirs, change. The death of the father sets a son (usually only the eldest) free to become proprietor or *waliy* of his father's flocks and herds: there is the saying that an eldest – and ungrateful – son, absent from home for a long time, returned to be told that his father had been dead awhile, and replied: '*al-hamdu li' llah rizqi halal*' (Praise be to God, my wealth is free). Of the eldest (or in some cases a younger) son, it is said that 'he took his father's position' (*akhadha matrah buhu*). The son inheriting this position is also given what is known as *kibr*, which, for the Bedouin, means some extra inheritance (Musil 1928: 663), and also importance, prestige and nobility. In material terms this gives him the right to his father's horse, cloak and seal – the speed to control external relationships, a garment to endow him with personality, and the seal to give the authority to negotiate relationships. With all this the son inherits his father's debt links, a most advantageous beginning, particularly if the son is adult but still young. This is the debt recognised in the annual sacrifice to God for the father. The son, however, inherits not only animals with which to make his future pattern of social relationships but, for most of his life, the debts of his father will continue to constitute part of the pattern of social relationships within his keeping. Implicit in these latter relationships is the element of property because, without it, the deceased could not have made debt relationships. Moreover, depending on the father's distribution of his surplus as debt links, the heir will receive a few or many animals during his father's funerary rites and, unless the father dies a pauper, he is likely to gain any number from an animal or so to several score of sheep. A mother, on the other hand, disposes of her property while still alive, hoping that her chosen son will support her in her old age. There is little point in her leaving her wealth in an intestate package because, if she does, it is absorbed into her husband's wealth and inherited with it. Hence, annual sacrifices to God are not performed for women. A mother receives her debt returns while she is alive, in the claims she makes on her beneficiaries. Alive, a father has no need to provide for sons making claims: he commands all his heirs.[6] Brothers cannot gift among themselves either. The death of a father frees one of them to become proprietor, and in moving into this status a new proprietory unit is formed over which he has authority. He will endeavour to hold the unit together as long as possible, sometimes until the brothers have reached old age. Such an arrangement is known as *al-halla al-wahida*,[7] the one cooking pot, meaning that their animal wealth is jointly held. Within this unit, gift giving is technically impossible, and should one of them die while their wealth is still undivided, they cannot contribute animals for the funerary rites. A funeral, in fact, always throws this property unit into relief; men thus conjoined do not bring gifts. But a surviving brother who succeeds in becoming *de facto* heir, as receiver of wealth also becomes indebted to the deceased, a death he redeems by making a marriage and naming a son after him. Whereas brothers cannot engage in debt relationships, at least while their wealth remains undivided, brother and sister are able to do so after the sister has married. On the first day of the birth of a son, the brother gives his sister the gift of an animal, known as *zaluf* (from the root *zalafa*, to get nearer, to aim for favour, and in this case, not only in relation to the sister but the affine as well), which for the first born son should be a sheep, if possible. Its issue is inherited by this son. Reciprocally, when the brother becomes father of a son, his sister's husband gives him a gift of an animal, known as *rabaiya* (from the root *raba*, to grow up, to increase), which should be greater than the original *zaluf*. The complexities in dealing with the handling of wealth among kinsmen are vast. The brief references made to the matter here have been included in the hope that they will suffice to show that the use of kinship as a gross term, undifferentiated with regard to sex, age or even the specific relation is not only unsophisticated but wrong; and any attempt to theorise from this grossness must be quite wrong also.[8]

Agnates are also subject to jural rules, albeit different from those obtaining in the father/son relationship. They cannot be the same since the latter is a specific kinship relationship with its associated rights to animal wealth, control of household labour, authority in a domestic unit, and the determination of marriage partners. Essentially, agnation has little to do with kinship. Its bonds are political, and they bind together – for certain purposes only – a corporation of men conceptually endowed by the Bedouin with a fiction of kinship but among whom are included consanguineously unrelated males. Their relations to natural resources, to external allies and enemies, to feuding, raids and war, to the responsibilities of paying and receiving blood money, to expulsion from a corporation, and their public attitude to political matters, all fall within the jural domain of agnation. There is clarity in these matters because rights against which claims can be forced are involved. This does not mean that exchanges are absent among agnates. At funerary rites they are the first to bring gifts of animals, and bring they must. An agnate who defaults in this is indicating that he no longer wishes to count himself as a member of the corporation. I was present at a funeral when a small group of men, resident a few miles away, failed to appear at the mourning ceremonies on the first day of a death. Concern was shown among the bereaved because they feared that neither they nor their leader would come, and that if they did now they might not bring an animal. It was explained that it is *wajib*, impellingly obligatory,[9] on all agnates to do so. The leader came at the end of a week of mourning, and did not bring an animal. The mourners knew that they would never be one again, that they had now split. During the first three days of mourning, when agnates of all the camps in the corporation's territory bring their animals, a man who was not an agnate but a neighbour brought a large goat, and it was immediately said about him that he had become an agnate.

Neither the agnate who defaulted nor the neighbour who gave broke an old debt relationship or started a new one; the former renounced an agnatic obligation and the latter showed that he wished to assume agnatic responsibilities. Passage of animal wealth among agnates does not therefore necessarily indicate the presence of a debt relationship. Another facet of this kind of transfer of wealth is sometimes to be seen during marriage negotiations or at wedding ceremonies. Among the Bedouin a man has prior right to his father's brother's daughter as a wife. If arrangements are made to marry her to someone else without the consent of her first paternal cousin, the latter can stop the marriage. My tent was used at a wedding for negotiations with a first patrilateral cousin who threatened to stop the proceedings just before the bride was due to enter the nuptial tent unless his claim to her was recognised. He was given some items of clothing and a few sheep, and the wedding proceeded. This was not an exchange for the purpose of creating debt between agnates; it was a demand for a *haqq*, or right, among men of an animal-owning property unit, a right which often appears when a man dies leaving sons who are minors and who, with their inheritance, are taken into guardianship by the father's brother. The latter diverts some, if not the major part of their inheritance to his stock, and the demand by one of them for his daughter is, in effect, an attempt to recover some of their lost property by defaulting on the bridewealth.

Bedouin are explicit on this point, stating that 'gifts among agnates must be equal', or that 'they only exchange (*tabadul*), among themselves'. In their status as agnates or patrilateral relatives there is an absence of debt relationships, but this does not mean that the differentiation which debt engenders does not exist among them. There is nothing to prevent one giving an animal to another in non-agnatic circumstances, such as the occasion of the birth of a male child, the kind of act which a shaikh of some standing usually performs. More commonly gifts of animals pass between agnates who are also affines or matrilateral relatives. Characteristically, these gifts are returned with increment, whereas an agnatic return is made without it. Agnation is a denial of choice, and the enforcement of duties. Debt allows a man the choice of differentiating among his agnates and it adds to his rights and duties the essential component of expectations. Since Bedouin expend much of their marriage linkages within the corporation, then – bearing in mind that these linkages include at least two generations – virtually all men are interconnected in ways other than by agnation. The social weight of these links, their number, and their duration are not the same for all men. Consequently nuclei of close-knit links appear among agnates of a single corporation, and it is within these that debt relationships will tend to be most active. While it is essential to temporarily separate debt and agnatic relationships for analytic convenience, it is imperative that they be seen together as the joint assets of all individuals of a corporation. Any man is linked to others in a corporation in a number of different ways, one of which, agnation, itself containing a cluster of rights, is common to all members; but how these rights are used, when they are forced, when they are waived and to whom they are transferred are all aspects of daily living, which are to be understood only partly in terms of agnatic and patrilineal relationships, but must be taken together with affinal and matrilateral relationships if they are to be understood fully.

Every marriage is preceded by a statement of bridewealth, whether the bride is a first cousin or quite unrelated. The amount varies from a sheep or two to twenty camels, the highest actual amount recorded. A large or small amount is not an estimation of the bride herself, and there is no stigma attached to marriages made with a very small amount of bridewealth. Amounts are not to be correlated with the durability of marriage either. But a large amount is invariably associated with a marriage linking people for the first time, people between whom there is no known previous history of kin relationships or among whom such a relationship has long been defunct. People, like agnates or patrilineal relatives who are already linked promise small amounts of bridewealth for marriages among themselves, and this small amount is sufficient to mark the fact that the change in relationships which marriage institutes is of an additive nature. Any 'marriage is a making of a relationship'. The word the Bedouin have for marriage is *nasab*, which itself means relationship. Enquiry about marriage takes the form of asking with whom is a relationship being made. Since bridewealth makes relationships, variations in amounts within the considerable range indicated are indices of the kind of relationships set in motion by it. Where marriage serves as an important link the bridewealth promised is usually very large, an earnest that the parties wish to enter into relationships to that amount of debt. A man who promises this kind of bridewealth always seeks to offset this against a similar promise for his daughter, making it known well in advance that 'her bridewealth is to be like her mother's' (*shartha kaif shart ummha*).[10] Major political alliances are made by marriage, and the large amounts of bridewealth provide them with the necessary strength and durability from the outset. Marriages within a corporation are also of prime significance in their effect on the social relationships of agnates and patrilineal kin. As an agnate, a man can demand his equal share of well water and ploughland, but no more, irrespective of the size of his herd or the number of his children. Bridewealth debt enables him to inject differentiation into a set of relationships which otherwise would be frustrated by the uniformity and stalemate of equality. In practical terms it means that a man who wishes to expand his flocks and herds expends part of his marriage assets by marrying a daughter within his corporation, often to a poor man, thereby giving him preferential access to agnatic sources. The phrase '*amm samm* (a male patrilineal relative is poisonous) is one curtly spoken, in some parts of the Arab world, with some point to it. Marriage with the daughter of an '*amm* takes some, at least, of the sting out of the relationship, and the birth of children transmutes it; affinity and matrilaterality expand the latitude of choice, and enable claims to be made which are excluded by agnation.

Bridewealth creates debt in any form of marriage, although, obviously, the type of relationship it stimulates so significantly (depending on the previous condition of relationships, the status of the individuals concerned, and the size, power and resources of the corporations) that it will be imperative later to discuss the sociological disparateness of this variety. But, for the time being, our concern is still with the processes of debt. Debt enters into bridewealth because it is rarely given in its full amount. During negotiations the conditions attaching to its payment are stated: an agreed part 'in front of you' (*qadamak*) and the rest over a number of years in case of 'shame' ('*aib*, i.e. adultery) or 'absence' (*ghaib*) through death or desertion. In effect very little more than the first part is given as actual bridewealth. This first part is unlikely to reach the bride's father, the receiver of the bridewealth, until a year of marriage has elapsed, and if it has resulted in issue by then, this part is given in good quality animals – but in one case where the bride had produced a still birth, one of the bridewealth camels was so diseased that it collapsed on the periphery of the camp as it was being driven to her father. As long as the marriage prospers, further demands for bridewealth proper are not continued, because by this time the debts between the two parties will have engulfed the debt of bridewealth. The bridewealth of the Bedouin works its purpose only when most of it is left as a layer of debt in which relationships can flourish. Significantly, the most final form of divorce is for a man to pronounce that his wife is like his mother (thus placing her in the category of incest) and to give the entire bridewealth promised for her. This is final severance, since, all debts paid, there is now nothing further to discuss. Payments terminate relationships; to honour a debt with exact repayment is to dishonour a relationships with insult.

The debt of bridewealth is the nexus which holds affines together. A father-in-law tests out his son-in-law during this period in many ways. Choosing his moment, he 'descends' (*nazala*, to descend or to dismount) on him, saying nothing, but expecting to be given a sheep or goat. And he is usually given one. A favourite time for this is the Great Feast. Fathers of married daughters visit their affines, who make off hastily to theirs. One sheep, sometimes, passes through several hands on a line of affinity, with no material loss to any but with amounts of social gain dropping at each point in the handling of the animal. Affinity in this probationary period of marriage is fraught with difficulties, the predatory father-in-law openly assessing his son-in-law, and the latter reluctantly conceding to him the claim to do so, a concession he signifies with the gifts he gives. Affinity retains its frailty until the birth of children turn debt partners into kin. But it is not the only debt that links affines. Unlike the debt created by a single slaughter for a guest as an opening of the way, preliminary reciprocal gifting will have taken place already; and the first formal stage in the marriage negotiations is the occasion when selected kin of the groom visit similarly selected kin of the bride with gifts of animals known as *siaq* (from *saqa* to drive along), the exact number and kind being determined by the number of certain kinsmen on the bride's side, and the status of the marriage. Later, those receiving gifts on this occasion are expected to return them in fuller measure. The marriage ceremony itself is one of the prime occasions for giving gifts in return for gifts previously received or as initial gifts. At the feasts given after the birth of children the series of gifts which pass between affines herald the new stage reached in the development of relationships. Marriage is the culmination of the debt process, although, of course, the debt in marriage is only one of its many aspects. Prior to this the debt relationship hangs on the willingness of the partners to retain an interest in its perpetuation, but it can always be abrogated. Marriage disperses debt over a wider range of people, the birth of children deepens their engagement in debt relationships; but it introduces new components of morality among people who are now kindred. A single marriage thrusts relationships on to a distinctively different plane of morality from that associated with debt, for while debt can be denied or denounced, it is impossible to opt out of consanguinity. A successful first marriage is soon followed by a second, either in the same direction as the first or vice versa, according to the availability of suitable spouses, so that the people thus connected are said to have become 'reciprocally interrelated' (*tanasabu*). Multiple marriages confirm the continued desire to complicate inter-linkages, until it becomes appropriate to refer to a kinship structure between people – a vastly different situation from a debt relationship or only a few marriage connections. With their flair for playing with words, the Bedouin speak of the latter as *tanasabu* (they intermarried), and of a kinship structure as *tanashabu* (they have become entangled). This kind of durability in their relationships is expressed as: *ruh bi-ruh*, soul by soul, and *'azm bi'azm*, bone to bone.[11] Debt continues to interlace relationships, its strands multiply, but it no longer stands exposed as a single voluntary relationship. The changed context has changed debt itself to one of a bundle of divers relationships adding a specific characterisation to each of them and deriving mutual support from all of them.

The end result of a successful debt relationship is an elaboration of a structure of relationships. Along the route that leads to this kind of firm and lasting relationship, there are several clearly defined stages. The initial step is the exploratory gift. Debt is instant, but it is still too early to speak of 'debt between them'. A confirmatory return gift, showing an increment, moves the relationship forward to reciprocity. Further, similar acts of reciprocity establish *dain* relationships. Even prior to marriage, a continu-ing debt relationship is a sufficient lien on people for one to speak of the other as an ally, *ribat*, even though the alliance thus formed is, perhaps, only temporary and for a specific cause, or of such a generalised kind as to permit sociability without any power to compel political action. Marriage marks the inception of a new morality, and debt expands to encompass negotiated contractual relationships. These latter insert rights and duties into the relationships for both parties; specific claims against outstanding bridewealth can now be forced, and fulfilment of contractual obligations by a wife and her kin can be demanded. An increase in marriages with a particular corporation establishes the next stage of reciprocal interrelated-ness, *tanasub*. Multiple marriage gives interrelatedness its durability, strength and persistence, *tanashub*. Save for occasional, and largely (but not wholly) casual dealings with the authorities, these seven stages, taken together with patrilineality and agnation, mark out the total field of Bedouin relationships in which some measure of co-operation is required of people. Or, to put the point in another way, assuming membership of a corporation, these seven debt stages represent the entire universe of any individual's co-operative social relationships. Moreover, of these seven stages, the first three are successively developed forms of debt relationships, uncomplicated by relationships of other kinds. Peripheral in the sense that they are all unguarded, exposed still to the buffetings of idiosyncrasy, they are by no means inconsequential. They represent those areas in relationships where the ambiguities implicit in competition lurk. They are the soundings taken by men who wish to extend or alter the existing configurations of their relationships. This aspect of debt is best seen in its differential use by men of status, and it is the weapon which a man with the ambition to become a shaikh, or a shaikh aiming to enlarge his power domain, must use and use with dexterity. The discussion that follows relates to the position of the shaikh in relation to debt.

A visitor, anticipating hospitality at a camp, makes for 'the tent of the man he knows to have most sheep'. This man is almost invariably the shaikh.[12] His tent stands out from the others because of its size and general appearance, and if the shaikh owns a horse it is tethered in front of his tent. Consequently, most of the animals given as sacrifices for visitors are provided by the shaikh. Visitors closely related to the people of a particular tent are given hospitality by their specific relatives, but if they stay the night it is likely that they too will be given hospitality by the shaikh the following day. The animals allocated for sacrificial purposes, although drawn from his flocks and herds, are part of the pool of gifts he has received on other occasions. These occasions when gifts of animals on the hoof are given are infrequent, but when they occur they add significantly to the shaikh's flocks and herds. On the first half day after the death of his brother, with whom he shared ownership of their joint animal wealth and whose sons were still minors, a shaikh received thirty sheep, yet during the seven days of mourning he slaughtered only five sheep and a few goats; his total gain in sheep and goats given as gifts over the whole mourning period was very much more than this. Wedding festivities for celebrating the marriage of a shaikh's son bring together upwards of a hundred people, and last for seven days. The amount of meat, water and other foodstuffs consumed are prodigious; the gifts of animals brought by the guests outnumber those slaughtered many times. Return after a long absence is a third occasion when gifts of sheep or goats are given to a shaikh, and the hearsay evidence on the gifts given to a prominent shaikh, on his return from exile, indicates that these gifts alone made him a wealthy man. A shaikh of much lesser stature increased his wealth by roughly a hundred sheep and goats on a similar occasion. Rare though these occasions are in the lives of shaikhs, the amount of wealth gained through them is enough to significantly affect their careers. Collection of blood money is done in the name of the shaikh, no matter who in a corporation the offender might be. The first people approached are the debt partners, and the evidence shows that many more animals are collected than are given as blood money.

Other events, like circumcision of a young son, the purchase of a horse, recovery from illness and so on, afford people the opportunity to gift the shaikh. Granting that the animals slaughtered for hospitality or given as gifts represent a much greater liability on the shaikh than the calls on the animal wealth of any of his followers, nevertheless the gifts received are usually well in excess of those given. Established shaikhs manage to strike this kind of materially favourable balance – a statement amounting to a truism, since failure to do this soon topples a shaikh. Upstarts are much more prone to serious losses of material wealth through engagements in gift giving. Over-eager to advance from a lowly position and unable to command much of an in-flow of gifts during the early stages of their careers, they soon find themselves impoverished. The temptation to bid for a following is ever present, requiring little more than a marginal surplus of wealth to make a start. Moreover, most of the occasions available to a shaikh for gathering in gifts are available to any of his followers. But the art of disposing of wealth for a return in social relationship is a skill that can only be learned in a costly apprenticeship. A shaikh, spontaneously generous as he might appear as host, must weigh his outlay against his anticipated returns, and he must be wary in accepting hospitality. If the volume of gifts flowing towards a shaikh is a flood, the turn of the tide might sweep him away to political oblivion: one semi-literate shaikh, living encamped on the outskirts of a township, kept a written tally of his debts so that 'I will not forget whom I must gift and with which animal', but also to provide him with a ready reckoner of his debts and credits. Debt drags men down, as surely as it promotes others to power positions. Some of the more prominent shaikhs have adopted the habit of spending much of their time in the villages and small townships dotted intermittently along the skirt of the semi-desert, in pursuit of their involuted *shughl*, business. Administrative affairs require them to be there occasionally, it is true, but one of the effects of absence from the camps is that they are less accessible, they cannot be gifted easily, and they are therefore better able to control their debt relationships. They chose their moment to ride into their camps with a flourish of white robes and a pounding of horses' hooves, their arrival an occasion in itself. The sacrifice that follows makes of it a major matter, as with one stroke of the knife across an animal's windpipe he puts a number of men into his debt, or adds to the accumulation already existing between him and his followers.

This necessity to keep strict control over debt links is, perhaps, best seen in the use of a horse. Any serious aspirant to the status of shaikh aims at buying one. With it, he is given a much more precious asset than relative comfort and speed in travel. A lengthy journey on foot, donkey or camel is slow, and to get from one place to another is not only tedious but takes time, and this means that a shaikh has to spend the night in camps on his route – a journey from some of the remote camps to the nearest village takes three days on foot and makes an overnight stop virtually certain even when a camel is used.[13] The speed of the horse allows the shaikh to eliminate hospitality he wishes to eschew. Speed gives an added dimension of control to the use of debt. Equally effective is the mounted shaikh's ability to be present at short notice where he knows men are gathering for matters of import, increasing his renown over a wide area for the effectiveness he brings to his status. A horse gives greater strength to the elasticity in the bonds which hold men to their shaikh.

All men are discriminate in their use of debt. The shaikh must exercise great care in the use he makes of it. Any man is free to gift, to offer a sacrifice as part of the hospitality for a guest. A shaikh does not enjoy the liberty of this freedom; giving gifts is the mainstay of his status. Default in a debt relationship is diminution of power. Another man who defaults injures a personal link; the same act on the part of the shaikh damages him and his corporation. Containment of the claims that can accumulate rapidly against a shaikh is only possible by countering a gift with its reciprocal gift. Most men express anxiety about redeeming their debts, but very many take their time about it. A man of ambition seeks to do so as soon as possible. A shaikh has the means to return the gift immediately, and has the power to create the appropriate occasion. The impulse to repay debt is largely a function of ambition and status.

'Agnates are equal', is a statement the Bedouin never tire of repeating. With regard to certain defined rights and duties, certain jural relations, the statement is true. Factually, it is equally true that each camp, however small, has its shaikh. The presence of shaikhship is clear evidence of differentiation within a corporation of agnates; and moreover, this differentiation is largely within the area of those very relationships subsumed under agnation. An aspirant to shaikhship must accumulate animal wealth above his immediate needs, and if he is to rise above the leadership of a small camp of, say, five tents, he needs to accumulate this wealth to an amount that is well in excess of his needs. To achieve this, he must gain differential access, in his favour, to the agnatic resources of land and water which, subject as they are to agnatic control, are available in equal amounts only on an agnatic distribution. Therefore, leadership of a camp of any size implies that a man has successfully penetrated the agnatic barrier of equality with a differentiation derived from non-agnatic origins. Important among these latter is debt. Expressed as it is so often, within a corporation, as marriage, its prime importance as a device which configures networks in this context lies in the fact that it is bundled together with others sets of relationships – such as the various and diverse constraints contained in affinity and the variety of kinship forms which marriage precipitates – for debt, acting alone, lacks the compulsiveness of claims which grant to a man the capability of transferring the shares of others to his own use. In this sense, debt, as a single-stranded relationship, is tactically useful; it has to be woven with others if it is to provide the durability necessary to plan a strategy. It follows from this that a shaikh, if he is to successfully hold his status and mature in it, aims to strike up a debt relationship with all his followers, and with key men among them is anchored in a bed of multiple relationships. A shaikh must largely carry his followers in several respects: he is the main provider of meat in a camp; he gives freely but carefully of his supplies of wool, milk and clarified butter; he provides camels for transport; and he is expected to provide for the poor on occasions such as the Great Feast, weddings, funerals, and for the numerous contingencies which befall his followers. Each camp, then, is a cluster of tents around a nucleus of surplus, and the shaikh stands at its centre, acting, in one of the aspects of his leadership, as the banker for, and the distributor of, surpluses. Being a follower means much more than extracting gain from a leader. The leader needs to differentiate among his agnates to acquire access to the natural resources, to possess some of the shares of his agnates in them, and thereby gain the power to distribute products, to accede in a *de facto* sense to proprietary control over them. But to maintain the increase in the flocks and herds which this kind of access permits, he perforce needs to command a labour force, which, in the circumstances, can only be made up of followers. Gifts of the kind mentioned, which pass from the shaikh to his followers, are payment in kind for the labour of some of them[14] – although it is important to add that among his followers there are always some men, and women, who, by virtue of age and infirmity, are too old to provide labour at least for the purpose of exploiting the natural resources.

The shaikh is, thus, both proprietor of much of the animal wealth of a camp, and the manager of a labour force. Show of strength by a shaikh in hostilities, disputes, negotiations, and *vis-à-vis* the administration, is the index of the resolve he is able to impart into his two roles of proprietor and manager, and the degree of firmness is partly a function of his deployment of debt links. Success in this raises a shaikh to the leadership of his corporation, an enviable position since at this point all the debt strands in the corporation are gathered into a single knot. Command of this position delivers the external debt networks of followers to the shaikh. He is poised now to make moves with the total social capital of a united following at his disposal, and he becomes a force to be reckoned with at a level of power of a socially different span. Each of his followers is linked externally through debt of one sort or another, and these linkages serve to differentiate between corporations as effectively as they do internally. Possessed by shaikhs the interpersonal debt links of individuals become a corporative asset of a fundamentally different nature, presenting different possibilities of use. Debts of various types differentiate a corporation internally and penetrate into external relationships; status differences further accentuate differentiation. In any context, in anyone's hands, debt diversifies relationships which already exist. The shaikh is in a critical position in a debt network because he is in command of the greatest diversity of relationships of a group, whatever its nature or span. Diversity is the prod which spurs shaikhs to give up their animals as gifts; hence, a camp, from this view, is a collection of tents surrounding that of the gift-giving shaikh. The frequency of animal slaughter is a measure of the diversity of relationships wrapped round about the status in shaikhship.

In the argument thus far, weight has been given to the view that debt, as a single relationship, is unable to withstand the stresses and strains which, until it becomes tied in the bundle of others, continually threaten it. For in this exposed state, it is essentially a relationship of watchfulness in which accounts are still sufficiently few to be kept accurately in mind. Debt works best when it is submerged in a sea of other relationships. While acknowledging the force and the implications of this, it is also necessary to bear in mind that a number of qualities adhere to a debt relationship, many of which have been discussed previously. A quality particularly pertinent to this brief discussion of leadership, which has been implicit hitherto, needs now to be made explicit. Debt has a malleability about it which gives the shaikh the power to supply bend his relationships in chosen directions, moving away from those which are unsatisfactory to gather in new ones, abruptly curtailing the growth of claims on him by summarily indebting his followers, shifting his generosity from these individuals to those within his corporation, pressing this precious asset into different shapes while retaining its substance. Any relationship the shaikh holds in his keeping allows him a certain latitude, but most of his relationships are given such clarity that this latitude is marginal. In the hands of a shaikh, the malleability of debt gives it its great importance. Marriage cannot be summarily negotiated. Consanguinity cannot be contrived to meet a contingency. Agnatic status cannot be accorded except after protracted consideration and assent of all the members of a corporation. None of these relationships can be rescinded off-handedly. Debt enables a shaikh to move with alacrity among his social relationships and to meet the recurring twists and turns in them with a readiness other relationships do not afford. Herein lies the value of debt to leadership. It can never provide a structure of power, nor a basis for its erection; but what it lacks in staying power, in clarity of definition, it offsets with its volatility, running with the slickness of a lubricant where the fostering of relationships is required, but, when drained out of relationships, leaving them seized in aridity.

Before proceeding to treat the nature of constraints debt imposes on social relationships, one final field in which most of the parts of its process are manifest and most easily documented, needs to be examined: blood money payments (*diya* from *wada* to pay blood money; or *muwaʿada* agreement, from *waʿada*, to give one's word) after a homicide. The range of possible events which succeed a homicide are numerous. Here the concern is limited to three: part payment of the amount promised coupled with a marriage; full payment of the agreed amount within a stated limited period; the refusal to enter into a blood money agreement, resulting in a protracted state of hostilities known as feud. Variations on all three courses exist, but for the present purpose it is not necessary to include them in the discussion.

Despite the generally expressed sentiment that every homicide, no matter what the peculiarities of the circumstances, requires to be avenged, two of the courses which succeed a homicide in fact put a stop to killing, and one of them brings about conditions of peace. Blood money, given in animals, is thought of as a device for the restoration of previously co-operative relationships, or to create a condition of co-operation where hitherto it had not been tried. Where the urge to restore peaceable relationships exists within a few weeks of a homicide serious formal negotiations for a peace meeting begin. At this meeting an amount of blood money is agreed and witnessed by the distinguished shaikhs who attend specifically to assume this role. Prior to departure they mouth pieties, but add to these – and only in circumstances where they know that an enduring peace is envisaged – the advice that the two groups involved should marry with each other. The social anthropological definition of the circumstances in which fully effective peaceable relationships are sought through the medium of this kind of peace meeting is beyond the scope of this chapter. Suffice it to say that since homicide might occur in any set of relationships – although vengeance is not pursued except in very few – frayed tempers can lead to a fight at any time, and a fight can result in death, whether it is between full brothers or quite unrelated men. Granting this, then clearly the means must be available to damp down the threat of immediate furore and then to get relationships running smoothly again. A full payment of blood money would not achieve this result. Full payment leaves the parties nothing to talk about, a state of sullenness in which neither is sure what the other might do next. What happens here is that a small amount of the total blood money promised is given in the first year, and each successive year sees a marked diminution in the amount compared with the previous year until, after the lapse of a few years, formal payments cease altogether. In the meantime a marriage between the two groups will have been made, the victim's group taking a wife from the offender's group 'for nothing'. This latter phrase does not mean quite what it says. A wife cannot be given 'for nothing' in any circumstance. What the Bedouin mean when they say this is that an agreement has been reached on the amount of the bridewealth, but the offender's group will not ask for any of it, nor will the victim's group offer it to them. Instead it is allowed to remain as a debt between them.

Added to the debt of blood money and further marriges between the two, a general and reciprocal debt relationship develops, which, with the appearance of children and the new constraints they bring to bear on adult relationships, become securely embedded in what becomes a structure of relationships. The debt of blood money acts on relationships like a kind of motive force propelling them not to a point of *status quo ante* but into a realm of significantly different relationships where relatively large amounts of debt on either side endow them with greater intensity and virility than ever before. Tolerably amicable relationships prior to homicide have been presumed in this discussion of the use of blood money agreements to promote a debt relationship, but I recorded cases in which (according to hearsay evidence) these prior relationships, while not hostile, were distant and in no sense the relationships of allies. One of these cases involved what is probably the most powerful single corporation in the land, engaged in strife for several years with a large but weaker corporation, at the end of which men belonging to both corporations had been killed. The weaker corporation sought to end this state of affairs, a peace meeting was arranged, an immediate transfer of animal wealth was made to the powerful corporation, and within a year two wives had been 'given' to it. Since then ten reciprocal marriage arrangements have been made, for which I have genealogical evidence. I lived in the camps of both corporations, they were obviously closely connected, showing conspicuous ease in the informality of their relationships, and the shaikh of the weaker one was proud to tell me: 'There is no fissure (*khalal*) dividing us, and there is not hatred *karh*) between us, and the ('*iddiya*), enmity or hostility (common enemies, in other words) of other tribes is for us both'. Compare this case with that (referred to earlier) in which a succession of killings ended first in blood money, followed later by an attempted killing when a horse was shot dead, and an end to it coming about after a meeting at which an equality of losses by both sides was negotiated thus leaving only formality in relationships, and the difference in relationships where debt is present and where it is absent becomes readily intelligible. Unless it is left as a debt, blood money does nothing to promote a flow of relationships. On the contrary, it breaks them. Left largely as a debt, it acts to persuade people to maintain connections, opening the way to possibilities of social prosperity between corporations. The debt of blood money makes a *nasab*, relationship.

Save for those which involve members of the same corporation, all homicides are referred as *dain*, debt, by the Bedouin. When a man 'brings vengeance' (*thar*) it is not said that he killed a man but that he redeemed (*salaka*) the debt. When a man kills another, the idiom used is: 'He took a soul' *akhadha ruh*), an act of robbery (*nahb*). Once the debt has been redeemed, there would appear to be no reason for further killing. But in a feud, 'a soul for a soul' is not the rule that is followed. Instead the details of each killing are carefully recounted, the status of the victims is stressed and the exact circumstances of the killing are noted. Statements which the killer made before killing, whether the victim stood at the entrance to his tent or seated inside, whether he was a camp shaikh or a more important leader, and so on, are the kind of details used to discriminate one killing from another: the statement might have added insult to vengeance, the place of the killing might have added a breach of taboo to it, and a vengeance killing might have been the death of a shaikh of a little more importance than the previous victim. The difference between one killing and another is the debt which makes feud so distinctively different from homicide vengeance. Like the debt recognised in animal slaughter, bridewealth and so on, it is nothing more than the somewhat marginal difference between one act and another, but it is a social difference of sufficient magnitude to keep relationships moving in a set direction, so that the Bedouin, thinking in terms of social debt, do not find it necessary to be numerically accurate when they say: 'There is still a man left over' (*lissa fi rajul taul*), by which is meant that another killing must be made to redeem this debt.

As in the processes of all debt, killings in a feud rarely accelerate sharply, for a steep rise in the number of victims is avoided precisely because the differences between them are marginal – indeed, were it otherwise, the successively increasing numbers of vengeances would soon become a holocaust. Periodically several men are known to have been slain in one incident – at the time of my fieldwork, a man was responsible for killing eight men of another group – but these killings are outside the field of debt and comprehend a fundamentally different type of relationship. The debt in feud ensures that hostility remains purulent. Although the point has already been made when discussing debt in other contexts, lest there should be any misunderstanding of its significance in this context, it is necessary to make it again: the debt in feud is not alone in precipitating homicides and perpetuating them in a patterned manner; it is always present among other factors. Obviously Bedouin would not continue to kill interminably merely to achieve exact equality. Feud is essentially a patterned mode of competing for resources. Priority, analytically, must always be given to this fact in considering successively linked killings between corporations. Bedouin are aware that in particular circumstances there is fierce competition for a particular well or ploughland. They are not aware that feud is part of the problems in the relations of all Bedouin to available resources. Consequently feud is a specific relationship, and debt is the cultural mode of conceptualising general relationships particularised by their participation in them. 'The debt of a bone', 'the debt of blood' are freely used idioms in reference to feud, but killings occur in other sets of relationships in reference to which these idioms are omitted. Thus a killing within a corporation is neither the debt of bone nor blood, for all its members are conceived as 'one blood, one bone, one body'. Debt enters only where it is conceptually necessary to differentiate identical acts in terms of known disparateness in social relationships.

In the discussion thus far some of the circumstances in which debt of various sorts is recognised have been given. There are many more. I list here some of the suitable times for giving a gift either as a slaughter or a live animal, to give some idea of the frequency of opportunity there is for giving and receiving, although the list is not exhaustive. At a birth of the firstborn son an animal slaughter is referred to as *'aqiqa*, although a man might vow to kill an animal for the birth of a child regardless of its sex, and this is then referred to as *nadhr*, vow or votive offering. Before, during and after a marriage many gifts are passed between certain specified kin of the bride and groom, and many animals are brought by those who come to attend the celebrations. The bride, aloft on a camel, sometimes with a little boy seated behind her, is led round the nuptial tent seven times, and shortly after she dismounts, an animal is slaughtered, known as *da'irat al-bait*, the circling of the tent. Shortly after the wedding, the bride's mother is given what is known as *suwar al-halib*, literally the armlet of the milk, although this gift is always given in sheep or goats. Both parties exchange formal visits after the marriage, and bring with them an animal as a gift, *diyafat al-ziyara*, the hospitality of the visit. The third life crisis, death, is an occasion for receiving and slaughtering many animals, and the terms for some of these sacrifices have already been given. On the feast of the dead a sacrifice known as *waqfa*, literally standing or pause or station, but implying here a consecration, is made. An offering (*sadaqa*) to God, for the sake (*khatir*) of a deceased person can be made at any time by his nearest male kinsman, but it is likely to be performed only when this kinsman considers that the mind (*'aql*)[15] of the deceased is 'unhappy' and that therefore he is likely to cause disturbance among the living.

A number of their animal slaughters are associated with their pastoral and cultivating activities. Immediately after a cistern has been cleared out one of the men circumambulates the well with a sheep or goat which is then slaughtered, a sacrifice referred to as *da'irat al-bi'r*, circling the well, or *zarda li'l-jahara*, a feast for the cleaners of the well. Whether or not a well has been cleaned out, when animals begin to use it systematically with the onset of drought, a sacrifice is performed. In summer, after the barley has been harvested, threshed and put in store, an animal is slaughtered at the threshing floor, and this is known as *da'irat al-majran*, circling the threshing floor. Sheep shearing requires a sacrifice, and reapers are given a sacrificial meal after their work is done. Any help is acknowledged with a sacrifice. To be added to these are irregular occasions such as incorporating a man into a corporation, for any group of male visitors, for female visitors, for certain matrilateral relatives, when a mare drops a foal, for a vengeance killing, for a wife after a severe quarrel, at circumcision, and so on. In all this wide range of debt dealings, a transfer is being made; it takes the form of a live or slaughtered animal, and the transfer carries with it the recognition that a moral relationship, expressed as *dain*, has arisen between the giver and the receiver. The same can be said of bridewealth, blood money, homicide, vengeance and feud.

Throughout this entire range of disparate circumstances, common to them all is the giving or seizure (in vengeance and feud) of a life, whether it is the life of an animal as a surrogate, or the life of a human being. Blood, life's very substance, brings people together in a relationship by imposing moral constraints on their behaviour. People, particularly in the rough and tumble of camp life, give and take in a manner familiar to situations where human beings live in close and intense relationships. The wealthier among the Bedouin give to the poorer among them a few fleeces after shearing, some milk to those without animals, dates to those too infirm to fetch them from the distant oases. The loan of a camel to a man who has none or to one whose herd is not near at hand, grind-stones among the tents in a camp and so on, are acts among neighbours important for the purpose of characterising relationships in a local community; but these are not debt relationships. A man giving a few fleeces to a widow in his camp described the act as *minha*, an act of kindness, and denied that it created debt between them. If, however, a person of this small community gives another an animal or slaughters one for him, then, decisively, debt has differentiated their relationships from the consociation of common residence previously obtaining between them. Mere exchange is not the same as reciprocal motion in relationships begun by debt. The difference between the two is not one of nuance, but it is a fundamental difference in the nature of constraints on behaviour. Without the moral notions bundled together in Bedouin sentiments about blood, life, wealth, and sacrifice, gift giving would be an incredible altruism or a wasteful outlay in very expensive hospitality with only the speculative possibility of any sort of a return. (The price of a sheep when I worked in Cyrenaica, before the discovery of oil, was about £4. By 1972 the price rose to between £20 and £25. For those unfamiliar with living costs during the 1948–50 period, the 1972 price gives an accurate measure of the burden of hospitality in earlier times.) In order to appreciate the nature of the constraints in debt relationships it is necessary, therefore, to examine what the Bedouin think – or rather what they say they think – when they give or slaughter an animal for someone else.[16]

After we had spent some months among the cow and goat herding plateau people of Cyrenaica, we returned to the camps of the camel/sheep people of the semi-desert. The question we were asked many times was: 'Did they give you meat on the plateau?', and when I replied in the affirmative, my reply always evoked the rejoinder: 'But what they gave you yonder was meat they bought from the market. The flesh from a butcher's might have belonged to anyone. We give from our wealth' (*rizq*). Herein lies a critical and revealing difference. The consequences of the acceptance of a meal among the plateau people are easily neutralised by the countercheck of assessable amounts of material goods, animal flesh, tea, sugar and so on. When the plateau people purposefully use the word *dain* for the most part they are thinking in terms of measurable gain. They, like people I worked with in South Lebanon, have a commercial idea of investment and its corollary interest, *ribh* or *fa'ida*. In both communities a few men grow rich through usury of one concealed kind or another.[17] Meat with a meal among the plateau people is part of an account in a sheep, and its counter is the price of sugar and tea. Among the semi-desert Bedouin we used prodigious quantities of tea and sugar, but this could never redeem the blood of a lamb. The cost of a sheep is assessable, a bill can be made for it. There is no bill for blood. A somewhat fastidious eater, the small quantities of meat I ate at sacrificial meals perplexed and distressed the Bedouin, but they never failed to emphasise that the power or value (*qadar*) given to me was in the blood of the sacrifice, not in the meat. Now when a man slits an animal's throat, as he does it he says: *bismi'llahi' allaha'l-akbar*, 'In the name of God, God is most great'. This invocation is always pronounced whenever an animal is slaughtered, whether it is the wild gazelle or the domesticated sheep or goat, and this pronouncement makes the meat of the animal permissible (*halal*) to eat. It does not convert slaughter into sacrifice. The ritual transformation, possible only when an animal from an individual's *rizq* (wealth) is used, is effected by a statement of the purpose of the slaughter. Ritualisation robs a slaughter of its commercial value, and replaces it with a bundle of sentiments about sacrifice. The key to an understanding of these sentiments is given in the Bedouin version of Abraham's sacrifice: God said to Abraham that he must have a sacrifice from him. He could not give Him bread. He had to give an animal from his own flock. But he had no sheep. So, he decided to sacrifice his son. He was about to kill him when two rams appeared out of the sky, and he sacrificed these instead. 'And now', as one man said, 'when we want to do something great for a person we take a sheep from our flock and slaughter it. This is the meaning of the slaughter we made for you, and which we make for anyone'. An animal slaughtered for a guest is a surrogate for a human life, a life over which the giver has proprietary control but which is part of his own life. The sacrifice of a sheep is the giving, in symbolic form, of a part of the life of the giver.

This intimate connection between the life of an animal and the life of its owner, between *rizq*, wealth, and *nafs*, soul or life, is the essence of the gift of sacrifice. Bedouin make the connection quite explicit. I quote a young shepherd who feared that a badly damaged finger would prevent him from watering his flock. When I asked him why he was so anxious to be with his flock constantly, he said: 'Last year, I was given goats for herding. This year I will have more. With them I will get sheep, and many sheep will get camels for me. When I have camels I can get a wife. And a wife will bear sons for me. Look. Animals make sons. I am here because my father gave animals for my mother'. All life is placed in a continuum, the life in one kind of body passing into another, to 'make' a son, who grows to the maturity of authority over the lives of animals. But the owner of an animal does not shed its blood wantonly, only for the purpose of eating flesh, for example.

Blood – any blood (*damm*) – is *haram*,[18] that which is sacred, inviolable, interdicted, sinful, forbidden and the other meanings which are included in this significant concept, which is rendered – sometimes as little more than as a manner of speaking – in our literature as taboo, and which is one of the words (without its long vowel, but having the same meaning) used in sacrificial acts. The stain of the blood of the sacrificial victim in the sand is left visible, so that people may ask: 'For whom is the blood?'

Therefore the slaughter of an animal is always purposeful, and the purpose is pronounced during the sacrificial act. Usually it is expressed as *qadar al-daif* (power of the guest) and sometimes as *qadar wa-haram*. The word *qadar* means fate, but it also means power, status, and measure of a man, and these are the meanings given to it in the context of sacrifice. Coupled with *haram* there is in sacrifice the idea that the guest's status, *qua* his position as guest (and only additionally as a person of general social renown), demands a reverence and a recognition of his power, and this demand can only be met by the host (*mudif*) giving away part of his *nafs*, life. The sanctity of sanctuary, stressed so much by Bedouin, is rooted in the idea that a guest holds part of his host's life, so that 'if anyone strikes my guest he strikes me also, in the same way as the shedding of the blood of an agnate is the shedding of my blood'.[19] Danger, respect, the being of a person are all caught up in the relationship between a host and his guest. The blood which spouts from the immolation does honour to the guest and exalts the dignity of the host. A man's measure is diminished by the loss of a life (animal) from his *rizq*, wealth, but his whole being is enriched, his life amplified, because it is now blended with another. The man of eminence, known for his generosity, is he who sacrifices for many, freely giving part of his life, and at the same time achieving a coalescence of souls to augment and enlarge his person. A third word which I often heard in situations of sacrifice is *khatir*, when the slaughter would be said to be 'for the sake of . . .' (*min sha'n khatir*), as the phrase is often translated; but *khatir* also means character and standing, and the root from which *khatir* is derived has in it meanings of danger, gravity, significance and the like, as the Bedouin make clear; there is doubt about the guest himself, and the danger that he will not reciprocate. In all the referents in the concept of sacrifice, the consistency of the ideas of the host giving part of his life, the recognition that the guest is to be feared and respected, and the intimacy between the two through animal blood, are striking.

The statement of intent, however, is always prefaced with the phrase: *sadaqa li-wajh Allah*, 'an offering for the face of God'. Bedouin give to God, in the first place, as part of their statement of intent; they also state for whom they are offering the sacrifice in the second part of the statement.

Since everything comes from God anyway, then how is it possible for a Bedouin to give what belongs to Him? Whatever the theological niceties in arguments about sacrifice in general, the Bedouin have no doubt in their minds that they are free to choose between giving or withholding, and for whom to give or not to give. Every sacrificial act is thus a trinity of the giver, the receiver and God. The inclusion of God transforms what would otherwise be a slaughter into a sacrifice, creating a bond of blood between guest and host, safe in God's keeping. In short, the power of the sacrificial act is the power of a covenant (Pedersen 1940: 657, 660). It is, of course, possible for men to break their covenants, but to break these is falsity, deception (*khiyana*), irrespective of the circumstances in which they were made. That is to say, while men break covenants when it suits them, breach is followed by consequences in social relationships appropriate to an act of treachery.

Many other acts of exchange might shuttle to and fro between two men, only to be severed by one of them abruptly, without any dire consequence for their relationships. Thus, a man, when he gives hunks of gazelle meat to others, does not alter his relationships with them except possibly to a fractional extent; nor can he expect for a piece of protein a return either in kind or in a permission to make requests, except of a very limited and relatively trivial kind – and if even these are refused he has no recourse to any kind of pressures. Sacrifice is not the re-distribution of protein to achieve a fairly equable amount for the maximum number of people; were this so there would be no difference between this and distribution of gazelle meat, haphazardly, and as the whim of the moment directs a man's choice among his neighbours. Sacrificial meat cannot be eaten by one man alone. All his camp neighbours share the commensality of the meal. Although eating sacrificial meat is surrounded by a number of distinctive conventions, the meal itself is not the essence of sacrifice. Commensality is imperative, as an adjunct to sacrifice, inseparable from it, but vested with its whole meaning by the ritual preceding it. The bond in sacrifice is a beginning of a new relationship among men: the commensal meal, following quickly after the act, is evidence of the good fellowship which it is intended to produce, and the emphasis of this the saying I so often heard at these meals: 'Eating around the same wooden bowl (*qasʿa*) is the emblem (*'alama*) or the blessing (*khair*).' Men enjoy the good fellowship of the meal because the impediment in their relationships, whatever its source, has been removed by a sacrifice.

Any domestic animal is a worthy sacrificial victim. It is the blood that counts, not the kind or size of the animal, and, among the plateau peoples, bread is sometimes used as a substitute, just as among the Nuer a cucumber serves sacrificial purposes (Evans-Pritchard 1956: 279). In his relationships with God, it may well be that man's intention is all that matters, and whether the victim is a scraggy goat or a prime ram is immaterial. But among men the difference is of critical importance. Bedouin assert that there is a ritual difference between a goat and a sheep, partly because the ram is said to have been used by Abraham as surrogate for his son's life, but also because the wool on the sheep's back 'was given blessing (*baraka*) by God from yonder', and sheep, in a general way figure largely in their religious sentiments. The implication of this view, however, is that, as emphasised earlier, both sheep and goats when used in social relationships are graded according to age and sex and, consequently, when a sheep is given in return for a goat the increment is not merely a matter of a different kind of meat, or of a commercially more valuable animal, but a difference of ritual state, and *a fortiori* a sacrifice of a sheep represents an intention to advance a relationship morally.[20]

It is not suggested that the meaning of sacrifice is wholly incapsulated in its ritual significance. It would be quite spurious to maintain that its ritual precedence eliminates any other significances. Some sacrificial acts have patently political purposes. As an example, I quote the use made of sacrifice between two ex-Bedouin competing for leadership on an olive plantation in 1964. One accused the other of embezzling a large sum, part collection and part grant, for the purchase of a modern olive press, by having the documents of purchase made out to him personally so that the capital investment and future profits would accrue to him. The accuser invited the Director General of Agricultural Co-operatives, in origin from the locality, to investigate the accounts. I had seen the various letters and bills of the transactions, and there was no doubt that there was evidence of impropriety. The accused heard of this, so he invited the Director to eat with him and all the members of the co-operative committee, of which he was then the self-appointed Chairman. For the meal, the accused killed five sheep. The accuser had to attend or put himself beyond the pale, but after accepting a sacrifice which was partly for him as an invited guest, he could not then press his accusation, or else he would have appeared to the Director and the committee as a cheat, prepared to go to the length of treachery in his dispute with the accused. The latter, during the chatter after the meal said, by the way, that some errors had crept into the accounts, but that he would give them his attention. That night the accuser resigned from the committee; his rival was elected President of the Co-operative a few days later. I was told that the accused was planning to snuff out the political threat the accuser had been posing for some time. The accused had the material means to do so; the accuser, heavily mortgaged, had little chance when the stakes were as high as five sheep. Similarly when excessive or insufficient gifts are given material assessments are present, and manifest or explicit objective overlie the religious content of sacrifice. In all sacrifices, however, the ideas about the significance of blood are always present, and it is precisely because these ideas are present that the gift permits people to anticipate behaviour and achieve their ends. The President of the Co-operative did not stop the mouth of his rival with meat; however replete he, the Director, and the rest might have felt after their gourmandising; he silenced him and frustrated his political plans with sacrificial blood.

The gift of blood,[21] of life, is a *dain* which establishes a relationship or transmutes what relationships already exist. The relationships thus engendered are of a moral order, and therefore they have moral sanctions imputed to them. In this they are quite unlike many other forms of relationships in which transfers of wealth, of one sort or another, occur. To sharpen the significance of debt, a brief comparison with bribery is useful. A bribe (*bartil*) moves men to do specific things, but its effect is limited to the actions specified. Debt acts in the opposite way to lower the curtain of formality and open up an extending vista of relationships. Bribes rise sharply in amount as the expected returns rise in magnitude. As a steering device in relationships, bribes are too costly to be in common use among the Bedouin; a debt gift is within the reach of virtually everyone and there is no defined limit to its return. A bribe is an immediate payment for a hazard of a known kind, and the lien a bribe gives ends with the cessation of the hazard. Debt is not specific and it constrains beyond the situation which created it. Bribery is a subterfuge, secretive and immoral. Debt is morally meritorious, deployed openly, enhancing a man's lustre. Bribery brings a known result. Debt has the potential to gather untold riches of relationships.

I have cited bribery because, to my mind, much of what has come to be treated as gift giving in the literature, should, with greater discrimination, be included within its meaning. Gift is to be characterised by the constraints it imposes. For this reason, an explanation of Bedouin sacrifice has been given. Mauss (1954: 1) asks the question, at the beginning of his analysis of the gift: '*What force is there in the thing given which compels the recipient to make a return?* (his italics)' In this chapter the concern with sacrifice is the same as that in Mauss' question, save that it has been put as an enquiry about the constraint an animal slaughter puts on the behaviour of people. The 'force' that Mauss sought he found to be the 'spirit', the 'religious' element in 'the thing'; so that: 'The obligation attached to a gift itself is not inert' (*ibid*.: 9), a view repeated a second time: 'The thing given is not inert' (*ibid*.: 10). Among the Maori, 'the spirit of things' is referred to as *hau*, a concept in a text of Best's, which, for Mauss, was 'the key to the whole problem' (*ibid.*: 8). Firth, with a flourish, sweeps aside Mauss' views about *hau* as misinterpretation, confusion, interpolation, linguistic lapses, and as 'his own intellectualised interpretation of it' (1929: 412–15). Yet in his writing on theories of gift exchange (*ibid.*: 417–20), save for a second and repetitious dismissal of Mauss (*ibid.*: 419), its absence urges one to exclaim – if the reader will forgive an apposite vulgarism – how about *hau*! What Mauss sought was the sanctions on behaviour, as he made explicitly clear in reference to the Trobriand *kula*: 'Unfortunately we know very little about the sanctions behind these transactions' (Mauss 1954: 24). Neither Malinowski nor Firth saw the significance of the constraints in gift exchange which Mauss seized on, and which Pedersen (1926–40: 296–306, 330, 657–60), publishing in 1920, two years before Malinowski's 'Argonauts' (1922) and five years before Mauss, so brilliantly analysed in his work on the gift. Malinowski does say however that before sailing the perilous seas to 'a land of danger and insecurity' (1922: 42), the leader feasts his followers off the pork of piacular pigs (*ibid.*: 209, 171, 213).

Struck by the pageantry of the overseas *kula*, Malinowski says relatively little about the organisation of followers, of which the internal *kula* was probably an important part, or of the obligations whereby followers were committed to a leader. The latter constituted the basis of a structure of leadership; the external *kula* was a brandish of the fact that a man had acceded to a leadership in which debt relationships among co-residents played such a crucial part. Men did not sail the oceans for the purpose of dominating, politically, leaders resident in other remote islands. The technology would not permit it. Each island enjoyed a high degree of political autonomy.[22] When, therefore, a leader took an expedition to another island to exchange *vaygu'a* – themselves heirlooms or, better, bundles of social relationships – his aim was aggrandisement; for the exchange of *vaygu'a* was a recognition by a leader, outside his political domain, of his right to claim this status, and the 'value' of the objects exchanged served to measure the extent of his aggrandisement. This 'value', however, was clearly related to the span of a leader's power in his own political domain: 'With reverence he would name them (the *vaygu'a*), and tell their history, and by whom they were worn, and how they changed hands, and how their temporary position was a great sign of the importance and glory of the village' (Malinowski 1922: 84). Indeed, the authority of a few leaders became so permanently dominant that the *vaygu'a* in their possession became so charged with social relationships that they were 'set apart as a special class', and were 'once and for all out of the *kula*'.[23] The basis of the analysis should have been the structure of the local leadership, and then the various kinds of leadership typified by their span. If Malinowski had done this the different sorts of *kulas* would have fitted into their proper places. As it is, he gave us a diversionary amount of froth and foam, comparable in its overstatement to some of the earlier writings on the potlatch,[24] thus giving the whole business a wrong focus. But had he looked closely into local leadership he might have given an analysis of the various constraints on behaviour, on which leadership structures, anywhere and at all times, rest; instead the virility of different forms of debt relationships are erroneously and superficially accredited to 'the love of give and take for its own sake', 'giving for the sake of giving' (Malinowski 1922: 173, 174), and they are classified on a basis of banality which makes the classification little more than descriptive repetition.[25]

Since the constraints which the variety of forms of reciprocity impose on relationships are rarely analysed, the danger is that sociologically disparate relationships remain undifferentiated. Unless some sophistication is introduced into the analysis, then all relationships become part of the common stock of reciprocity, and reciprocity in turn becomes synonymous with relationship.[26] In this state, reciprocity cannot contribute to, much less form, the basis of a structure, as Blau claims (1964: 2). 'Any interaction', as Cohen (1968: 124, 125) says in reference to Blau, 'can be treated as an exchange in which all parties receive something in return for what they have given', and 'when exchange theory is applied to the intrinsic benefits which men obtain from an adherence to an ideology, religious faith or ritual activity, the results are unenlightening or even absurd'.[27]

I myself have to admit to writing the statement: 'Where there is no debt, there are no relationships' (Peters 1951: 338). As a conversational manner of speaking, or used as banter, the statement has its uses. Analytically, I now consider it irresponsible. In a few limited situations, debt is at work in Bedouin relationships, virtually on its own; in most, it is interwoven with others, and there are situations from which it is absent. Among them, it is the prerogative mainly of males for, while women enter into the relationships it evokes, and while they are crucial in many of them, their ritual status and their relation to property disables them from the control of social relationships because it is so distinctively different from others. Its hallmark is the conventional bond the gift establishes between the giver and the receiver, and which Chelhod (1955: 188) argues endows the gift with its motive power, releasing a current which flows incessantly between the two. Without its conventional support there is no reason why a gift should hold men conjoined beyond the duration of the meal. It is this aspect of gift which, perhaps, prompted Cohen (1968: 125) to ask implicitly of Blau, in relation to his 'exchange' analysis – as he could well have done of the increasing number of authors writing about 'exchange' relationships – why does the relationship endure? And until this question is answered, Blau has no answer to Cohen's other question: 'How much power is actually created in this way?' (*ibid.*: 122). For, until greater precision is shown with regard to the specific areas of social relationships affected by exchange, and the kind of constraints which hold persons in some kind of bond, the constituent elements of power will necessarily remain unknown; and if these are unknown, the characterisation of various types of power, which is an essential part of its analysis, cannot be undertaken.

Consequently, exchange theory, so-called, restricts the investigation of power to certain of its types only and, more restrictively, to one – sometimes not the most important, or even an inconsequential – element. The result is that the theory becomes irksomely reductionist. Exchange might be present in all sorts of power, but it takes more than a nod or a wink, a little gift for a frivolous favour, to command an army to go to war, or to conscript a generation of men for an army, or for a Trobriand leader to gather and organise a body of men to set forth on a *kula* expedition. The same criticism can be levelled at Lévi-Strauss (1969), who reduces the whole of marriage to one of its constituent elements, exchange. Fortes (1953) gives the measure of the error: 'The transfer of rights in a woman, let alone in her unborn offspring, is a different thing from an exchange of woman for woman. The concept of rights refers to an isolate, to a special kind of social relation between two parties which is enforceable by sanctions. As soon as we put it this way, we see how different is the level of the analysis from that involved in reducing marriage to a special form of exchange. The patient observer can almost literally see bride price being exchanged for a woman. To arrive at "rights" he has to examine the whole range of social relations in which the married couple have joint and separate roles, and also consider marriage as a developing process through a stretch of time.'[28]

What led me into the error of saying that where there are no debts there are no relationships is the fact that debt penetrates so many and such diverse relationships. It was for this reason that Mauss (1954: 76) claimed that 'The facts we have studied are all "total" social phenomena.' He meant by this that in them 'all kinds of institutions find simultaneous expression: religious, legal, moral and economic' (*ibid.*: 1). In his analysis, however, these priorities are reversed, for here he demonstrates that the gift with its associated reciprocity appears in the institutions he cites, and not that these institutions find expression in the gift. But by thinking explicitly of institutions as being simultaneously captured by gift, reciprocity becomes what Hobhouse (1915: 12) called 'the vital principle of society'. The ascription of this significance to the gift led Mauss to think of a general theory of reciprocity, collecting bits and pieces of data from here, there and everywhere, and to encourage Lévi-Strauss to even greater excesses in his world-wide travels through the ethnographic literature (1969: 52ff). The omnipresence of reciprocity and its relations to social systems have been noted by many scolars,[29] and there has been much said about the theory of reciprocity or the theory of exchange. Mauss gave us a number of analytic thumb-nail sketches of great beauty, relating to a range of sociological problems in many societies, but sadly, when he came to making theoretical statements, they degenerated into a homily about substituting gift for war (1954: 80). The suggestion that gift exchange can be a 'surrogate for it' (war) appears in Young (1971: 356) and in Strathern (1971: 54) who considered moka gifts as a true functional alternative to warfare, and this is a lapse in two works which are so full of data and analysis.[30]

Fortunately few of the other writers on gift exchange have followed Mauss in his concern with the substitution of war by gift; but his idea that gift is a total social phenomenon has tempted many to give it an unwarranted primacy and, hence, to attempt general theories of reciprocity. Sahlins (1965), in a carefully considered argument, attempts to classify (as one would expect of an evolutionist) gift exchanges according to several scales: the mechanics of exchange, kinship distance and closeness, wealth, segmentary societies, and types of reciprocity. His classifications are, however, so crude, that the rest of his argument is denied its basis of support.[31] This is not to say that any kind of classification is crude – anatomical classification, for example, is precise, whether the classification, is of general structures or of specific parts. Kinship distance and kinship closeness are not general features but the lumping together of disparate acts of behaviour, in an effort to arrive at some form of generality, which can only result in analytic crudity.

In this chapter only some of the forms of kinship have been dealt with briefly, in their relation to debt, but sufficient evidence has been presented to make the view clear that to leave kinship undifferentiated is to make an initial error of such magnitude that any argument of Sahlins' kind must necessarily be invalid. Indeed, the argument becomes bewildering when an attempt is made to connect reciprocity to areas of intense relationships (close kinship), and to connect its decline in importance with distance in kinship. Why should reciprocity, the instrument for selecting relationships, for exerting choice, be so lavishly used where an abundance of relationships of other sorts already exists, but not used in areas where social relationships are weak? There is no answer to this in Sahlins' argument, save that reciprocity contributes to the solidarity of the kin group (as if there is insufficient solidarity without it), as yet another trowel load of social cement. It has been argued that, among the Bedouin, debt appears among agnates as an agent of differentiation, and among other kin, particularly at the inception of affinity, to hold people as yet unbound in a moral tie until other forms of relationships supersede it and render it redundant, finally burying it beneath the weight of durable claims, rights and duties of a different order. Debt also deals with peripheral relationships, knitting together their ravelled ends, as a first step in patterning a new design. Debt affects a range of relationships. The work it does is not more, nor of greater significance among kin, whether they be agnates, patrilineal relatives, affines, matrilateral relatives, affines who are agnates (common among the Bedouin) or any of the vast range of kinship complexities which stem from patrilineal parallel cousin marriage, than it is between non-related peoples. As a connection, it is tenuous in reference to the specific relationships it affects; how it affects relationships is not a matter of placing on a scale of importance; what is interesting about debt is that it has the capacity to do so many different kinds of work in so many social anthropologically disparate situations.

The view pressed against Sahlins' argument amounts to saying that a general theory of reciprocity is not possible. Smith (1962) gets to the root of the matter when he states: 'Gifts are indirect investments in social relationships of varying function and form.' Granting that the social relationships in which debt appears among the Bedouin are 'of varying function and form', then debt itself is not the same thing, social anthropologically speaking, when it is found amongst these disparate social relationships. Except in the relationships between a father and son, debt occurs, sometimes momentarily, sometimes ephemerally, sometimes persistently throughout the whole range of Bedouin social relationships. A theory of debt would have to comprehend in it virtually the entire universe of Bedouin social relationships; but since debt is one component among many in any set of social relationships, it is part of a multitude of discrete problems which cannot be wrapped together in a single theory.

Debt in any particular culture is not the mainspring or basis of the structure of a society, any more than, say, agnation, because it sprouts among so many relationships, is the main principle of something called Bedouin society; and matrilaterality, because it is lodged in the vital interconnections between individuals and groups of people who would otherwise remain either discrete in their relationships or suffer a critical lessening of choice in their behaviour, does not thereby become the key to all social processes. Debt (like agnation and matrilaterality) constitutes a part of as many problems as the large number of situations in which it takes root. The ubiquity of a form of relationship does not warrant its elevation to the status of a general theory. The attempts to compare the reciprocity in gift exchange or debt cross-culturally, run into graver difficulties than attempts to theorise from the facts of a single culture. The grand sweeping cross-cultural comparisons of Sahlins – to stick to the example already cited – is sometimes little more than the associative link of words like gift, debt, exchange, and reciprocity, used by authors for acts they have observed in various countries, or translation of words they have heard, and which are heavily loaded with cultural content: and we know that any attempt to compare cultural realities perforce ends in a catalogue of acts of behaviour and beliefs showing which of them are alike and which are unlike.

Thus, it would be futile for me to compare, for the purpose of arriving at generality, the debt that Arensberg (1937: 147–75) writes about in the countryside of Southwest Ireland with debt as it works among the Bedouin, although we both use the same word. Debt among the Irish presumes a heavy dependence on external economic relations, for most of their debt is anchored in the local shops. Some of these shops survive for long periods. The owners of these shops flourish because they control a flourishing network of social relationships and the clientele composing this network are largely the kin of the shopkeeper: farmers who are 'chronically in debt' to him (*ibid.*: 170). The shopkeeper, however, has to pay his suppliers' bills. The debt here is not only the debt of social relationships, but monetary debt as well. If, therefore, a shopkeeper is to guard against the threat of perpetually increasing debt, he must allow for it in his profits. Arensberg states clearly that business 'is no frantic search for better qualities at lower prices', (*ibid.*: 155, 156). And that the owner of 'crossroad shops' charge 'a bit more', and that in the larger country shops, 'The farmers know they pay more' (Arensberg and Kimball 1940, Reprint 1948: 129, 296). It is a common characteristic of this kind of shop that the customers who are fleeced are the shopkeeper's nearest and dearest among his kindred and friends. Some shops weaken and die (Arensberg 1937: 155), and there are those which fail (*ibid.*: 152). These are probably the small shops which are set up in private houses and which, because they are supplied by the larger shops (not by producing firms) operate on slender profit margins; unable to carry the chronic debt of the countryside, they are doomed to die. Suppliers' bills cannot be paid by networks of social relationships. That is to say, the debt relationships of the countryside are not accepted.

Bedouin debt relationships work within a closed circuit where a uniformly accepted morality exists. I have worked in Libya since oil was discovered, and when many Bedouin had migrated recently to towns, villages and plantations. Armed with the morality of the pastoral area they would attempt to establish connections in their new surroundings by giving their sacrifices in the hope that reciprocity, as well as blood, would flow from them. Men who were expert in these techniques looked inept in these changed circumstances, and they could only stand bemused when the realisation that they had made a moral shift as well as a territorial move was forced upon them.

Superficially, there are similarities between the Irish and the Bedouin with regard to debt. Among both it occurs in marriage arrangements; but among the Irish the transfer of wealth is in the form of dowry and among the Bedouin it takes the form of bridewealth; and the social anthropological significance of marriage in the two areas is so widely different that comparison does not suggest itself as a feasibility. The 'non-monetary cooperation', expressed as 'cooring', which Arensberg and Kimball (1948: 75) cite, could be paralleled among the Bedouin, in terms of factual similarities, but when acts of co-operation are placed in their respective Irish and Bedouin contexts, they are seen to be non-comparable, for similarity at an immediate cultural level is not social anthropological comparability. In Ireland the mystical sanction of the curse guards the debt relationships between a shopkeeper and his customer (Arensberg 1937: 174), and ' . . . failure to fulfil the pattern of conduct demanded by extended family obligations leads often to punitive action on the part of the aggrieved party', and this action might take the form of a beating for the defaulter (Arensberg and Kimball 1948: 71). Among the Bedouin the sanction of the curse is present, and I have recorded cases where failure to fulfil debt expectations led to fracas and, in one case, homicide; but the consequences of the curse and the punitive actions are quite unlike. Among the Irish, debt is deep in kinship, as it is among the Bedouin; but it affects the agnates of corporations among Bedouin, and matrilaterality in its significance as the connection between them, to mention only two sets of kin links; among the Irish, corporations are absent and, therefore, matrilaterality is of different significance. This list could be extended *ad nauseam*. This abbreviated list is amply sufficient to dispel any notion of direct comparability between the Irish and Bedouin forms of debt.

In this chapter the concern has been to analyse the Bedouin concept of *dain*. It is based on incremental returns, whether the reciprocity is intended to indicate good will or hostility. It is used to accelerate, retard, suspend or reverse relationships. It is used to perpetuate hostility. It is used to create good fellowship and co-operation, but, because it is selective, the result of deliberate choice, it also makes enemies. It is hedged around by moral constraints, without which it would lose its meaning. It is found among different categories of kin doing different kinds of work. It is used to differentiate among people and, therefore, intimately related to personal status, and to micro-structures of power. Competition between corporations is expressed through it. The perpetual state of hostility in feud is emblematised as *dain*. It precedes marriage and grows with its success. To all relationships, where it occurs, it contributes movement. Debt among the Bedouin is a multitude of problems.

8

Family and marriage

Marriage and the father-son relationship

When a marriage takes place among the Bedouin of Cyrenaica, a nuptial tent is set up some distance away from that of the groom's father.[1] There is no particular significance about the nuptial tent itself, but it must be pitched at a distance so that the father 'will not see it' – although, obviously, in a country of large level plains, it stands out conspicuously. This pretence that the tent remains unseen by the father is pushed to the point of his denying any knowledge of what is afoot. A middle-aged or elderly man with a family adopts a similar attitude to any marriage in which his son participates, as groom or as guest. An elder, the father of three unmarried sons (one of whom, in his late twenties, was known to be getting impatient about marriage), when I asked after his eldest son, insisted that he was away with the camels, although the son was conspicuous in a semicircle of young men encouraging a blindfolded maiden in the movements of her seductive dance outside a wedding tent in his full view. Prior to the wedding festivities, the father will have participated in negotiations, although even in these he will have remained silent, leaving an affine, as a rule, to arrange the details with the girl's father and his kinsmen. The father feigns aloofness from the start of negotiations until after the wedding celebrations have ended. Before inquiring into this seemingly odd behaviour, a few further details of marriage ceremonies need to be mentioned briefly.

The bride is carried to the nuptial tent on a camel, seated in a cagelike structure placed on the camel's back, this canopy covered over with carpets and at least one long blanket – later to be used to divide her tent into male and female quarters – which constitute part of the goods given to a woman on marriage. On her arrival, while she is still seated in her canopy, the camel is led round the tent seven times by a small boy. She then descends and is hustled into the tent by a number of women who make a show of their attempts to conceal her from view. Inside the tent the bride is enclosed in one corner in a kind of cubicle partitioned off by a length of blanket.

In the meantime, the groom has affected to escape, but is 'caught', while running away, by his fellows, who 'compel' him to return to the nuptial tent, to the accompaniment of their lewd songs telling of the sexual pleasures awaiting him. Much of this is horseplay, but the young men carry it out brazenly and the groom is required to show reluctance to continue with the ceremonies. His entry into the nuptial tent is marked by an expectant hush that falls over the crowd of men gathered, as they await the result of the virginity test the groom is about to perform, which he does by wrapping part of his toga round one of his fingers to pierce the hymen. Sharp shrieks from the bride give the signal that the test has been undertaken; not a stir moves the crowd until evidence of its success has been publicly displayed, which is given by the groom hoisting the blood-stained portion of the toga through the corner of the tent on a pole, followed by firing three shots from his rifle. Jubilantly, the men gathered fire volley after volley from their rifles just over the nuptial tent, and the seven-day celebrations begin.

A full descriptive account of a marriage, or many of the ritual details woven into it, need not be given here. What is included is intended to illustrate certain relationships between father and son, and between one generation and another. In this connection two further points are appropriate. First, during the week of festival, young men gather outside the nuptial tent each night to encourage a maiden in her dancing, clapping their hands to the point of injury 'so that we will have a wife soon'. The celebrations belong to the bachelors, and they are the only ones to engage in the singing and hand clapping. It is they too who stop the bridal camel on its way to the nuptial tent to recite obscene rhymes to the bride, and they also shout their rather dubious consolations to the bride who, during the virginity test, crying out for her mother, is assured by them that the night holds promise for her which her mother could never extend. The married men, particularly the close senior agnates of the groom, stay away from it all, discussing matters unconnected with the affair.

Second, the fiction that nothing has happened, which characterises the father's behaviour, does not cease with the termination of the celebrations. Each morning, soon after daybreak and before the camp is astir, the groom must leave his bride and repair to his father's tent to lie at his father's side 'as he always had done in the past, as if he had not left him'. This conventional ruse is followed, not just for the seven days of wedding festivities, but after the groom has moved back into the camp proper, and pitched his tent alongside his father's, with the ropes of the two tents crossing.

In matters other than sleeping arrangements, this fiction that 'nothing has happened' is maintained. Marriage does not mean the immediate creation of a wholly separate domestic unit. Save for the appearance of an additional tent, the ordinary run of daytime activities is scarcely altered. To mention perhaps the most important feature of the relationships between father and son, the groom continues to eat with his father. As yet, the son does not use his own bowl,[2] and may not, indeed, do so for several years. The important symbolism of 'eating together' or 'eating out of the one bowl', the act of commensality creating a bond of fellowship about which Robertson Smith[3] wrote so eloquently can only be referred to here in one of its many aspects. Bedouin themselves stress that eating together is a strong bond, and the communal meal is always used for this purpose after the settlement of a dispute, or at the conclusion of a blood money agreement, and so on. It is significant also in the sense that those who partake of a meal accept the authority of the host; he becomes their protector, and a blow against one of them is struck at him also. Even if the guest is an enemy,[4] as long as he has eaten from another's bowl his life is safe.

The slaughter of an animal for another person creates a bond which has its roots in the intimate connection between man and his animals. In a very vivid way, the Bedouin view their animals as part of themselves, as part of their *rizq*, their general wealth, in which their sons are included. It is this mystical association between a man and his animals which distinguishes a meal consisting of the meat of an animal slaughtered from one's own flock or herd from a meal consisting of meat bought from a butcher's shop – often given by the plateau peoples of northern Cyrenaica to their guests, but which the camel-herding Bedouin of the south regard as despicable hospitality. A slaughtered animal is the food, *par excellence*, which establishes this bond between man and man, although the various cereal dishes which constitute their regular meals are said to have a similar effect.

The son who continues to eat with his father 'as he always had been doing', also continues to accept his authority. Indeed he could do little else at this stage, for he lacks the economic means to cut away. Neither at marriage nor after is there any transfer of wealth from father to son. The new tent recently pitched is no more than a dormitory to which the young couple retire at night. During the daytime the son is still to be seen in his father's tent, and, in the male quarters, things appear to be much the same as before. In the female quarters, the only superficial change is the more frequent appearance among the women of one who, before marriage, often sat among them if she had been a close neighbour or a close cousin previously; or of an additional helper if she had come from afar. On the surface things remain 'as they always have been', although in fact, a whole set of changes have been initiated.

Rites de passage are few among the Bedouin. A man's progress in life is ceremonially marked by only four events: his birth, circumcision, marriage and burial. His development into manhood is not marked by clearly defined stages. About the age of seven, the henna markings on the front of a boy's shirt for protection from the evil eye are not renewed, the cowrie shell stitched to the front of his cap as a kind of talisman against the evil eye is removed and he is no longer permitted free access to the women's quarters. As he grows older, he will be instructed in goat-herding, and later taught to follow the sheep. In his late teens he will have to undertake the more arduous and responsible task of herding the camels. Coincident with camel-herding, he may be given a gun by his father. Shortly afterwards he must undertake the stringent test of manhood, a journey to a distant oasis for dates. These changes are not marked off by a *rite de passage*. The rites a man undergoes during the course of a lifetime are minimal, and in the sense that they are concerned with only the basic events in a man's life anywhere (save for circumcision, which is a minor celebration anyway), they are irreducible. Moreover, the rituals which exist do not comprehend the same multiplicity of relationships as rituals which occur in many other African societies.[5] It is true that the ceremonies referred to in this chapter by no means include all the Bedouin rituals. It is also true that the events mentioned vary in elaboration, and in the number of symbols present in them, but they are not multiplied or reduced for different people.

In this context it is important to stress that we are here dealing with a lineage society where social differentiation is not built up into differences of rank, where the roles to which a man succeeds are almost wholly captured by his kinship relationships with other men and which are sociologically to be distinguished from the roles a man enters into by acquisition of office, membership of associations and so on. The statuses a Bedouin achieves depend not on an ordered acquisition through the inheritance of roles or election to them, but on his personal manipulation of linkages in his jockeying with others. Rites are minimal because there are few defined statuses an individual can predictably acquire. The equalitarianism of the desert denudes the Bedouin of ritual riches. Complementarily, rites which do occur are thrown into exaggerated relief by the absence of others, and in their isolation, become not merely a 'passage' but a cataclysmic change. Marriage and burial both comprehend limited fields of relations, but accompanying ceremonies may bring several hundred people together, people who otherwise rarely gather in these numbers to meet one another as kinsmen and neighbours, and it is suggested that the emphasis given to the events dramatises the significance of the changes they produce. In the discussion of the changes brought about by marriage, the Bedouin view of what is entailed will be considered first.

The Bedouin view of marriage

After marriage, the Bedouin argue, a son has a tent of his own, a woman over whom he has authority and soon children to make him a father. Marriage causes split, branching. A new family is created, holding the potential of a new lineage. The separation is so painful a matter for the father that he cannot contemplate it, hence his pretence that he has no knowledge of wedding festivities, and his subsequent attitude that nothing has happened.

Interestingly, there are two other occasions when this attitude is to be observed. When a man kills within his corporate group,[6] he may flee his tribe or he may be compelled to leave; later he is likely to return and, when he does, he is received with a minimum of show. Every attempt is made to suppress knowledge of the event.

Again, if incest occurs, the memory of it must somehow be suppressed, and it is an ever-present danger. Men, permitted four wives simultaneously and also able to engage in a plurality of marriages through divorce or death of spouses, may have children showing an age difference of two or three generations. Thus it comes about that a man may be of an age in relation to his father's sister which permits them as children to behave as if they were first paternal cousins. As an adult, the preferred spouse for a man is a father's brother's daughter. In terms of relationships between adolescents the situation in which a man is of the same age generation as his father's sister is fraught with danger. In one such case, between a man and his father's sister, the male child of the union was put out in the desert to be devoured by wild animals, the girl was 'given'[7] to a close cousin who had shot his sister. Both now reside with an enemy tribal section. The two acts were equated. They were similar to the extent that both created a situation which defied institutional resolution. The culprits were exorcised. The girl's lover remains with his group – the odium for the male is incomparably less than for the female, since, while maternity is easy to establish, paternity is frequently shrouded in doubt – and during the months I lived with this particular group, there was never a mention of the affair. It was as if 'nothing had happened'.

If asked why these two events cause such profound distress, the answers the Bedouin give are twofold: they can do nothing about them, and they cause split. By split in this context they mean split in the lineage; split in the case of homicide because it may lead to a demand for blood money which is payable only between corporations, and split in the case of incest because it causes chaos in relationships. Marriage, in one sense, their reasoning runs, is similar, for it too causes split. Whatever may be the analytic strength of the arguments that homicide and incest precipitate splitting, the argument that marriage does so is spurious. In what sense can marriage mean split? Bedouin men marry 'so that we may beget many sons, to make a big lineage later on'. The worst fate that can befall a man as a result of his son's marriage is that he, in later generations, will become the focal point in a series of branching descent lines. The alternative – that his sons remain unmarried – can only mean that his name would disappear through want of successors to carry it on, which is one of the greatest evils which can befall a man, according to Bedouin sentiment: better split than oblivion. If the key to the interpretation of the father's attitude to his son's marriage is not that it causes split, it must lie elsewhere in their relationship. What marriage does is alter the distribution of authority between father and son. In order to pursue this, it is necessary first to clarify the types of authority involved, and then assess them in a post-marital situation.

The division of authority between the family and the corporation
Politically, a person's status is determined for him at birth. At this time a man has the right to accept or deny paternity. Denial is tantamount to an accusation of adultery by his wife. In practice, once a wife has given birth to a male child, whatever doubts people may harbour regarding paternity, the husband accepts the child as his. 'The boy for the bed', is a saying often heard among the Bedouin; but it remains the husband's prerogative to invest the child with legitimacy, hence, political status. Only if a husband becomes aware that he is publicly considered a cuckold, or if he catches his wife and a lover *in flagrante delicto*, is he at all likely to take action. Otherwise he may indeed welcome unfaithfulness on his wife's part. If a man is very old, and his wife very young, it is likely that she will entertain lovers; if a man leaves camp for a long absence his wife may not remain chaste. In both cases, if the liaisons lead to the birth of a child, particularly a male, the husband greets the news with unrestrained enthusiasm – 'praise be to God', as their saying goes. Incapacity[8] to produce offspring, if a husband is convinced of it, may lead him to delegate a kinsman to serve his wife for procreative purposes: he has the legal authority, as husband, to do so, and to require his wife to submit, for the only alternative, if he is not to die without 'issue', is to 'take' a son from his brother and fulfil the obligations towards this boy required of a pater, namely, attend to his

circumcision, provide him with teaching in the Koran (a duty neglected by most) and give him the wealth with which to marry.

Granting the acceptance of paternity, whatever the circumstances of conception, a male child, *ipso facto*, accedes to membership of a corporation, and is subject to the authority of that group in a number of matters. In many situations it would appear that a son is under the father's political control. At a moot, the son, if he speaks at all, will do so only to corroborate his father. Discussions among men in a small camp evoke a similar pattern of behaviour. Until the father becomes senile or dies, a son cannot publicly pursue an independent course, but he desists by virtue of his relationships with his father *qua* pater, not because of his father's political power to coerce. All men of a corporation, in any event, 'speak with one word' at a moot, and a son, by his assent to the common view, also supports his father; in so doing he yields to the political authority of his corporation, and not that of his father.

Membership in the corporation invests a man with other privileges and duties. Protection against external enemies comes within the corporation's jurisdiction, although in a particular situation, the father may well be the person who dispenses it. Complementarily, if a man commits an offence against a person not of his group, whatever private thoughts his father may have about the act, the responsibility lies not on his shoulders but on the group, and he is compelled to share this responsibility equally with all other members. For example, if a son commits a homicide the father bears the same legal responsibility for the act, and is under obligation to contribute the same share of blood money as he would if the act had been perpetrated by any male of the group other than his son. Even in a narrower field of relations between father and son the group exercises its authority. Acting as pater, a man may punish his son, physically or otherwise; he may not do so to the point of injury, for personal injury comes within the legitimate sphere of the corporation. A man's 'bone' belongs to his group; he is an integral part of 'the one body'; events which affect a man in this context lie outside a father's field of jurisdiction. The political authority vested in a corporation acts to circumscribe the authority of persons in other fields.

Other rights stem from political membership. As a person with a defined position in a lineage corporation, a man has the right to use the natural resources of its territory. A father, although he instructs his son where to plough and when to water the animals, cannot deny him access to wells, pastures and ploughland. Economically, a son is independent to this extent, although his ability to exploit his right to the natural resources is restricted by his father's control of animals. Ultimately, however, this restriction cannot amount to stultification, because a man has the right to demand food. In practice, a poor man staves off hunger with donations from this or that individual, and superficially it appears that he is dependent on the personal charity of his fellowmen. This is not so, for what is implicit is that the parcels of wealth controlled by individuals are the possessions of the corporation. It is not accidental that poor people do not go hungry. During my entire stay among the Bedouin I never saw one of them beg or suffer hunger, however marginal the diet of many. Clearly, those with a surplus can and do use it for personal advantage, but the extent to which they can do so is circumscribed by the legal claims which members of a corporation have on the parcels of moveable property held by each of them.

Control over the wealth, whether it be animals or the procreative functions of women, rests, in the final analysis, in a corporation. Inheritance laws specify that women are not legal heirs,[9] and that all male children are equal heirs. Women do, in fact, come to control property, and it is rare that wealth is equally divided among male heirs. The precise details of inheritance may partly be decided by a father, but he is limited in his actions. Most of the time inheritance disputes are not of the kind which require action by the corporate group; a case which occurred while I was resident with the Bedouin did, however, invoke immediate action. A man, who had left the desert to live in a village on the plateau, had only one daughter. He made it known that he intended to will his entire property to his daughter. When the news was brought to the camps of his fellow agnates, there was great consternation, because, as became clear in their lengthy discussions, the threat now existed that a substantial parcel of property would be removed from the group, a threat made real by the proposed marriage of the daughter to a man of another tribe. The court would have to recognise the daughter's right to some of the property, and the members of the group reluctantly had to concede that there was little they could do about this, but they had one action left to them – they decided that her nearest agnate should demand her in marriage. Usually, the choice of husband for a daughter is a decision her father takes, but in certain critical situations he can be relieved of choice if the interests of the group as a whole are at stake.

Political authority is the preserve of a corporation, and its exercise leads to invasion of a man's authority in the field of domestic relations. This does not mean, however, that discrete areas of authority do not remain with the father. In the tent his authority over his son is so overwhelming as to keep the son in almost complete subordination. The son is referred to as a slave, and in daily life he has to behave as one. He must obey every command, for were he to rebel, he would find little or no support among his agnates, whatever the extent of the provocation. Retreat from his father is hardly an alternative, since, while his father is alive, he has no animals of his own, and to leave camp would only mean that he would have to move outside his group to seek employment elsewhere as a shepherd. If he did this he would forfeit status, and almost certainly cut himself off from property which would fall to him after his father's death. A man who 'denies' his father loses too many privileges for the practice to become widespread.

Caught in this dilemma, a son's predicament is worsened by the fact that he cannot initiate marriage negotiations – to be able to do so requires some animals to offer a girl's father. Through his mother's brother he has the means of bringing pressure to bear on his father, but the latter can resist for years. Finally, a marriage is arranged for him. It is difficult to convey the yearning of young Bedouin for marriage. They discuss it among themselves *ad nauseam*. For the most part their talk is about the sexual aspect of marriage. Premarital sex relations are strictly controlled, and the movements of each young girl are carefully guarded because, if on the day of her marriage the test shows that she is not a virgin, she not only brings disgrace to her family, but the marriage may be revoked and her worth as a bride for another man seriously diminished. Nevertheless premarital relations do occur, if not between youths and maidens to any extent, between young men and married women.

The question still remains: why is marriage the occasion of such ebullient celebration? The formal authority a father exercises over his son changes little on marriage. Economically the son is still harnessed to the father. The latter still shouts his orders at him, and obedience remains unaltered. Any sign of an independent view on a matter is met with a gruff rebuff. If the marriage turns out to be disagreeable to the father, he has the authority – if not always the power – to break it. Marriage does not mean a change in the general mode of behaviour between the two; the legal relations remain unaltered, albeit modified in practice, as the married son matures in age. But marriage does mean the acquisition of rights and status previously denied a son. Henceforward, he has a domain of his own. This is high drama, indeed, for although every effort is made to give substance to the expressed view that 'nothing has happened', for the first time in his life the son has seized publicly, amid the jubilations of his fellows, a status which hitherto was the possession of the father.

Until marriage the changes in a man's life have been in the nature of an ordered sequence of development from a child to be cared for – the only time in his life when a father, without inhibition, showers on him his love and affection – to one who, by degrees, makes an increasing contribution to a production unit. Marriage necessitates that a man pitch a tent for himself.

With a tent he becomes a potential host and protector of others. The local idiom for marriage is 'to set up a tent'. It would be quite improper to use the verb 'to marry' when inquiring whether a marriage has taken place since this verb also has the meaning of 'to have sexual intercourse'. Instead the euphemism, 'Have you pitched a tent?' is used. The Arabic word for a tent in this context is *bait*. It is not used to refer to a military tent, nor to the small tent which shelters only a widow. It is reserved for the Bedouin tent, which usually has a wool top, and, most importantly, holds the promise of the continuation of life, whether it shelters a newly married couple, a mature family or young unmarried people. (The word *bait* represents a complex concept, and it would be too much of a diversion here to discuss the various points of its significance. It is essential to understand that its meaning is not confined to a tent in the physical sense.) Its top has *baraka* (divine goodness) in it; the quality of *haram*, which makes it possible for the tent to be used as a sanctuary, is associated with it and this quality of *haram* extends, moreover, to the ropes of the tent, so that anyone who clutches them comes under the protection of the owner. In it, the wife must permanently reside and her husband has the legal right to insist on this. In it too, he has the legal right of sexual access to a woman, his wife. Any children born in it he can claim as his own. With the erection of a tent the son reaches adulthood, and it is in this sense that he can be said to have acquired a domain of his own.

Marriage gives a son greater freedom and less dependence on his father in another sense. A second euphemism used for marriage is 'making a relationship', specifically an affinal one. Relationships between a man and his father-in-law are diverse and are used in various ways in different situations. Here, the particular aspect which needs to be stressed is that a man can cajole his father-in-law, and (through his wife) wealth, in the form of animals, may pass from the former to the latter. Reciprocal gifts are passed between affines on certain occasions, but in addition small amounts may pass which are not connected with the formal occasions of exchanges. Debt lies between them. It begins with the initiation of marriage negotiations, when the suitor's kinsmen take a prescribed number of sheep to present to the girl's father if negotiations are successful. They promise to transfer bridewealth[10] to the girl's father. A few weeks after the marriage, the husband is required to take gifts to his mother-in-law in recognition of the fact that she nourished his wife as an infant (the literal meaning of the word used for this gift is 'milk'). A return visit is made and gifts are given to the daughter. When the first child is born an animal is presented by the affines, and if the child is a male, the gift may be several sheep, or even a few camels if the father-in-law is very wealthy. Formal exchange of gifts continue, but, in addition, informal transfers are made. Moreover, if relations between a man and his father-in-law develop favourably, it is not uncommon for a young husband, during the early years of marriage, to move away from his father and pitch his tent alongside that of his father-in-law. Marriage gives a son affinal relations of his own. Affinity can alleviate the dead weight of paternal authority.

It is suggested that the crisis which the marriage of a son assumes for a father is the shift it entails in the distribution of authority. This is borne out by other details in the marriage ceremony referred to earlier. Ordinarily, young men dare not sing within earshot of their senior agnates. Far from allowing obscenities, agnates of the ascending generation would not allow even a mention of women to be made by young men in their presence. In a group consisting of young men and an agnate, I chanced to use the noun for woman and immediately my tent was cleared of all but the senior agnate. At a wedding the young men revel in their lewd songs and shout their obscenities for all to hear. The senior agnates stand aside and make a show of ignoring the proceedings. And well they may, for each marriage is a challenge to the exclusive authority they have enjoyed; each nuptial tent is an invasion of the domain of which they have been undisputed masters. Marriage is the only occasion when the men of one generation can clap and sing their defiance of an older one, and give warning of the changes which must be accommodated however great the pretence that nothing has happened.

Marriage ceremonies dramatise the clash between adjacent generations over the distribution of certain forms of authority. If this authority is as overwhelming as has been suggested, and if it is so deeply resented, how is it that life is endurable for juniors? Relationships between junior and senior agnates are so restrictive that they almost amount to what Professor Fortes has suggested I view as a form of avoidance relationships. Juniors must always defer, they must obey commands promptly, they serve their seniors, they must accept a lead when it is given and the restrictions on conversations exclude all reference to women, marriage or sex. These are not simply a set of general guides for behaviour, they are rigidly applied rules, deviation from which is countered with rebuke or greater severity. It would appear from this that young men spend their premarital lives in an environment of unmitigated agnatic hostility. Greater substance is given to this view when it is realised that agnates live together. The residential concentration of agnates in Cyrenaica exceeds 80 per cent. I wish to stress that this figure is based on the universe of the small camp, and the only males included as agnates are those who are consanguinely related. Over 50 such camps were used in arriving at the figure. Obviously, the figure of agnatic concentration will vary depending on the universe. If all men who claim to belong to a tribe of, say, 15,000 souls, who claim that they are agnates in a political sense are included, then the figure will not be the same as that derived from a small group where the criterion for inclusion is consanguinity, not mere political affiliation. It is necessary to make this clear to emphasise that the Cyrenaican figure is unusually high, and also because the modes of behaviour between consanguineal and political agnates differ critically. Granted the hostility built into agnation, and recognising in addition the significance of the high degree of agnatic concentration, unless there are other factors present in the situation, life would be intolerably burdensome. Parallel-cousin marriage comes to the rescue.

Parallel-cousin marriage

Among the Bedouin the prohibited degrees of marriage are few. A man may not marry within a closer range than first paternal or maternal cousin; he cannot marry a woman of a senior generation, nor a woman known to be older. He cannot marry the daughters of a woman who has acted as wet nurse to him or to any of his brothers and sisters. Otherwise he is permitted to marry any other woman. Marriage with the first paternal cousin is preferred, and is more than a sentiment. A man has a right to his father's brother's daughter, and before a marriage is arranged with anyone else, the girl's father seeks the opinion of his brother's son. If he neglects to do this, or if he flouts the opinion offered him, he runs the risk of the marriage being brought to a halt on the very wedding day. I have witnessed this. In most of the records I possess, it usually happens that the brother's son is bought off with a few sheep (about five) and some articles of clothing. Here the brother's son was seizing the occasion to extort from a father's brother wealth which he considered was due him from an earlier inheritance dispute. Occasionally the intervention is genuinely designed to prevent a marriage; if the girl refuses to marry her father's brother's son, he can force her into spinsterhood. Men exercise their right to marry their first parallel cousins. They also marry other parallel cousins. The significance of parallel-cousin marriage varies with the exact degree of the relationship. First- and, say, third-parallel cousins are sociologically different in a number of respects, and in relation to specific problems these differences may assume major importance. In the present discussion the various degrees have this in common: that whatever the precise relationship, all parallel cousins are the daughters of agnates and, in view of the high agnatic concentration, the daughters of agnates who are co-residents as well. Parallel-cousin marriage therefore creates affinity between co-resident agnates.

The rate of parallel-cousin marriage is high, producing such a density of kinship relationships as to afford a reliable index for defining the agnatic corporation. As a form of marriage it persists; genealogical records clearly demonstrate this. Frequency of parallel-cousin marriage taken together with its persistency, means, above all else, that it makes an agnatic group a cognatic group as well. The matter is put in this way to suit the general development of the argument, but it would be a serious error to think that this means I am giving priority to agnation and that I am considering cognation as intrusive, or that, in this society, agnation can stand on its own because it has a kind of absolute significance other forms of relationship do not possess. Both forms exist in reality.

The great Bu Bakr of Cyrenaica's most celebrated lineage is alleged to have exhorted his fellow tribesmen to 'marry your father's brother's daughters and then your paternal relatives and your maternal relatives will become one'. Whether he had given the advice or not, the Bedouin, as their society is constituted, would marry them anyway. The Bedouin form of agnation without its accompanying parallel-cousin marriage would impose impossible restrictions, if indeed there is any point in attempting to conceive of a situation so remote from reality. With parallel-cousin marriage present in the corporate group, men referred to as agnates are not agnates only; each and every one of them is the centre of a bundle of roles, each role potentially as important as the other. It would be false to argue, moreover, that complexities of relationships can be unravelled by analytically separating them, giving precedence to the agnatic role in an 'agnatic' situation, the mother's brother's role in a domestic situation and so on. An agnate who is also a mother's brother is never the same, in any situation, as an agnate to whom one is not otherwise related. The prime significance of parallel-cousin marriage is that it creates a complexity of linkages which almost amount to confusion, thereby maximising the choice available to individuals to meet whatever contingencies befall them.

The only area of relationships left relatively undisturbed by parallel-cousin marriage is the son, father and father's brother triangle. Freed of the complications stemming from parallel-cousin marriage, agnation can here approximate its true form. Other complications arise out of marriage. A few are listed here: father and son marry a mother and her daughter; a form of exchange marriage between first parallel-cousins occurs; two brothers marry two sisters; the marriage of two brothers to two sisters is followed, in the succeeding generation, by the son of one union marrying the daughter of the other, making this latter a double first parallel-cousin marriage – both a father's brother's daughter's and a mother's sister's daughter's marriage. These forms can all occur within a corporate group. No citadel of agnation can withstand this attack. All forms of marriage combine to break the grip of agnation on the members of a corporate group and give it a taproot of diversity whence it derives its strength, and which makes of it 'the one body', conspicuous, in comparison with other societies, as the corporate group *par excellence.*

The sister's son-mother's brother relationship

Previously the mode of relationship associated with agnation and affinity has been briefly discussed. In order to appreciate the effects of parallel-cousin marriage, some remarks concerning the sister's son-mother's brother set of relationships must be included here. Bedouin contrast the mother's brother with the father's brother; their sayings and proverbs afford a wealth of verbal documentation on the contrast. With the mother's brother a man enjoys all the freedoms he is denied in his relationships with his father and father's brother. He is permitted to joke with him; they indulge in exchanges of obscenities. When the sister's son wishes to marry, he is permitted to discuss the matter with his mother's brother and can urge him to intercede with his father on his behalf. Two men thus related are readily recognised in the camps, because in their acts they are required to show affection by displays of innocent horseplay, pranks or mild practical jokes. Small boys pursue their mother's brother, feign to kick or strike him, and he takes it all in good part.

The external aspects of this behaviour are deceptive. Joking of this sort creates the image in which the relationships are conceived; what is equally striking is its compulsiveness. Obviously, mature men are not always in the mood to be teased, but if they are, they must respond appropriately. Their relationships are unmistakably onerous. This remark applies not only to the external forms of their behaviour, but also the favours a man is permitted to ask of his mother's brother. A brief amplification will make the point clear. Demands can be made of agnates, but only in situations of serious contingency. Day-to-day needs are met, not by appeals to the rights of agnation, but from the expectations linked to the mother's brother. If these expectations are withheld, the sister's son may be left in a quandary. Interestingly, in the records of homicides I gathered, three (in the contemporary population) were concerned with the killings of mother's brothers by sister's sons. Homicide within this field of relationship is difficult to comprehend unless it is appreciated that expectations are as compulsive in the daily life and the general well-being of people as are the rights and duties associated with agnation.

These general remarks apply to the relationships irrespective of the lineage origin of the mother's brother. The similarity ends there, since the nature of the expectations, their urgency at any given moment and the kind of favours which are granted vary with the group identity of the mother's brother. A mother's brother who is a member of ego's corporate group may be expected to give the sister's son small quantities of flour, favour him in all sorts of petty ways, listen to his grumbles about his agnates, interfere on his behalf in petty camp quarrels, shield him from the disciplinarian father and guard his property interests against the predatory father's brother; if the mother's brother dies without heirs, the sister's son can reasonably expect at least a share of his wealth. When the mother's brother is a member of a different corporate group, a sister's son cannot possibly expect to inherit from him in any circumstance.

The mother's brother may reside in a camp too distant to be of much effective direct help in day-to-day living. His relative remoteness gives the relationship other possible opportunities, however. Rainfall in the semi-desert area of Cyrenaica is highly variable, both from year to year, and from place to place in any given year. As a result this shallow saucer of a depression may have sufficient rain to supply both the water needs of animals and crops, while an area a few miles distant will have inadequate water supplies for either. The mother's brother-sister's son link can mean water for animals and a crop of barley for both when, in successive years, the resources of one area or the other are inadequate.

The differences in the relations between men and their mother's brother do not end with a characterisation of their antipodal forms. The demographic structure of a group may be such that one man may have a number of mother's brothers, another only one; one man may have to share with several brothers, another may be an only son. Complications of this sort determine the precise relationships between men, but however intricate these may be, each corporate group has its matrilateral links with a group occupying a slightly different ecological area, and it also has a plurality of matrilateral connections within it. Further, if a direct connection is not available to any particular individual he can use an indirect link (e.g. father's mother's brother or mother's mother's brother) to satisfy his needs.

The preference for males

Thus far the family and the social matrix in which it is embedded has been discussed in general terms, most particularly in reference to several selected sets of relationships. I wish now to place these relationships in a more specific setting with a brief discussion of the composition of a small camp of a group inhabiting the arid areas of central Cyrenaica. When the Bedouin give their views on the structure of the family in Cyrenaica they speak of it as consisting of a pair of spouses and about ten children, mainly males. The emphasis on males is not mere sentiment, overwhelmingly though it favours them against females. Additional males in a family increase the productive possibilities of a family in the sense that more herdsmen become available and larger ploughing commitments can be undertaken; an increase in the number of females has small effect on production since they are precluded from any direct participation in these activities. Both sexes, ranging in age from about seven years to mature adulthood, are necessary if a family is to constitute a viable economic unit; and if it is to expand, the number of males must be increased disproportionately compared with females. Since the structure of this 'ideal family' (which in the sentiments of the Bedouin is the only family) is based on the division of labour, some details of the tasks and their allocation among members of a family are included to estimate the importance of this notional 'ideal family'.

The division of labour, by sex

The tasks women perform are almost entirely associated with the tent. They make the tent top, and the gaily coloured carpets which cover the sandy ground in the men's quarters. They also weave the material for making sacks, and nose bags for horses and camels. Throughout the year a piece of weaving is always on the loom waiting, and while any women of the tent may take a turn at weaving, the mother decides what is to be made, its pattern and colours and in general directs operations. Women also pitch the tent when the camp is moved; they do so unaided by the men. It is a task which requires considerable strength and only grown girls and mature women can assist in this; younger girls scour the vicinity in search of stones to hold the sides of the tent on the ground after it has been erected. As soon as pitching is complete, the floor of the tent is brushed clean before carpets are spread and the few articles of personal belongings placed in their proper positions.

Next, brushwood must be fetched in large quantities for fires. Apart from cooking needs and winter warmth, the fire of each tent is in constant use for preparing the sickly sweet tea, almost the consistency of syrup, which is drunk several times a day regularly and which is made again for even the casual visitor. The task of fetching brushwood is performed daily, and each load takes a few hours of a woman's time to gather and bring back to the tent. Bushes are uprooted with the aid of a long-handled adze and piled together, to be carried on her back for the homeward journey. The load is cumbersome and heavy; only girls in their late teens and mature women can cope with it.

All cooking is done by the women. Most meals consist of cereal dishes of various sorts, so that grinding, using heavy millstones, is a perpetual activity to satisfy the demands for large quantities of flour. Millstones are bought in the villages. In most small camps there are only one or two sets, so they are passed round from one woman to another. The stones are very heavy but when they are carried from tent to tent men offer no assistance.

Each tent also requires large quantities of water for human consumption. If the camp is located near a well, water is drawn in small quantities, frequently. Young girls and boys take a donkey to the well, fill a couple of jerry cans with water, wait for an older sister to load them on the donkey and then drive the beast back to camp. After a fall of rain, while puddles of water remain on the ground, mature women make haste to gather the surface water in jerry cans, bringing them back to the tents, one at a time, on their backs. Clothes are kept clean in the desert, and the women do the washing.

The care of children from birth until they are a few years old is the responsibility of the woman. Childbirth causes a minimum interruption in the daily sequence of a mother's activities. The child is breastfed if the mother has milk; if not, a wet nurse is sought or goat milk is substituted. Other than the time given to feeding it, the infant does not take up much of the mother's time. It is placed in a hammock slung between the centre poles of the tent and rocked by the mother as she passes to and fro. If nursing in illness is required, the mother devotes herself to it; her other tasks must then be performed by another woman.

As children acquire mobility, and at a time when, perhaps, the mother is pregnant again, they become so fractious one with the other that if help was unavailable the nervous strain could seriously disrupt the normal routine of work. During the early years of marriage, when daughters are still too young to look after their small brothers and sisters, the grandmother's help in child-rearing is invaluable. Too old for the arduous tasks of the daily routine, she may assist in teasing and spinning the raw wool, but it is in her role as nursemaid that she assumes importance. Children of both sexes are given the comfort of suckling at her breast, receiving attention and care for which the young mother could not possibly afford the time.

Caring for children takes up little of a man's time, and is mostly incidental. The woman, on the other hand, devotes relatively little of her time to the animals. She does the milking in spring – of camels, sheep and goats – but herding is not her responsibility, save for partly tending goats. Goats, when they are in the vicinity of the camp, are looked after by boys and girls of about eight to ten years of age. In springtime when they have dropped their young, or if some of them have to be retained in the camp at night for various reasons, the woman makes a brushwood enclosure at the side of the tent and sees the goats safely inside before nightfall.

A catalogue of the tasks for which women are responsible may not seem very impressive; the number of tasks is not excessive, but the persistence of the routine bends the backs of most women. Paradoxically, any suggestion that men should take over female tasks would strike them as absurd. Assistance from one of the same sex is always a welcome relief, but the abrogation of a particular task by men would be interpreted by women as the loss of a right. For, in the division of labour, it is not merely that tasks are allocated between the sexes for expedient reasons, or in consideration of the labour involved or because tasks which can be performed in the vicinity of the camp are left to women; division of labour would not make sense on these grounds, however strong they may be in Bedouin sentiments. Each task which falls to the lot of woman constitutes a right exclusive to her. Fetching firewood is not only a chore; it is a woman's prerogative. The insistence that only a woman can undertake certain tasks has nothing to do with her liking them or any innate aptitude for them; this insistence is an index of the jealousy with which she is prepared to guard her rights. Each right derived from this or that small task is an extension of her control over the male.

The force and significance of this control are, perhaps, best seen in a woman's right to cook. At marriage a woman must have at least the minimum of cooking utensils, and one of the rights a man acquires in a woman is that she cooks for him. This is something a man cannot do for himself. Therefore, when a man ill-treats his wife or threatens her with divorce, she can retaliate by refusing to cook, or leave the tent altogether to return to her father. A man bereft of this service is in a very sorry plight indeed. The legal dominance of the male, seemingly autocratic, is reduced at every point by the control a woman exercises through her exclusive right to perform tasks. The limits to the area of her coercive powers are significant. They are confined almost wholly to domestic relationships. Legally, women suffer such disabilities that they are almost of the status of minors; in reality, their day-to-day living is far from intolerable because they are able to control males over a wide field of relationships.

Men, excluded in the main from domestic duties around the tent, perform tasks to which their legal rights are tied. While women have access to wells for water used by human beings, the transport of larger quantities of water over longer distances, requiring the use of camels, is a task which falls to the men. Watering of animals is done by men. Only they can slaughter the animals for food. The meat of an animal slaughtered by a woman is not 'free', in a ritual sense, for human consumption. In an extremity only, a woman can, in effect, kill an animal, but the knife which cuts its throat must be held in a male hand, even if it is the hand of a very small boy. The exploitation of the land is also the males' prerogative. They plough and sow the grain; incidental help may be provided by wives working alongside their husbands during the early part of reaping, but the main reaping is done entirely by men. Transportation of grain to the mounds is also carried out by men, and it is they who have access to the grain stores when quantities are withdrawn for family use. Sheep-shearing is carried out entirely by males, the fleeces are stacked by them and the distribution and sale of these is directed by the male head of the tent.

Additional to these major tasks which males undertake are a number of minor ones. Men sew strips of cotton together to make clothes for both sexes. They also make rope of grass, albeit in a desultory sort of way, by twisting together the strands between the palms of the hands. A number of other tasks fall to the men by virtue of the fact that the sexes are separated in the tent by a divider of blanket material, which may be taken down when only members of the elementary family are about, but which is put in position immediately anyone else appears at the entrance to the tent.[11] Women cook, but they do not serve the meal to males, nor are they responsible for the distribution of meat among them. Parts of an animal are carefully specified, and the various portions distributed at a meal carry with them a great deal of significance. A host can honour, flatter, disappoint or even insult his guest, depending on the precise distribution of meat he adopts. Designated portions should go to certain kinsmen if they are present, but this still leaves a wide margin of choice, and a host can use this choice as part of the many means at his disposal for directing his relationships with other men. A political link can be forged or another snapped by the distribution of portions of meat at the commensal meal.

The Bedouin ideal type of family as a unit of production
This account of the division of labour is far from inclusive of all the tasks carried out. The details given are only barely sufficient to provide some indication of the necessary composition of a family. Referring again to the Bedouin sentiments about the matter, it is now possible to give it some numerical precision. The number of females should be a minimum of about three, including a mother, a teenage daughter and a child of about eight years. Males should number about six: a father, relieved of most chores to act as director; a son in his middle to late twenties, to plough; a second son, in his early to middle twenties, to herd the camels; a third, in his late teens to early twenties, to shepherd the sheep; a fourth, middle to late teens, to look after the goats; and a younger son to fetch, carry and run errands about the camp. The family of the ordinary Bedouin, they say, shows this sex and age distribution, although they recognise that a politically ambitious man with the wealth to match his aspirations would require more of both sexes – particularly women, since the burden of entertainment increases rapidly with a man's climb to power and fame.

Clearly, the basis of Bedouin sentiment concerning family structure is its approximation to an ideal production unit. Some families display the features of this ideal, but even they enjoy the productive benefits of this composition for a very limited period only. The family, as described above, can only be an ephemeral unit, since the age structure constantly changes, women are removed by marriage, men move away and death affects it at any point at any time. The Bedouin family is a fiction in the sense that it can be said to have a characteristic composition. The mistake they make is to conceive of it as a particular kinship structure related to production. The substance of what has been referred to as a fiction is that, if viewed as a productive unit, it bears close consistency with reality. Freed of the need to examine it in terms of specifically limited kinship relationships, and no longer anchored to the inhabitants of a single tent, the distribution of people according to sex and age depicted in their notion of a family is meaningful. It follows that, since this unit will not be clustered in one tent, but distributed over several, each small community must be so constituted that links people can use to claim the services of others must exist, and that, since claims can be made against various sorts of kinship relationships, each small camp will have predictable kin links. It follows, further, that since age, sex and number of people are significant, a small camp will have a characteristic demographic structure; each tent in a camp will display developmental changes, and particular tents may be shifted from one camp to another, but if a livelihood is to be gained in this semi-desert environment supporting its mixed pastoral-cum-agricultural economy, then at any given time the small camp must have certain fixed features in its composition. The elementary family is subject to far too many vicissitudes to exist on its own. It now remains to demonstrate this general argument by examining the details of one of these small camps.

A particular camp viewed in detail

The camp was one of 12 which constitute a minimal tribal section. In genealogical terms its male members were genealogically linked through an ancestor five ascending generations from living males of about 20 years of age. Usually, in summer, camps of this sort move to the vicinity of a large watering point; in winter, this larger community breaks up into a number of smaller ones as men and animals move off further south to the pastures. The total living population of the tribal section to which this particular camp belonged was 524.

Linked patrilineally, its male members were also linked in a plurality of other consanguineal ways. Primarily, this plurality was brought about by parallel-cousin marriage. The incidence of this form of marriage for males of this group was 48 percent[12] of the gross total of 234, derived from their marriages over three generations; that is, the generation of males entering into marriage, and the generation which has begun to die out are included with the generation of middle-aged males. This means that practically every male is related to others in a number of ways, and it is necessary to point this out now because the details to be given presently will show only the more immediate, but not all, existing connections. Plurality of links, moreover, is not the only consequence. Parallel-cousin marriage is a transmuting agent, creating a diversity of links. Each and every link carries with it specific modes of behaviour, which in turn means that each individual has a wide variety of different claims he can press on his co-residents. Marriage connections also exist with other sections of the same tribe. Their proportion is 28 per cent of the total. Demographically, it would be impossible to satisfy all marriage expectations of men within the universe of the minimal tribal section. For this reason alone external links are inevitable and persistent. Also, the small territorial strip such a group claims as a homeland produces an economy which, in this environment, is unstable. Additional security is gained by making connections with other tribal sections, each with its specific ecological character. Men also marry into their client groups. The proportion of these for this camp was 9 per cent of the total. From these links they gain economic advantages, they can claim services and a client-following is politically significant. Finally, 7 percent of the total[13] are marriages with women of other tribes, which again not only reduces the instability of the economy (in that a large tribal area suffering near-famine conditions has access to areas of markedly different ecology), but also provides political connections for men whose power ambitions have passed the point of leadership limited to their own tribes. In one way or another all these interests are manifest in the small camp and attention is now directed to the latter.

The disposition of people in the camp is represented diagrammatically in fig. 8.

The nucleus of the camp is Tent A. Its owner (1) was a powerful shaikh, the son of a famous father. His marriage represents a political link with a group of one of the primary sections of his own tribe. His father died only a few years before I recorded my census, and the large amount of moveable property he left had still not been divided among the sons; the owner of the tent, as eldest brother, still controlled the flocks and herds. Most of his time he spent away from the camp engaging in political intrigue. His two younger brothers lived in his tent, but the second (5) would not remain there long because negotiations for his marriage had been started. His father (2) married a parallel cousin; she died and shortly afterwards he took her sister (3) in sororal union. When this occurred an amount of bridewealth was agreed, but instead of giving any of it to her father, the entire amount was 'put in front of her' (that is, the animals were allowed to remain with her husband's flock), and these animals she had marked with her brother's tribal sign to distinguish them from those of her husband. It was widely known that she was going to leave these animals to her husband's second son, for although she could not transfer them to a male outside her husband's corporate group, she could decide who, among his heirs, should inherit.

During my stay in this camp, her brother's (4) son came as a temporary resident for a month. Since he was poor, the purpose of his visit was to capture some of his aunt's wealth while she was still alive and the possibility

Figure 8.

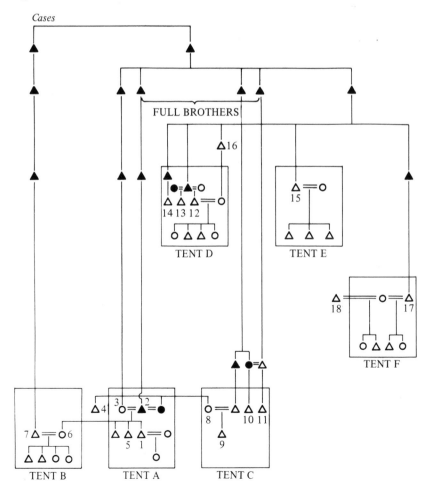

still existed. During his stay he was fed well but did not work. His kinsmen found his company tiresome, so, to cut short his stay, and after consulting her nominated heir (5), she gave him three grown goats. Also when an occasion arose for an animal slaughter, she provided the sheep, and since meat is shared by all the people of the camp, her wealth was partly dispersed among her poorer kinsfolk.

The location of Tent B was determined by the fact that the wife (6) was the niece of (3) of Tent A. Her husband (7) had moved into the camp a few years earlier as a result of an inheritance quarrel with his elder brother who robbed him of his fair share. This husband (7) gained in two ways from the move. Although poor, he had a small flock of his own, too small to justify its own shepherd, but which he was permitted to include with his wife's aunt (3) flock for shepherding. If the flock had been larger he would still have had difficulties, because at some times of the year, save for short occasional visits to camp, the shepherd is with his sheep for several weeks, day and night. He (7) had three sons, still far too young to follow the sheep, but when they become of age to do so, his dependence on Tent A will cease, for then he can begin to gather the small flocks of other kinsmen around his own, his sons can shepherd them all and he can begin to enjoy the benefits to be derived from dependents. In addition, he enjoyed the lavish generosity dispensed by the members of Tent A, and fed far better than would have been possible otherwise.

The location of Tent C was also determined by a link through women. The only female (8), living in this tent, a middle-aged widow, was the sister of (3) and aunt of (6) of Tents A and B respectively. Her teenage son lived with her. They possessed only a few sheep, which were put with the flock of Tent A for shepherding. The son, (9), spent some of his time herding for Tent A. With the mother and her son in Tent C were two other kinsmen. One, a poor man, (10), was this son's first patrilateral cousin, and they both were the only surviving sons of their respective fathers. He, (10), was the main shepherd of Tent A. The third male, (11), also poor and nearly blind, was a close patrilateral cousin of both, but his sister was also 10's mother. All occupants of Tent C were almost entirely supported by Tent A. Relieved of the necessity to live off their own resources, the two young men (9 and 10) were afforded the opportunity of building up their flocks for the day when they would be able to negotiate their delayed marriages.

Tents A, B and C sheltered men who were agnatically closely linked. More important, their grandfathers, three sons in a family of 19 children, were full brothers. The latters' mother's name was used when referring to these three tents as a group. During the past few years, many changes have occurred within it, and the death of the pivotal woman, (3), of Tent A might well disperse this small cluster. Further, the nuptials of her heir, (5), were anticipated, and this event, itself likely to precipitate division of his father's (2) wealth, might also lead to further residential rearrangements.

The owner of Tent D, (12), a man in his later thirties, son of a slave mother, was at loggerheads with his father's brother, much more senior in age. The owner's father, one of a family of 24 children, had been a wealthy man and died leaving a substantial herd and a large flock, but he, (12), was bereft of most of this wealth by the father's brother. His first successful strike against his uncle was the demand he made for his daughter as a wife. Earlier, when (12) had demanded his father's wealth, his father's brother, who had for years acted as his guardian, replied, 'It is in your stomach', (meaning that it had been expended on his upbringing). Later, after the marriage had taken place, when the uncle demanded payment of the bridewealth his own words were thrown back at him, but this time with the meaning that the bridewealth had already been paid. While I was resident in this area, the two men met occasionally: each meeting was hostile, for (12) was encouraging his half-brother, (13), (also the son of a slave mother) to demand a second daughter as a wife. Included in this tent was a third adult male, (14), virtually a pauper, reduced to this state by the same grasping father's brother. His link with (12) was their closeness of relationship (first paternal cousin), together with the fact that all three males, (12, 13 and 14), had suffered privations and were allies against the common enemy, their father's brother.

Associated with them for the same reason, was the owner of Tent E (15). Genealogically he was their father's brother, but he was of their same age and generation, and behaved as if he was their agnatic equal. Towards his own brother, (16), he behaved as if the latter were his uncle, for he was much his senior in age and had virtually brought him up from boyhood. They had quarrelled bitterly because his brother, (16), had given him only a fraction of his inheritance, which he himself, in turn, should have shared with his young full brother (not shown on the diagram) but he did not do so. This youngest brother left (15) for this reason and now resides with (16), his full brother's enemy. Two of the men, (14 and 13), of this group of four were the chief herdsmen of the camp, although they were assisted for short periods by (12) and (15), who also helped tend the camels in other ways. Their connection with the group centred on Tent A was a mutual close link to a politically powerful person (not shown on the genealogies) to whom they were deeply loyal and who, while I was among them, was actively opposed to the common political enemy of them all, (16), and who in earlier years had challenged the leadership of (2) of Tent A. There is also the fact that they were all linked within a closer range of agnation. This linkage included, too, the owner of Tent F, (17), not in fact the descendant of the man shown in the diagram – he was the son of a slave wife; his genitor was a slave, but his mothers master reared him, freed him and he is now given as his son in the genealogy. He lives with his wife, of client origin, together with her children. Aging, he no longer acted as a regular herdsman, but relieved other men in the camp, and also spent some time shepherding.

The details given of the strands which run through the camp to tie these particular people together are so few that, like the Bedouin plough, they do no more than scratch the surface, but they are sufficient to permit a few general statements. The camp, and particularly the precise disposition of its tents, shows a group of males clustered together to share two of the main economic tasks: shepherding and herding. The physically strong adult males of Tents D and E shoulder the burden of herding all the camels of the camp, and the men of Tents B, A and C shepherd all the sheep, with (17) of Tent F serving both purposes. This number of men allows some to remain in the camp at all times, to free one of them for a journey to the distant market when supplies of sugar and tea are necessary, and to enable one or two men, at short notice, to hurry away on horse or camel to search for lost animals.

Economic determinants of the general structure of the camp

It is also clear from these details that, given the disparities in wealth (although all men have some wealth), the diet of most is considerably ameliorated in its protein content, particularly by the generosity of the occupants of the nucleating Tent A. Not that they are the only ones who ever slaughter their animals for food. Others do so, albeit much less frequently. Whoever kills an animal, everyone present in the camp is given a share, and the men always eat in the tent of the donor, sitting around one bowl. Thus, the surplus that builds up at one point is redistributed among those suffering a shortage, and meat, in a society where the climate and way of life militate against its storage for more than a few days, is more efficiently used. Many other general economic points could be deduced. These general statements could, however, be made of practically any camp, whatever the specific differences.

Affinity and matrilaterality in the structure of the camp

Economic considerations determine the general structure of these small camps, but do not account for the particular people gathered in them. Perhaps one of the most striking features of these camps, which comes out clearly in the one discussed here, is the confined agnatic span which links the males. Lest it be underestimated, I wish to stress the profound significance of this fact. While granting its importance it is equally necessary to stress that the span, potentially, could be considerably reduced; in some camps it is. Many of the closer agnates of the men of this camp are not shown on the genealogy included with the diagram; (7), (15) and (16), for example, all have brothers, (12) has a large number of first paternal cousins and so on. Therefore, this particular cluster of agnates formed for reasons other than agnatic ties. The most direct single thread connecting Tents A, B and C is that which runs through women. Men of many other camps are all linked in this way, directly. Five tents of this camp are connected through a female link to a common ancestress, whose name still defines the group, two ascending generations from one adult male, three from others and four from others. If greater elboration could have been shown on the genealogy without confusion, additional links through women could have been demonstrated. Affinity and matrilaterality are the prime movers in bringing agnates together as neighbours.

Other factors affecting the structure of the camp
Other considerations narrow the area in choice of residence. The quest for power where every man entertains hope of achievement, where ambitions are not stifled by the rigour of rank and a small amount of wealth provides a basis for a beginning is also a significant factor in considering the composition of camps. The generosity of the people in Tent A was not entirely altruistic. Justly, it had won them repute, but the repute itself was an important aspect of the political power they enjoyed. They also acquired the services of several men to manage their animals, an impossible strain for them alone. And with their shepherds and herdsmen they secured devoted followers. It was hinted in discussing the structure of the camp that changes were imminent, because the marriages of two of the men were anticipated, two others harboured more distant hopes and boys in all the tents would soon be youths. The composition of this camp, caught at a moment in time, was a function of the age and sex distribution of its inhabitants. All camps show regularities in their structure, but their content is dynamic. Certain general features persist, but the alignments of people undergo change with equal persistency. What priority is given to each of these considerations, which component occupies the nucleating centre for others, will depend on the problem under analysis, for while I have stressed that this or that is important, I do not wish to suggest that any single factor has an absolute importance compared with others, except in relation to a specific problem.

9

Bridewealth

Bridewealth, coupled with exogamy, has long been viewed as a means of bringing together otherwise unconnected lineage segments or clans. The overall effect of these separate alliances is seen as 'knitting the whole system together'.[1] Several assumptions are contained in this view. First, it assumes that the political separation of segments in a lineage system is so complete that groups are left virtually isolated. Second, it is only marriage, and the property transfer it entails as bridewealth, that can interlace these groups, by the kinship it creates: in some societies, kinship appears to be so urgent a necessity that even affinity passes for it. Many who would vehemently deny the mystique which, allegedly, Fortes bestows on kinship, ascribe to it in this context, with a curious twist of logic, a binding force which would probably make Fortes himself demur. Third, despite the immediate effect attributed to exogamous marriage, and its extension through delayed transfers of bridewealth, the bond it creates must be short-lived, since each and every marriage must be exogamous and connect otherwise autonomous peoples. The power of the link, that is to say, resides almost exclusively in affinity, and when this becomes transmuted into kinship it ceases. Fourth, to give the link strength the wife must be incorporated into the receiving lineage. Gluckman (1950) attached such importance to this that the stability of marriage in African societies, in his view, was based on the extent to which wives were incorporated, the bridewealth being the main instrument in this, with other forms of marriage (levirate, sororate and so on) serving as corroboration.[2] Fifth, since exogamy with bridewealth knits, binds or cements 'the whole system', then exogamous marriages need to be dispersed to the maximum extent – and it is worth noting that precisely the same metaphors are used to explain the function of bridewealth among Arabs, who marry their first or other patrilateral parallel cousins![3] Bridewealth is thus spread like a blanket over the whole population, since the number of clans is always limited. Sixth, although exogamy is accompanied by other marriage rules (which, if taken together, would appear to make the task of finding a marriage partner difficult or impossible), precedence is given to exogamy, certainly in explaining bridewealth. In the effect on marriage patterns, it is suggested that this is unwarranted precedence, because the accompanying rules relating to prohibitions of certain kin are equally important, and in some cases the latter might be more selective, in practice at least. Seventh, stress is placed upon exogamy because anthropologists give it its full jural force as an implacable rule; people practising it might view it differently, not only as one rule among many, but as a rule of thumb possessing considerable mutability. Finally, the assumption is made that exogamous marriage interconnects people throughout all the clans in a maze of cross-cutting ties, whereas a few well chosen links with otherwise unrelated groups would be much more effective. Why should a particular lineage need to have links into all clans and, indeed, into most of their segments?

While assumptions of this sort are regularly made, the details of particular cases lead to quite other views of exogamy. Thus, although Nuer clans and lineages are exogamous,[4] the prohibition on marriage to daughters of clansmen applies with equal force to all kin of any kind,[5] even if the relationship is through a third person.[6] Yet, a Nuer is able to establish kinship with any other Nuer he meets at any time during his life, anywhere in Nuerland.[7] Obviously, if the rules, taken together, were applied, Nuer would be unable to marry. Evans-Pritchard is careful to qualify the rules – or, to be more precise, to add other rules – relating to kinship, in the statement that different ranges of kinship are recognised for different purposes, and that known kinship can be ignored as easily as tenuous kinship can be made crucial, as suits the circumstances.[8] Even the boundaries of clans and lineages are not inviolable, and if there is ambiguity about a particular case of marriage, it can be resolved by ritually splitting a gourd: clan exogamy is 'not unalterable'.[9]

There is no suggestion in this that the rules matter so little that they are given to whimsical alteration. The suggestion is that any of the rules are of importance in circumstances where their application is required. Clan exogamy ceases to be a bar when people decide that the agnatic relationship is too distant, or when they reach a local consensus about restricting the span of a clan. Similarly, kinship can be adjudged to be too distant to impose a bar on a marriage. In short, particular cases require to be negotiated by taking account of all the rules – a wholly different matter from manipulating the rules to suit individual convenience.

This does not mean the absence of an exogamous unit among the Nuer.

Represented in a village is an agnatic core, with a gathering of cognates around it. The people residing in it are drawn together by tribal 'bulls',[10] who rally the agnatic core of which the 'bull' is the leading member, and which includes some of his affines and matrilateral relatives.[11] Among these co-residents kinship is close, possibly according to the degree of consanguinity, certainly in a general social sense. It is this effective kinship which composes the local community into a *de facto* exogamous unit.[12] That is to say, the rules of thumb which prohibit marriage between clan members and kin are subject to rules relating to propinquity. Consanguinity and residence both count – members of a local agnatic core come under the ban of exogamy, whether the agnatic connection be close or relatively distant, and kinship further excludes marriage, however it is traced, directly or indirectly, or through affinity. What makes exogamy (with regard to clan origin or kinship) effective is co-residence.

It is characteristic of the Nuer that they move about a great deal. Seasonal variations in climate, vegetation and water compels annual transhumance from the wet season villages, above the floods, to pastures, as the waters recede, and thence to waterholes or streams during the winter drought. During these moves people from different villages spend time together, first in small camps at the beginning of the drought, and in winter kinsmen of different villages may spend the season together in a large camp. Apart from these seasonal moves, Nuer also change their village residence.[13] All Nuer aim to become 'bulls' – to be able to lead a local community – having as followers a few agnates, maternal relatives and affines; and in furtherance of this aim brothers and cousins part company.[14] The manner in which village communities split is patterned. Nuclei of kin form, and congregate to occupy different sections of a village.[15] These same people marry outside the bounds of their village to people in neighbouring villages, so that kin in the latter aggregate to a kin nucleus in the former. When a 'bull' emerges, he takes with him his local nucleus and the aggregated kin from elsewhere, thus constituting a new residential unit of pre-determined and effective kin, exogamous from the outset, but enjoying a new freedom to marry in the neighbourhood because of the shift in residence. Effective kinship is intense among the people of this newly constituted residential unit, bridewealth cannot be passed between them, and in its absence they have become exogamous.

Bridewealth, even where a rule of exogamy exists, does not act as a palliative gift or compensation for the acquisition of rights in the daughters of enemies, despite the abundant proverbial wisdom often quoted to this effect. 'Enemy' is, perhaps, an inappropriate translation anyway, since words of this kind have a plurality of meanings; the reference is more likely to be to lineage discreteness only, and lineage relations never subsume all relationships anywhere. Further, most marriages are not alliances in any meaningful sense of the word, although a few are. Since people marry people with whom they are familiar already, as inhabitants of a common area, or with whom they have some kind of relationship, then bridewealth must serve to alter pre-existing relationships or to create a specific set of new ones. The Bedouin case might assist in identifying the different kinds of relationships which bridewealth regulates.

The Nuer case is used for comparative purposes for four reasons. First, it is well documented:[16] Evans-Pritchard began writing about bridewealth in 1931, published what has remained an important article on the subject in 1934, and continued his interest in a number of subsequent publications. His writings were also the source of many later ideas. Second, the Bedouin and the Nuer bear a superficial resemblance: they are both transhumant pastoralists, they are arranged in corporate groups, they possess elaborate lineage structures and, although culturally quite disparate, some of the details of their behaviour, the sentiments they express about various matters – among them, marriage – are, at least at first flush, uncannily alike. Comparable in general in many ways, the Nuer stand in sharp contrast to the Bedouin in that they observe a form of exogamy, and this would seem to be critical in assessing the significance of bridewealth. Third, both employ the same general type of bridewealth. The only similarity between the many forms of property transfers at marriage, about which anthropologists write, is the English word bridewealth. There is little point in attempting to give an analytically specific definition of this descriptive term here, but it is necessary to limit its meaning to those transfers in which several categories of kin of both spouses are involved, thus distinguishing it from transfers made between the two spouses only, or with the assistance of their parents, or varieties of these. The differences are so fundamental that to lump them all together under the same term is confusing, and misleading when comparison is attempted. Those like Fox,[17] who deprecate the inclusion of details of the collection and distribution of bridewealth, are clearly ignorant of the basic fact that it is not just one thing but a bundle of parts, and that a particular bundle is characterised by these details. Omission of the latter is bound to lead to a reductionist argument. Hence the absurdity of the stance taken when bridewealth is reduced to the status of a device for forging an alliance. Fourth, there is no well documented Arab case available for comparative purposes.

The Bedouin of Cyrenaica are neither exogamous nor endogamous. The bars to marriage can be stated under three sets of general rules. First, consanguinity. Anyone in ego's descent line, in the ascending or descending generations, is excluded. Siblings of the father and mother are also debarred, a relationship which causes most difficulty because siblings sometimes range in age from about twenty to over sixty years, with the result that, not uncommonly, uncles and aunts are of the same age or younger than nieces and nephews. Reared in the camps in the social context of first cousinship, the danger of breaching the ban on sexual relationships between such relatives is evident, and it is stressed by Bedouin, and it is subject to dire penalty.

These are the main bars to marriage.[18] They define the range of incest as well. Sexual intercourse with grandparents is dismissed as laughable, with parents it is regarded as unbelievable; but it is admitted as a possibility with the siblings of parents, between siblings, and with the children of siblings; and for these reasons feelings of horror, disgust and outrage are expressed in talking about its taking place with any of these three categories of kin. Represented diagramatically in fig. 9, for a male, the simplicity of the arrangements becomes evident at once.

An extension of this range of bars is that marriage with lineage collaterals of the same generation as the parents should not occur. It does, because not only are genealogical and age generations confused, but there is also such marked ambiguity that sometimes it cannot be resolved. In effect, unless there is known close consanguinity, the rule has no force. Indeed, the records show that marriage sometimes occurs where it is known, as in the instance of a man marrying his grandfather's brother's daughter. The same can be said of the general rule that a man should not marry a woman older than himself, since their time reckoning is inadequate for this purpose: unless there happens to be certainty about the order of birth, an estimation based on general appearance suffices to settle this issue. Women marry men who are both older than them, and who might also be of one or two generations up from them. Some sense of the complexities of separating generations and ages can be gained from a small segment of an actual genealogy, of part of a camp, as in fig. 10.

Second, affinity. A man is prohibited from marrying any woman in his wife's own descent line – that is, her mother, grandmother, daughter or

Figure 9.

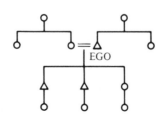

grand-daughter. Also applicable is the rule that a man should not have two wives simultaneously who, had they been of different sexes, would have been unable to marry – two sisters, for example. In Hanafi law[19] this is regarded as irregular, but not sufficient cause to make a marriage null and void. Most Bedouin regard this with repugnance, but it is known, although of infrequent occurrence. Some view sororal marriage with distaste also, but this form is common.

Third, other bars. Children who have been suckled by the same woman cannot marry. This foster relationship is known as *rida'*. The bar is strictly observed by the Bedouin for, as they see it, such infant nourishing puts people in a sibling relationship. A wet nurse is usually a relative and, unless her own child is a still birth or dies young, her natural child and foster child share her milk. Fosterage affects two or three pairs in practically all corporate groups, and has the effect of reducing, slightly, the number of possible spouses. The effect is more if the wet nurse is of another corporation, since the possible spouses here are much more limited in number.

Figure 10.

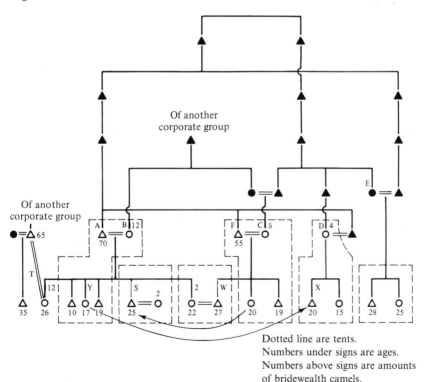

Dotted line are tents.
Numbers under signs are ages.
Numbers above signs are amounts
of bridewealth camels.

After divorce or death of a husband a period of sexual continence, known as '*iddah*, must be observed by a wife. The concern here is with paternity and, consequently, if a woman is not known to be pregnant already, three menses must pass before she is free to re-marry. In the event of pregnancy, conventions are recognised for the rearing of children.

After a triple divorce re-marriage is not permitted until the wife has been married to another man, divorced, and then observed the period of '*iddah*. Much is made of this in some Arab countries, and a 'young donkey' is used to perform the service of freeing the wife from the bar. Among the Bedouin, although they maintain that the rule must be obeyed, the divorce pronouncement is used so frequently that it is much of a manner of speaking, used to bring pressure on someone, or to let off steam, or as a threat.

Men are permitted a maximum of four wives simultaneously, but a woman – a rule that rarely receives mention – is allowed only one husband at a time.[20]

These three general categories of rules cover all marriage bars as the Bedouin know them. Disagreement about the appropriateness of a possible match sometimes occurs, but the instances of this are very few, to do with the kind of ambiguities cited earlier or, at most, with irregularities. Compared with reports about other peoples, Bedouin (and other Arabs for that matter) devote little attention to problems arising out of the rules when they discuss marriage, perhaps because they are so straightforward and so few, and permit a great range of choice. Unlike Jewish law,[21] Islamic law does not permit marriage between relatives as closely consanguineous as nephews and nieces, but the closeness of permitted degrees is not exhausted by the statement that they can marry a first cousin on either side – that is the four first cousins, a fact which requires to be stated because of the overwhelming primacy given, in the literature, to marriage with the father's brother's daughter. Indeed, in the majority of cases, relatedness other than first cousinship pre-exists first parallel cousin marriage. Thus, for example, a favoured marriage is a first parallel cousin marriage between the son and daughter of two full brothers who had themselves married first parallel cousins, as shown in fig. 11.

Almost invariably, these three kinds of marriage are described as first patrilineal parallel cousin marriages, as if this is the only relationship.[22] The majority of first patrilineal cousin marriages contain a plurality of connections: A and B are related as first patrilineal parallel cousins, as first maternal parallel cousins, as children of their fathers' sisters-in-law, as children of their mothers' brothers-in-law, as children of grandfathers who are brothers; they have common paternal and maternal grandparents, and they are both great-grandchildren of C. These seven different modes of relationship are, by no means, the maximum possible number, but they will suffice to substantiate the point that cousin marriage among Arabs is a much more complicated matter than is generally assumed, particularly when people are well aware of these plural connections, and regularly use them to account for details of their behaviour.

This tendency to expunge the complexities in Arab marriage by reducing it to cousin marriage is only possible if women are omitted from consideration. The expression 'first patrilineal parallel cousin marriage' refers to three men, and the one woman included as a wife is there only to complete the diagram, so to speak. The importance of including all the components that enter into marriages, to subsequently affect behaviour, can be made clear with reference to the data in fig. 10. The six tents shown are situated very closely together in a large camp of which they are a part. The people in them had lived in exile in Egypt together, along with some of the people shown as dead, and others who are not shown. They went into exile together, and returned to their homeland as a group.[23] Since A is the shaikh of the corporate group of which the inhabitants of the six tents are a part, it would appear that his ability to hold the group together, as a small nucleus of power, rests on his command of close agnates, their wives and children, while his wealth in animals provides him with the additional economic assets to exercise his power. The agnates show in the diagram. are not all his nearest, and his hold over those who are not shown is much more tenuous.

In this statement there is no intention of diminishing the significance of agnation as a force for drawing men together, but it is imperative to note, also, that there is a selector at work, which discriminates among men who are equals (*aswa'*) to persuade some of them to stand together through all kinds of vicissitudes. Some of these agnates, to be sure, are poor; other

Figure 11.

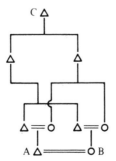

agnates are equally poor and equally close, or closer, patrilineally. The shaikh is well off; other agnates are as well, or better, off. It is the thread running through women which pulls the men of the six tents to knot them securely together, a fact recognised by all: hence the parallel cousin marriages in the succeeding generation, with the addition of a proposed marriage between X and Y, and possibly another similar one or two, still to come. The eldest of these women is the wife of the shaikh. She is mother's sister to C, the first parallel cousin of D, and sister-in-law's sister to E, who was father's sister to C and D, and who, although now dead, lived as a widow, with two young children, for twenty years, with this little group, sure of its mens' help in herding her few animals, and of their generosity in giving her gifts of wool, meat, clarified butter and barley. A basic element in the shaikh's structure of power is this group of faithfully devoted followers. Without the linkages between them, and through them between men, it would not be possible to account for his full brother's constant co-operation, much less that of any of the other people. Yet women are disinherited both as daughters and wives. Thus disabled, it might appear that women could not expect to exert more than a mild form of pressure on men, petticoat influence at best. Their positions in fig. 10 make it abundantly clear that they are part of a pattern of relationships, which rests not on fortuitous friendship or anything as casual as that, but on selection of spouses by men and women together. Their strength, their ability to insist on a meaningful say in affairs, lies in bridewealth.

Figure 12.

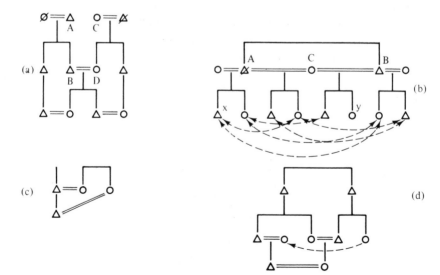

A few more examples are given in fig. 12 to illustrate the closeness of spouses, which appears in many marriages, but which is concealed when they are designated merely as parallel cousin marriages, and to provide a more realistic context for bridewealth.

In fig. 12(a), a father (A) and son (B) marry a mother (C) and her daughter (D). The children of B and D marry the children of their brothers, one of these marriages being to a first parallel cousin, and the other to a cross cousin. All four spouses are also the grandchildren of A and C. There are fourteen forms of affinity shown in the diagram. The total number of relationships is formidable.

In fig. 12(b) two brothers, A and B, marry wives who are themselves closely related, and who are closely related to their husbands. Both beget children by these wives. The elder brother A marries a second wife, C, begets children by her, but pre-deceases her. His brother B marries his sister-in-law in a leviratic union, and begets children by her. Among the four sets of children of these three men and two women, six first parallel cousin marriages are possible, although only four can be, and are, realised in practice. These marrying pairs are related in a variety of other ways, and in the following generation the relationships become even more intricate.

The marriages shown in fig. 12, (c) and (d) are included as variants of the same theme.

Stress has been given, thus far, to the closeness of kinship in marriage. The closeness, however, is not consistently within a limited patrilineal range, for many of the more crucial marriages are to women of other corporations, that of the woman B in fig. 10 being a good example. At the heart of the agnatic group, therefore, there are always women possessing connections with other women and men, some of them the daughters of agnates, others from outside the group but linked to women inside it as matrilateral relatives of one sort or another. Apart from this, there is a consistent tendency, once a link with another corporation has been established, to replicate the original marriage with a succession of cross cousin marriages in the same generation or the following ones. When these sorts of marriages are reciprocated, as they are so often, then the interconnections become as intricate as those resulting from marriages within the corporate group. Occasionally marriages occur between people whose homelands lie far apart, with 100 miles or more between them: one went right across country, from the southwest to the Aulad 'Ali tribe in Egypt. These are major alliances between two important corporate groups, and once made appear to have the durability to last for two or three generations.

Obviously there is no question of this marriage pattern approaching an endogamous condition. The fiction that Arabs marry endogamously has been perpetrated by many anthropologists.[24] Marriage is permitted within the patrilineage, but there is no rule which prescribes it, and marriage outside it is also permitted. Statistically the corporate lineage group is not an endogamous unit either. Preference is expressed for the father's brother's daughter, and a man can force his claim to her, although this would be conceded to only one of several brothers. Preference is also expressed for the mother's brother's daughter – who, the Bedouin say, 'is sweeter than milk' and, in physical conditions where the water is brackish, this is sweetness indeed – but she cannot be claimed in marriage by the father's sister's son. The only motive for viewing parallel cousin marriage as endogamy is the wish to simplify marriage problems by focusing the attention on men, and defining the marriage universe so widely and imprecisely that the majority of marriages are bound to be to parallel cousins of one sort or another, despite the fact that consanguinity between the spouses cannot be demonstrated;[25] and by thoughtlessly casting aside the other relationships between spouses, sometimes when one of these is the nearest in terms of degrees. Such perversity robs Bedouin marriage of its considerable interest, and the bridewealth associated with it is denuded of its full meaning, to be explained as an insignificant amount, or is not given.

There are three conditions to be satisfied for a legal marriage, irrespective of the closeness of consanguinity between the spouses: consent of the spouses, a statement giving the amount of the bridewealth, and a witnessed contract.[26] Consent is assumed by those who initiate the process, the fathers of the spouses if they are alive, or if they are dead, the spouses' guardians. Much trouble originates in guardianship. A boy, when he matures to manhood and demands his inheritance, might be told that it has been expended on his rearing, or that he must wait. If he insists on bridewealth for marriage, his guardian (his father's brother or next nearest agnate) might comply, but the amount of wealth he releases might be small, depriving the ward of choice, since it is the guardian who conducts the negotiations.

The witnessed statement of the amount of the bridewealth constitutes the marriage contract, but it is only a part of the bridewealth process. Prior to this the contracting parties will have been known to each other, either because of existing kinship, common residence, or propinquity. When approaches are seriously being considered, occasions are found for mutual entertainment, whether the parents reside in the same camp and are agnates, or live in camps set apart by some distance and are of different corporate groups. These preliminaries, during which soundings are taken to ascertain the exact amount and details of the wealth required, constitute the first sign of the changes in the relationships which marriage is to bring about; for entertainment is not proffered to those with whom casual relationships already exist and are to remain unaltered, or to those with whom relationships are not desired. If things go well, several of these reciprocal exchanges of hospitality are likely, especially if the bridewealth is likely to be large, while all the time negotiations are afoot, without the principals (the fathers of the future spouses) mentioning the matter of the marriage they have in mind. This process ended, the scene is now set for the formal public negotiations to take place.

The bride and groom do not enter into these negotiations, nor in those that follow, and only become the principals when they are brought together on the first day of the nuptials. During the preliminaries, both are told who the spouse is to be, and if the bride vehemently objects – and it is the bride, not the groom who most usually raises objections – every endeavour is made to reconcile her to the decision her parents have made. If she remains obdurate severe measures might be taken against her, although the threat of spinsterhood, and the commiserable status it implies, is usually enough to move her to acceptance. She would be left without the support of unpaid bridewealth to sustain her for life, and without a son to care for her as she ages. For a woman, while she can be reasonably certain of marriage, cannot demand it. She has to receive a proposal (*talab*), whereas a man has the right to demand that his corporate group provide him with the wherewithal to marry (if he is bereft of animal wealth himself), and with it he is able to initiate a proposal. A woman is free to object but must yield; a man is not permitted the indulgence of obstructing his father's plans, yet marriage for him is certain. Both come under the father's authority, but with different effects. The father can delay a son's marriage, since it is he who is ultimately answerable for the bridewealth; if a daughter is adamant in her refusal she may not be given another chance to marry.

The appropriation of choice by the parental generation does not mean that parents act only in their own interests. When A in fig. 10 arranged to marry his eldest daughter to an important shaikh for a large bridewealth, self-interest was not his motive. He was too advanced in age to be swayed in his choice by personal gain of either a material or status kind. He was a shaikh of some renown, but since the days when his marriage proved to be politically rewarding – and fructive to boot – circumstances had so changed that an immediate renewal of this link in the next generation had been rendered unnecessary. Consequently, he sought a different external connection for his son, through his eldest daughter, T. The latter was disconsolate when told who her husband was to be, and prayed that her first cousin, W, would assert his right to demand her for himself. This was unacceptable to her father, who had refused this demand only a year earlier. She (T) had been reared in her mother's image, a confident and distinguished personality, something of a grande dame, fit to be the wife of a shaikh. And this was the rub; everyone knew that the most threatening challenger to the shaikhship, in the succeeding generation, was the first cousin, W, and to have agreed to this parallel cousin marriage would have been to improve his chances markedly. In giving her as a wife to a shaikh of another corporation A was not only ensuring that his son would enjoy the benefits of an important political connection, but that his sister had the strength of personality to dominate it. The shaikh's concern was to provide as much of a structure of power, while he was still alive, for his eldest son, as a kind of inheritance, much as townspeople attempt to give children a preferential start in life with a good education or a trade.

The first formal move towards marriage is the arranged appearance, in the bride's camp, of a delegation from the groom's camp. The groom's father accompanies these men, but says nothing during the negotiations. The delegation consists of four or five men, as a rule, the most important of whom is the man who is to do most of the talking, a mother's brother of the groom if one is available or, if not, a close friend. This spokesman is the sponsor, or guarantor (sometimes referred to as the *kafil*). The father's brother, although present, is not used in this role, because he and the father are unlikely to have divided their inheritance of animals at this stage in their lives, and since the negotiations turn on the amount of this wealth to be transferred, better to exclude both of them.

Witnessed statements concerning the amount of bridewealth must be made in advance of marriage taking place, no matter how close the relationship of the spouses. Before the formality of negotiation and witnessing begins, a number of animals known as the *siaq* (from the verb *saqa*, to drive or to herd cattle) are given 'to the bride's tent'. Contributions to the *siaq* come from several kinds of relatives, among whom the father's brother (unless he is the groom's father) and the mother's brother are counted, but otherwise the precise category of kin is of no consequence. The number and kind of animal varies. The largest recorded was fifteen sheep. A camel was delivered as *siaq* at one of these meetings. The more usual number ranges between three and seven, sometimes made up entirely of sheep, sometimes a mixture of sheep and goats, and sometimes three goats only if a man is poor. At least one of the animals of the *siaq* is likely to be slaughtered for the feast provided by the bride's father for the delegation, to mark the successful conclusion of the contract. The rest are distributed among kin, whose specific relationships, as described, are to the bride and not to the parents, brother or guardian. The mother's brother almost invariably gets one, and so does the father's brother, unless he happens to be the groom's father. Otherwise, the exact kinship category of the recipients is unimportant. People are free to choose according to their own assessments of the needs of others, their friendship with them, and whatever personal considerations they think should influence them; thus the wife of S in fig. 10 gave one to her mother, 'her mother's sister's tent', and 'to the tent of the children of' E; two of the animals she retained for herself, branding them with her mother's brother's sign.[27]

The significance of the *siaq* is not to be dismissed as an inconsequential part of the bridewealth process. Until these animals are delivered, the formal negotiations cannot commence. At their conclusion, by way of celebrating the institution of new relationships or of putting existing ones on a new footing, one of these animals is slaughtered for the commensal meal. It would be too much of a diversion to enter into a discussion of the significance of animal sacrifice among the Bedouin here, but it is necessary to note two points about the slaughter of a *siaq* animal. When a man gives or slaughters an animal 'from his own wealth', it is a surrogate for a life, his life, which is in the blood of the animal and, in this sense, what he gives is, vicariously, part of himself. The receiver is said to be in debt to the giver, and it is a debt which cannot be 'redeemed' until an appropriate occasion occurs later on: to return a slaughter without cause for doing so would be gross insult in normal circumstances; its return, the redemption of the debt, in the correct context, is meritorious, enabling further relationships to proceed in a spirit of amity. At the commensal meal, the slaughtered animal is one that is given and received by both the giver and the receiver, a permitted haste of return indicating the urgent desire that both parties should become instantly enmeshed in their new relationships. Although the whole of the *siaq* is slaughtered at the celebrations only if both parties are rich, it is thought to be a generous act, bringing people closer, and specially propitious for the marriage and the other relationships which are to stem from it. The one camel *siaq*, mentioned earlier, was slaughtered at the celebrations, but this was a marriage between a shaikh and the daughter of a shaikh; it was considered magnanimous, befitting a shaikh of some standing.

The *siaq* represents the first transfer of wealth between the parties. It is not included in the contract, and the amount given is the giver's estimation, based on information he has gathered, of the number of people to whom the receiver wishes to give an animal. The fact that the *siaq* is not a contractual obligation makes it all the more important. It is always confidently anticipated, but it is regarded as wealth which can be withheld or varied in amount and, to this extent, it is a measure of the relationships into which the giver wishes to enter: the larger the amount given, the greater the number of animals slaughtered for the celebrations (if the giver's expression of his intentions are to be reciprocated), and the greater the number of people partaking of the commensal meal, itself an act rich with meaning. It is also the first public commitment to proceed with a marriage, binding in the sense that should anything baneful happen between the negotiations and the nuptials, or during the nuptials, it is returnable in full – the bride's father has to take the risks that his daughter is a virgin, that she is not frigid, and not sexually malformed.

The choice people exercise in deciding to contribute to the *siaq*, and in its distribution, means that, in advance of a marriage taking place, contributors and recipients are singled out from potentially much larger numbers, for more intimate involvement. These are the effective affines through whom future relationships are expected to pass. The spouses, it must be stressed, have yet to meet, and although the principals at the negotiations can be said to be representing the bride and groom, the *siaq* is delivered before negotiations start, and they meet in order to discuss how marriage will realign relationships. Later, affinity will be claimed by a vastly larger number of people on both sides, but for the first difficult year or so of the new marriage, it is this select group of people who will bear the responsibility for all going well. The delivery of the *siaq* is the occasion, *par excellence*, for getting to grips with affinity, and for this reason, it is different from any of the succeeding arrangements.

The negotiations take on a set form. First, the delegation's spokesman calls out the name of the bride's father. He feigns not to hear. There follows a repetition of this. At the third calling, he 'hears' and responds. The spokesman now asks for the daughter, and the conventional reply is given: 'Welcome, if you have camels.' The number demanded in the first instance is several camels in excess of expectations. This is reduced according to accepted conventions. A shaikh of standing begins by requesting that two camels be removed from the total for his sake, and the request is promptly granted. A second shaikh requests a like reduction, and this too is granted with equal promptitude. Then a 'client of the goodness' asks for another one to be taken off, and this too is conceded with alacrity. Finally the spokesman requests a last reduction, in favour of the gathering – a gathering of men, particularly if one of two shaikhs are included in it, confers honour on the host – and this cannot be denied. Although this apparent bargaining is strictly conventional, it is not without meaning. Each time a shaikh asks for a reduction in an amount of wealth to be transferred, whether it be bridewealth or blood money, he incurs debts. They are not held against him in the manner of a debit accounting, but as concessions which require concessions in return. Hence, the shaikh must be a person who can be approached by the bride's father at some future date, a shaikh within a structure of alliances between corporate groups; but he must also be of a stature to be able to accept debts of this sort with aplomb – a shaikh from among the small fry would be quite unacceptable for the job. Part of the measure of a shaikh's puissance is the frequency of calls made on him for such purposes. Likewise, the 'client of the goodness' must be one thought genuinely to possess *baraka* (blessing), and not one with dubious credentials.

Moreover, once the formalities have ended all the men present rise, kiss each other on the head, and go out into the open, to 'read' the *Fatiha* (the opening sura of the Quran), palms of the hands upturned, much as they do when the formalities of blood money negotiations are concluded. The women herald the end to the agreement by the excited trilling of tongues, which they reserve for an action which can be said to be something of a triumph, or to urge a person forward in a hazardous undertaking. The kissing of heads, followed by the *Fatiha*, has a singular significance, without which the Bedouin do not accept an agreement to be binding; a peace brought about by the intervention of government officials, concluded in an office, is thought to be no more than an expediency, lacking the compulsive force of moral authority, to be kept only for as long as it suits both parties. The kissing of heads, and repeating the *Fatiha* endows an agreement with this authority, and thus makes it lasting.

Prominent in the formalities, and the subject of the genuine negotiations which precede them, are the animals which are to constitute that part of the bridewealth known as the *sahiba*.[28] The word has several meanings, but the connotation it carries in this context is that of master or owner, although neither of these words express its precise meaning. Insistently, the Bedouin affirm that a woman's 'bone' belongs to her natal corporate group, and that if she is killed in homicide the blood money goes not to her husband, but to its members. (Anthropologists see this as evidence that she is not fully incorporated into her husband's lineage.) In practice, the matter is not as simple as this. If the bridewealth has 'died', the blood money might be given to the wife's father, but only for him to transfer it to the husband. If the marriage is only two or three years old, and only one payment of bridewealth has been made, the wife's father must compensate the husband for the loss of bridewealth, and argument about the rights of the wife's children is likely to ensue. The most satisfactory settlement is that the wife's sister (or her father's brother's daughter) is given in sororal marriage, with an agreed *sahiba* equivalent to the dead sister's, with the difference that none of it will actually be given to the father. What is certain is that both bridewealth and blood money will not accumulate on one side. Neither, it is said, have *baraka* in them. They are for disposal, not for keeping. Bridewealth should be kept until given for another marriage, and the best thing to do with blood money is to use it as bridewealth at the earliest opportunity. Replacement of a human being is not a matter of material assessment, but of using material goods to beget another. That is to say, the issue is never one of a fracas over animals, or of the degree of incorporation into a family or group, but in establishing who has what rights over women and men at particular stages in their lives. Indeed, the issue of incorporating is irrelevant since almost half of the women marry men of their own corporate groups.[29]

If there is any substance to the meaning 'owner' given to the word *sahiba*, it is that the husband acquires certain limited rights in his wife. No one but a husband has the right of sexual enjoyment with his wife, and her procreative powers are his. This gives him the liberty to allow another man sexual congress with his wife if he deems it necessary, but any issue she bears is his – 'The boy for the bed' (*al-walad li'l farsh*), as the saying goes.[30] A woman, in other words, can be accused of adultery; if caught in *flagrante delicto*, and unless her husband is in connivance with her, she risks her life – I recorded several cases of husbands who had suffered cuckoldry, killing their unfaithful wives. By the same token, a wife has a right to sexual enjoyment and to pregnancy, and if it is demonstrated that the husband fails to satisfy the wife on either count, she can demand that he makes arrangements to provide her with this satisfaction, or that he frees her. Whereas sexual abnormality in a woman leads to a summary termination of a marriage – there is a virginity test on the first day of the nuptials, and consummation takes place that night – the consequences for a man need not necessarily be as severe. As owner of her sexual and procreative powers, he can solicit the aid of another man, but if a woman is sexually abnormal she cannot provide a substitute woman. Further, while a wife's issue jurally belong to her husband, and remain under his authority for his lifetime, a woman has the right to rear her children, strictly until they have been properly weaned and, in practice, long afterwards;[31] and she also has the right to live with them, if their father leaves them, or after they have reached maturity. In short, a wife has a right to motherhood, in its procreative and social senses. Complementarily a husband has the right to expect it of her. The rights of the *sahiba* are not exclusively the husband's. They are distributed between both spouses to form the symbiosis which is the very minimum requirement in any marriage.

The camels (often used as a generic term for animals, enabling camels to be compounded for sheep, goats or some of all three) are never given immediately, nor, when a transfer is made, are they all given at one time. The terms of reference in the agreement are: 'We will put "so many" in front of you (*qadamak*), and leave "so many" in case of '*aib* or *ghaib*.' The word '*aib* is given very many nuances of meaning; here, it is intended as the shame brought upon a husband if his wife flaunts her sex persistently, or has sexual congress with another man, so that she is publicly thought of as an adultress or is one in practice, and makes a cuckold of her husband. The word *ghaib* means absence, either through death or desertion. None of the bridewealth is given for about a year; 'in front of you' is taken to mean after the next lambing or next harvest, but, in any case, after sufficient time has elapsed to determine whether the union is fertile. The initial *siaq* is in respect of affinity (*nasab*; an affine is called a *nasib*. The same root can also be used in a generic sense to refer to affinal and cognatic connections between groups); the *sahiba* is tied to parenthood.

Women are proud to boast that the *sahiba* is 'on their backs'. All of it will not come their way, since that which is 'put in front of you' (the fathers) is soon expended on another marriage. People implore God to give them boys. But without girls the boys might well be unable to marry, particularly boys of the poorer families. Women do not gain materially from bridewealth. The giving of bridewealth is a process whereby relatively small numbers of animals are circulated among large numbers of people, leaving in their trails no appreciable amounts of individual gains in animals, but huge accumulations of relationships. As far as a woman is concerned a portion of these relationships are contained in the rights she acquires over her husband, her father, and the brother who marries with her bridewealth; for it is the promise of bridewealth for a daughter which prompts the father to make an acceptable promise of bridewealth to get his son a bride. If a husband does not bring a trinket or a dress length for his wife, after returning from a visit to town, she can demand such things of him: bridewealth gives her just cause for doing so. If her husband abuses her in any way, she has the right to return to her father or brother, who can demand justice. (The word *haqq* is frequently used for this, and it has an abundance of related meanings. In this context, the word *insaf* is preferred. It is used to refer to the wealth a wife receives as 'justice'.) Depending on the seriousness of the complaint, the *insaf* varies from one to about five sheep or goats. Let it be clear: the *insaf* is not a gift; it is a claim to the husband's property which is made against the wife's bridewealth; and it goes to her. The animals are then branded with the personal sign of her mother's brother, so that there will be no fear of them being merged into her husband's or father-in-law's flocks. There comes a time, however, when a woman finds the company of neighbours so congenial that she will not leave it, after her children have survived the perils of infancy and are growing into maturity, and when it matters little any longer if her husband abandons her for a young wife – he does not divorce her after the menopause; 'he throws her off his back'.

At about this time even the most dogged among fathers will have relinquished all hope of receiving any more bridewealth. Instead, the father insists that the portion reserved to meet the contingencies of adultery, death or desertion is now put 'in front of her', and on these animals a wife again brands her mother's brother's personal sign. The brand does not give her complete ownership of the animals; it does separate her rights in them from those previously held by her husband, and thereafter, she is free to will them (together with any of the *siaq* or *insaf* animals) to her sons, as she wishes.

There is point in delaying the transfer of bridewealth. The initial amount is usually only a portion of the total contracted amount, and this is stated at the formal negotiations. It will not be transferred until the wife is pregnant, or preferably after childbirth. The rest is left. While it is still unpaid the husband can expect formal but unannounced visits from his immediate affines, when he is expected to display his generosity. At first, when the son-in-law sees or hears that his father-in-law is approaching his tent, he skedaddles to hide in another tent, or to his sister's husband (in the hope of getting something from him) because he knows full well the purpose of the visit. After some years have passed, and the marriage is prospering, relationships move to another stage at which affines meet each other more as equals, and a spirit of give and take grows between them. Nevertheless, the contract remains, to be evoked whenever trouble arises between the spouses. Its importance, however, lies in the fact that it is allowed to remain unfulfilled. Completed to the letter it would act to sever relationships. Left over as a debt, bridewealth incites people to indulge in continuously changing relationships.

Included in the *sahiba* is a detailed list of items the bride is to receive, and which, when they are given to her, are called the *kiswa*. They can all be seen at any wedding as the bride, riding high in a canopy on the hump of a camel, is taken to her wedding tent. All she wears, boots, cummerbund, dress, silver bracelets and so on will have been given her as part of her *kiswa*. Draped over the canopy are the hand-woven carpets for her tent, and a straw mat (*dis*), in a roll slung in front of the canopy, and, hanging over the side, a few pots and pans. All part of the wedding gaiety it would seem, but nonetheless important for that: the groom pays the cost of all the clothes his wife wears to her wedding, and he must continue to clothe her hence-forward; the straw mat they will lie on together and any children born on it are theirs, since no other woman has the right to lie on the mat, not even another wife of the husband; the carpets are provided to start married life, and thereafter the husband must provide wool to make others; the wife must cook for her husband – it is her right to do so – but he must buy the utensils. These details of the *kiswa*, so carefully listed during the bride-wealth negotiations, are not intended merely to give the young couple a start; they define rights and responsibilities for both for the rest of their life together. Such is the importance attached to the *kiswa* that the nuptials cannot begin until every item has been bought and delivered to the bride.

There is still the bride's mother. She gets nothing specifically earmarked for her until the bride becomes a wife. As soon as possible after the nuptials are over, the husband and wife along with the husband's mother, sister and sister-in-law, pay their first visit to the wife's mother, taking with them one or two sheep or goats, one of which will be slaughtered; the intention of which is 'to seal the affinity'. Months later, certainly if the wife is now pregnant, the mother will receive her due, *haqq al-halib* (right of the milk) or *suwar al-halib* (silver bracelets of the milk). In practice, it is unlikely that a husband, however well off, would be so rash as to buy his mother-in-law a pair of very heavy bracelets (they weigh about half a kilo), but if his relationship with his wife is thriving he might give up to about five sheep – animals which are again given a mother's brother's brand, and disposed of among her sons as she wills.

In giving these details pertaining to the woman's rights that are caught up in bridewealth it is not the intention to overstress them, but such emphasis is placed on rights accruing to men in bridewealth, in the literature on Arabs, that an attempt to restore the balance is necessary. Women are not being irrational or unrealistic when they reiterate the statement that the bridewealth is on their 'backs', and add that it goes to their fathers. What they mean is that authority over the bridewealth is held by the father, but the rights which are derived from it are carried by the wife. They last until the bridewealth is 'dead', by which time they have become defunct or the spouses have entered the stage of connubial companionship for the rest of their lives. Unless this were the case bridewealth associated with father's brother's daughter's marriage would not make sense.

In one way or another a considerable amount of property is needed to make a marriage, and the details already given are ample evidence of this. During the nuptials, the consumption of food is prodigious. Whatever a man's status, the number of guests is always high. About a hundred people assemble on the first day of the nuptials, and a score or so are present on each of the remaining six days. The guests at an important marriage are considerably in excess of these numbers. Five to ten sheep or goats are likely to be slaughtered during the week's festivities; some 100 kilos of flour, 50 kilos of rice, 25 kilos of sugar, 5 kilos of tea, and 100 gallons of water are used. This represents a modest estimate of the average consumption for an ordinary wedding, the sort of entertainment provided by the owner of five to ten camels and about 100 sheep. For a man of these means, the expenditure represents roughly a third or more of his total wealth. For a man of poorer means the proportion is likely to be much higher. When a shaikh marries, the expenditure is likely to be double the amount of most other marriages, although the proportion might not be as high. Clearly, this scale of expenditure would be an intolerable burden for most individuals. During the festivities the guests themselves bring animals, sugar and tea, each group of men from a camp bringing one animal between them, or a few kilos of sugar, as they judge to be fitting. Men from the groom's camp are also likely to contribute. All in all, the groom's father – or the groom himself – is likely to gather more wealth than he dispenses during the nuptials, and if he is a shaikh he will probably gain a substantial number of animals. Direct contributions are also made to the bridewealth, and both father's and mother's brothers are picked out as those who are most obliged to give. Others contribute as well, but it would be wrong to categorise them in specific kinship terms. Agnates do not contribute because they are agnates, no more than do matrilateral relatives. Agnates, matrilateral relatives and affines might contribute, not because they fall into these kinship categories, but because they are differentiated from the other people of all three categories, as a result of a history of relationships which have brought them closer together to form a distinct nucleus of more effective kin. They are self-selecting because they are caught in such an entanglement of any or all of these three types of relationships, with the bride or the groom, or both, that they are susceptible to as many pressures to give as there are strands in their relatedness.

The upshot of all this is that the number of people directly involved in any marriage is high, and the crowds at the festivities are eloquent testimony of a wider involvement. The number directly implicated varies considerably depending on the particular circumstances. It is known to rise to as high as fifty, if men and women are counted; it would be an odd sort of marriage if it dropped to under a dozen, especially if the bride were a maiden. These people help for one prime reason: to promote the success of the marriage. They are always available to advise – gratuitously and abundantly, very often – and to assist in all sorts of ways. They are intimately concerned because their contribution has made new, or renewed old, relationships. It is they who make personal enquiries about the wife's condition, who watch every detail of the spouses' behaviour, and so on. It is not the material value of the animal given as a contribution that they have in mind; uppermost in their minds are their social relationships, for which a breach in the marriage would be disruptive. Assuming sexual compatibility between the spouses, the fertility of both, and a minimum of social compatibility there is no reason why any Bedouin marriage should not endure. The demands on the spouses of a marriage are few and they are not onerous. They can be met by the vast majority because the foundation of marriage lies in a stable social environment. This stability is the major contribution made by those directly implicated, with the animals given serving as emblems of their intentions.

A more general context of stability is created by the guests at the festivities. They come, kith and kin from round about, with their gifts, to join in the jollifications, and to display their public pleasure with the match that has been made. At dusk, when they dance in a crescent formation, led by a virgin, they clap until their hands become very sore. Unless they do this, they will not, they say, get a bride; although they know full well that hand claps, however vigorous the effort, will never fetch a bride: they also know that without the support of others they cannot hope to marry and remain wedded. From the outset, a marriage is ringed around with two defences, an inner one of intimates, the contributors to the bridewealth, and an outer one of friends, the wedding guests. Bridewealth, *per se*, has little to do with marriage stability. Marriages which carry a bridewealth of five sheep are as stable as those carrying twenty camels. Animals, as material goods, do not hold human beings together. Despite the arguments in the literature pertaining to the amount of wealth transferred and the difficulty or ease with which it can be retrieved, when spouses are determined to part, they are not thwarted by considerations of this kind. The animals are there as symbols of the nature of social relationships. Marital stability is rooted in the moral context created by a community, symbolically expressed through the animals which change hands at the several stages on the way to a union.

The number of animals promised as bridewealth is not the same for all marriages. The range is considerable, as it is among most peoples,[32] despite the predilections of some authors to iron out the differences, to arrive at high bridewealth here and low there, ascribing these unwarranted evaluations to societies as it suits their arguments.[33] Among the Bedouin, it can drop as low as about five sheep, and soar as high as twenty camels.[34] But the range in the number of animals delivered to the fathers of brides is much less than this. For example, if the promised number is twelve camels, the number handed over after a year of the marriage has elapsed is four; if it is six camels, the number handed over is likely to be three; if it is five sheep, the probable number a father gets is three or four. This does not mean, however, that the wife's rights contract correspondingly. 'The camels on her back' is the total number promised at the formal negotiations, and it is this total which symbolises her rights, not the number required by her father to set in motion arrangements for marrying off one of his sons. Nevertheless, the discrepancies in the total amounts would appear to affect the rights of wives in a like order of magnitude, since there is a close correspondence between the bridewealth and the rights a wife derives from it. Some wives, it would seem, are provided with a greater store of rights than others. Why should there be this apparent discrimination among women?

The saying is that a woman's contract should be the same as her mother's (*shartha kaif shart ummha*). As well as meaning contract, the word *shart* also means crevice, and is used indecently, in this context, to mean vagina, but, like all proverbial wisdom, it tells only part of the truth. A father always attempts to get a promise of bridewealth for one of his daughters, at least equal to the amount promised for his wife, particularly if the latter was a big bridewealth, say, eight camels or more. In fig. 10, shaikh A delayed his eldest daughter's marriage until he received an offer equivalent to her mother's twelve camels. His stature would have suffered had he accepted less; his ability to command bridewealth is a test of his power. His second daughter was married soon after the eldest with a bridewealth of only two camels. His eldest son, heir to the shaikhship at that,[35] married a wife who was promised only two camels – telling evidence to show that the direct status effect of the amount is attached to the wife, and to throw into relief the pivotal position a wife occupies in affinal relations. A man's status is affected indirectly by the control he commands over affinal links; therefore, it is largely fortuitous whether the bridewealth promised for the wife of a leader is big or small. An upstart shaikh, exulting in his new-found status, endeavours to command a big bridewealth, if not in his own marriage then through one of his kinsmen or kinswomen.

Status differences affect bridewealth in other ways. Daughters of clients are married to freeborn men for very little bridewealth, but clients who marry daughters of freeborn men have to make large promises. Both rules apply to grafts, co-residents who are nothing more than neighbours, and shepherds from elsewhere. In a rough and ready fashion, status sought means promising a large amount, and status granted the opposite. Actual arrangements are subject to the contingencies of the circumstances: a wealthy client would not give his daughter to a freeborn nonentity for five sheep; whether a shepherd would promise much or little would depend entirely on the particulars of his relationships with the girl's father and his agnates, and so on. In one way or another, status considerations impinge on all bridewealth arrangements, but in ways too complicated to allow a list to be drawn up showing the appropriate bridewealth for each status. Bridewealth and status do not necessarily match. Were this so, then an important element in the power structures of individuals would be permanently fixed, frustrating any shifts in power, and relegating those without it to persistent deprivation. But power does shift; some men without it succeed in capturing it, and some of those possessing it fall into decline. A detailed listing of each arrangement does not reveal much about power, for what matters most is not their social order but their configurations, and the command of these configurations by individuals.

The suggestion advanced here is that the seeming differentiation of women by bridewealth is not attributable to a single cause, such as status, but to the kind of social relationships already in being or desired. Very many of these are encapsulated in property, and before proceeding with the argument it is necessary to point to some of its characteristics. As a preamble, it must be stressed that women are implicated in property, however circuitously. They are not denied their rightful status as heirs, to leave them bereft of all property relationships, and it is flimflam to say otherwise. Apart from their claims to bridewealth, they critically affect the use to which corporate resources are put.[36]

Land and water are owned by males collectively. Corporate property is available for use as a right by all adult male members of a group, and because they are equals, in this respect, they cannot transfer their rights to others *qua* their status as agnates. Agnation does not provide for preferential access to corporate resources, and were agnation the only means of control, any unexpendable shares would revert to the agnatic pool without much gain to anyone: individuals would not be able to grow more grain, nor increase the size of their flocks and herds with this trivial additional access to resources, and little reliance could be placed on it in any event. Affinity and all forms of matrilateral kinship, however, are recognised as legitimate grounds for temporarily relinquishing rights in resources to others. In this way, an agnate can give the use of his right to another agnate, as long as they are otherwise related. Poor agnates can be valued affines. A shaikh who controls a number of such links is able to expand his flocks and herds, and enlarge his grain store appreciably. There would be little point to this expansion if the continuity of additional supplies rested entirely on local resources. It is a characteristic of the Bedouin economy, due to the vagaries of the rainfall, that insufficient rain might fall, in a season, to fill the well or to permit ploughing. In order to maintain sizeable flocks and herds, or increase them, it is imperative to have access to the natural resources of other corporations, in order to make good local deficiencies. Affinity and matrilateral kinship open the way to the resources of agnates in other corporate groups. The term for affinity, *nasab*, is applied to all affines, whether they are within the corporate group or members of others, irrespective of generational differences, a usage consistent with their behaviour as equals. Generations are not merged in the term (and its derivatives) used for matrilateral relatives, but the term is used to cover them all, whether they are of the same corporate group or of others. As a result of selected marriages within a corporate group and connections to others outside – links which, moreover, are both replicated – corporate groups come to be differentiated internally, forming two or more kinship clusters, and demarcating the lines of division, if and when the pressure on resources rises to an intolerable level.[37]

Animal property is individually owned, in that there is an individual proprietor. The Bedouin make much of the joint ownership of livestock (*halal wahid*). The small group based on this kind of ownership does not last for more than two generations; more often it breaks up after brothers have married. Its interest here is that while it lasts, there is much more likelihood of first parallel cousin marriage occurring than when brothers have divided their inheritance. In fig. 10, the shaikh, A, was the proprietor of all the animals in which the occupants of all six tents shown in the diagram had claims. Before arranging the marriage of his eldest daughter for a large bridewealth, he consulted his nephew, W, who agreed to the match on condition that he should be given the second daughter. Previously, the shaikh's eldest son, S, was confidently expected by his kinsmen to marry the daughter of a shaikh of another corporation. As soon as the shaikh's nephew, W, demanded the second daughter, he arranged for this nephew's sister to marry his eldest son. One other first parallel cousin marriage had been agreed, and there was talk of one more. If the latter were consummated, the number of first parallel cousin marriages would have reached the maximum for this small group. Equally interesting is that not one of the five seniors of the group married a first parallel cousin.

In discussing the two major types of property, the outline of the marriage pattern has emerged. To give it more sharpness the main directions of the links are now summarily given. Highly selective first parallel cousin marriage occurs when there is a connection in the ascending generation other than the sibling link, giving genealogically localised spots of intensity, interspersed with its partial or complete absence. Selective marriages with parallel cousins other than the first are numerically more common, and the majority of these are between people related in other ways, as matrilateral parallel cousins, cross cousins of both types, or as affines. Marriages into other corporations are roughly equal to internal marriages, but they are restricted to a limited number of groups.

Variations in bridewealth, while not matching the marriage pattern, are consistent with it. In most corporate groups, there is general agreement as to what the bridewealth should be. One such group gave it as 'two female camels and a pair of silver bracelets' (*naqatain wa-suwar*) for the daughters of agnates; another as four camels. Differences arise because a new link with agnates, previously known to be related patrilineally only, commands a higher bridewealth than a renewal, other things being equal. The number of animals given is more of a maximum than a fixed amount, many falling below it. There is also a general consensus that an initial marriage link with another corporation requires a large bridewealth of ten or more camels, and records confirm this. If it is followed by another marriage, the bridewealth drops by about a third until, after a succession of reciprocal marriages has erected a kinship structure to span the two groups, the amount declines further until it becomes like the bridewealth of corporate parallel cousin marriage.

Property relations, marriage patterns, and variations in bridewealth are of a piece. In some instances, first patrilineal parallel cousin marriage is open competition for property. A man who thought he had been denied his proper inheritance by his guardian, his father's brother, demanded the latter's daughter in marriage, and deliberately defaulted on the bridewealth (*naqs al-haqq*; literally, defective justice). Another man, a weakling shaikh, spoke of such marriage as vengeance (*thar*), albeit later he had suffered the indignity of his brother's son entering his tent and throwing his toga over his daughter – a conventional way of asserting the right forcefully; still enraged, after some time had elapsed, he swore he would compel his son to do the same. Further, it is common for a man to remain demure while preparations for the marriage of his first paternal parallel cousin are afoot, only to appear in high dudgeon as the nuptials are about to begin, and to assert then his prior right to the bride. It is known in advance that this disturbance might arise, and provision is made to buy off the recalcitrant cousin with some garments and a few sheep.

All first paternal parallel cousin marriages are not as hostile as these. In fig. 10, the brothers A and F concurred in the marriages arranged between their children. Nor is it true to say that such marriages are invariably rooted in gain, greed or competition. They are often evidence of the will to co-operate, to allow one brother to rise above the other, or because women want their chosen children to remain with them. Hence the exchange marriage (*tabadul*), shown in fig. 10, in which the men received nothing; but bridewealth was promised for both wives, giving them their separate rights in the common property – since exchange marriage is frowned upon in Islam, the elder brother 'put five extra sheep on his son's wife, but they will never be given to her father nor his brother'.

In first or any other parallel cousin marriages the redistribution of property between men is of small amounts, or none at all. But then bridewealth is small, and men get only a part of it anyway. It gives women rights, through property, in their relationships with men, and puts men on a new footing with one another. Women and men also have rights in each other as members of the same corporate group. The alteration in their relationships adds a new component to these. And if the marriage breaks, the other relationships endure. The bridewealth is small, to match the dimension of change. By the same token, where there has been neither affinity nor kinship before, a commensurately greater number of animals must be proffered. A large bridewealth is earnest that the people involved wish their relationships to grow to the richness of the wealth put into it. Only when there are no relationships is there no bridewealth – save where relationships are those of chronic enmity.

The stress given to bridewealth, in this chapter, has been on its power to generate relationships between men and women, separately and collectively. There is little else available for the purpose. The relationships are essential. Men meet in the pastures, or when they go in search of straying animals, or go to market. They need access to the resources of other groups, and the means must readily be available when contingencies arise. The economy does not coerce groups to co-operate on a permanent basis. Each corporate group has the labour force to tend its animals and grow a crop. The products, however, are uniform throughout the land, and few in kind – barley, wool, milk products and meat. These cannot be used for regularised exchanges between groups, since they are not required on an ordered basis. But the need for maintaining production is regular, and it necessitates that men are free to call on others to provide them with the basic resources of production, at short notice and in unpredictable quantities. Affinity and kinship create the context in which these needs can be met. Marriage within a corporate group cannot resolve the problems arising from the equal rights to resources, frustrating some people who might suffer deficiencies, and others who have assets they cannot use. Marriage into other corporate groups resolves the problem of giving stability to the local economy. The prime mover, in this type of environment, is the right of access to the resources of others, and only by marriage can it be achieved and securely held. This is not to say that precedence is given to affinity, and the relationships which issue from it, in other conditions, where various forms of differentiation might be marked; but it is suggested that the precedence given to affinal relationships, *per se*, among the Bedouin, is intimately related not so much to the paucity of the economy, but to the recurring fluctuations in usable resources.

With parallel cousin marriage among the Bedouin, and exogamy among the Nuer, both put into their perspectives, the two cases have been brought within the bounds of comparability. Evident differences exist, and the temptation is to put them down to major cultural dissimilarities. Thus one might argue that the Bedouin are Muslims and, as such, they perforce include a statement about property transference in their marriage contracts. There would be a point to this argument if property arrangements in marriage were uniform throughout Islam. They are not; on the contrary, the variety of these arrangements is impressive. It is not suggested that cultural differences are of no importance for comparative purposes, but to evoke them when confronted with the slightest difficulties, particularly in the general terms of a religious culture which subsumes a vast disparity of social conditions, is bound to be abortive. Data on Arabs is rarely used for comparison by specialists in other cultures.[38] This is unfortunate, since they afford such useful test cases for many hypotheses.

If maps were available showing the distribution of actual marriages for the Bedouin and the Nuer, it is probable that the patterns would show similarities, especially with regard to the dispersal of connections. The reasons for the kind of dispersal, if not completely consistent in both cases, would be well within the bounds of comparability. But whatever comparisons might emerge, the fact remains that there is an exogamous group among the Nuer, while among the Bedouin there is only a limited incest group. Or, to put the matter in question form, why do Nuer stop marrying locally as kinship intensifies in a locality, while Bedouin regard this kind of intensification as a good reason for augmenting it? Part of the answer might lie in those very external links which make the Nuer marriage pattern comparable to that of the Bedouin. If these have to be widely spread to deal with the contingencies of meeting with unrelated people, as a regular feature of their lives, it may well be that so much of their marriage capital, so to speak, has to be dispersed in this fashion that it would be a waste of a valuable asset to expend it within a local community. This, in turn, raises several issues, the most immediate one, obviously, relating to the differences in the form of pastoralism. The Bedouin occupy areas they call their homelands. They are notoriously footloose within them, some tribal sections moving considerable distances seasonally. They are not compelled, however, to move into other territories and join the groups occupying them. Their moves into other territories are temporary, mainly for two or three weeks of ploughing, and of a similar duration for harvesting. The Nuer, it would appear, not only mix with diverse people in their seasonal movements, but they leave one local group to join another with ease; local communities split up and the nuclei fuse with others to form new ones, without the constraint of residential or descent rules to give the composition of territorial units much stability. But these differing modes of pastoralism raise further issues related to economic differences. In Nuerland, there is a greater evenness in the distribution of resources, there is greater differentiation in them, they occur in greater abundance, and there is greater reliability about them than there is in Cyrenaica. These factors, taken together, obviously affect inheritance. Land is not vested in a corporation of agnates as securely among the Nuer as it is among the Bedouin. Animal wealth is attached to individuals among the Bedouin, despite the common ownership in which animals are sometimes held; among the Nuer, it would appear that herds of cattle are not divided into individual lots. Division of animal wealth on an individual basis makes bridewealth transactions intelligible. Among the Nuer, bridewealth transactions among kin, who own herds in common, might be practically impossible.

10

The status of women

In the four Arab communities of this study the position of women varies considerably, both with regard to their influence in domestic and political affairs and in their social relationships with men.[1] Islamic laws and traditions are frequently evoked to account for behaviour among Muslims, particularly behaviour between the sexes, and, since much scholarship on Arabs has until recently been drawn from literary sources, the weight given to the determining influence of Islamic culture has been considerable.[2] Indeed, the uninformed impression in the West is still that all Arab women occupy a position of unmitigated servility: they are completely dominated by their men and kept out of sight most of the time, only to appear in public when they are completely veiled.

The four kinds of Arab communities examined here include the Bedouin of Cyrenaica (Libya), where the people are Sunni Muslims; a horticultural community of Shiite Muslims in south Lebanon; olive farmers, Sunni Muslims, in a plantation area in Tripolitania (Libya); and a Maronite Christian village in central Lebanon.

Among the Bedouin, women are excluded from inheritance, whether as wives or daughters. Their domestic status is high, and the veil is only situational, though women are excluded from the company of men in public. Politically, their status is high, and marriage alliances are crucial, although women have virtually no direct say in the choice of spouses. Women among the Lebanese horticulturalists inherit both as wives and daughters, and although marriage constitutes an alliance of sorts, its main effect is on the redistribution of plots of land rather than on political groupings. Domestically, women's rights over their husbands are fewer, but wives are more independent of their kinfolk. Women of the peasantry spend most of their time unveiled, but women of high status are heavily veiled (save for the few Christian Arab women, who are unveiled). In all cases, social access of men to women in their households is extremely difficult, even for family friends, unless they are kin. On the Tripolitanian olive farms, women are for the most part isolated from other women, and their subservience to their husbands, even though they are involved in property matters, is conspicuous. Left alone on the farms by their husbands most of the time, this separation of women amounts to a segregation I have not witnessed elsewhere in the Middle East. Christians living in this plantation area observed limitations on the social behaviour of women, particularly among the Sicilians, of whom there are many. They contrast markedly with their counterparts among Maronite Christian women in central Lebanon, whose freedom to mix publicly with men and whose social maturity is not only conspicuous in the Middle East context but is of an order that might be regarded as libertarian in many Western communities.

The concern here is with differences between communities, and it will be seen that an explanation of various forms of behaviour is to be sought neither in Islamic culture nor in its adaptation to local needs. This is not to say, however, that Islamic culture is not a force in the behaviour of people, no more than it would be profitable to argue that Christianity is inconsequential for studies of Christian communities. By the same token it would be as unrewarding to claim that social behaviour in Muslim communities can only be understood in terms of the Quran and the traditions that have grown around it as it would be to say that behaviour in European communities can only be understood by reference to the Bible and the vast body of interpretative literature accumulated over centuries. Two of the communities under discussion belong to different divisions of Islam: the Bedouin are Sunni Muslims, and the south Lebanese are Shiites. Differences in law between Sunnis and Shiites are profound, particularly as the law affects the status of women as heirs. Yet any attempt to treat the differences described herein as resulting from these sects would be as barren as the attempt to interpret behaviour in general Islamic terms. For, while Shiite law could be used to explain many details of behaviour in the south Lebanese village, the Bedouin neglect their Sunni law in many important respects. In Lebanese Shiite law, persons related through women are put on an equal footing with those related through men as far as the designation of heirs is concerned. Women can be sole heirs to property. Practice conforms closely to law; consequently, women regularly and legally come to hold proprietary rights in all forms of property. Sunni law is emphatically agnatically weighted for inheritance purposes, and women not only stand to receive less than men, but their designation as heirs is much more limited and tied to agnatic relationship. In practice, Bedouin women do not inherit either as wives or daughters. Lebanese Shiite women are heirs, in accordance with law, but some other Shiite peoples do not observe the law: from an account of Iraqi marsh dwellers, who are Shiites (Salim 1962), it appears that their women are disinherited; and the details Barth (1961) offers of inheritance among the Shiite Basseri indicate that their practice is inconsistent with any school of Islamic law. Some Sunnis behave more in accordance with the law than do the Bedouin, although showing inconsistency: the people of the Palestinian village of Artas provide an example (Granqvist 1931–35). The differences among these five peoples cannot be resolved in terms of their codes of law. It is of interest to note that a comparative review of Muslim communities shows that some Sunni communities are closer to some Shiite communities in their practices as regards inheritance of property than they are to other Sunnis, and vice versa.

Broad cultural traits, such as those embodied in the great traditions of Islamic religion, have, therefore, little explanatory value for the analysis of differences of behaviour between peoples. Instead, the discussion becomes limited to general characterisations that rarely match actual behaviour, save as they haphazardly correspond to disconnected acts of behaviour in this or that community. It is for this reason, too, that discussions of sex differentiation are so often concerned with equality. Whether a woman's status in particular social relations is judged to be equal or unequal depends not only on the sex of the observer but also on the observer's cultural background – class, status, rural or urban origin, religious affiliation, and natal country.[3] Equality or lack of it will, therefore, not be assessed, since it is virtually impossible to evaluate. Even when both sexes hold the same right, this does not give equality, because the particular right is part of a cluster containing many others, and if the total clusters are not identical then there can be no equality of specific rights. For the significance of a particular right lies in its relation to others; detached, it is no more than a piece of information.[4]

The mode of investigation adopted here, therefore, aims to examine the rights of both sexes and seeks an explanation for the different ways in which rights cluster in one community compared with another, and of how these clusters are related to the social order. In doing this, the initial approach will be made through the life cycle, because the status of males and females, whatever other statuses may be available for capture, will inevitably vary with age. There is no such thing as *the* status of women – or of men for that matter – and to lose sight of this elementary fact leads to serious analytical distortion (see Fortes 1949, 1958). In what is to follow, the developmental cycle of the Bedouin is given in detail, thereby facilitating comparison with the other communities.

Bedouin of Cyrenaica

Among the Bedouin, there is little social differentiation among small children. The birth of a boy is the occasion for celebration and feasting. Any birth is a matter of joy because it establishes the fertility and sexual compatibility of a married pair, but when a daughter is born an animal is not usually slaughtered, as for a boy, and the expressed wish is that the next birth will be a male one. There are a number of reasons why sentiment should weigh heavily in favour of male children: there is an urgent need for the additional labour a man can command directly if he is to enlarge his economic assets; a daughter is excluded from succession; a mother has no guarantee of support in a son-in-law; and an aged man is unable to activate his agnatic rights fully except through a son (see chapter 8). By comparison, a female child does not hold the same potential, although, as the Bedouin are well aware, she holds other promises for them. Children of either sex, during the first seven years or so, spend most of their time in the female quarters of the tent under the mothers' control, playing in the camp together, running minor errands, or doing small chores. A father fondles both sexes of this age, but he is more lavish with his affection for his small son. He takes little part in the children's education, which is left to the mother, and disciplines the children only if they become obstreperous in or near the tent.

At about seven, the amulets (often a cowrie shell sewn onto a cap) worn by a boy to avert evil or misfortune are removed from the clothing, and his clothing is now of a kind that makes him more distinctively male. In keeping with these changes, the young boy frequents the men's part of the tent more and more, and the young girl keeps more to the women's part. There is no exact age when these changes occur; nor do they come about overnight. The culmination does not occur until a boy has reached his teens and a girl has entered puberty. Meanwhile, both sexes continue to move between the male and female quarters of the tent, and even when a boy has passed the age of ten he is often seen sitting on the divide between the male and female quarters of the tent, intently absorbing all that goes on on both sides. Moreover, at this age the roles of the sexes are interchangeable with regard to their tasks. Thus, they may tend the fire together or herd a few goats or sheep on the edge of the camp, or they may go to a nearby shallow well to collect small quantities of water. Close as they may seem to each other, the small boy nevertheless begins to assume authority by instructing his younger sister, and she begins to obey.

From the age of about seven until manhood, the transition for a boy is gradual and unmarked by any divisive event. In his middle teens a boy may handle a rifle and is encouraged to do so; unless his father is very poor he wears a toga and a red felt cap; he keeps to the male part of the tent; and goat herding now becomes an allotted regular task. He is still not involved in the main herding activities; the number of animals in his charge are few and he remains within sight of the camp. When he reaches the age of seventeen or eighteen, he is given a small flock of sheep to herd, wandering with them away from the camp and remaining with them during the night. After this training with goats and sheep he moves on to camel herding. Success as a camel herder is one of the chief qualifications for the beginning of manhood proper, and it is often marked by a present of a rifle and sometimes, within a year or so, a horse. By this time the youth has matured into an agnate in a corporation of agnates, responsible enough to sit with his seniors when they discuss matters of ploughing and watering rights, and to dispute with other people, adding corroborative weight to the decisions they reach.

A young girl when she reaches puberty passes much more abruptly from one status to another than does her male agnate. Henceforth, she lets her hair grow, she has to wear a head covering, and as she moves from tent to tent she draws her silk head shawl across the side of her face at the approach of males, except her closest kinsmen. Her movements are now much more restricted. She is no longer permitted to play freely with boys. Increasingly, she participates in activities of the tent, learning its intricate details; she has to spin wool, grind flour and cook, milk animals, and help to weave tent tops and carpets – all tasks that require skill and a long training period. Collecting brushwood for fire is an arduous task and carrying it back to camp is back-breaking; the unmarried daughter is usually responsible for this.

Most noticeable in a young girl, from an age soon after puberty until marriage, is her partial retirement from the general social life of the camp, lasting until she begins a new participation after the birth of children. Girls are not married until their late teens or later, and, since a young girl just past puberty is not looked upon as immediately marriageable, the restrictions placed upon her, her use of a head scarf to hide her face, and her contribution to tent duties, are all part of a growing process by way of induction into womanhood, rather than an abrupt alteration of status that accompanies a *rite de passage*. Entering into the age of puberty is a kind of acquisition for a girl since she has become capable of producing offspring. In Bedouin culture this acquisition remains potential only, until she reaches the age of about fifteen or sixteen, by which time she is kept under close surveillance. A sexual relationship between a man and an unmarried girl carries with it severe penalty, to the point of killing the culprits, as well as a rupture between the male kin of the lover and those of his accomplice; but if a man seduces a girl who has only recently entered puberty, his act is regarded as heinous, while the girl can be partly excused on the grounds of ignorance.[5]

Nubility in Bedouin Cyrenaica begins from about fifteen years. During this period the greatest threat to a girl's chastity exists. A maiden, since precedence is accorded premarital chastity, possesses the honour of her male kinsmen. If she conceives out of wedlock or is seen having sexual intercourse, she suffers, it is true, but it is her brothers, and to a lesser extent her father and her first parallel cousins, who shoulder the main burden of disgrace. Nubile women are subject to restrictions because they possess what can be regarded as a kind of commodity: the ability to bear children. Like other commodities, it is owned by males, and its transfer from one set of males to another is a contractual arrangement. Until a contract has been concluded, a male who has exclusive usufructuary rights to a woman's reproductive capabilities has not been designated, and it follows that a woman's issue lacks designation also. Despite the public virginity test – an essential part of the marriage ceremony for all young girls which must act as a restraint on premarital intercourse – the circumstantial evidence is that pre-marital intercourse does occur, on however small a scale. Bedouin, although they would not give specific evidence, admitted the possibility when explaining that if a man had enjoyed sex relations with his bride before his nuptials he would draw blood from his nose or otherwise stain his toga to conceal from the public the failure of the virginity test. Indeed, I was present at a wedding when the virginity test was a complete failure in that the groom failed to produce a bloodstained cloth by any means; the festivities turned into a fiasco of bickering on the first of the seven days of celebrations, and although the groom suffered the opprobrium of his age mates, a year later when I visited the camp, the matter was not mentioned and the couple had remained wedded. Clearly, despite the emphasis on female chastity, the concern is not so much with the act of sexual relations but with its results. Hence, the overwhelming importance attached to the designation of an individual as possessor of a woman's procreative facilities. Young men cannot act independently toward women because they lack control over property and cannot, therefore, meet the cost of their amours.

One of the effects of puberty is that female social maturity is accelerated, compared with the progress of a boy of the same age. The onset of puberty is the beginning of womanhood, with the prospect of marriage and a wholly new status only five years or so ahead. A male child remains a boy and by the time his sister has entered full womanhood in marriage, he has only reached the stage of being a youth with little prospect of marriage for three years or more. Moreover, how soon a man leaves his youth behind depends very much on his sister's development, because his marriage is delayed until a partner has been found for her. Obviously, the details of marriages depend largely on order of birth and on age differences between children, but save for the chance of children of one sex, it is true to say that the marriage of at least one male is directly affected by his sister's marriage, and others are indirectly affected also. Thus, it is common for an eldest son's marriage to be delayed until suitable arrangements have been made for his eldest sister; and once this hurdle has been successfully surmounted, the next sister will soon be married off, to be followed quickly by the next son. A father, in other words, plans his children's marriages, and the first move is critical for the success of the others. For these reasons, the age of marriage is not the same for males and females; women have several years' start over men in the race for adult status. Paradoxically, women, derisively referred to by men as irresponsible, are quickened into the responsibility of control of a domain of their own while males still suffer the status of irresponsible youths, lacking authority.

The years before marriage are a training period for assuming authority. In early life the contribution of both sexes is peripheral, in the sense that their tasks could be done by adults without seriously dislocating their main productive activities. I do not wish to diminish the significance of the contribution of child labour to a production unit; the regret voiced about a childless couple is that they have no one to fetch and carry for them. A man without sons may 'borrow' one of his brother's or sister's small sons, rewarding him later in life with a gift of animals or by making him his heir. Nevertheless, the main productive tasks do not become the responsibility of children until they reach their teens. Strikingly, the separation of the sexes now becomes pronounced. Previously, interchangeability character-ised the relations of boys and girls, both often working together at their small tasks, sitting together in the tent, and even sleeping together. Puberty parts them. Henceforth, they are separately inducted, not merely into different pursuits, but into the fields of authority to which they will ultimately succeed. As if to clarify the distinction, the separation of the sexes is at its maximum during this premarital period. Women are not, however, completely secluded and wholly bereft of male company. Men see their sisters with their faces uncovered, converse with them in the female part of the tent, confiding secrets that they could not broach even with the confidante of all men, the mother. Men of this age discuss their love yearnings and marriage hopes among themselves; such discussions, whatever their emotional value, do not bring marriage a day nearer. The subject of marriage between proximate generations is disallowed. Between father and son, avoidance of anything relating to sex or marriage is strictly observed. Only one male, the mother's brother, is free to discuss these matters and present a case for marriage to a father on behalf of a son. Men also have access to their fathers through their sisters, who are free to discuss any matters relating to male-female relationships with their mothers, and the latter, in turn, press fathers to marry off their sons.[6] While men at this age are cut off from their senior agnates in this important field of relations, young women of the same age enter fully into these relations with their seniors.

Neither young men nor young women have any authority to dispose of or manage property. Ultimately, both sexes are under the authority of the head of a tent, a male, although a young woman is effectively under her mother's authority. Lacking any control over property, they also lack the means to make claims for themselves. Both are key helpers in production. Men herd the animals, plough, reap, store the grain, and transport it to the tent as and when it is needed; it is they who water the animals during the dry months and bring water to the camp for domestic use and consumption. Women spin and weave the tent strips, together with all the carpets and bags that are found inside. Anything that needs to be done to a tent – adjustments for wind changes, repair of ropes, pitching and dismantling – is done by women exclusively. Cooking is entirely their concern. They also do all the milking.

At this age, more than at any other time, interchangeability of roles or cooperation in joint activities is reduced to a minimum. This is not just a matter of convenience. Men are not permitted to interfere in women's work, any more than are women permitted to encroach on male tasks. The effect of this clear cleavage in the division of labour, as Durkheim long ago taught us to appreciate, is to create a solidarity stemming from the symbiotic relationships of men to women, and both to the land and the animals it supports. It also means that in every camp, whether small or large, a minimum number of men and women of this age will be present. Division of tasks between the sexes at about this age is the most important single element in determining the demographic constitution of local settlements, and this in turn is critical in marking out the pattern of social relationships in the universe of each group.

The consequences do not end here. A dependence is created in the division of labour between the proximate generations of both sexes. Young women are as valuable to their seniors in domestic work as males are to theirs in herding. Throughout the developmental cycle in production units, the period during which a male and female can perform all the necessary activities, without aid, is of very short duration. The arbitrariness of the authority vested in the senior generation is constrained by demands they have to make on the younger generation for labour. Tasks performed by young men and young women entitle them to food, clothing, and shelter, and, as long as they make their appropriate contributions, their fathers must yield to their marriage demands sooner or later. If need be, the pressure built up by son and daughter can be staved off temporarily with gifts – silver bracelets or earrings in the case of women, and a horse in the case of men. It was not without point that an elder, when I urged him to consider his son's desire for marriage, replied that he had already bought him a horse and the elaborate accoutrement that went with it. Nor is it fortuitous that gifts of this sort are made to sons and daughters whose marriages have been delayed considerably due to the father's holding out for a high bridewealth. Beyond a certain period, dutiful sons and daughters are considered to have done more than earn their keep; either marriage must be arranged or some of the paternal wealth must be distributed to them, although neither son nor daughter is free to dispose of these gifts by selling them to begin gathering a flock.

Prior to marriage, therefore, both sexes are held to be responsible beings, and through responsibility they acquire a limited measure of control. They fulfil their responsibilities, however, under direction. They have yet to accede to managerial status and the prospect of capturing proprietary rights is still more remote. Late adolescence to early adulthood is the most difficult period in the life cycle of the Bedouin. Physically they have matured into adulthood and their activities compel them to carry the heavy responsibility of adulthood, but the legal right to assume the status is denied them. I wish to stress that these disabilities are suffered by both sexes, because it is at this time of their lives that women are said to 'suffer' most. I hope the details given here suffice to show that the restrictions are not reserved for women only and that they share a developmental status with their brothers of similar age. There is no question of subjugating women as a category. Both sexes come under the same authority, and although sex necessarily determines many of the specifics of behaviour, the constraints placed on both are concerned with moving them forward from one status into another – a kind of long, drawn out *rite de passage*.

Granted this high degree of premarital constraint in sexual, productive, and authority relations, a constraint not limited to single areas of social life but pervading a whole range of relationships, it follows that the changes brought about by marriage must be most profound if the long and careful preliminary discipline that both sexes perforce undergo is to make sense. What is at stake in marriage to make the training period for it so protracted, so constricting socially, and so heavy an emotional burden to bear? I suggest that the clue lies in the fact that a multiplicity of social relationships are absorbed by persons of both sexes as they grow, and that these rapidly coalesce at a point in time, coincident with marriageable age, to make marriage an important moment in change of status. It is because premarital control covers so many sets of relationships and is so strictly applied that the marriage ceremony has to comprehend a wide range of issues, and is a major event in Bedouin life. This can be documented by considering some aspects of marriage, beginning with the marriage ceremony itself.

Nuptials, and the seven festive days that accompany them, are preceded by weeks, sometimes months, of negotiations. The bare formalities are the same whether the bride is a kinswoman from within the lineage or an unrelated person of another corporation. Over these weeks of negotiations gifts are passed, to mark the beginning of the new relationship that entry into marriage involves. Bridewealth itself varies conspicuously from about two camels to twenty.[7] When marriage occurs within a corporation the bridewealth is small, and when an exchange marriage is arranged, the difference between the amounts promised may be as little as one sheep, although it is important to realise that both parties to the exchange promise more than this amount.[8] Some internal marriages carry a small amount of bridewealth, but external marriages command large amounts. This variation in amount is not a reflection on the bride or her kin. A parallel cousin marriage contracted with an agreement to pay two camels is not less important, as a marriage *per se*, than a marriage that has twenty camels attached to it. Stability of the union is not affected by the amount of bridewealth promised: a parallel cousin marriage, especially to a first cousin, leads to serious difficulties if it is broken, and although the bridewealth is small these marriages are as stable as those where the bridewealth is twice as much or more.

Bridewealth is concerned with social relations, and if this variation in amount is to be understood it must be viewed in terms of the nature of the relations that are initiated through marriage, whether these are new, with previously unrelated people; or are old ones being revived; or new ones being perpetuated. Thus, where strong links are already available – as with agnates within a corporation – the relatively small bridewealth documents the desire to add to relationships that already exist by transmuting some of them into affinity. A bridewealth of two camels is a measure of the value of affinity added to agnation. Where there is an absence of a marriage link between two corporations and an alliance is sought, then the bridewealth is likely to be massive – twenty camels if the bride's group is politically powerful. What this indicates is that a corporation wishes to build up relations of this magnitude. The exact number promised, whether it is eight, ten, fourteen, or twenty, depends on the value the suitor's group attaches to the alliance. An initial link of this sort commands a large bridewealth; in a succeeding link, say a marriage to the sister of the first spouse, or, in a succeeding generation, to a cross-cousin such as a mother's brother's daughter, the bridewealth is of a considerably reduced amount – perhaps four camels. But this second bridewealth is earnest that the now established relationships are desirable and that the intention is to consolidate and perpetuate them. The amount of bridewealth is a most valuable indication of the change expected in a set of relationships. Further evidence in support of this view is given by the status conferred on women who carry a high bridewealth. A high bridewealth endows a woman with high status, enabling her to become a kind of chief woman of a camp; she occupies this role because the responsibility of mediating a major political connection has been allocated to her.[9] Women are not merely links, providing the cross-cutting ties that bind men together. Their positions constitute the reference points on the map of any corporate group's political relationships.

After the successful conclusion of bridewealth negotiations the nuptials take place as soon as the groom has been able to collect a number of articles, together forming a separate part of the bridewealth, which, unlike the promised camels, must be given at the time of the marriage ceremonies. These articles consist of a complete outfit of clothes for the bride, a carpet and a straw mat (the 'bed'), a length of cloth to divide off the female quarters from the rest of a tent, cooking utensils, and a pair of heavy silver armlets. For the first time in her life a woman now has property over which she has proprietary rights. As long as she remains married, the consumable items in this part of the bridewealth must be renewed by her husband. Wives do not own their own tents,[10] but, save for the help they may be given on marriage, they weave them from wool provided by husbands. A tent means security of shelter for a woman, and it is interesting to note that at any time during her life a woman can demand shelter, whereas a male may be unable to make this demand for certain limited periods of his life. A bachelor is not always able to find tent accommodation, and perforce sleeps against the side of a tent to gain some shelter from the elements. This arises out of the fact that in a tent a woman is provided with her own private domain – the female third of a tent – but she also possesses access rights to the male quarters, since it is here that the 'bed' of sexual intercourse is laid out. A wife is thus able to exclude her husband's brothers from nocturnal shelter, from a home in fact; but because female quarters are exclusively for use by women, women cannot be excluded by males.

During his lifetime a husband remains titular head of a tent as long as he has a wife in control of the female quarters. Without the services of a woman, a man surrenders his title to headship: there is point to the saying, 'a woman is to a man as the tent pole is to the tent'. Indeed, a woman can become head of a tent herself: if she is widowed, but still active, with a young child, she can recruit bachelors or widowers from among her kinsmen, give them shelter in her tent in exchange for their labour, and enjoy dominion over them until the unit is split on her son's marriage. Much attention is given in the literature to the care and protection provided for widows and old women; the provisions that have to be made for bachelors and aged widowers are more difficult to meet because the availability of a woman of the right age and status is a minimal essential in any domestic unit. A woman possesses both the right to a separate part of the tent and the right to control all the activities that go on there. The preparation and cooking of food, weaving, gathering tinder – all those activities without which the round of everyday living would come to a halt – are exclusively female tasks. Males are excluded from participation in these activities, and since they are barred from the female part of the tent, a woman must be present in all tents. A widower with or without young children, or a man who has hastily divorced his wife, is in a predicament that can only be resolved by the immediate recruitment of another woman, or else he must face the dispersal of the unit and the possibility of remaining homeless for a long period. Moreover, a widow, after her son has married and broken up her home, may go to live with her son, but she can also live in a tent on her own (see S. Peters 1952). A man cannot do this.

For a tent to be more than a dormitory, both sexes must be present. When, therefore, a bride is presented with domestic utensils and a tent at marriage, they are not for herself only: the husband gains possession of the domestic services of a woman. Part of his social life comes under his authority for the first time. Immediately after marriage, this authority is not effective if a man's mother is alive, because the latter anxiously awaits the arrival of a daughter-in-law to close the gap in domestic help created by the loss of her own daughter in marriage. Even in a case of first parallel cousin marriage, when the natal tents of both spouses are adjoining in a small camp, the new wife takes her place with her mother-in-law, and meticulously observes her new station. Until a child is born, then, a man shares his wife, domestically, with his mother, and only exerts effective authority over her sexually. Also, because the tent of a newlywed couple is used only for sleeping, the husband is still part of his father's domestic unit, and is, therefore, under his authority. It is not until the birth of a child – or the death of the parents – that the new couple are liberated to become tied to their own tent.

Thus far, of the changes precipitated by marriage, only those relating to limited aspects of bridewealth have been discussed. A full account of the marriage ceremony and its symbolic riches is out of place here. The discussion now turns to property and its distribution.

Males acquire their proprietary rights to animals and land by transmission through males. Women do not inherit. Bedouin are aware that in thus dispossessing women they are contravening the Shari'a law, but to do otherwise would result in an uncontrolled alienation of property from the corporate group where ownership is vested. Bridewealth effects the transfer of property from one corporation to another, but the transfer is controlled. Since women are free to be married by men outside their natal corporations (nearly half their marriages are of this sort), female inheritance would mean an uncontrolled run on corporate resources. This would be serious enough if only mobile property were involved, but if land were threatened in this way also, the entire basis of corporate life would collapse. Therefore, the lack of status of women as heirs is, among the Bedouin, related not only to the status of individuals as heirs, but to the nature of the property-owning group.

The property-owning group among the Bedouin is a corporation of males clustered together on the basis of what is conceived of as agnation. Moreover, the relation of these groups of males to permanent property is a fixed one; the economy of mixed agriculture and pastoralism in Cyrenaica permits agnates to remain assembled on their homeland, absences for economic purposes occurring only two or three times a year and for such short periods that it is unnecessary to move tent and family. This relationship to land persists from generation to generation, since the virilocal marriage arrangements, while they may not always be patrilocal, confine residence in the majority of cases to a homeland, the territory of a corporate group. By comparison, women are much more mobile. Marriage takes many women away from the natal homeland, and the mothers of women who marry within their corporation may well have been recruited from other corporations. If one views the matter in terms of one generation, some women, coincidentally as it were, remain attached to their homeland; this is too fortuitous to allow us to speak of a fixed relationship of women to land, and when successive generations are taken into account the relationship is seen to be even less permanent. Women are thus precluded from constituting permanent groups with enduring ties to parcels of land.

Mobile property in the form of animals is the other side of the coin: denied permanent rights to land and water, women (as a category) lack the basis to rear flocks and herds, since if they are to keep animals they can only do so through the good offices of men. Some women contrive to control a small flock of sheep or a few camels, but if they were allowed to inherit and to transmit freely, this, in effect, would be an invasion of the natural resources of a corporate group. Hence, proprietary control of both these major forms of property, and the transmission of this right, rests with males. In this respect women never reach full legal majority. On the other hand a man does not acquire proprietary rights until his father has died.[11] With regard to natural resources and mobile property, women of all ages and men – married and unmarried – who have yet to inherit, are together under the authority of senior males.[12] Marriage, retarded by senior males, as others in the community think, is a public challenge to this authority. The unendowed – males and females – combine at a wedding ceremony to announce that one of the bastions of authority is falling. Senior males stand apart from the festivities, overbearingly disregarding the warning there is in them. Inasmuch as rights to property are not and cannot be compromised, their disinterestedness is fitting; but since social relationships are not all subsumed under these rights, and because the authority, which stems from these rights, seeps its way into diverse fields of relationships, marriage leaves the rights intact but erodes the domain of authority. One aspect of marriage is the transacted transfer of property between two sets of senior males. It is the wedded couple who are instrumental to this transfer. Since they are implicated in this way, the interests of the senior males are delegated to them for fulfilment.

After marriage a son has a claim to his father's goods. The young man's wife and children must be clothed and fed, and wool must be made available for weaving purposes. Claims to these goods are made by a wife on her husband, but he has to get them from his father, who is compelled to give. By this time a father will have probably retired from the arduous duties of herding, thus relinquishing effective managerial control of the animals to his married son, so that claims to goods are a recognition of rewards due for different services: at an earlier age, the son's labour was rewarded by his keep, but now his needs have expanded considerably, and his services have grown in status to match. A married couple, especially after they form a separate domestic unit, dismantles the authority of the family head and win a stake in his property, thus advancing toward greater independence. In this area of relationships, the couple act jointly to cream off as much as they can of the patriarchal wealth. Independent claims are also secured by the wife through bridewealth. In order to appreciate this, reference must be made to another aspect of bridewealth.

At the bridewealth negotiations, the details of the wealth to pass from the groom's kin to the bride's father and selected members of his kin are stated and witnessed. These negotiations are concluded by an advance 'gift' of a few sheep,[13] which, assuming the marriage prospers, commences a series of gift exchanges that continues for years. The main part of the bridewealth payments is not given for about a year. Depending on the fertility or barrenness of the marriage, the first amount to pass will vary, but it will not amount to more than a small fraction of the amount promised, in either event. The remainder is left over as a debt, and may never be paid over to the bride's father, certainly not if relationships between the two sets of kin develop favourably. Against this remainder, the girl's father and brother can make claims on the services and good offices of the husband and his father. Also, a wife is enabled to extract wealth from her husband. The manner in which this is done follows a conventional pattern of behaviour. A wife, as a result of a quarrel with her husband during which he insulted her, or particularly if he struck her, goes back to her father in anger. The word commonly used for the state to describe a woman who leaves her husband in these circumstances is *za'alana*.[14] She refuses to return until she is placated with a 'gift'. Sometimes this 'gift' is a valuable pair of silver armlets, or one or more sheep. It always represents a redirection of property in favour of a wife. In later years, a wife no longer resorts to this ruse for extracting property from her husband, for the bridewealth debt has by now been buried beneath an accumulation of social relationships. The wife's father is well aware that further payments will not be forthcoming, and he formally renounces all claims by requesting that the bridewealth still outstanding is to be 'put in front of her' (his daughter). It is not given to her outright, but she insists on marking an agreed number of sheep with her father's or brother's personal brand: she holds the right to nominate an heir, among her sons, to this property. A similar arrangement is practised in a sororal and leviratic marriage; an amount of bridewealth is stated, but the woman's father agrees to leave it 'in front of her'. In some cases, women amass sufficient property in animals (their silver armlets and anklets they tend to sell for animals as they reach old age) to affect significantly the distribution of inherited wealth among a man's sons, and in doing so give one of them an advantageous start in the struggle for power.[15] These rights are not to be dismissed lightly as peripherally influential, but should be seen as rights that determine relations.

It is now necessary to clarify the relation of women to property. Both wives and daughters are disinherited, contrary to Islamic law, and they are well aware of this. But women do not meekly surrender such a prime right because they are submissive by nature, as some writers on Arabs seem to believe. They renounce rights – whether they are Bedouin or of the other Arab communities discussed below – and in return they are able to make claims against the males who hold their property rights. This ability to press claims applies to heritable property and to bridewealth. These claims are neither 'submerged' nor 'shadowy', as Goody writes (1959). They are asserted by women unambiguously. Hence, when a man among the Bedouin seeks access to ploughland or water in his mother's brother's territory, or asks for a share of his animal products, the mother's brother must yield because his sister can make demands against him. Similarly, when a mother's brother assists his sister's son by making a significant contribution to his bridewealth, or to a blood money payment, he does this not out of sentiment – which varies with the individual in any case – but in recognition of his sister's due share of his property. It is for this reason that the mother's brother, in Cyrenaica, is of such high import to the sister's son, not because he stands external to the affairs of the corporate group – often he is a member of the same group – but because the intricacies of property relationships compel him to participate in the affairs of the group into which his sister has married. Lest it be thought that a woman, as sister or mother in this context, merely acts as a channel along which relationships between mother's brother and sister's son flow, it must be made explicit that this is not so: a woman has her own defined position in relation to property. This is to be seen, also, in her diverting property from her natal home to her husband, according to her wishes, and if she is disinclined to effect this transfer, her husband will not receive the property.

Dispossessed of proprietary rights, women nevertheless help to shape things in all fields of behaviour, and not only within the limits of small domestic groups. This women achieve without recourse to revolt, either of a ritual or a nonrational kind. What they do is force claims that they support with their rights. Their claims are not arbitrary; they are commensurable with their rights, otherwise they could not be sustained. For this reason unmarried women do not press claims, although during the years before marriage a woman is more restricted socially and has less status than at any subsequent time. If demands are to come from any females, if revolt is to appear among women, it is from this 'deprived' group that either or both could be expected.[16] In fact, demands come from married women, and with good reason: the 'deprived' group has not been deprived in the sense of being divested of rights; they have not acquired any yet. Women cannot rationally make demands against nothing. Backed by bridewealth and the rights with which they are thereby endowed, they have no need to make demands; they can force claims.

Bridewealth has further implications. Left largely as a debt it becomes almost a synonym for reciprocal obligations, for social relationships, that is to say. Indeed marriage is commonly referred to as 'making relationships'. What bridewealth and marriage do is to initiate a set of social relationships in which claims and counterclaims can be made against forms of property. Two parties of senior males assume the responsibility for initiating the relationships, which they have decided are in conformity with their interests, and thereafter they relinquish the future of these relationships to a pair of spouses, who, in some cases, have never met before.

It is necessary to interrupt that argument to point out that the question of social compatibility seldom arises as a serious issue (see Freedman 1967). The tent is divided into male and female parts, and for most of the daytime, at least, the sexes occupy their own areas of the tent. On the first day of the marriage ceremonies, sexual compatibility has already been tested, albeit in a preliminary manner. The virginity test is not only a witness to premarital chastity; it ensures also that the bride is not suffering some sort of sexual malformation. On the first night of the nuptials the marriage is consummated, and the following day the spouses are questioned about it by males and females respectively. The spouses continue to sleep together for the test period of seven days – the duration of the wedding festivities, in fact. Consummation reveals that the bride is sexually normal and that the groom is not impotent. If either defect is present, the arrangements are summarily terminated. Also, if these first seven days pass without impediment, it augurs well for future sexual compatibility. It is indicative of the relatively minor importance attached to social compatibility that little provision is made for it before marriage or during the nuptials. A married pair is not compelled to remain in each other's company at any time during the day, not even for meals, which men always take separately and, if necessary, alone. They sleep together only for sexual intercourse. Social compatibility matures as time passes, and as the spouses associate socially to an increasing extent. In the early years of marriage, at a time, that is, before companionship has had a chance to take a strong grip, and when divorce, for personal reasons, is most likely to occur, the need for continuous social relations does not exist. Social compatibility of the spouses is peripheral to the matter of marital stability. This point is stressed in order to throw the critical importance of the young spouses, particularly the wife, into relief. Whether the relationships initiated by marriage prosper is too important an issue to be left to the chance of two individuals of opposite sexes getting along together. In the final analysis, it is left to the considered adjudications they make, separately or jointly, on the relationships that they mediate.[17]

The priority given here to mediation, compared with linking and communication, arises from the consideration that while the latter are operative in marriages between corporations, they are largely irrelevant where the spouses are the children of a pair of full brothers or of close cousins resident in the same small camp of a few tents. The argument that a woman in marriage mediates relationships comprehends all marriage, whatever the particular form it takes or the territorial distance it covers. This becomes clear upon consideration of the interests served by marriage within corporations and between them.

Property rights within corporations entitle all agnates to an equal share of land and water resources. Inheritance rules make the male children of a man equal heirs to his property. If this equality were to be realised in practice, then it would mean an absence of social differentiation. It can be stated as a fact that while class does not exist, differentiation on the basis of wealth and status does. The main way in which this is brought about is by men struggling to break out of the treadmill of equal shares to capture more than their legal agnatic right. Part of the point of parallel cousin marriage is that it assists the unequal allocation of resources, because matrilateral and affinal connections among agnates can be used to make requests not permitted within agnation; and because agnates have the same rights to resources but not all of them have a sufficient number of animals to use their full share of water or the wealth (in the sense of money to buy seed and labour to plough) to grow a large crop, trading of resources between affinally and matrilaterally related agnates appears. An agnate cannot alienate his share to another agnate, since as agnates all men of a corporation have a legal claim to the surplus. Marriage thrusts a wedge of differentiation into agnation. A power seeker who marries one of his daughters to a poor agnate gains through her the unexpended surplus of a fellow agnate, thus enabling him to increase the size of his flocks and herds. With regard to animals, the distribution among heirs is rarely equal; the eldest son, for various reasons, is in a position to appropriate more than an equal share. In the succeeding generation, this unequal distribution can be partially corrected if an heir who loses property to his eldest brother marries his son to the eldest brother's daughter and defaults on the bridewealth; and this daughter has the ability to divert more of this wealth. The success of attempts to skim off surpluses from fellow agnates, and the readjustments in the distribution of inherited mobile property, hinge on the willingness of a wife to remain with her husband. A wife has the power to make or break a relationship.

The capture of unequal access to agnatic resources is the immediate aim of men. Assuming a man achieves this, he is then in a position to expand his animal wealth. Large flocks and herds, in a country where climatic vagaries lead to concentrations of surplus water here and deficiencies there, in any given year, can become a serious liability unless secure links to the resources of other corporations are available. For what such links mean is that local surpluses that accumulate in corporations can be redistributed by permitting affinal and matrilateral kinsmen to water their animals there when they are short of water in their homeland, or by granting them the use of ploughland when they are experiencing a shortage of rainfall, or an unsuitable regime for raising a crop. It is partly for this reason that links leapfrog collateral sections (or neighbouring corporations) where conditions are likely to be identical, and are dropped into selected sections at greater distances. Women residing in other corporations secure continued economic stability, where otherwise all corporate groups would be exposed to the persistent threat of local economic instability. Economic stability must be anchored in affinity and kinship. Contractual relations alone are too frail to provide the security required. In other areas of relationships, the ties of debt – essentially arrangements imposing obligations, but of a kind that can be summarily renounced – appear to be sufficiently strong to maintain them. They are, however, tenuous relationships, lacking the jural durability of those tied up in marriage.

Relationships do not, however, begin and end with the economic distribution of wealth. The member of a corporation who succeeds in capturing the equal shares to resources of fellow agnates also commands a following, since, in return for the shares, food and wool are given, creating dependency. First parallel cousin marriage, by converting an agnatic nephew into a dependent affine, can thwart the nephew's power ambitions, and leave the field clear for his wife's brother to conquer. Women positioned in other corporations also secure the political allegiance of a number of corporations: the extent of the spread of external marriages that a man of power possesses is an accurate measure of the span of his power. Whether one considers the case of a man who has succeeded only in dominating his brothers, or of one who has enlarged his field to the extent of a small camp, or another who can boast of the allegiance of several corporations, the domains of each are delineated by women.[18] If this view is valid, then women are not mere links, they are the points of articulation in combinations of corporate groups, which constitute the political structures and which form the basis of all political activities.

Finally, to complete the details of the developmental cycle for Bedouin women, a few further remarks are needed. As women age, their daily relations with men of the camp are easier than before. They rarely cover their faces, they go into the male part of the tent more often, they are free to talk with men of all ages, and curtaining off the women's part of the tent is limited to the infrequent occasions when a gathering of strangers meets in the male part. Past childbearing age, a woman, who previously argued with males within the limits of her own domestic unit, now engages in public discussions, voicing opinions that may be backed by other women in the camp. It is wrong to suppose that because women are not among men during discussions they are no more than isolated units and wholly unrepresented. In most camps a leading woman is present, usually the wife of the camp shaikh, who greets guests on their arrival and entertains visitors in the absence of males. These female leaders rely on women for support; leadership among women is not given them *ex gratia* by males. Just as most men in most camps are agnatically related, so too, women, drawn from a wide range of groups, are also related consanguineously and affinally. Men are masters of the art of reckoning agnatic connections among males; women are equally adept at finding their way through a labyrinth of ties to establish links among themselves. Those women who rise to prominence in the camps are not isolated individuals who have been thrown into totally strange surroundings by marriage.[19] They lead connected groups of kinswomen. But they lead among men of a corporation other than their own natal one. Their presence there ensures that the interests of their natal corporations are respected and included in the deliberations of the corporations where they live as wives. They are mothers as well as wives, and guard the rights and well-being of their sons, as their participation in nuptials makes abundantly clear. They are included if inheritance disputes arise; and if, through her own efforts, a woman fails to gain her ends, she can call on her father or brother to assist her to deal, as an affine, with her husband or others of his close kin who threatened her son. If a man gives preferential treatment to one son in distributing his property, against the wishes of his wife, she is able to adjust the balance by giving her property to another son; or, if she wishes, she can tip the balance still further by giving it to her husband's preferred heir. Therefore, women are not intrusive to agnation. They do not constitute a category in opposition to males. They insist that their claims are met; so do men; neither forces claims in the absence of rights. The male-female dichotomy is false when applied to Bedouin life (see Evans-Pritchard 1934). There are not two worlds, one for men and one for women. The sexes combine to form a single community, where women do not consistently press female rights, any more than men consistently press male rights, but where both sexes – amid the uproar of disputes and the calm of reconciliations, the growth of new relations and the breach of others – recognise a convergence of interests and attain a tolerable social life.

Shiite villagers of Lebanon

The Shiite Muslim village of south Lebanon has a multicrop economy, with a variety of over twenty fruits and vegetables.[20] The population is divided into three ranks, distinguished by dress, occupation, and style of living: the

Learned Families (as they like to speak of themselves), who live a leisured life, comprising roughly 20 per cent of the population, owning roughly half the cultivable land and deriving additional income, in various ways, from the religious status accorded them in the village; the petty traders, who own the fourteen shops, and who, as a group, are better off than those whose income is derived almost solely from cultivation; and the peasants or labourers, who constitute the vast majority of the local population, who work their own land and that of wealthier people and are engaged as casual labourers in the coastal towns during the agriculturally slack period in midwinter, and among whom there are considerable differences of wealth. The discussion begins with the peasant group.

Until they reach the age of about seven years, boys and girls are treated in similar fashion to their desert cousins. From the age of about ten and onward, children of both sexes run errands about the village, or carry parcels for unrelated people and shopkeepers. In summer, when people from the coast flock into the hills and rent houses, or live with kinsfolk for two to three months until the worst of the heat and humidity on the coast has passed, children, especially boys, are kept busy daily. They are paid for their services. The payments are trivial for each task, but it is possible for boys to accumulate the equivalent of several shillings in a day. For this is a cash economy, and one of its features is that trivial payments can be made for trivial tasks. Among the Bedouin, children are fortunate if they are rewarded at all, and what they receive can only be a piece of bread or meat, or the rare luxury of a sweet after a father has made one of his infrequent visits to market; the reward is eaten immediately. Among the Lebanese children the small coins they are given can be saved and later used to buy an article of their own choosing. From an early age these children learn to use wealth independently, and to gauge the value of their labour and the goods they see. This interest in evaluation is implanted at a young age, in a multicrop economy, when the value of one product has to be assessed against that of another, for exchange purposes; the absorbing interest in money and prices, which both sexes of all ages show, is a noticeable feature, and the inquiries they make are not moderated by considerations of privacy. This early training makes them well fitted for the kind of property relations they enter into a few years later.

Children who have reached their teens follow their fathers and mothers to the gardens and begin to learn methods of cultivation. At the same time boys continue to earn their small amounts, but girls of this age do not frequent the marketplace. Instead, they learn to sew, to make preserves, and other household skills; they also act as domestic servants for other people.

All these are spare-time activities until the age of twelve, since both sexes attend school compulsorily. Thereafter, the tasks they perform become differentiated, except that at this age all garden tasks are interchangeable. Where the differentiation is apparent, however, is in the household. Young girls assist their mothers with the cooking and bread-making, and they help keep the house clean. But it is not wrong for a boy to join them, particularly when the house has to be swept. Among the Bedouin the differentiation between the sexes is clear-cut by this age, whereas, in Lebanon, interchangeability continues to characterise the relationship between the sexes in the growing and harvesting of crops. When they enter their late teens, sons and daughters are full-time members of a production team and spend long hours in the gardens working together. A full discussion of the multitude of tasks required in any economy, of the horticultural richness of this village, is outside the scope of this study: suffice it to say that harvests run in an uninterrupted sequence for nine months of the year, and even during the slack winter months vegetables are being picked. There are some tasks, however, that are exclusively the work of males; there are others that are allotted to women, but men are not barred from any of these.

An examination of these points of departure between the sexes leads to interesting results when compared with the Bedouin. Lebanese males plough the land; in this women have no part. Many of the terrace walls on the steep slopes collapse in winter. If only a few stones have tumbled, women may assist men. Major repairs to large gaps in the walls are carried out by men only. Plots that have fallen into disuse are broken up laboriously with an adze by men, although it must be added that an adze is not a peculiarly male instrument, and is used by women for a number of purposes, such as splitting firewood. Much of the land has to be watered at regular intervals. Men do this work, sometimes having to rise in the middle of the night if the time allotted happens to fall at that inconvenient hour. The tasks listed are done mainly by males and are referred to as men's work; it is not wrong for women to help, and no evil will befall people or crops if they do. The same remark applies to women's work. Distinctively, this is weeding, but men can weed with women, or without their help for that matter. Add to this interchangeability between the sexes the fact that there is no differentiation of garden work according to age, and it can readily be appreciated that a small family is a highly efficient productive unit, maximising its labour potential, and at the same time creating a high degree of cooperative dependency among its members. Nevertheless, there are three tasks that women do not undertake on their own – ploughing, terrace repairs, and irrigating the plots. In these specific relations to property, women must depend on men.

Domestically, also, the cleavage between the sexes is not nearly as sharp as in Cyrenaica. The Lebanese housework is mainly woman's work. Yet men are not removed from the preparation of food in the sense that any help or interference would bring bad luck. The separation of the sexes in this context is most at the meal, when, as in Cyrenaica, they eat separately even within the intimacy and privacy of an elementary family: the women sit in the centre of the room and the father sits in the right hand corner facing the door, his two shoulders resting against two walls, and his sons beside him. Women control the kitchen, but just as men are not wholly excluded from the preparation of food, so they are not compelled to reside with women, as in Cyrenaica. A bachelor can live on his own. Life is not intolerably difficult for a man who wishes to remain a widower or unmarried. But if men can live alone, so can women. They do not plough but they can hire labour, in the same way as men can employ girls as domestic servants, there being a sufficient labour surplus to provide for the needs of both. Both sexes can live apart, many of them remaining unmarried because such a conspicuously high degree of interchangeability between the sexes exists with regard to productive activities and domestic tasks. This raises the question: why should the interchangeability of these roles be maximised in this south Lebanese village, and reduced to a minimum among the Bedouin?

The critical productive activities in the Cyrenaican economy are ploughing, herding, watering animals, and, to a lesser extent, gathering the harvest. Ploughing, assuming favourable conditions, must be completed in a fortnight or three weeks, and during this time men work hard from early morning to sunset. Herding animals causes men to be absent from camp for several successive days, and when the pastures dry up as summer approaches, they are away for longer periods, dropping in at the camps for short respites only. Watering a flock of a hundred sheep takes several hours, and watering a herd of twenty camels is long and exacting. Barley is gathered as it begins to ripen, but when the whole crop is ready, it requires work of several men for several days or weeks, depending on its size. To briefly characterise the effort required: concentrated and intense labour is needed urgently twice during the year, and if this kind of labour is not available, the crop is lost; regular labour must be at hand to give constant attention to the animals and to wander with them in search of pastures. Women cannot provide this kind of labour. They milk the animals, a relatively easy task for which substitution is possible. They can also tend a small herd of young goats with the help of young children. But the main tasks of production are beyond their capabilities, if they are to bear children as well. The nature of production shuts women out of a major role as producers. The economy also lacks diversification. Composed of only one crop and of animal herding, it is too concentrated to offer any alternatives for women: they, therefore, only process the products.

In the Lebanese village, there is a wide range of crops. Temporary incapacity is not catastrophic. If a woman has to hire labour for one harvest because she is incapacitated by childbirth, she is often fit enough to deal with the next. Infants add a burden to labour but they do not prevent it. A family of children is an asset, because even young boys and girls can pick fruit, assist with grape packing, and the like. Women's childbearing role does not preclude them from sustaining production. In an economy as diversified as this, the range of opportunities available to women is wide enough to minimise the dislocative effect of their biological role. And to make their participation effective they engage in the full range of tasks save for those that require immediate and continued attention for limited but critical periods. Therefore, in Cyrenaica, little economic diversity, coupled with the concentrated effort required for two short periods of the year, are important factors in the marked sex differentiation and the little inter-changeability of roles; in Lebanon, conspicuous economic diversity promotes interchangeability of roles and minimises sex-differentiation.

Neither the Bedouin nor south Lebanese peasant women cover their faces, except in limited situations: since they both engage in tasks publicly, a veil would be an intolerable encumbrance. Nevertheless, Bedouin girls during the period of nubility are restricted in their movements and draw the head scarf across their faces at the approach of all males save for those of their immediate family, while south Lebanese peasant girls during the same period are no more restricted in their movements nor do they cover their faces more than at any other time in their lives. Why this difference between the two? Bedouin marriages are arranged by the parental generation, for the reasons already given. There is urgent need, therefore, for them to control their nubile daughters. Covering the face is an essential part of this control. The marriages of peasant girls in the south Lebanese village are not strictly arranged; many of them follow premarital pregnancies, and, in cases where the parents take an initiative in arranging a match, the daughter must concur in their choice. But these Lebanese girls are to be distinguished from Bedouin girls in two important respects. They inherit as wives and daughters, and they receive a settlement on marriage. They also contribute significantly to productive labour. Bedouin girls do not inherit, they are not given their bridewealth, and they only process the products of male labour. In all these respects, Lebanese girls achieve an independence of status not granted to their Bedouin cousins.

Young women of the Learned Families in the south Lebanese village behave quite differently. Like their menfolk, women of the Learned

Families do not work on the land at all. In public they are permanently veiled. They are distinguishable from other women by the black garments they wear, and the veil shows that they do not engage in agricultural activities: more important, the veil is meant to ward off the attentions of men. Women of the Learned Families remain indoors most of the time, and when they go out to visit, they go in small groups or with a male escort. Any women who brazenly frequent the village centre would be suspected of concupiscence, but peasant women move freely out of doors: they must do so since almost daily they go to and from the gardens – some of them distant – and during these excursions they converse with men, call out greetings to them, and avert their gaze or draw their headcovering across the side of their face only when they pass adult male strangers. Women of the Learned Families are much more secluded, and they are brought up to regard unveiled female faces and the appearance of women in public places as vulgarity. Ascent in status places greater restrictions on the behaviour of women.

In both classes, women inherit as wives, mothers, daughters, and sisters. The discussion of the division of labour shows the vital role peasant women play in relation to property. It is suggested that the rights held by women in property are derived from the contributions they make to production, for, unlike Bedouin women, their activities are not confined to procession products handed over to them by men. Learned Families' women do not produce; neither do the men. Both absorb the surplus of male and female peasant labour, and both inherit. Therefore, the two distinct patterns of differentiation in this Lebanese village cannot be a matter of inheritance alone, even though a comparison between peasant and Bedouin women suggests this as an immediate possibility. Since inheritance is not the only critical variable, why is it that control is exercised over the general behaviour and marriages of women of the Learned Families, while women of the peasantry are allowed a considerable measure of freedom in both these areas of their lives? Part of the explanation of these differences is in the nature of the property groups to be found among the Learned Families and the peasants, respectively.

The rank of the Learned Families is founded in property ownership. Their disproportionate share of property in land allows them to hire labour and detach themselves from agricultural work. But the balance between them and the peasants, who get for their work half the products of the land, is a delicate one. Alienation of land is a threat to their rank. This threat occurs in two ways: men can sell land, and women transfer it through marriage. It is met by tying land to an association of males, with the authority to threaten disciplinary action against those who are tempted by rising prices to sell and, also, by controlling marriages. Because women must be prevented from dismembering the estate of the Learned Families they are denied free choice in marriage. The same applies to men. It is in the interests of both sexes to marry within their land association, for the threat comes as much from a man's marrying a peasant as it does from a woman's marrying a peasant – and this needs to be emphasised, since in most anthropological works, particularly those on Arabs, marriage arrangements are seen in terms of male interests, rarely female. The population of the Learned Families is, however, only about two hundred and twenty.[21] Therefore, the high marriage rate within the group in the village – over 60 per cent for males and over 80 per cent for females – can only be achieved with an accompanying high spinster and bachelor rate, for demographic reasons. The precedence given to the maintenance of the total land holdings of the Learned Families is evidenced by the large number of unmarried people of both sexes, and this in turn shows the control of marriages of both sexes.

Among the Bedouin, only one spinster was encountered during a stay of over two years – she was found to be sexually deformed on the first day of her nuptials. Lacking any property rights, she was forced to rely on the compassion of her kinsmen, for the claims that other women enforce accrue to them from marital status. Spinsters of the Learned Families are not doomed to commiseration. They become leaders of congregations of women that meet to mourn the death of one of the early heroes of Islam. They have the wealth to pay for a pilgrimage to Mecca or to other shrines venerated by Shiites. A spinster is also a benefactor for many men and women of her class; they vie for her favours. She becomes a sort of revered aunt credited with neutrality because, without husband or children, she stands in the same relationship to a number of people; she is endowed with neutrality, also, because the competition among her potential heirs, particularly those who are unlikely to receive much if she dies intestate, tends to inhibit her from decisively discriminatory decisions. Hence, spinsters act as foci for small groups within the Learned Families, consulted on important matters and serving as the repositories of troubles for their kinsfolk. Where women inherit and wealth is available for transmission, spinsters are likely to hold high status.

Comparatively, the differences between the Sunni Bedouin and the Shiite Lebanese can be summarised as follows. Among the Bedouin there is little separation of the sexes until girls become nubile, but from then until they marry the behaviour of young women is strictly controlled. Marriages are arranged for both sexes by senior males. After marriage the formality in male-female relationships decreases. As men mature into managerial responsibility for flocks and herds, ploughing and harvesting, women increasingly take over the management of the domestic unit, including the children, especially sons. Women agree to renounce their inheritance and assent to the transfer of their bridewealth to their nearest kinsmen. Both these rights to property they compound for claims against their kinsmen and their husbands. At marriage, women assume a political status, and some of them rise to positions of leadership.

In the south Lebanese village, women of high status wear the veil from infancy for their whole lives, their movements are restricted, and they do not associate with men. Peasant women wear a head scarf which they draw across their faces in certain circumstances only; they are much freer to move in and around the village, they work alongside men, and they engage in brief conversations, publicly, with virtually any village men. The majority of men and women of the Learned Families marry within their rank. Peasants have a much wider range of choice in marriage, and their marriages are often love matches. Although neither sex among the Learned Families engages in productive activities, there is interchangeability between them regarding domestic tasks, sufficient, at least, to allow some men to live alone. The peasants show great interchangeability between the sexes regarding production activities, and on a reduced scale regarding domestic tasks. Women among both the Learned Families and the peasants inherit, and they are accorded the same precedence as males in reckoning heirship. Sometimes women relinquish their property to a brother, and this is reported in the literature as a denial of inheritance – as if they would simply give away their most valuable material assets due to meekness, submissiveness, or some other quality peculiar to them. My evidence is that women who do this reside in coastal towns and are unable to manage their plots of land in the village. The kinsmen who receive benefices of this kind are obliged to maintain their sisters and their families for three months during the summer months, when there is a general exodus of people from the heat of the towns to the cool of the hills. These sisters, when they return to the coast, take with them enough fruit, nuts and preserves to last for months. In return for the land they 'give' to their brothers, they receive annually some 30 per cent of their subsistence needs.

The control of marriage exercised by the Learned Families is to be seen in terms of the threat of alienation of property that the free choice of partner would pose. For the Learned Families the threat is immediate since both sexes inherit. Moreover, the threat is all around them, since they are a small minority of the village population, and, demographically, it is hard for them to maintain the integrity of their group. The fact that there are only two extant marriages for men and one for women outside their group is ample evidence of the success of the socialisation they receive from childhood. The Bedouin do not have to concern themselves about the alienation of natural resources because they are of a kind that makes individual inheritance impossible. Animal property, together with cereals, is the basis of Bedouin subsistence, and if either of these forms of wealth is to be distributed outside the corporate group, this must be done in a planned way, such is their importance. Moreover, as I have stressed, their women have claims on men, and, given the scarcities of the semi-desert, it is of critical importance that these claims be controlled also. By contrast with both the Bedouin and the Learned Families, the peasants are not constrained within the boundaries of large groups; instead, they are fractionised into the small groups of individual families. Since both sexes inherit, each marriage effects a rearrangement of plots, and, as either spouse views the matter, one adds to the holdings of the other. In these circumstances, the control of marriage can safely be reduced to a minimum. Therefore, when property is held by a collectivity, whether it is individually transmitted or corporately owned, the premarital behaviour of women is restricted and marriages are arranged. When property is individually transmitted and individuals do not constitute a collectivity, premarital control is lax and the choice of partner is permitted.

In this comparison the issue of political status remains. A paradox of combinations can be expressed: low jural standing but high political status for Bedouin women, and the appearance of leadership among them; high jural standing but low political status for women of the Learned Families and the peasants, and an absence of political leadership. Clearly, the resolution of the apparent paradox is to be sought in the power of women to bring groups of people together. In this respect the women of the south Lebanese village are at a disadvantage, compared with Bedouin women, because their jural status is so sharply defined in law and practice. This defines their social domain as well. They represent a known quantity, so to speak, and when they enter marriage their contribution is individual and measurable – as, indeed, it is for males. The status of Bedouin women in relation to property is characterised by ambiguity. Moreover, they are born into corporate groups. When they marry they bring together two groups, or if they marry within their natal corporate group they knit together people whose interests coincide, in one way or another. Inheritance is not the only relevant factor here, however: transfers of wealth at marriage are also significant, and serve to demonstrate the differences between women in the two communities with greater clarity.

In the south Lebanese village, the property transferred at marriage is land. It is given to the bride as a marriage settlement (*mahr*), and it is registered in her name. The plot is provided by the groom himself, and, almost invariably, it represents an advance of part of the inheritance he is to receive from his parents. This marriage settlement is enlarged by a grant of land to the bride by her parents, and this, also, is given as an advance of part of her inheritance. Further, it is an accepted arrangement that both spouses, when they become heirs to their parental property, will have preferential claims to the land lying adjacent to the plots brought together by their marriage. In this way, they come to own a small joint estate when they begin their married life, which they work for themselves, thus achieving a measure of economic independence. They remain heirs to parental property after marriage, but the grants of land made to them at marriage considerably lessen their dependence on their kin; and, since these grants are part of their rights as legal heirs, they do not create a tangle of obligations. Marriage brings together two individuals, and the redistribution of property it occasions does not have the effect of uniting large numbers of people. A marriage settlement has the inherent tendency of isolating spouses from their kin.

Bedouin women are not given a marriage settlement. The bride's father is promised a bridewealth (*sahiba*), but he receives only about a quarter of it, after the lapse of about a year. The remainder is left as debt between the parties. These parties, however, are not two individuals, but two groups of people. The total number of people directly involved in contributing to bridewealth and receiving it varies, but can be as high as fifty and is rarely below twenty. This does not take account of the people involved indirectly through their gifts during the nuptial festivities; these usually number no less than a hundred and often very many more. Bridewealth, in contrast to marriage settlement, creates a structure of social relationships, or adds to one already in existence. It is in this context that a woman is placed upon marriage; she not only serves as a means of conjunction between groups, she also mediates the relationships between them. In saying this, it must be stressed that these wives are not merely 'women in between' (M. Strathern 1972), conveyances of sorts. A mediatory position is one that possesses an integrity of its own. In this sense, all Bedouin women achieve political status, whether they marry within their natal corporate group – for a man, if he is to dominate his corporate group, must command the affinal alliances within it – or into another. The mediatory role is the foundation on which the power of women is built. The ambiguous position they occupy in relation to property, coupled with the demands they are able to make on their own and their husbands' kin, permit them to elaborate this structure, and reach political prominence. Clarity in the definition of their legal status, and the isolating effect of marriage settlements, rob the south

Lebanese women of this kind of political opportunity. Spinsters sometimes achieve political importance, but the span of their effectiveness is limited to their competing heirs.

Olive farmers in Tripolitania

Olive farms in Tripolitania (Libya) were owned until 1959 exclusively by Italians. Thereafter, the Italians began to sell their farms until only about a quarter of the 186 farms remained in their possession by 1964. They were bought by Arabs, mostly of Bedouin descent, with the financial contributions of men and women;[22] for the latter, in the pastoral areas of Tripolitania, inherit and transmit rights in animals and landed property.

Olive growing requires little labour, especially now that tractors can plough the strips of land between the lines of trees. Ploughing is carried out about six times a year by those who are conscientious about it. The labour of one man for eighteen days, at most, is needed to complete the annual ploughing required for a farm of medium size. Harvesting takes a little less time. Groundsheets are spread out under the trees, which are then thoroughly shaken. On a few of the farms, the fruit that falls outside the groundsheet is gathered by women. The only other labour is loading the fruit onto hired trucks, which transport it to olive presses on the plantation. Apart from olives and a few almonds, Arabs cultivate no other crops. Italians cultivate vines and press them for wine on the farms; they also have kitchen gardens, near the farmhouse, in which they grow vegetables and flowers. Arabs have pulled up their vines and do not keep kitchen gardens. Both Italians and Arabs keep a few sheep, but the number in a flock does not exceed twenty, so they can be left in the care of young boys without worry.

The participation of women in production is largely a function of economic differentiation. Arabs have essentially reduced the economic diversification introduced by the Italians to one crop. Consequently, Arab women are unnecessary for production purposes on the farms. The only tasks required of them are those that have to be done within the house. Further, the amount of time men devote to farming each year is about a month. The astonishing amount of time in which men are free from farming duties is used to visit the pastoral areas to the south, to attend markets, and to sojourn in Tripoli, where many men have erected tin shacks in the shantytowns on the periphery of the capital. As a result, most men spend very little time on their farms. The prolonged absence of men – and even young boys – from the home heightens the isolation that women on the plantation suffer, and the vicious pye-dogs, which lurk near farmhouses, discourage all but the most resolute callers.

As explained earlier, in the camp life of the semi-desert, women are tolerably free socially and go about unveiled. When they travel from camp to camp, however, they travel with male escort and cover their faces. The norms of behaviour for women among the Arab farmers are similar to those of the semi-desert. That is to say, the change is in the situation, not in the norms. For women who have migrated to the plantation, the camp has shrunk to a single household and freedom is enjoyed only within its confines. In some parts of the plantation, the farmhouses are clustered in fours, although most occur in pairs. There are a few instances of a small group of kin owning a pair or a cluster of farms. Mostly, neighbours are strangers, of tribally heterogeneous origin; and often Italian families are interspersed among them. Only occasionally, therefore, are women permitted to move among the farms in one cluster, and they can rarely move from farm to farm along the roads. Segregation for most women is complete. The retention of norms of behaviour befitting camp life, in conditions that do not require the participation of women in production and where the population is heterogeneous in origin, diminishes the status of women to the point of degradation.

Italian women are much more favourably placed. Their relationships with Arabs of both sexes are either minimal or nil. But they perform diverse tasks, helping their husbands with the hoeing, pruning, and scything the grass that grows between the olive trees (the Italians tend their farms meticulously), pressing grapes, and growing garden produce. They also sew and embroider – household skills the Arab women still have to learn. In family groups they frequently visit their compatriots in the area. They often accompany their husbands to the capital, where they sell their wine, vegetables, meat, and flowers to relatives in business there. On Sundays almost all the Italians go to church, and gather together after the service.

Cultural differences between Arabs and Italians are so obvious that, it might be argued, there is no need to seek further explanations of the difference in status between their women. The importance of culture here is not being minimised: it certainly keeps Arabs and Italians apart socially. But there are differences other than cultural ones, and these have been shown to bear directly on the issue. Indeed, if the beliefs about differences among Italian women are true, they are to be understood not in terms of general Italian Christian culture, but whether women came as immigrants from industrial families in Milan, or from vine-growing villages in Tuscany, or from peasant homes in Sicily, and so on.

Maronite Christian villagers in Lebanon

The impact of emigration on women is another variable that can be introduced in this discussion. The Maronite Christian village of central

Lebanon is situated in an area from which people leave for the United States, Brazil, West Africa, Kuwait, Saudi Arabia, Australia, and other countries. Only in exceptional cases have women emigrated alone. When they emigrate they leave with a family. Many men, however, emigrate alone, some for short periods, some for twenty years or more. There are numerous instances of men marrying locally, begetting children, then leaving them and their wives to go to work in a foreign country, and returning to the village after an absence of one or two decades. Other men find work in countries nearer to Lebanon, and visit their homes for short periods once or twice annually.

Ecologically, this area is broadly similar to the area around the south Lebanese village. There is almost as wide a range of altitude, and the range of crops that can be grown is as great as in the south. Horticulture, however, is no longer the basis of the economy. People still grow vegetables and fruit near their houses, and some of them press their own olive oil and enjoy the freshness and quality of home produce. However, the worth of the land is now in its value as real estate. In the village itself house building sites are very costly. Also, the village is only about eighteen kilometers from the centre of Beirut, and its lands stretch as far west as the suburbs of the city. Recent industrial and other developments on the western boundaries of the village have meant that previously low-priced land now fetches astonishingly high prices, and many people who until the late 1960s enjoyed no more than a tolerable rural standard of living have become wealthy: about half a dozen are said to be dollar millionaires. Differentiation had been present before the boom condition of recent years, but the general social conviviality among the people did much to obscure marked differences in wealth. Contemporarily, differentiation is hardening into stratification, and the social ease in relationships between rich and poor, which gave an added pleasure to life for everyone, is becoming increasingly impeded by class differences. This tendency is exacerbated by occupational differentiation – the village is near enough to Beirut for people to commute to work and, if the number of men and women working there continues to rise, it is possible that the village life will degenerate – it will become more and more like a dormitory. Higher education is accelerating these processes. The educational facilities available locally have long been of an unusually high standard, and a large percentage of the population has benefited from them. In recent years the number of youths entering university, either in Lebanon or the West, has risen sharply, and they are joined now by young women. During the past decade women have found employment in Beirut mainly as shop assistants and as secretaries. Higher education is professionalising them, and providing them with a greater diversity of occupational choice.

Males assert that women were not heirs to property, and males of peasant origin insist that the position is still unchanged. They point out that, until the end of World War I, they had been under Turkish rule, and that the Turks applied Sunni law in matters of inheritance, which, as they misunderstand it, denies women inheritance. The fiction of the transmission of property in the patriline is founded on the superior managerial status of males, not on proprietary rights. The facts are that abundant evidence shows that women did inherit in the past; many current disputes over inheritance originate in the property holdings of aging women or of recently deceased women, and the contemporary status of women, as heirs, is remarkably high. There is no reason for inheritance practices excluding women: they cultivated the plots of land alongside their men, and some older women, at an age when few people of either sex bother to work the land, find it hard to abandon the habit.

In the ordinary course of events, the status of women would have been high. The frequent, and sometimes prolonged, absences of men from their homes makes it higher. While a wife is still young, her husband might emigrate for a few months, a few years, or for a decade or more, and these forms of emigration affect families irrespective of wealth. Women are left at home to manage the affairs of the family entirely on their own, not merely in that they rear the children, prepare food for them, and attend to household chores, but that they budget the family needs, employ men to keep the house in repair, and deal with business matters that arise. The wives of men who do not emigrate are familiar with the same kind of responsibility, because men's occupations take them away from their homes for most of the day, but they require that someone be available there to answer queries. This is particularly necessary for men who work in the building trade, in transport, as taxi drivers, or as masons. Effectively, these wives act as secretaries, and since literacy is almost universal in the population by now, they are highly efficient in performing these duties.

A priori reasoning suggests that, in these circumstances, all women are potentially significant in politics. In fact this is so, and the fact is given public recognition. Several women who for various reasons command a bundle of kinship and affinal connections are acknowledged by both sexes to be of critical importance in configuring political alliances, and to be among the leaders of local political parties. They enter the fray of argument with as much gusto as men. This status is achieved, moreover, without bridewealth or dowry. To assist a young woman in finding a suitable partner, her parents register a valuable piece of land in her name, making her more attractive – it is true – to men who weigh such considerations heavily, but also providing her with an additional asset with which to make a choice. Young women are as analytically perceptive in estimating the worth and the consequences of a match as are young men. At least until 1974 the weaving of the threads of affinity to create the affinal sets was done by both sexes (see E. Peters 1976), but the pattern of the alliances conformed to male business interests. As yet, women are not sufficiently professionalised to determine the pattern of these affinal sets, but many of them represent the knots in the strands, which hold men and women in a set and which give it its durability.

Politically, the status of Christian Lebanese women resembles most that of the Bedouin women, but the political contexts are widely disparate: among the Bedouin, politics is within and between corporate groups, founded on collective ownership of natural resources; among the Christian Lebanese, politics is chiefly the creation of groups, and individual inheritance prevails. Otherwise, they present a contrasting pair: among the Bedouin, marriages are arranged for both spouses, without consulting them, and, once the negotiations have ended, they are summarily instructed to proceed with the nuptials; among the Christian Lebanese young people are permitted a considerable latitude of choice in marriage, and marriage is preceded by courtship, sometimes for a period of years – but, then, unlike the Bedouin, social compatibility is a grave consideration for them.

Concerning choice in marriage and the courtship that precedes it, Muslim Lebanese peasants are akin to the Christians. They differ with regard to political status. Here the Christians are unencumbered by rank, which, until recently, in the Muslim village strongly militated against the peasants' advancing politically. Some Muslim peasants of the south Lebanese village emigrate, but emigration is on a much smaller scale compared with the Christian village, and its rewards in most cases are almost inconsequential. There is far less occupational differentiation in the south Lebanese village than in the Christian one, and consequently women there are not drawn into the same diversity of activities. Finally, although basic literacy was widespread among these Muslim women, the education they received was – until a few years ago – vastly inferior to that provided for the Christian women, and a university education has been beyond their reach. The Muslim women of the Learned Families are taught basic literacy and they are given a Quranic education privately. Privacy characterises their style of living. Like the Sunni Muslims on the olive farms, their labour for horticultural purposes is not required, and in both cases seclusion of women is practised, but with a difference: the Lebanese Muslim women live in a nucleated village, where it is easy for them to meet amongst themselves, and to join congregations of women for ritual purposes; the Muslim women on the olive farms live in an area of dispersed habitations, where most of the inhabitants are immigrant strangers, and where the conditions convert the tolerable seclusion of the Muslim Lebanese women into commiserable segregation.

The styles of life in the four communities are markedly unlike. The nearest in this regard are the two Lebanese communities, but the sophistication of the Christian women gives their lives a qualitatively different texture. In this discussion attention has been drawn to a limited range of problems. Cultural nuances, as seen in the behaviour of women in these four localities, have scarcely been touched upon. The appeal to general cultural traits was discounted at the outset on the grounds that they fail to account for obvious differences. But certain similarities of behaviour exist in all three Muslim communities, which, perhaps, defy sociological analysis. Thus, in each, males and females take their meals separately, households have a male part and a female part, and mothers sleep with daughters and fathers with sons. Perhaps the similarity is only in the form of behaviour and analysis would reveal sociological differences of content, but it is not possible to pursue this major issue here. The subject of differences in the social positions of males and females is a field of study, not a problem. The inclusion of issues raised in this discussion is a matter of personal choice, and is intended mainly to clear the ground for further investigation.

Notes

1 The Sanusi order and the Bedouin

1 The first version of this chapter, entitled *Libyan Kingship*, was read to a seminar at the Center for Middle East Studies, University of Chicago, to which I was invited, in 1968, by the Director, Dr W.R. Polk. I am grateful to him, and to the several anthropologists present at the seminar, for the considerable stimulus I received from them.

2 The Grand Sanusi himself travelled across the Cyrenaican desert through the oases on the 29° N parallel of latitude, along the coast from Tripoli to Benghazi, the plateau area to the south, the desert to the west and south of Tobruk, the western desert of Egypt and the Arabian peninsula. See Evans-Pritchard 1949: 11–19 and Ziadeh 1958: 44–50.

3 I did not see a Bedouin drink alcohol during the twenty seven months I lived among them. Women, particularly the older of them, enjoyed a pinch of snuff occasionally, and men were given to smoking. Young men in love sang their hearts out when out of range of the camps, and at weddings, when there was dancing, also singly it is true, but nevertheless, sinuously voluptuous. At funerals women danced, and on one occasion I saw the head of a lodge stop a death dance. Otherwise the ecstatic dances and the various other exercises associated with certain dervish orders are alien to Bedouin culture. One such dervish visited a camp in which I lived, when we had gathered at a saint's tomb, and put on a show of ecstatic dancing and drum beating, followed by balancing a heavy sword on his eyeball, then thrusting it through his stomach sideways. The Bedouin watched distractedly. Although many authors stress the austerity of the Grand Sanusi's puritanism, Hamilton (1856: 286) writes: 'The Sanusi is represented to us as all that an Arab Saint should be – exact in observances of religion, gay, and a capital shot; he rides a horse of the purest breed, and of great value, dresses magnificently, paints his eyes with khol and his beard with henna'.

There are numerous references to Sanusi behavioural norms either in directives sent as letters by the head of the Order to heads of lodges, or in interviews with one or other of the heads of the Order. Such references can be found in: Duveyrier 1884, especially pp. 1–12; Rinn 1884: ch. 31; Le Chatelier 1887: 12–19 and 257–263; Hassanein Bey 1925: ch. 2; Hachaichi 1912: ch. 3;

Giglio 1932: 13–30; White 1899: 117–20; Bourbon del Monte Santa Maria 1912: 100–135; Adams 1944: 22–40; and Ziadeh 1958: ch. 3.

Sanusi teachings, at least as far as Bedouin are concerned, are summed up by Le Chatelier (1887: 256): 'Cheikh Senoussi est surtout proposé de rendre à l'Islam la pureté littérale des temps primitifs, de faire revivre les grandes lois sociales, morales et religieuses instituées par le Prophète, de les défendre et de les propager'.

4 There are many descriptions of Jaghbub, most of them second hand. Descriptions by travellers who have visited the oasis include: Hassanein Bey, 1925: 61, 68–71 and Forbes 1921: 293–299. Pictures of it, one an aerial photograph of 1930, are to be found in Piccioli 1933: 156–9. In 1926 the Italians sent part of an army (shown in the pictures) to capture the place: 'Alle ore 12 del 7 [February] la occupazione era un fatto compiuto. La bandiera d'Italia, sventolava dalla più alta torre della Città Santa' (p. 161) – and pictures are provided to prove it.

3 The tied and the free

1 I have discussed the matters raised in this chapter with Professor Gluckman, and I wish to record my thanks for the criticisms and suggestions he has made.

2 The majority of references to Marabtin in the literature are to this class. Lévi-Provençal (1953) and Marçais (1953) for example mention only these 'holy men' Marabtin. Some of the remarks made about them by other authors are queer. Dubois (1897) writes that they are men who make a profession of devotion, who go on pilgrimages, and visit universities, and proceeds to claim that 'A cerebral refinement was thus produced . . . which has had surprising results . . . and which gives the categorical lie to the theorists who insist upon the inferiority of the black races' (p. 278). The celebrated traveller, Lyon (1821: 9), divides these 'saints' into two classes: idiots, and rogues who juggle and conjure. Piccioli (1935: ch. 5) gives an embellished account of the doings of men that the Bedouin would speak of as dervishes. Occasionally, a wandering dervish visits the camps and stages a performance, during which he perspires copiously from beating his drum and feigning to pierce his body with a sword – his *baraka*, he claims, protects him from harm, and his sweat is *baraka* exuding from his body which he can transmit to others by contact. The Bedouin are singularly unimpressed by these ecstatic excesses; as far as they are concerned *baraka* is the divine blessing bestowed on man by virtue of his birth and origin, and is made manifest in the good works of its possessors.

3 Cf. de Agostini, 1922–23. From his extensive population survey, the clients of the goodness constituted 3 per cent of the population, and approximately 11 per cent of the client population.

Agostini's survey is used because the Government census (United Kingdom of Libya, 1959) does not categorise the population in this way, and my own census material is not sufficiently extensive to offer a general figure for the number of Marabtin in a total population of 291,000.

4 I heard of these designations when the Bedouin were recalling them for my information, and on one or two occasions when they were used insultingly in hot temper, and in a derogatory sense when ridiculing a client who was also a simpleton.

5 Cf. de Agostini, 1922–23: 31.
6 de Agostini, 1922–23. According to his survey, they constituted 38 per cent of the clients of the fee.
7 I lived with the people of a client tribe of this sort, the Zuwayya. Its territory formed a large triangle, with the powerful water resources and market facilities of Ajadabiya at its apex. Its population numbered nearly 4,000 souls (some of whom lived in the distant oasis of Kufra), and that of its patron tribe, the Magharba, 12,000.
8 de Agostini, 1922–23. The total number he gives for these clients amounts to 16 per cent of the population. My estimate, based on censuses taken from sections of four noble tribes, is substantially lower than this: around 10 per cent for the clients of these sections resided on the plateau sections of their patrons' territory, and the number among the noble tribes of the plateau is higher anyway than among the noble tribes of the semi-desert. Also, included in Agostini's figures are clients resident outside Cyrenaica, and in the oases. But, allowing for these distribution difficulties, my rough estimate of 10 per cent is more realistic for the proportion of small client groups to patron groups in the semi-desert areas.
9 Evans-Pritchard (1949: 53) quoting Agostini's figures, seems to suggest higher figures for what I have called buffer client tribes, but these figures do not represent the number concentrated on a homeland. The Qat'an, for example, are shown to number 5,850; over 1,000 live across the border in Egypt, over 1,000 are distributed among the Magharba tribe in the West, about 1,000 live among the Bara'asa, many hundreds more are dispersed among several other noble tribes, and only a relatively small proportion of them are concentrated. Indeed, many of the Marabtin tribes listed by Evans-Pritchard are not tribes in the sense that they are gathered together on a strip of territory which they regard as their own, but are fragmented groups dispersed widespread throughout the country, knowing of no connections themselves, but brought together by the anthropologist under a common ethnic name.
10 Cf. for example, Savarese 1928: 55–57; Agostini 1922–23: 28–31; Chemali 1916: p. 59–63. All three authorities subscribe to the conquest theory to account for what they speak of as the subjection of the Marabtin to the noble tribes, although their argument rests less on historical fact than its apparent correspondence with contemporary reality, as Agostini admits.
　　Murray (1935: 41) quotes King Idris I, the present King of Libya, as suggesting a Yemenite origin for the Marabtin.
　　Kennett (1925) offers a very fanciful theory. Originally the Marabtin were holy men, exclusively preoccupied with their religious devotions, and using the Sa'adi as herdsmen. The latter became hardened into warriors, as a result of their open air life; their conquests made them rich and they came to be feared by the Marabtin, who were now glad to pay for protection. Later, after long enjoyment of the services of Marabtin, the Sa'adi shed their warlike characteristics, until, in recent times, the distinction between them has almost disappeared. Kennett's theory lacks any plausibility.
11 Ibn Khaldun (1925: 34): ' . . . les familles hilaliennes se précipitèrent sur l'Ifrikia comme une nuée de sauterelles, abîmant et détruisant tout ce qui se trouvait sur leur passage'.

12 Volnay (1805: 73) comments on the use of the term 'westeners' for designating people when he travelled in Egypt at the end of the eighteenth century, and Murray (1935: 275) reports its use in Egypt in modern times to indicate servile status.

13 I recall this happening. A nobleman insisted that a client, who asserted to me that he was of noble lineage, should give his line of descent. After giving the names of four lineal ancestors he hesitated, wondering whether it would be prudent to latch on to the freeborn line at this point; he decided against the move, and went rambling on in a state of evident distress, until I had counted over thirty ancestors, when he threw caution to the winds and linked his line on the Sa'adi, the founding ancestress. The noble tribesman derisively dismissed the client's claims, and pointed out that to arrive at Sa'ada it was necessary to reckon through well-known lines of ancestors.

Even when clients have resided for a long time in a tribal territory and have become noble tribesmen to all intents and purposes, they are still most reticent to make a claim of nobility in the presence of true Sa'adi tribesmen.

14 Fustel de Coulanges (1864) attaches considerable importance to genealogical exclusion in Roman clientage, and argues, like the Cyrenaican Bedouin, that it makes the relationship an enduring one: 'Le fils d'un client, au contraire, si haut qu'il remonte dans sa généalogie, n'arrive jamais qu'à un client ou à un esclave. Il n'a pas de *pater* parmi ses aïeux. De là pour lui un état d'infériorité dont rien ne peut le faire sortir.'

15 Cf. chapter 5.

16 Cf. Ibn Khaldun 1925: 28 ff.

17 Since land is not individually owned, but resides in tribal corporations, there is fixity in the relative positions of names in the genealogy above those which mark off these corporations, but below them reshuffling of names is a continuous process, for it is here that the shifts in the population are comprehended. Cf. chapter 5.

18 I must point out that I heard client origin admitted unashamedly by Sa'adi tribesmen only twice; once by the tribesmen of a famous lineage mentioned on p. 45 and again by men of a politically dominant group of clients on the plateau whose translation was so recent that they could not conceal the fact, even if they wished to do so.

19 In one case I recorded of *sana'* payments, the paying group was, when I worked among its members, wealthy in animals and numerous in membership. The demand for *sana'* was aggressively made and the alternative, of feud, was made clear. Many of the offender's group wanted to withhold payment, but the shaikh thought it prudent to pay a small amount on this occasion once more, because he was standing as a candidate in the parliamentary elections which were about to be held. This payment could only achieve a postponement of hostilities, for the obligation to pay *sana'*, once accepted, is a committal in perpetuity.

20 Savarese (1928: 55–57) – probably the best among Italian authors who have written about clients – stresses their landless state, likening them in this respect, to the clients of ancient Rome.

Fustel de Coulanges (1864: 262) also assesses property as highly significant in his analysis of the ancient Roman client status. See also Glotz (1929: 36), and Declareuil (1927: 38).

21 Human needs are relatively small compared with the large quantities required to maintain a herd of, say, 50 camels, a flock of 300 to 400 sheep and a herd of 100 goats, plus, perhaps, 2 or 3 horses.

22 Fustel de Coulanges (1864: 271–272): 'La propriété de la famille appartient tout entière au chef, qui d'ailleurs en partage la jouissance avec les branches cadettes et même avec les clients.' After pointing out that younger branches had a right to this property, he adds: ' . . . le client ne peut jamais devenir propriétaire. La terre qu'il cultive, il ne l'a qu'en dépôt; s'il meurt, elle fait retour au patron . . .'

23 The Italians invaded Cyrenaica in 1911, and managed to subdue the Bedouin by 1931. Thereafter, they pursued a policy of pacification until they were finally ejected by the joint British and Sanusi forces in 1943.

24 I do not wish to suggest that the Marabtin, as a class, were unpatriotic, and welcomed the Italians for the gains they could win: some of Cyrenaica's most celebrated heroes came from their ranks. It is true, however, that some of them gained materially, and they are aware that Italian rule afforded them new opportunities. For their part, the Italians saw the division between the clients and the nobles as an opening for a wedge to cleave the Bedouin population. De Agostini (1922–23: 31) wrote (probably quite genuinely) of the necessity to eradicate the inequalities in the population: 'Le instituzioni italiane fondate sul concetto della perfetta equaglianza vano a poco a poco cancellando le antiche disparità sociali, e molti nuclei marabutici già sottomessi ebbèro nell'organizazione delle tribù capi propri ed anche rappresentanti al Parlamento Cirenaico.'

25 Many writers on feudalism have emphasised the importance of land and some of their remarks are most pertinent for the present discussion. Maitland (1960: 205) argues that 'landed endowment' confers political liberty, but that if land is distributed wholesale, the result is 'a freedom of movement . . . akin to anarchy'.

   Vinogradoff (1908: 347), also points to the importance of the tie to land. Bloch (1961: ch. 14) gives an excellent analysis of the changes in social relationships brought about by the alienation of land to vassals, reducing the lord to the position of an equal competitor with his vassal for the purchase of land formerly in his patrimony, and concluding with the remark: 'Fealty had become an object of trade.' Ganshof (1952: 140) misquotes the remark but improves on it, thus: 'mise dans le commerce'. He, too, brilliantly illustrates the consequence of altering landed property relations; speaking of vassalage, he says: 'When it became attached to alienable property, however, instead of to property which could be alienated only with great difficulty and which had been simply intended to facilitate the service of the vassal, it virtually ceased to be a personal obligation and became no more than a commodity which might be sold to the highest bidder . . . It lost in consequence all its stability and perhaps even the very reason for its existence.'

26 During the early years of the Italian wars some of the men who were then middle-aged were killed in battle, but, because they arranged for other men of the group, together with women and younger children, to take refuge in Egypt, many of these children, now men in their twenties and thirties, survived. When the group reassembled after World War II, only two of its men were too old for work on the land or with the animals, and even they were sufficiently robust to participate as leaders at political disputes.

27 The group was caught out in this way while I lived there. Five men of another tribal section visited the camp to discuss political problems, but all the men of the camp were away. Later I heard the visitors grumbling about the lack of hospitality, and although the men of the camp smarted under the insult, they had to accept that when several men visit a camp together an animal slaughter is unquestionably called for, whoever they may be.

28 They could not, for example, take the initiative in entertaining a distinguished visitor; indeed, it would be gross insult if a guest permitted precedence to a client; even a client's relative calls on the patron shaikh first. Hospitality in a camp must be seen to be provided by the shaikh although the fare may be provided mainly by his clients.

29 Fustel de Coulanges (1864: 274): ' . . . ses parents, ses clients même lui font cortège et marquent sa puissance.'

30 Cf. p. 41 ff.

31 Cf. p. 49.

32 It is not the place here to enter into a discussion of the content of kinship terms. Generally, in anthropological literature, the concept of kinship has been much abused, and a kind of mystique has been given to consanguinity which is quite unjustified. It would be absurd to argue that kinship has little to do with consanguinity, but it is only one component among many and its significane is no more than contextual; the other aspects of kinship must also be given their full analytical weight. The many meanings which are held together by any particular term have cultural characteristics in common, but it is essential to distil the sociological meaning from each. Earlier writers were aware of this and insisted on the separation. For example, Fustel de Coulanges (1870: 270–271) said that patron, in Latin, was synonymous with pater, and that pater referred to the family chief, who 'présidait au sacrifice, disait la prière, jugeait, gouvernait. [. . .] car ce mot (pater) qui désignait la puissance et non pas la paternité. [. . .] Ses fils, ses frères, ses serviteurs, tous l'appelaient ainsi '.' . . . le *pater* ou *patron* exerce la triple autorité de maître, de magistrat et de prêtre'. Cf. also Smith 1903: 156. The word used for agnates in Cyrenaica is *khut*, a plural which is also used to mean brothers in a consanguineous sense, and which is also used to mean patrilineal relatives, men who share rights in land and who have a claim on the inheritance of mobile property; also people who pay blood money together, people who give unexpectedly generously at funerals, clients, Laff, and followers in general. Conversely, a consanguineous brother who fails in the duties expected of him is said not to be a *khu* (singular of *khut*). Among the Rwala Bedouin the word *khuwa* (derived from *akh*, meaning brother) means tax or tribute and a tribute paying tribe is known as the *akh* of its protectors.

When the word agnate is used, therefore, it is important to bear in mind that it has many meanings, and in this context the shaikh was using what we call a kinship term to speak about property, not consanguinity.

33 The daughter could not significantly affect either form of wealth in her husband's favour because women do not have rights in the natural resources, nor do they inherit.

34 Cf. pp. 42ff.

35 I do not wish to exaggerate this mobility. I mean that patrons are loathe to detach their clients, but I have witnessed it. The patron group was one of the most powerful in the land with relatively vast land resources under its control.

But in 1950, when the first parliamentary elections took place (discounting what went on during Italian rule) the resources of the group were over-extended to meet the heavy costs of electioneering, and at the same time there was a contraction of water supplies due to drought. Usually, if pressure builds up on local resources, the first step taken is to use links with matrilateral relatives in other groups to provide relief supplies for agnates; if this fails to solve the problem, other debt relations are tried. If all else fails, and only then, clients are told to leave. A camp of clients had to leave the powerful patron group in 1950. The patrons were very worried, and with good reason, because their clients joined the opposing candidate's group. A few days before the election I was asked to guess the result. I recorded the voters on the genealogies I had taken of the two groups and saw that, in numbers of agnates, they were very close, with a slight advantage to the opponent. But my records of the clients (like their clusters) were fragmentary at the time. Clearly the issue would be settled by the way clients voted. Some men in our camp insisted that clients were compelled to vote with the patrons to whom they had been tied, but others of them knew that no such provision had been made by the Government. It was decided that one of the men should hasten to Benghazi, the capital, to discuss the matter with a relative in high office. The opponent was defeated.

All the candidates, for the semi-desert areas, were noblemen, in the election of 1950. Clients still did not contribute any candidates for these areas, but if they had ever been political pawns in the past they were no longer in that category.

36 Cf. Mair (1961: 315), whose minimum definition of a patron-client relationship is 'a relationship of dependence not based on kinship, and formally entered into by an act of deliberate choice'.

4 Aspects of the feud

1 The chapter was presented in its first form to a seminar at Manchester University. Modified versions were read at Oxford and Cambridge and at University College London in 1963. In a Manchester seminar, Professor W.J.M. Mackenzie raised issues which led me to reconsider my mode of analysis. Professor Ely Devons read a draft, and offered valuable suggestions. I also wish to thank Professor Gluckman for many profitable discussions.

My interest in the feud stems directly from Evans-Pritchard's work on the institution among the Nuer. I am most grateful to him for his help and encouragement while I was pursuing my researches. Anyone writing on the feud must acknowledge the contribution made to its understanding by Dr. Elizabeth Colson.

2 Evans-Pritchard 1940. The feud might have been present among the Nuer. Exogamy and the other rules of marriage which obtain among them create a dispersion of ties, which superficially appears to militate against a condition of feud. But a dispersal of ties does not mean that they necessarily act as a pressure for peace. Moreover, the exogamous links may link limited numbers of groups only, leaving others with sufficient discreteness to pursue feuding relationships as they are described in this chapter.

3 See chapter 5.

4 Many sections trade fleeces for dates with the folk of distant oases, but the sections do not trade among themselves.

5 I recorded one case of a man who was expelled from his group and the tribes around were warned that the rules of sanctuary were not to apply to him. He is said to have died from grief and hunger. The reason given for such drastic action is that he killed a first cousin in cold blood because of a dispute between them over the ownership of a new-born kid. Although this was the only reason given by the Bedouin other considerations were involved – the victim was said to have been a fine person, and his killer a constant trouble-maker, and so on.

6 See for comparison Robertson Smith 1903. The tent is an area of sanctuary, and this extends to include the ropes also.

7 This statement requires more documentation than I am able to give to it in this chapter, but the descriptive details given hereafter give it some substance. See also Smith 1956.

8 It is necessary to add here that these clients do not assume coercive powers. They are granted the power to curse, but the curse that is feared is the curse of their dead when an oath is given at a saint's tomb. When they know that groups wish to make peace they assist as messengers in bringing people together, but they do not use their power to curse as a pressure.

9 This point becomes clearer when considered in the general context of debt relationship among the Bedouin. Marriage payments, gift exchanges, hospitality, various forms of help, and so on are all aspects, with blood money, of an intricate and fascinating web of debt relationships.

10 See chapter 7.

11 A marriage is not legal unless at least a promise to hand over wealth has been made beforehand. In the case cited the amount promised would be no more than a token – a sheep or a goat.

12 Dr. Paul Bohannan has distinguished in his writings between what he calls folk systems and analytical systems. The distinction, as he sees it, is set out clearly in the statement 'a certain field of Nuer relationships is explained by Nuer in terms of an agnatic genealogy. This is the folk system. The same field is explained, in English, by Professor Evans-Pritchard, as a lineage system based on the principle of segmental opposition. This is an analytical system' (Bohannan 1957: 5). What is the difference? Is it only a difference of language? Bohannan's analytical statement is little more than a generalisation of what is in the folk system. An analytical system, in his hands, is a sophistication of a folk system, for it is the latter which provides him with his analytical framework. The act of creativity on the part of the social anthropologist about which he writes (Bohannan 1963: 14) is the revealing of a folk system through analysis. But he does not depart from the framework set by informants – the agnatic genealogy is the lineage, and the fission and fusion of parts, the opposition of like segments and so on is explained by informants in different languages as adequately as it is explained by social anthropologists in English. Bohannan's viewpoint is made clearer, perhaps, in his discussion on the arrangement of facts relating to Tiv law. Here he considers what he should do once he had elicited all the facts, and he argues against setting them out as an arrangement of the procedural law of Tiv courts because, 'The error would be that the arrangement is not part of *the Tiv way of looking at it*, and hence would be false' (Bohannan 1957: 69. Italics mine). Why? The Tiv are not the social anthropologists. Is the test of an analytical model its consistency with a folk comprehension?

13 Fortes 1945: 30.

14 Smith and Porcher 1864. These two archaeologists met this leader and continued their archaeological researches around Cirene only with his goodwill, although the site is not on the territory of his tribe as I knew it in 1950. They also speak of him as inhabiting a castle which also lies outside the modern territory of his tribe. See also Hamilton 1856.

15 Evans-Pritchard 1949. In this book a brilliant account is given of the development of the Order and how it came to unify and provide centralised political leadership for the tribes.

16 Leach 1961: 6.

5 Proliferation of segments

1 Much of the work I have done on genealogies was included in a thesis presented for the degree of D.Phil. at Oxford University in 1951. The ideas included in this thesis I developed more systematically in a course of lectures on the Bedouin which I gave at Manchester University during the session 1953–4. I subsequently read papers around the problems discussed in this chapter at Oxford and Cambridge Universities. I am grateful to Professor Gluckman for reading this chapter in manuscript, and for the numerous discussions I have had with him on problems relating to lineage organisation.

2 One of these, the 'Ailat Fayid, now only numbers about 150 souls, and although it is given the structural position of a tribe in the genealogy, it scarcely merits this distinction in practice.

3 This part of the discussion is necessarily brief, but further amplification will be found in chapters 2 and 5.

4 I use the word hierarchy here since, although segments of any order display many like features, the orders represent distinct and progressively more embracing interests, and these differences are of such consequence that to consider one order of groups as a facsimile of a superior or inferior order can only lead to confusion. A tertiary group, that is to say, may possess many of the characteristics of a secondary group, but the one is a fundamentally different sort of group from the other. (cf. Smith 1956.)

5 This statement does not apply to the Darsa, and the Hasa tribes, two of the plateau tribes in Cyrenaica. The statements in this chapter are confined almost exclusively to the camel herders of the semi-desert.

6 This, admittedly, is too general a statement to make about such an important issue, but I would prefer to leave its documentation and precision for an article on the analysis of the composition of Bedouin camps.

7 e.g. Burckhardt (1831) speaks of the *khomse*, the five generation group, as very widespread among Arabs. Murray also reports the use of the word *khomsa* among the Arabs of the Sinai desert to designate the blood-vengeance group, but the term used by the Aulad 'Ali tribe, the cousins and Egyptian neighbours of the Cyrenaican Bedouin, he gives as *awlia'-ed-dam* (which simply means 'blood kindred').

8 'It is evident, moreover, that since the minimal lineage consists of four or five actual steps in ascent, there has been telescoping of the agnatic line from the founder of the minimal lineage further up the line of ascent to the founder of the clan, for the founder of the minimal lineage was himself the extremity of another minimal lineage which has, by increase in generations, become the minor

lineage, and so on' (Evans-Pritchard 1940: 199). Since Evans-Pritchard first wrote on the telescoping of genealogies among the Nuer, other anthropologists have discussed the process in various systems. Fortes, Richards, Laura Bohannan, Cunnison, and Mitchell in their writings on the Tallensi, Bemba, the Tiv, the Luapula people and the Yao respectively, are notable examples, reference to which is made in the bibliography. As the mode of manipulation of Bedouin genealogies is marginal to my present problem, the main comparison is not with these works but with Evans-Pritchard's earlier work on the Nuer, because the Bedouin and Nuer lineage system have more in common than either have with the other systems, excepting possibly the Tiv.

9 The prefix *bu* is used by the Bedouin to mean 'son of'.

10 To avoid confusion, it ought to be made clear that this is not ghost marriage. As I understand ghost marriages from Evans-Pritchard's (1951) account, two main conditions must be satisfied: (i) that there should be inherited wealth to make a marriage, and (ii) that the wealth remaining after the ghost marriage has been made is inherited by the ghost children only. In Cyrenaica, wealth thus inherited becomes part of a man's total wealth and is not reserved for a ghost marriage and its issue.

11 It is necessary here to warn the reader that, brilliant an ethnographer as Agostini undoubtedly was, his grouping of tribal sections is not always correct. I had his book (Agostini 1922–3) with me in the field and checked his tribal survey. I found that at several important points his ordering of the segments was incorrect. I should add that the differences between Agostini and myself are not due to the kind of changes discussed in this chapter.

12 Barsha's position is incorrectly given as a sub-group of Haiba; it should be shown as structurally equivalent to Haiba. See also note 11.

13 The situation is not always as simple as this. Cross-cousin marriage may take more than two directions, and marriage within the segment might bring about great complexity, but the argument put forward above is not seriously affected by neglecting these details here.

14 A goat is inferior to a sheep in gift exchanges.

15 The naming of groups within a tertiary segment is an interesting study in itself, but it would be outside the limits of this discussion to make more than a brief mention of it.

7 Debt relationships

1 I wish to thank Miss Laurie Arnold and Mr Paul Nurick for a number of suggestions they made when presenting papers on general problems of gift exchange at post-graduate seminars in Manchester during the 1971–72 session; and Mr Khatir Abu Habib for the many interesting discussions we have had about key Arab concepts relating to debt and sacrifice.

Dr A.F. Heath gave me a copy of his unpublished article, 'Theories of gift exchange'. I am most grateful to him for this.

This chapter includes information which my wife gathered or helped me to gather. I am grateful for this, but I am also grateful to her for shielding me against the pressure to eat excessively at the numerous sacrificial meals we attended, for eating food is not my forte, and eating large quantities distresses me. And she bore the brunt of our debt relationships which, if one is to live successfully among the Bedouin, soon become part of the daily hurly-burly.

2 The use of the word receiver is deliberate. It conveys the meaning of a person receiving with full knowledge of the consequences, whereas a recipient can be quite innocent of any foreknowledge.

3 Accompanied by three young men of our camp, we visited a camp some distance away, where, after we had taken tea it became clear to them that a sacrificial meal was not to be given us, so we all rose to depart. As we were leaving, we could hear some women berating the shaikh for his stinginess, and as we got to the perimeter of the camp, one of them hurried after us to urge my wife to accept a few eggs. The three young men on our way back dubbed the camp 'the egg camp,' and in a short time the news and the nickname had been passed on to many camps over a wide area.

4 Although *bu* means father, when used as the prefix to a name, among the Bedouin, it means 'son of . . .'

5 I have known cases where a father has bought a horse 'for his son', as people might say, speaking in the context of the use of the animal. But in reply to an enquiry from a stranger, they are more likely to refer to it as the father's horse. The latter retains control over it, sometimes disciplines it himself, uses it as he wishes and tethers it outside his own tent. On the father's death, the horse should count as part of his eldest son's inheritance; disputes invariably arise over this, and other like issues, which the eldest son usually wins.

6 Asad 1970: ch. 4: 'Institutional Sources of Domestic Power'. The chapter is critical to the theme of the book, but misses key distinctions in the domestic relationships of kin in his anxiety to corroborate Sahlins' obfuscating notion of generalised reciprocity. The term *haqq* he correctly translates as justice and right (p. 86) only to confuse its meaning a little later by making it almost synonymous with generalised reciprocity. He gets himself into deeper analytic distress when he includes under the umbrella of generalised reciprocity, along with various kin relations, the contractual relationships between a man and his hired herder. The *haqq* throughout this chapter is a right which implies duties and obligations; and the performance of these, in turn, grants rights. Complementarity in relationships must never be confounded with reciprocity as Gouldner (1960) has pointed out in his admirable analysis.

7 The phrase *al-qidr al-wahid* was also given to me. A *qidr*, like *halla*, is a cooking pot, but larger in size. It implies a unit larger than brothers, but I have no evidence of a large group of patrilineal kinsmen holding undivided animal wealth as a single unit.

8 I have in mind here the chief and most recent in a long line of offenders, viz. Sahlins (1965). This passing reference only is made here, because his views are examined towards the end of the chapter.

   I will not be dealing with all forms of kinship with respect to debt relationships. In particular, only reference is made to the mother's brother, for to analyse his position systematically would be beyond the scope of this chapter.

9 The word *wajib* carries strong moral force, but it is not the impelling duty imputed to *fard*, a religious obligation which does not admit compromise, and which, in a gift context, I heard in reference to gifts to God only, e.g. the slaughter at the celebration of the Great Feast.

10 The word *shart* means contract. It also means crack, crevice or slit, and it is used by the Bedouin to refer, in conversational rollicks, to the vagina. In bridewealth negotiations, both senses are included.

11 Both phrases are also used when incorporation into a corporation occurs.

12 The word shaikh has a variety of meanings in Arabic. Here it is used to refer to secular power only.

13 These journeys, if one is determined, can be done in shorter time, but the delays of hospitality normally add many hours to the time taken over a journey.

14 Some men are so deeply indebted to their shaikh that they become pliant and he is able to order them about with impunity.

15 The mind is thought to survive death.

16 This was by no means easy to investigate, largely because the Bedouin, once they had made known the purpose of the sacrifice, were more interested in its meat than in its ritual. I give here an example of the way in which some of my enquiries foundered.

One winter's night we were all gathered in a tent for a sacrificial meal to celebrate the safe return of a flock of sheep which had been lost for a second time in three weeks. After the meal and before the tea and talk, with the determination of a novice bent on getting to the root of the matter, I began pursuing enquiries about the sacrificial act which had provided the meat of the meal we, together with all the men of the camp, had been eating, seated around 'the one bowl'. Later in my fieldwork, I knew better than to make enquiries during this interval: experience taught me that it is the time when men are too preoccupied in dealing with problems of flatulence to bother. Eructing in peal after peal, each man, as he did so, emitted praise to Allah in a *basso profondo* of remarkable rotundity and resonance, assuaging the coarseness usually associated with this bodily function, and giving the phrase a grandeur of sound, which, when otherwise used, falls on the ear with the paucity of a piety. No-one took any heed of my questions, and I became agitated – until the dear elderly Salima, standing her full stature above us like an eucalyptus tree, brushed them aside and began a conversation with my wife, which ran as follows:

> Salima: Oh Stella, does a person do a *fusa* in London yonder? (I apologise for the use of indelicate English in translating *fusa* as noiseless fart, but to use a euphemism would be to lose the smell of the campfires altogether.)
> Stella: No. We have it as *'aib* (shame).
> Salima: Same here. If a little baby does it on your hand it does not matter, of course . . . But Muhammad yonder has been striking the ground with noiseless farts, in his toga, all night.
> Muhammad: I have never farted noiselessly in my life.
> Salima and the men cry out in protest, and collapse convulsed in waves of laughter.
> 'Ali: Oh Muhammad, you must not go to Stella's tent often. She will have to throw too much incense on the fire!
> Salima (to Muhammad): You are striking the ground through your toga now.

More laughter as Muhammad, inclining towards me, in between wheezes of laughter whispered one of his favourite obscenities in my ear, and lost control completely in doing so. I thought it prudent, now, to discontinue my enquiries, and, instead, joined in the ribaldry with gusto.

This was not an isolated incident. After a sacrifice, and after a commensal meal had been taken, the interval before the elaborate tea making began was often given over to some sort of ribaldry (obscenity, I think, is too strong a word to be used here). Commensality, as I have argued in the text, is the manifest liberation of relationships made possible by a sacrifice. Significantly, the first effect is this ribaldry – a marked contrast to behaviour during and before the meal, and usually absent from the talk over tea. Men in company show familiarity before entering upon more serious discussion. Among two or three men, privately, the same conversational exchanges would be obscenity, not ribaldry.

17 Usury is prohibited in Islam, and I saw no evidence of it among the Bedouin, although they were aware that loans with heavy interest were available in the coastal towns. Both in these towns and among Muslims in south Lebanon (where I have worked), the way round the prohibition was to make a loan for a stated period and include the interest in the amount of the loan. Thus, a man borrowing £100 from a usurer at 60 per cent interest would sign a document for a loan of £160. Since usury is prohibited, the interest charged by usurers is usually greatly inflated. The few men who practise usury are despised, and are subject to many jibes. Just as they conceal their usury in the amount of the loan so too jibes can be wrapped up in an idiom which inhibits them from taking retaliatory action. At a funeral I attended in south Lebanon I walked with two men, one of whom was a usurer who, on any religious or ritual occasion, was given to mouthing pearls of piety in a loud voice, ending each with praise to God. The other man was a peasant, with a local renown for his wit. The usurer finished one of his pieties with a saying from the Koran, thus:

> '*al-hamdu li'llahi rabb al-'alamin*', Praise be to God Lord of the Universe, which the peasant turned into a rhymed couplet, adding '*alli yirzigna bi-mi'a sittin*', who enriches us sixty to the hundred.

18 All sacrifices among the camel herding Bedouin are blood sacrifices. They acknowledge that bread can be used for the purpose, and I have evidence for its sacrificial use among the cow and goat herders of the northern plateau area. But in the south, the camel herders insist that the only true sacrifice is one in which blood is spilt. A poor man among them, wishing to perform a sacrifice, is given an animal by a richer relative or his shaikh. The stress on blood is dramatically highlighted in the recounting of an incident in the late nineteen twenties when a group of guerillas under 'Umar al-Mukhtar, hemmed in by the Italians and cut off from their flocks and herds, took a traitor and sacrificed him, exactly as an animal is sacrificed, as an offering to God on the morning of the Great Feast.

19 Many authors (e.g. Burckhardt 1831, Chelhod 1955, Dickson 1949, Doughty 1936, Jaussen 1908, Mueller 1931, Murray 1935, Musil 1928, Smith 1927) report various durations for the sanctuary granted by a meal. Cyrenaican Bedouin gave slightly differing periods for the length of sanctuary conferred by a sacrificial meal. Since I did not get any evidence of this claim on time for sanctuary, and since I am satisfied that it is not a practical issue, I do not wish to give the matter the prominence it has been accorded by other authors.

20 See Hubert and Mauss (1964: 13). Sacrifice 'modifies the condition of the moral person'.

21 Many scholars are agreed that the gift element is strong in sacrifice. Robertson

Smith (1927: 388 ff) considers the gift theory of sacrifice to be inadequate, but admits the element of gift. Grey (1925: 40) writes ' . . . in the course of history the idea of gift in connection with sacrifices strengthened its hold on its domination over other ideas in a variety of ways'. Chelhod (1955: 189), discussing sacrifices given as hospitality, writes: 'L'hospitalité n'est en dernier ressort qu'une forme particulière du don . . . Comme lui, elle met des forces en mouvement. Mais c'est parce que ces forces penêtrent plus intimement en nous, qu'elles produisent une fraternisation temporaire, presque jamais violée, une fusion des élements en presence.' Evans-Pritchard (1956: 276) says: 'Now every Nuer sacrifice is clearly a gift of some sort . . . Moreover a gift is far from a simple idea. It is a symbol which may have many different meanings and shades of meanings.' Pedersen (1940: 322–3) views sacrifice as a gift, which makes (p. 660) and strengthens a covenant (p. 330).

22 Evans-Pritchard (1951: 95), in his cogent criticism of Malinowski's work on the *kula*, says of it: 'There is consequently no real standard of relevance, since everything has a time and space relationship in cultural reality to everything else, and from whatever point one starts one spreads oneself over the same ground . . . Malinowski might have started from chieftainship and described the *kula* in relation to that institution . . .' And, 'It is because he seldom made abstractions that Malinowski failed to see clearly what is perhaps the most significant feature of the *kula*, the bringing together, through the acceptance of common ritual values, of politically autonomous communities.'

23 Malinowski (1922: 94) attributes their removal to the fact that they were 'specially fine' specimens. But since their fineness was the quantity and quality of the social relationships they emblemised, Malinowski was thinking, here, as in so much of his writings, as a Trobriander, and in this role he is very good indeed. This is not to deny that some specimens were of superior craftsmanship, but it is significant that 'only one or two' were of this admirable quality.

24 Several writers have, in recent years, endeavoured to cut the potlatch down to size. Drucker (1967) casts doubt on the vast excesses said to have been involved in the potlatch. Others are tending to take the view that earlier writings about it amount almost to a hoax.

25 Malinowski (1922: 156–194). See also Heath (1969: 5–8), and Sahlins (1965), especially p. 146.

Fortes (1953: 4) finds Malinowski's work commendable on one count: 'When we speak of the "family" or of "sacrifice" we are referring to descriptive not analytical units. But when Malinowski wrote of "reciprocity as the basis of social structure . . .", he was developing isolated concepts.' I will argue later in the chapter that Malinowski was using the term reciprocity in a descriptive sense to refer to many discrete kinds of relationships which he lumped together by their most obvious observable characteristic.

26 Blau (1964) is not the only culprit. Parsons and Shils (1952: 105–107) fail even to distinguish reciprocity from complementarity.

27 Heath, an economist, in both his works cited in the bibliography offers critical appraisals of Blau's work. In his 1972 review article, he says: ' . . . of those of Blau's arguments which I have summarised above, a number seem to be trivial or false while, of the more interesting ones, the majority certainly need more empirical support before they can be accepted and probably need some

modification too' (p. 110). Heath alights, in this quotation, on one of the serious weaknesses in sociological works, viz., empirical inadequacy. Much of the data on exchange and reciprocity is little more than casually observed items of behaviour picked up in the ordinary course of events, or of responses, robbed of any riches, to questionnaires – a technique of investigation which yields data of much mass but little meaning.

28 Burling (1962: 807), with quixotic hebetude, writes: 'Brides are frequently paid for, but because of our ethnocentric view that brides are not an economic commodity anthropologists have resisted the idea that women can be bought and sold, and that it is somehow nicer to speak of "bridewealth" than "bride-price".' He is led to this folly by a desire to isolate some behaviour as economic. Bohannan and Dalton are also concerned to carve behaviour into separate spheres. It is a pleasure to read that Joy (1967: 40–41), a professional economist, argues against this, admitting to 'constraints' on behaviour, but not allowing 'the attempts by some researchers (e.g. Bohannan and Dalton) to distinguish *separate* "spheres" of activity.'

29 Gouldner (1960) refers, in this excellent article, to many of them. Others are to be found in the bibliography.

30 Both A. Strathern (1971) and Young (1971) have collected excellent material on exchange, and focus the analysis of this specifically on problems of leadership. Moreover both explicitly deny that exchange represents the totality of leadership, although, in the analyses of the many problems they treat, such precedence is given to gift exchanges that they come to assume the status of being the main prop of leadership, if not its totality.

31 Heath, in his two articles cited in the bibliography, gives a valuable critical appraisal of Sahlins, along with Malinowski, Firth, Homans, Blau, and selects from their works hypotheses he considers to be useful. There would be little point here in offering a critique of a critique; with many of his criticisms I would agree, but I think his pursuit of Blau's 'self-interest' and 'trust', although they loom large in Blau, is to impute motives which cannot be empirically demonstrated.

8 Family and marriage

1 I wish to express my gratitude to R. Werbner for reading this chapter in manuscript.

2 When Bedouin take their meals, they eat from large wooden bowls imported from south of the Sahara. It is a matter of custom that a man does not eat alone unless it is unavoidable, a custom of such strength, that when one day only an elder, occupying a tent the ropes of which were crossed with mine, was left in camp, he brought his bowl into my tent 'so that I will be eating with a man'.

3 Robertson Smith 1927.

4 A stranger entering a camp is under no obligation to give his identity. Few do so until they have partaken of a meal. In the past, the Bedouin claim, the period of anonymity could last for 40 days, but nowadays they say they limit it to two only. I have known strangers enter a camp, receive entertainment, and leave without offering any specific identity.

5 See, for example, the elaboration of rituals discussed in Gluckman 1962.

6 Bedouin are disposed in groups which, in summer, usually constitute a single community, around or near a watering point. The men of this group are interlinked by reference to an ancestor ascending four or five generations, reckoning from the generation of men of about 20 years. When, elsewhere in this chapter reference is made to corporations, it will be to groups of this kind.

7 A marriage is illegal unless it is accompanied by an agreement to transfer wealth to the girl's father.

8 Impotency is a special case, because it is dishonourable for a woman to remain wife to an impotent man. She cannot divorce him, but her father can insist on a witnessed test of impotency and, if it is proven, the husband is compelled to divorce her. Barrenness, obviously, is a different matter.

9 The Bedouin are Sunni Muslims, and, as Sanusi, belong to the Maliki school in legal matters. According to court law, women are heirs. However, actual Bedouin practice is contrary to law. For if women were permitted to inherit, since many marry outside the corporation into which they were born, they could alienate its resources.

10 I use the word 'bridewealth' because it has become so familiar in the literature, but the only similarity between the *sahiba* of the Bedouin and the bridewealth of many African societies is that wealth is transferred. Obviously, in societies where the rules of exogamy compel a dispersion of links outside a man's own clan, what is involved in this transfer of wealth cannot be sociologically similar to one in which marriage to the first cousin on either side is permitted.

11 This is the general rule. In practice, the use of the divider can indicate an intimacy or distance in relationships most subtly.

12 As a matter of interest, the figure for marriage to the father's brother's daughter is 50 per cent of the figure for parallel cousin marriage in general, but the consequences of these figures are beyond the scope of the present discussion.

13 The remainder is made up of marriages to the daughters of men incorporated into the lineages.

14 There is little point in seeking the lost animals themselves in the first instance. A man travels from camp to camp asking for information, and when he has gathered his clues, he searches a neighbourhood.

9 Bridewealth

1 Leach (1976: 67). Fox (1967: ch. 7) elaborates this view; and, of course, Lévi-Strauss (1949) devotes a stout volume to it. In addition to these three arbitrarily chosen contributors there have been many others.

2 Lewis (1962: 41–43) effectively demolishes this argument.

3 The offenders, with regard to writers on Arabs, are legion. It would be unfair to single out anyone; save for Marx, 1967, it would be difficult to cite anyone who has not used parallel cousin marriage to add a bit of cement to the system. Writers on non-Arab peoples, who peddle this view, are equally numerous.

4 Evans-Pritchard (1940: 225): 'A man may not marry into his clan and, *a fortiori*, into his lineage.'

5 Evans-Pritchard (1951: 30) mentions six categories of kin among whom marriage is prohibited and confirms this on p. 34.

6 Evans-Pritchard (1951: 8). In this context he is discussing *mar*, kin. He includes in this category a person related 'through a third person who is in different ways

related both to himself and the other person'. I assume that when he refers to marriage bars between kin, persons thus indirectly related are included.

7 Evans-Pritchard (1951: 8). I assume that he does not mean that consanguinity can be demonstrated. He adds the rider: 'For all social obligation of a personal kind is defined in terms of kinship.' The kinship he is speaking of here is not of blood, but of idiom, a manner of speaking – a most important point with regard to the view of exogamy I offer.

8 Indeed, a bar can be evoked just to rebuff an undesirable suitor.

9 Evans-Pritchard (1951: 30). He also refers to the ambiguities in the field of kinship.

10 Evans-Pritchard (1951: 27). These 'bulls' are not necessarily real aristocrats, but they are accorded this status when they become bulls.

11 Evans-Pritchard (1951: 9). Here, he gives ethnographic evidence on 'bulls' and the composition of the localities in which they are dominant. See also pp. 16, 23 and 58 for further evidence.

12 Evans-Pritchard (1951: 35, 47). Although rules are not based on locality, they are so composed that marriage is excluded within local units.

13 Evans-Pritchard (1951: 24): ' . . . relationships change from year to year and from season to season inasmuch as Nuer frequently change their place of residence'. On p. 28 he refers to the freedom with which Nuer change their residence and the ease with which they attach themselves to new neighbours.

14 Evans-Pritchard (1951: 2). Village splits are due to rivalries. See also pp. 20, 24 and 28.

15 Evans-Pritchard (1951: 2). This is most notable in larger villages, but it appears to be common.

16 In saying this I am not suggesting that there are no other good accounts: Harris (1962), La Fontaine (1962), and Lewis (1962) are all admirable – a vintage year, in sooth!

17 Fox (1967: 233). ' . . . this kind of thing has been called "the right foreleg of the ox" school of anthropology'. It is just as well that there are some who know the difference between one end and the other.

18 Fyzee (1949: ch. 2) gives a good summary account of formal marriage laws.

19 The Turks (who colonised Cyrenaica until 1913) follow the Hanafi school of Islamic law, and the Sanusi, to whose religious order the Bedouin belonged, follow the Maliki school. The Bedouin were unversed in either.

20 Religious bars also exist, but they are irrelevant since all Bedouin are Sunni Muslims.

21 Epstein (1942: 274). Attempts to reform this law began some time ago.

22 I suspect this results from the use of questionnaires.

23 These people, along with many others, were forced to leave their territories during the wars with the Italians from 1911 to 1931. This group left in the late twenties, returning in 1944.

24 There are so many offenders, in this respect, that it would be absurd to give specific references. The sloppiness of thought implied by the use of the term endogamy to refer to Arab marriage leads to serious errors.

25 This stems from the habit of confusing agnation and patrilineality, I suspect.

26 Witnesses are required by Sunni law, but not by Shiite law, although, in practice, Shiites use them as well.

27 With this mark, the animals are distinguished from those of her father-in-law and husband. If she used her father's or brother's mark, the animals could be claimed by either of them, or if the spouses' fathers had not divided their inheritance then the possibility of ambiguity in the rights to animals is serious. The mother's brother cannot lay claim to the animals either, because his mark, which they bear, is added to that of the husband's. Both marks on the same animal leave little scope to dispute rights to it.

28 The word *hulwan* is used among cow herders in the northern plateau areas, and is known throughout the country. The word *mahr*, common in other Arab countries, is not used among the Bedouin.

29 Since this chapter is not meant to be an analysis of marriage patterns, this statement is given only as a guide. The incidence varies from group to group.

30 There is little point in discussing these rights at length, since so much has been written about them already. Fortes (1962 and 1969: 18–84) gives admirable summaries of the issues involved in these rights – and of issues relating to bridewealth in general.

31 Weaning can be delayed for several years. The Bedouin believe that a long period of breast-feeding produces strong males.

32 Nuer bridewealth is negotiable (Evans-Pritchard 1951: 83). It is also negotiable in many other societies: see Lewis (1962: 39 ff).

33 Most of those who participated in the arguments, which appeared mainly in *Man*, concerning the relation of the amount of bridewealth to marriage stability, were guilty of this kind of gross evaluation of amounts.

34 As a guide for conversion, about six sheep would buy a grown camel, in the market. Nowadays the value of sheep is relatively higher.

35 He has since come to be acknowledged as the shaikh of his corporate group.

36 See chapter 10.

37 I do not, as Khuri (1970: 604) claims, attribute lineage proliferation to parallel cousin marriage: on the contrary, I stress in chapter 5 that lineages split when the relation between the carrying capacity of the resources and the population living off them becomes seriously imbalanced. When a split occurs the seceding groups are composed of cognatic kin, linked partly by parallel cousin marriage, mostly by matrilateral marriages, and their external marriage links assist in the process of severance.

38 Lévi-Strauss (1969) in his massive writings on marriage neglects the data on Arabs almost entirely. Were he to take it into account he would have to revise some of his hypotheses. Goody (1976: 32, 104–110) suggests that the plough and dowry go together, and are spread throughout Eurasia. The other combination suggested is African hoe agriculture and bridewealth. Into which of these combinations do the people who are spread from Morocco to Iran belong, among whom many communities practice some form of bridewealth, and where the plough has long been used? Pitt-Rivers (1977) is one of the few non-Arab specialists to give data on Arabs his serious attention.

10 The status of women

1 I worked for twenty-seven months (between 1948 and 1950) among the Bedouin. This research was made possible by an award made by the Emslie

Horniman Trustees, and by a senior studentship from the Scarborough Committee for Studentships in Oriental Languages and Cultures. The same studentship enabled me to undertake my first research in south Lebanon in 1952-53, when I was given an award by the University of Manchester. This university sponsored my research on the Tripolitanian olive plantation in 1964. The Social Science Research Council sponsored the eighteen months of research I have done in the Lebanese Christian village, between 1969 and 1974. I wish to express my gratitude to all these bodies for making the research possible.

My wife and I worked together in both Cyrenaica and Lebanon. Much of the information I have used in this essay would have been inaccessible to me had I been working alone; she also helped me to correct the bias in statements made to me by males.

An early vision of this chapter was read as a paper at a conference in Athens in 1966 which was sponsored by the Wenner-Gren Foundation, and convened by Dr J. Peristiany. I am grateful to Dr R.P. Werbner for many profitable discussions concerning the issues raised in this article.

2 See Antoun (1968). His analysis is based partly on citations from the Quran, and partly on observations. As he views the matter, the problem is one of accommodating the great tradition to various localities in the Muslim world.

3 Both Evans-Pritchard (1965) and Gluckman (1954) have stressed this defect in discussions of the position of women.

4 Benedict (1967) takes equality to mean an equivalence of rights and duties. Thus, chastity, because it applies to women but not to men, implies inequality to him. Chastity, however, implies a number of things, including the right of a woman to withhold herself sexually from males until she has been married by a man who, thereafter, has strict obligations toward her.

5 When I related that an elderly townsman had married a girl barely thirteen years of age, the Bedouin were disgusted and disinclined to accept the information. One of them claimed that a Muslim would not do this – he knew nothing of infant betrothal, nor of early marriage, in other parts of the Muslim Middle East.

6 It is interesting to note, in this context, that unmarried men discussed matters of sex and their marriage aspirations with my wife because they were too 'shy' to discuss them with me.

7 To give some idea of the amount involved, the cost of a camel varied from about £18 to £25. Nowadays, they cost more than £150.

8 Exchange marriage, the Bedouin know, is illegal. They circumvent the law by giving a promise of bridewealth for both marriages, and by making one of the promises marginally more than the other.

9 Other women may succeed in becoming prominent among women in camp life, but if they achieve political significance recognised by both sexes, it is usually a result of their husbands' rise to power.

10 When a tent is pitched in a camp for the first time, the young men course their horses and fire their rifles over the tent as they gallop past. This they do in honour of the woman of the tent, even though she is not its owner.

11 The Bedouin relate a tale of a man, who, returning to his camp after a long absence, is told of the deaths of various types of kinsmen. He expresses condolences in each case, consistent with the commonly held sentiments about

the different types. Finally he is told that his father has died, to which he replies, 'Praise be to God, my property is free.'

12 See Rosenfeld (1960). He attaches great significance to property as a determinant of male-female relations; indeed his argument is almost reductive. I, too, attach significance to property, but whereas Rosenfeld considers its legal aspect, I view it as a bundle of social relationships caught in a matrix of many others, and, therefore, not meriting the analytical precedence Rosenfeld gives it.

13 This part of the bridewealth is known as *siaq* – the animals that are driven, on the hoof, to the meeting. The number given is usually about four to five.

14 See Rosenfeld (1960). He discusses this as a condition peculiar to women. The word has a number of meanings: annoyed, angry, vexed, put out, sad. It is applied to men and women, but not with the meaning of spirit possession of any kind.

15 I was present at the witnessing of a will when a woman stated she wished her youngest son to inherit her five camels, and all present repeated her statement.

16 See Lewis (1966). In his argument on spirit possession he attaches importance to the fact that when migrants return from towns, they bring back baubles for themselves, while women are deprived of the soap and scent they so desire. They are not 'deprived' of town goods: they have not acquired rights to them, either directly or through claims on men.

17 Marx (1967, 1987) has emphasised the importance of marriage in linking interests, and how it serves as a channel of communication between groups. I agree with him on both counts, but I prefer to give precedence to the mediatory significance it gives to women.

18 See chapter 4, where I discuss the political role of women in relation to the feud.

19 Several authors have referred to people's 'marrying enemies'. But marriages are made with chosen partners. Except in special circumstances, why choose enemies? People, for the most part, marry others with whom they wish to further existing social relationships.

20 See E. Peters (1963), where I give additional information on this village.

21 The population for this group and for the village as a whole varied between summer and winter.

22 Only one man signs the document of sale. Later, when inheritance issues arise, this is bound to cause serious trouble among the contributors to the cost and their heirs.

Bibliography

Acquaviva, S. 1917. *Il Problema Libico e il Senussismo*. Rome: Athenaeum.

Adams, C.C. 1944. The Sanusiya Order. In *Handbook on Cyrenaica*. D.C. Cumming, ed. Cyrenaica: British Military Administration.

Agostini, Enrico de 1922–3. *Le Popolazioni della Cirenaica*. 2 vol. Benghazi: Governo della Cirenaica.

Antoun, R.T. 1968. On the modesty of women in Arab Muslim villages. *American Anthropologist* 70: 671–97.

Arensberg, C.M. 1937. *The Irish Countryman*. London: Macmillan.

Arensberg, C.M. and S.T. Kimball 1940. *Family and Community in Ireland*. Cambridge: Harvard Univ. Press.

Asad, T. 1970. *The Kababish Arabs: Power, Authority and Consent in a Nomadic Tribe*. London: Hurst.

Ashkenazi, T. 1938. *Tribus Sémi-Nomades de la Palestine du Nord*. Paris: Geuthner.

Aswad, B.C. 1971. *Property Control and Social Strategies in Settlers in a Middle Eastern Plain*. Ann Arbor: University of Michigan, Museum of Anthropology.

Ayoub, M.R. 1959. Parallel cousin marriage and endogamy. *Southwestern Journal of Anthropology* 15: 266–75.

Barnes, J.A. 1954. *Politics in a Changing Society*. Cape Town: Oxford Univ. Press.

Barth, F. 1953. *Principles of Social Organization in Southern Kurdistan*. Universitetes Etnografiske Museum, Bulletin. No. 7. Oslo: Jorgensen.

1954. Father's brother's daughter marriage in Kurdistan. *Southwestern Journal of Anthropology* 10: 164–71.

1961. *Nomads of South Persia*. London: Allen and Unwin.

1973. Descent and marriage reconsidered. In *The Character of Kinship*. J. Goody, ed. Cambridge: Cambridge Univ. Press.

Barth, H. 1857. *Travels and Discoveries in North and Central Africa*. London: Longman.

Becker, H. 1956. *Man in Reciprocity*. New York: Praeger.

Behnke, R.H. 1980. *The Herders of Cyrenaica: Ecology, Economy, and Kinship among the Bedouin of Eastern Libya*. Urbana: University of Illinois Press.

Benedict, B. 1967. The equality of the sexes in the Seychelles. In *Social Organization: Essays Presented to Raymond Firth*. M. Freedman, ed. London: Cass.

Blau, P.M. 1962. Operationalizing a conceptual scheme: The universalism – particularism pattern variable. *American Sociological Review* 27: 159–69.
1962. Patterns of choice in interpersonal relationships. *American Sociological Review* 27: 41–55.
1964. *Exchange and Power in Social Life.* New York: Wiley.
Bloch, M. 1961. *Feudal Society.* London: Routledge and Kegan Paul.
Bohannan, L. 1952. A genealogical charter. *Africa* 22: 301–15.
Bohannan, P. 1955. Some principles of exchange and investment among the Tiv. *American Anthropologist* 57: 60–70.
1957. *Justice and Judgment among the Tiv.* London: Oxford Univ. Press.
1963. *Social Anthropology.* New York: Holt, Rinehart and Winston.
Bohannan, P. and G. Dalton, eds. 1962. *Markets in Africa.* Evanston: Northwestern Univ. Press.
Boissevain, J. 1973. Preface. In *Network Analysis: Studies in Human Interaction.* J. Boissevain and J.C. Mitchell, eds. Paris: Mouton.
Bott, E. 1971. *Family and Social Network* (2nd ed.). London: Tavistock.
Bourbon del Monte Santa Maria, G. 1912. *L'Islamismo e la Confraternita dei Senussi.* Citta di Castello: Corpo di Stato Maggiore (Italian Army publication).
Bulmer, R. 1960. Political aspects of the Moka ceremonial exchange system among the Kyaka people of the Western Highlands of New Guinea. *Oceania* 31: 1–13.
Burckhardt, J.L. 1831. *Notes on the Bedouins and Wahabys.* 2 vol. London: Colburn and Bentley.
Burling, R. 1962. Maximisation theories and the study of economic anthropology. *American Anthropologist* 64: 802–21.
Buxton, J. 1958. The Mandari of the Southern Sudan. In *Tribes without Rulers.* J. Middleton and D. Tait, eds. London: Routledge and Kegan Paul.
Campbell, J.K. 1964. *Honour, Family and Patronage.* Oxford: Clarendon Press.
Chapple, E. and C.S. Coon 1942. *Principles of Anthropology.* New York: Holt.
Chelhod, J. 1955. *Le Sacrifice chez les Arabes.* Paris: Presses Universitaires de France.
Chemali, I. 1916. *Gli Abitanti della Tripolitania.* Tripoli: Governo della Tripolitania.
Colson, E. 1962. *The Plateau Tonga of Northern Rhodesia: Social and Religious Studies.* Manchester: Manchester Univ. Press. (See especially 'Social Control and vengeance among the Plateau Tonga of Northern Rhodesia'.)
Cohen, A. 1965. *Arab Border-Villages in Israel: A Study of Continuity and Change in Social Organization.* Manchester: Manchester Univ. Press.
Cohen, P.S. 1968. *Modern Social Theory.* London: Heinemann.
Coon, C.S. 1951. *Caravan: The Story of the Middle East.* New York: Holt.
Coser, L.A. 1969. *Sociological Theory: A Book of Readings* (3rd ed.). London: Macmillan.
Cunnison, I. 1956. Perpetual kinship: a political institution of the Luapula peoples. *Rhodes-Livingstone Journal* 20.
1957. History and genealogies in a conquest state. *American Anthropologist* 59: 20–31.
1966. *Baggara Arabs: Power and the Lineage in a Sudanese Nomad Tribe.* Oxford: Clarendon Press.

Curtiss, S.I. 1902. *Primitive Semitic Religion Today.* London: Hodder and Stoughton.

Dalton, G. 1960. A note of clarification on economic surplus. *American Anthropologist* 62: 483–90.

1961. Economic theory and primitive society. *American Anthropologist* 63: 1–25.

1967. Traditional production in primitive African economies. In *Tribal and Peasant Economies.* G. Dalton, ed. New York: Natural History Press.

Davis, J. 1972. Gifts and the U.K. economy. *Man (N.S.)* 7: 408–29.

Deacon, A.B. 1934. *Malekula: A Vanishing People in the New Hebrides.* C.H. Wedgwood, ed. London: Routledge.

Declareuil, J. 1927. *Rome the Law Giver.* London: Kegan Paul, Trench, Trubner.

Despois, J. 1935. *La Colonisation Italienne en Libye.* Paris: Larose.

Dickson, H.R.P. 1949. *The Arab of the Desert.* London: Allen and Unwin.

Doughty, C.M. 1936. *Travels in Arabia Deserta.* London: Cape.

Drucker, P. 1967. The potlatch. In *Tribal and Peasant Economies.* G. Dalton, ed. New York: Natural History Press.

Dubois, F. 1897. *Timbuctoo the Mysterious.* London: Heinemann.

Dupire, M. 1962. The economy of the nomadic Fulani of Niger (Bororo). In *Markets in Africa.* P. Bohannan and G. Dalton, eds. Evanston: Northwestern Univ. Press.

Durkheim, E. 1933 (1902). *The Division of Labor in Society.* New York: Free Press.

Duveyrier, H. 1884. *La Confrerie Musulmane de Sidi Mohammed ben 'Ali es-Senousi et son Domaine Geographique.* Paris: Societè de Geographie.

Elam, Y. 1979. Nomadism in Ankole as a substitute for rebellion. *Africa* 49: 147–58.

Epstein, L.M. 1942. *Marriage Laws in the Bible and the Talmud.* Cambridge: Harvard Univ. Press.

Evans-Pritchard, E.E. 1931. An alternative term for bride-price. *Man* 31, no. 42.

1934. Social character of bridewealth with special reference to the Azande. *Man* 34, no. 194 (Reprinted 1965 in E.E. Evans-Pritchard *The Position of Women in Primitive Societies and Other Essays in Social Anthropology.* London: Faber and Faber.

1940. *The Nuer.* Oxford: Clarendon Press.

1944. Tribes and their divisions. In *Handbook on Cyrenaica (Part 8).* D.C. Cumming, ed. Cyrenaica: British Military Administration.

1947. Bride-wealth among the Nuer. *African Studies* 6: 81–88.

1949. *The Sanusi of Cyrenaica.* Oxford: Clarendon Press.

1951. *Kinship and Marriage among the Nuer.* Oxford: Clarendon Press.

1951. *Social Anthropology.* London: Cohen and West.

1954. Introduction. In M. Mauss *The Gift.* London: Cohen and West.

1956. *Nuer Religion.* Oxford: Oxford Univ. Press.

1962. *Social Anthropology and Other Essays.* New York: Free Press.

1973. Genesis of a social anthropologist: an autobiographical note. *The New Diffusionist* 3(10): 17–23.

Firth, R. 1929. *Primitive Economies of the New Zealand Maori.* London: Routledge.

1936. *We, the Tikopia: A Sociological Study of Kinship in Primitive Polynesia.* London: Allen and Unwin.

1954. Orientations in economic life. In *The Institutions of Primitive Society.* Oxford: Blackwell.

1967. Themes in economic anthropology. In *Themes in Economic Anthropology*. R. Firth, ed. London: Tavistock.

Firth, Rosemary 1943. *Housekeeping among Malay Peasants*. London: London School of Economics. Monographs on Social Anthropology, No. 7.

Forbes, R. 1921. *The Secret of the Sahara: Kufara*. London: Cassell.

Forde, C.D. 1948. The integration of social anthropological studies. *JRAI* 78: 1–10.

Forde, C.D. and M. Douglas 1967. Primitive economics. In *Tribal and Peasant Economies*. G. Dalton, ed. New York: Natural History Press.

Fortes, M. 1945. *The Dynamics of Clanship among the Tallensi*. London: Oxford Univ. Press.

1949. *The Web of Kinship among the Tallensi*. London: Oxford Univ.Press.

1949. Time and social structure: An Ashanti case study. In *Social Structure: Essays Presented to A.R. Radcliffe-Brown*. M. Fortes, ed. Oxford: Clarendon Press.

1953. Analysis and description in social anthropology. *The Advancement of Science* 10: 190–201.

1953. The structure of unilineal descent groups. *American Anthropologist* 55: 17–41.

1958. Introduction. In *The Developmental Cycle in Domestic Groups*. J. Goody, ed. Cambridge Papers in Social Anthropology, 1. London: Cambridge Univ. Press.

1962. Introduction. In *Marriage in Tribal Societies*. M. Fortes, ed. Cambridge Papers in Social Anthropology, 3. London: Cambridge Univ. Press.

1969. *Kinship and the Social Order*. London: Routledge and Kegan Paul.

Fox, R. 1967. *Kinship and Marriage*. Harmondsworth: Penguin Books.

Freedman, M. 1958. *Lineage Organization in Southeastern China*. London: Athlone Press.

1967. *Rites and Duties of Chinese Marriage*. London: London School of Economics and Political Science. Inaugural lecture.

Fried, M.H. 1957. The classification of corporate unilineal descent groups. *JRAI* 87: 1–30.

Fustel de Coulanges, N.D. 1864. *La Cité antique*. Paris: Hachette.

Fyzee, A.A.A. 1949. *Outline of Muhammadan Law*. London: Oxford Univ. Press.

Ganshof, F.L. 1952. *Feudalism*. London: Longmans Green.

Giglio, C. 1932. *La Confraternita Sanussita dalle sue Origini ad Oggi*. Milan: Antonio.

Glotz, G. 1929. *The Greek City and Its Institutions*. London: Routledge and Kegan Paul.

Gluckman, M. 1950. Kinship and marriage among the Lozi of Northern Rhodesia and the Zulu of Natal. In *African Systems of Kinship and Marriage*. A.R. Radcliffe-Brown and C.D. Forde, eds. London: Oxford Univ. Press.

1954. The nature of African marriage. *The Anti-Slavery Reporter and Aborigines' Friend*.

1955. *Custom and Conflict in Africa*. Oxford: Blackwell.

1955. The peace in the feud. In M. Gluckman *Custom and Conflict in Africa*. Oxford: Blackwell.

1958. *Analysis of a Social Situation in Modern Zululand*. Manchester: Manchester Univ. Press. Rhodes-Livingstone Paper, No. 28.

1965. *Politics, Law and Ritual in Tribal Society.* Oxford: Blackwell.

1965. *The Ideas in Barotse Jurisprudence.* New Haven: Yale Univ. Press.

1967. Introduction. In *The Craft of Social Anthropology,* A.L. Epstein, ed. London: Tavistock.

Gluckman, M. ed. 1962. *Essays on the Ritual of Social Relations.* Manchester: Manchester Univ. Press.

Goody, J. 1959. The mother's brother and the sister's son in West Africa. *JRAI* 89: 61–88.

1962. *Death, Property and the Ancestors.* Palo Alto: Stanford Univ. Press.

1976. *Production and Reproduction.* Cambridge: Cambridge Univ. Press.

Goody, J. ed. 1958. *The Developmental Cycle in Domestic Groups.* Cambridge: Cambridge Univ. Press.

Goody, J. and S.J. Tambiah 1973. *Bridewealth and Dowry.* Cambridge: Cambridge Univ. Press.

Gouldner, A.W. 1960. The norm of reciprocity: A preliminary statement. *American Sociological Review* 25: 161–78.

Granqvist, H. 1931–35. *Marriage Conditions in a Palestinian Village.* 2 vol. Helsingfors: Societas Scientiarum Fennica.

Grey, G.B. 1925. *Sacrifice in the Old Testament.* Oxford: Clarendon Press.

Hachaichi, Muhammad ibn 'Uthman 1912 *Voyage au Pays des Senoussia à travers la Tripolitaine et les Pays Touareg.* Paris: Challamel.

Hamilton, J.H. 1856. *Wanderings in North Africa.* London: Murray.

Harris, G. 1962. Taita bridewealth and affinal relationships. In *Marriage in Tribal Societies.* M. Fortes, ed. London: Cambridge Univ. Press.

Hassanein Bey, A.M. 1925. *The Lost Oases.* London: Thornton Butterworth.

Heath, A.F. 1969. Theories of Gift Exchange. (Cyclostyled article).

1972. Exchange theory. *British Journal of Political Science* 1: 91–119.

Herskovits, M.J. 1952. *Economic Anthropology.* New York: Knopf.

Hobhouse, L.T. 1915. *Morals in Evolution: A Study in Comparative Ethics* (3rd ed.). London: Chapman and Hall.

Homans, G.C. 1961. *Social Behaviour: Its Elementary Forms.* London: Routledge and Kegan Paul.

Hubert, H. and M. Mauss 1964. *Sacrifice: Its Nature and Function.* London: Cohen and West.

Ibn Khaldun, 'Abd al-Rahman 1925. *Histoire des Berbères et des dynasties Musulmanes de l'Afrique Septentrionale* (Transl. de Slane). Paris: Geuthner.

Jaussen, A. 1908. *Coutumes des Arabes au Pays de Moab.* Paris: Adrien-Maisonneuve.

Jochelson, W. 1910–26. *The Yukaghir and the Yukaghirized Tungus.* New York: American Museum of Natural History. Memoirs of the American Museum of Natural History, No. 13.

Johnson, D.L. 1973. *Jabal al-Akhdar, Cyrenaica.* Chicago: University of Chicago. Department of Geography Research Paper, No. 148.

Joy, L. 1967. One economist's view of the relationship between economics and anthropology. In *Themes in Economic Anthropology.* R. Firth, ed. London: Tavistock.

Kennett, A. 1925. *Bedouin Justice.* London: Cambridge Univ. Press.

Khadduri, M. 1963. *Modern Libya: A Study in Political Development.* Baltimore: Johns Hopkins Press.

Khuri, F.I. 1970. Parallel cousin marriage reconsidered: a Middle-Eastern practice that nullifies the effects of marriage on the intensity of family relationships. *Man (N.S.)* 4: 597–618.

Kuper, A. 1983. *Anthropology and Anthropologists: The Modern British School* (2nd ed.). London: Routledge and Kegan Paul.

La Fontaine, J. 1962. Gisu marriage and affinal relations. In *Marriage in Tribal Societies*. M. Fortes, ed. London: Cambridge Univ. Press.

Leach, E.R. 1951. The structural implications of matrilateral cross-cousin marriage. *JRAI* 81: 23–55. Reprinted in Leach 1961.

1954. *Political Systems of Highland Burma*. London: Bell.

1957. Aspects of bridewealth and marriage stability among the Kachin and Lakher. *Man* 57, No. 59.

1961. *Rethinking Anthropology*. London: Athlone Press.

1976. *Culture and Communication*. Cambridge: Cambridge Univ. Press.

Le Chatelier, A. 1887. *Les Confréries Musulmanes du Hedjaz*. Paris: Leroux.

Le Clair, E.E. 1962. Economic theory and economic anthropology. *American Anthropologist* 64: 1179–203.

Leone, E. de 1957–60. *La Colonizzazione dell'Africa del Nord*. 2 vol. Padua: Cedam.

Lévi-Provençal, E. 1953. Marabout. In *Shorter Encyclopedia of Islam*. H.A.R. Gibb and J. Kramers, eds. Leiden: Brill.

Lévi-Strauss, C. 1963. *Structural Anthropology*. New York: Basic Books.

1969. *The Elementary Structures of Kinship*. R. Needham, ed. London: Eyre and Spottiswoode.

Lewis, I.M. 1961. *A Pastoral Democracy: A Study of Pastoralism and Politics among the Northern Somali of the Horn of Africa*. London: Oxford Univ. Press.

1962. *Marriage and the Family in Somaliland*. Kampala: East African Institute of Social Research. East African Studies, No. 15.

1966. Spirit possession and deprivation cults. *Man (N.S.)* 1(8): 307–27.

Libya. Ministry of National Economy 1959. *General Population Census 1954*. Tripoli.

Lux, A. 1972. Gift exchange and income redistribution between Yombe rural wage-earners and their kinsfolk in Western Zaire. *Africa* 42: 173–91.

Lyon, G.F. 1821. *A Narrative of Travels in North Africa*. London: Murray.

Macbeath, A. 1952. *Experiments in Living*. London: Macmillan.

Maher, V. 1974. *Women and Property in Morocco*. Cambridge: Cambridge Univ. Press.

Maine, H.S. 1906. *Ancient Law* (with introduction by Sir Frederick Pollock). New York: Holt.

Mair, L.P. 1961. Clientship in East Africa. *Cahiers d'Études Africaines* 2: 315–25.

Maitland, F.W. 1960. *Domesday Book and Beyond*. London: Collins.

Malinowski, B. 1922. *Argonauts of the Western Pacific*. London: Routledge and Kegan Paul.

1926. *Crime and Custom in Savage Society*. London: Kegan Paul, Trench, Trubner.

1935. *Coral Gardens and their Magic*. London: Allen and Unwin.

Maquet, J.J. 1961. *The Premise of Inequality in Ruanda*. London: Oxford Univ. Press.

Marçais, H. 1953. Ribat. In *Shorter Encyclopedia of Islam*. H.A.R. Gibb and J. Kramers, eds. Leiden: Brill.

Marshall, L. 1961, Sharing, talking and giving: relief of social tensions among !Kung bushmen. *Africa* 31: 231–49.

Marx, E. 1967. *Bedouin of the Negev*. Manchester: Manchester Univ. Press.

1987. Relations between spouses among the Negev Bedouin. *Ethnos* 52: 156–79.

Mauss, M. 1954. *The Gift*. London: Cohen and West.

Mayer, P. 1949. The lineage principle in Gusii society. London: International African Institute. Memorandum 24.

Middleton, J. 1958. The political system of the Lugbara of the Nile-Congo Divide. In *Tribes Without Rulers*. J. Middleton and D. Tait, eds. London: Routledge and Kegan Paul.

Miner, H. 1953. *The Primitive City of Timbuctoo*. Princeton: Princeton Univ. Press.

Mitchell, J.C. 1956. *The Yao Village: A Study in the Social Structure of a Nyasaland Tribe*. Manchester: Manchester Univ. Press.

Moore, W.E. 1955. Labour attitudes toward industrialisation in underdeveloped countries. *American Economic Review* 45: 156–65.

Mueller, V. 1931. *En Syrie avec les Bédouins*. Paris: Leroux.

Muir, D.E. and E.A. Weinstein 1962. The social debt: An investigation of lower-class and middle-class norms of social obligation. *American Sociological Review* 27: 532–39.

Murphy, R.F. and L. Kasdan 1959. The structure of parallel cousin marriage. *American Anthropologist* 61: 17–29.

Murray, G.W. 1935. *Sons of Ishmael: A Study of the Egyptian Bedouin*. London: Routledge.

Musil, A. 1928. *The Manners and Customs of the Rwala Bedouins*. New York: American Geographical Society. Oriental Explorations and Studies, No. 6.

Nash, M. 1961. The social context of economic choice in a small society. *Man* 61, No. 219.

1967. The organization of economic life. In *Tribal and Peasant Economies*. G. Dalton, ed. New York: Natural History Press.

Oberg, K. 1940. The kingdom of Ankole in Uganda. In *African Political Systems*. M. Fortes and E.E. Evans-Pritchard, eds. London: Oxford Univ. Press.

Parsons, T. 1949. The professions and social structure. In T. Parsons *Essays in Sociological Theory*. Glencoe: Free Press.

Parsons, T. and E.A. Shils 1952. *Towards a General Theory of Action*. Cambridge: Harvard Univ. Press.

Patai, R. 1955. Cousin-right in Middle Eastern marriage. *Southwestern Journal of Anthropology* 11: 371–90.

Pedersen, J. 1926–40. *Israel: Its Life and Culture*. 2 vol. London: Oxford Univ. Press.

Peters, E.L. 1951. The Sociology of the Bedouin of Cyrenaica. D. Phil. thesis. Oxford University.

1960. The proliferation of segments in the lineage of the Bedouin of Cyrenaica. *JRAI* 90: 29–53.

1963. Aspects of rank and status among Muslims in a Lebanese village. In *Mediterranean Countrymen*. J. Pitt-Rivers, ed. Paris: Mouton.

1965. Aspects of the family among the Bedouin of Cyrenaica. In *Comparative Family Systems*. M.F. Nimkoff, ed. Boston: Houghton Mifflin.

1976. Aspects of affinity in a Lebanese Maronite village. In *Mediterranean Family Structures*. J.G. Peristiany, ed. London: Cambridge Univ. Press.

1978. The status of women in four Arab communities. In *Women in the Muslim World*. L. Beck and N. Keddie, eds. Cambridge: Harvard Univ. Press.

Peters, S.M. 1952. 'A Study of the Bedouin (Cyrenaican) Bait'. B.Litt. thesis. Oxford University.

Piccioli, A. ed. 1933. *La nuova Italia d'Oltremare: l'Opera del Fascismo nelle Colonie Italiane*. 2 vol. Verona: Mondadori.

1935. *The Magic Gate of the Sahara*. London: Methuen.

Pitt-Rivers, J. 1977. *The Fate of Shechem or the Politics of Sex*. Cambridge: Cambridge Univ. Press.

Polanyi, K., C.M. Arensberg and H.W. Pearson 1957. *Trade and Market in the Early Empires*. Glencoe: Free Press.

Quell, G. *et al*. 1951. *Sin*. London: Black.

Radcliffe-Brown, A.R. 1933. *The Andaman Islanders*. Cambridge: Cambridge Univ. Press.

1952. *Structure and Function in Primitive Society*. London: Cohen and West.

Rinn, L. 1884. *Marabouts et Khouan: Étude sur l'Islam en Algerie*. Algiers: Jourdan.

Robertson Smith. See Smith, W. Robertson.

Rosenfeld., H. 1957. An analysis of marriage and marriage statistics for a Moslem and Christian Arab village. *International Archives of Ethnography* 48(1): 32–62.

1958. Processes of structural change within the Arab village extended family. *American Anthropologist* 60: 1127–1139.

1960. On determinants of the status of Arab village women. *Man* 60: 1–5.

Sahlins, M. 1965. On the sociology of primitive exchange. In *The Relevance of Models for Social Anthropology*. M. Banton, ed. London: Tavistock.

Salim, S.M. 1962. *Marsh Dwellers of the Euphrates Delta*. London: Athlone Press.

Salisbury, R.F. 1962. *From Stone to Steel*. Melbourne: Melbourne Univ. Press.

Saverese, E. 1926. *Le Terre della Cirenaica Secondo la Legislazione Fondiaria Ottomana e le consuetduini della Tribu*. Benghazi: Governo della Cirenaica. Ufficio Studi, serieza, n. 9. Societa 'Arti Grafiche'.

Schapera, I. 1956. *Government and Politics in Tribal Societies*. London: Watts.

Schapera, I. and A.J.H. Godwin 1937. Work and wealth. In *The Bantu-speaking Tribes of South Africa*. I. Schapera, ed. London: Routledge.

Sillani, T. ed. 1932–40. *La Libia in venti anni di Occupazione Italiana*. Rome: La Rassegna Italiana.

Simmel, G. 1950. *The Sociology of Georg Simmel*. K.H. Wolff, ed. Glencoe: Free Press.

Smith, M.G. 1956. Segmentary lineage systems. *JRAI* 86: 39–80.

1962. Exchange and marketing among the Hausa. In *Markets in Africa*. P. Bohannan and G. Dalton, eds. Evanston: Northwestern Univ. Press.

Smith, R.M. and E.A. Porcher 1864. *The History of Recent Discoveries at Cyrene*. London: Day.

Smith, W. Robertson 1903. *Kinship and Marriage in Early Arabia*. S.A. Cook, ed. London: Black.

1927. *Lectures on the Religion of the Semites* (3rd ed.). London: Black.

Southall, A. 1956. *Alur Society*. Cambridge: Cambridge Univ. Press.

Stephenson, C. 1942. *Medieval Feudalism*. Ithaca: Cornell Univ. Press.

Strathern, A. 1971. *The Rope of Moka*. Cambridge: Cambridge Univ. Press.

Strathern, M. 1972. *Women in Between: Female Roles in a Male World*. London: Seminar Press.

Suttles, W. 1960. Affinal ties. Subsistence and prestige among the Coast Salish. *American Anthropologist* 62: 296–305.

Thurnwald, R.C. 1932. *Economics in Primitive Communities*. London: Oxford Univ. Press.

1934. Pigs and currency in Buin. *Oceania* 5: 119–41.

Turner, V.W. 1957. *Schism and Continuity in an African Society*. Manchester: Manchester Univ. Press.

Uberoi, J.P.S. 1962. *Politics of the Kula Ring: An Analysis of the Findings of Bronislaw Malinowski*. Manchester: Manchester Univ. Press.

Van Velsen, J. 1967. The extended-case method and situational analysis. In *The Craft of Social Anthropology* A.L. Epstein, ed. London: Tavistock.

Vinogradoff, P. 1908. *English Society in the Eleventh Century*. Oxford: Clarendon Press.

Volney, C.F. 1805. *Travels through Syria and Egypt* (3rd ed.). London: Robinson.

White, A.S. 1899. *From Sphinx to Oracle*. London: Hurst and Blackett.

Whyte, W.F. 1943. *Street Corner Society*. Chicago: University of Chicago Press.

Wilson, G. and M. 1945. *The Analysis of Social Change*. Cambridge: Cambridge Univ. Press.

Young, M.W. 1971. *Fighting with Food: Leadership, Values and Social Control in a Massim Society*. Cambridge: Cambridge Univ. Press.

Ziadeh, N. 1958. *Sanusiyah*. Leiden: Brill.

Index

adultery, 193–4
affinity (*nasab*), 238
  effect on camp structure, 213
  effect on wealth distribution, 126
  relationships within, 128
  rights associated with, 47, 73–4
agnation, 109
  as basis of property-owning group, 255
  versus cognation, 108–9, 221–2
  as political bond, 158–9
animal slaughter
  occasions for, 140–1, 172–3
  ritual attached to, 175–7
  at wedding festivities, 233–4
  women barred from, 50
  see also sacrifice
animal wealth, 48–54, 97, 120, 128, 166–7, 238

baraka (divine goodness), 26, 64
  of Marabtin bi'l baraka, 40
  of the Sanusi, 14
  of sheep, 36
  of tent, 197
blood money (*diya*), 61, 153–4
  for a client, 54
  payment of, 64–5, 77, 169–71
  for a women, 54, 69
bribery, 179
bridewealth, 214–42 *passim*
  amounts of, 235–6, 252–3
  components of, 226–33
  payment of, 161–2, 256–7
  statement of, 160–1
brothers
  competition between half-brothers, 104
  special position of eldest, 126, 157

camps, composition of, 106, 207–13, 221–2
chastity, 248
children, 202, 204, 246–8
circumcision, 90, 191
cisterns, 60
  ownership of, 49
clients, 40–58 *passim*
  categories of, 40–1
  group movements of, 48, 53
  marriage connections of, 54–5
  seizure of resources by, 45
  status changes of, 45–6
cognates, 75, 103, 109
corporate group (*'amara dam*)
  definition of, 134
  resources of, 129
  see also tertiary tribal section
co-wives, 103–4
cross-cousin marriage, 75, 102–3, 110–11, 223–4

debt, 138–87 *passim*
  in blood money payments, 169–71
  in bridewealth, 161–3
  in feud, 67, 171–2
  importance to shaikh, 122, 166–9
descent, *see* Sa'ada
disputes, 32, 79–80, 104, 108
division of labour, 203–6, 250
drought, 48, 93–4

ecology, 66, 75
  influence on genealogies, 86, 96–8, 135–6
  influence on marriage links, 131–3
economy, 23, 120, 265–6
endogamy, 217, 223–4

Evans-Pritchard, 1, 10–28 *passim*, 88,
    93–5, 115–19, 215–17
exogamy, 74
    in other cultures, 214–17, 241, 285
external marriage, 74–6, 78–9, 131–2

family, 202–3, 206–7
father's brother, 73
father-in-law, 197–8
father-son relationship, 7, 90, 105, 156–7,
    188–98 *passim*, 225–6, 256
Feast of the Flesh (*'aid al-lahm*), 36, 116,
    141
feud (*thar*), 59–83 *passim*, 171–2
freeborn (Hurr), 40–3, 47, 60, 99
    see also Sa'adi
functionalism, 2–3, 6
funerals, 52
    behaviour of kin at, 107

genealogies, 44, 84–111
    female names in, 85
    fusion of names in, 89–93
    in relation to ecology, 86–7, 96–8
    telescoping of names in, 88–9, 92–3
gifts
    exchange theory in other cultures,
        179–83
    occasions for, 172–3
    to shaikhs, 164–5
    see also reciprocity
graft (Laff), 47, 58, 99–100
grain, 130–1
    storage, 63, 120
guest (Daif), 58
    behaviour of, 55, 142–3
guerilla warfare, 116–17, 133–4

harvest, 34–5, 65
herding, 29–30, 86, 120
historical background, 10–20, 44, 82–3,
    112–13
'holy men' (Marabtin bi'l baraka)
    functions of, 40–1, 64
    see also saints
homeland (*watan*), 15, 32, 75, 87, 241
    see also territory
homicide, 61–3, 66–8, 78
    see also killing
horses, 55, 103
    importance for shaikhs, 121–2, 166
hospitality, 138–9, 144–7, 154, 164
hostilities, 32, 37, 51, 63–75 *passim*

incest, 192–3, 218
inheritance, 73, 126–7, 243, 255
Italians, 1–2, 8, 18–20, 26–8, 49, 82–3, 112

killing
    within corporate group, 192–3
    of father, brother, agnate, 76
    of mother's brother, 68–9, 72
    of woman, 69
    see also homicide
kinship, 109, 156–8, 223

leadership, 79–80, 115–17
Lebanese Maronites, 273–6
Lebanese Shiites, 113–14, 262–72 *passim*
lineage
    models, 59, 70–1, 76, 80–1
    in other cultures, 115–16
    proliferation, 111
    segmentary, lineage system, 22, 24, 81,
        114–115, 285

marriage
    links created by, 71–2, 75, 103
    negotiations before, 224–9
    preferential, 102
    women's rights in, 224–9
    see also patrilineal parallel cousin
        marriage
matrilaterality, 72–4, 126, 212–13
    see also affinity
mothers brother, 73, 105, 201–2
movements
    of clients, 51–2, 57–8
    of Sanusi headquarters, 14, 25
    of tribal sections, 30–3, 66

natural resources
    access to through affinity, 240–1
    needs for, 130–1
    ownership of, 47, 99, 125
neighbour (Jar), 58
nobles, *see* freeborn
    Nuer, 1, 88, 93–5, 120, 215–17, 241–2,
        284–5
nuptials
    ceremony, 188–9, 233–5
    cost of, 105
    gifts, 172–3

oases
    and the Sanusi, 11–26
    as source of dates, 75, 103, 132–3
oaths, swearing of, 92, 285

patrilineal parallel cousin marriage, 74,
102–3
affects of, 54–5, 66–7, 126–8
made for gain, 239–40
plurality of relationships in, 220–3,
238–9
patrons, 40–58 *passim*
as owners of land and water, 43–5,
47–9, 99
peace meeting after homicide, 63–4
pilgrimages
to saints' tombs, 16, 37–9, 107–8
ploughing, 34–5, 247, 250, 258, 260–1,
264–5, 269, 272
allocation of land for, 47
population, 57, 87–8, 93–4
power
of shaikhs, 114–137 *passim*
versus authority, 114
products of Bedouin economy, 120, 132–3,
240
property, 48–9, 237–8, 255–6, 260–1
women and, 257

quarrels, 46, 101
between agnates, 55–6

rainfall
causing summer camp break-up, 60, 106
importance for crops, 47, 130–1
variability of, 57, 94
reciprocity
in entertainment, 129, 144–5
in gift-giving, 139–41
inadequate, 150–2
requests for help (*talab*) 34
rites de passage, 191, 247, 251
ritual, paucity of, 22, 191

Sa'ada, descent from, 42–5, 47, 84–5
Sa'adi tribesmen, 42, 45, 47
see also freeborn, nobles
sacrifice, 37–8, 175–8
Abraham's, 175, 178
see also animal slaughter
sacrificial meals, 63, 177–8
saints (Marabtin bi'l baraka)
cult of, 16, 107
tombs of, 16–17, 37–9, 108
see also pilgrimages
sanctuary seeker (Nazil), 58
Sanusi Order, 1–28 *passim*
heads of, 10–11, 14–15, 19–21, 137

lodges of, 11–27, 82
spread of, 11, 21–2, 27–8
segmentary lineage system, 21–3, 84–111
limits to individual power in, 114–15
shaikhs, 112–137 *passim*
categories of, 133–6
trappings of, 120–2, 164
sheep, 29–30, 36
shearing, 35–6
spinsters, 268
status, 40–58 *passim*
change of, 45–6, 49
noble status 42–3
status groups, 99
see also women

tent (*bait*), 35, 55
position in camp, 106, 109–10
killing in, 68
of the shaikh, 120
pitching tent on marriage, 197
rights of husbands and wives in, 253–4
territory, 66, 74–5, 131, 136
see also homeland
tertiary tribal section ('*amara dam*), 61, 87
homeland of, 87–8
splits in, 97–8
see also corporate group
trade
trans-Saharan, 2, 14, 25–7
slave, 25
transhumance, *see* movements
tribes
organisation of, 60
ownership of land, 60
Tripolitanean olive-growing community
Arab women in, 244, 272
Italian women in, 273
use made of sacrificial meal in, 178–9
Turks, 17–19, 112

vegetation, zones of, 29
vengeance (*thar*), 60–1, 63–4
leading to feud, 63–4
vengeance group, 61, 87
virginity test, 189, 196, 248, 259
visits to other camps, 33–4, 129, 144–5,
164

war
inter-tribal, 68, 79–80
Italo-Sanusi, 18, 20, 26, 182–3
World War II, 20, 112

water supply
  allocation in dry season, 47, 125
  importance of, 31–2, 47, 57
  for man and animals, 130
  see also rainfall, wells
wealth
  of clients, 43–45 *passim*
  control by corporate group, 195
  importance to shaikhs, 122, 164–5
inherited wealth in marriage, 91–2
  see also animal wealth
weddings, *see* nuptials
wells, 31

cleaning of, 92, 104–5
competition for, 106
see also cisterns, water supply
women
  claims on men, 124
  as creators of marriage links, 71–2
  as heirs, 124, 243–5, 267–8
  older women 104, 261–2
  as property owners, 34, 124, 157, 255–8
  status of, 243–77
  as widows, 254
  as wives, 253–4

Cambridge Studies in Social and Cultural Anthropology

Editors: JACK GOODY, STEPHEN GUDEMAN, MICHAEL HERZFELD, JONATHAN PARRY

1 The Political Organisation of Unyamwezi
   R. G. ABRAHAMS
2 Buddhism and the Spirit Cults in North-East Thailand*
   S. J. TAMBIAH
3 Kalahari Village Politics: An African Democracy
   ADAM KUPER
4 The Rope of Moka: Big-Men and Ceremonial Exchange in Mount Hagen, New Guinea
   ANDREW STRATHERN
5 The Majangir: Ecology and Society of a Southwest Ethiopian People
   JACK STAUDER
6 Buddhist Monk, Buddhist Layman: A Study of Urban Monastic Organisation in Central Thailand
   JANE BUNNAG
7 Contexts of Kinship: An Essay in the Family Sociology of the Gonja of Northern Ghana
   ESTHER N. GOODY
8 Marriage among a Matrilineal Elite: A Family Study of Ghanaian Civil Servants
   CHRISTINE OPONG
9 Elite Politics in Rural India: Political Stratification and Political Alliances in Western Maharashtra
   ANTHONY T. CARTER
10 Women and Property in Morocco: Their Changing Relation to the Process of Social Stratification in the Middle Atlas
   VANESSA MAHER
11 Rethinking Symbolism
   DAN SPERBER, translated by Alice L. Morton
12 Resources and Population: A Study of the Gurungs of Nepal
   ALAN MACFARLANE
13 Mediterranean Family Structures
   EDITED BY J. G. PERISTIANY
14 Spirits of Protest: Spirit-Mediums and the Articulation of Consensus among the Zezuru of Southern Rhodesia (Zimbabwe)
   PETER FRY
15 World Conqueror and World Renouncer: A Study of Buddhism and Polity in Thailand against a historical background*
   S. J. TAMBIAH
16 Outline of a Theory of Practice*
   PIERRE BOURDIEU, translated by Richard Nice
17 Production and Reproduction: A Comparative Study of the Domestic Domain
   JACK GOODY
18 Perspectives in Marxist Anthropology
   MAURICE GODELIER, translated by Robert Brain
19 The Fate Shechem, or the Politics of Sex: Essays in the Anthropology of the Mediterranean
   JULIAN PITT-RIVERS

20 People of the Zongo: The Transformation of Ethnic Identities in Ghana
    ENID SCHILDKROUT
21 Casting out Anger: Religion among the Taita of Kenya
    GRACE HARRIS
22 Rituals of the Kandyan State
    H. L. SENEVIRATNE
23 Australian Kin Classification
    HAROLD W. SCHEFFLER
24 The Palm and the Pleiades: Initiation and Cosmology in Northwest Amazonia*
    STEPHEN HUGH-JONES
25 Nomads of Southern Siberia: The Pastoral Economies of Tuva
    S. I. VANSHTEIN, translated by Michael Colenso
26 From the Milk River: Spatial and Temporal Processes in Northwest Amazonia*
    CHRISTINE HUGH-JONES
27 Day of Shining Red: An Essay on Understanding Ritual*
    GILBERT LEWIS
28 Hunters, Pastoralists and Ranchers: Reindeer Economies and their Transformations*
    TIM INGOLD
29 The Wood-Carvers of Hong Kong: Craft Production in the World Capitalist Periphery
    EUGENE COOPER
30 Minangkabau Social Formations: Indonesian Peasants and the World Economy
    JOEL S. KAHN
31 Patrons and Partisans: A Study of Two Southern Italian Communes
    CAROLINE WHITE
32 Muslim Society*
    ERNEST GELLNER
33 Why Marry Her? Society and Symbolic Structures
    LUC DE HEUSCH, translated by Janet Lloyd
34 Chinese Ritual and Politics
    EMILY MARTIN AHERN
35 Parenthood Social Reproduction: Fostering and Occupational Roles in West Africa
    ESTHER N. GOODY
36 Dravidian Kinship
    THOMAS R. TRAUTMANN
37 The Anthropological Circle: Symbol Function, History*
    MARC AUGE, translated by Martin Thom
38 Rural Society in Southeast Asia
    KATHLEEN GOUGH
39 The Fish-People: Linguistic Exogamy and Tukanoan Identity in Northwest Amazonia
    JEAN E. JACKSON
40 Karl Marx Collective: Economy, Society and Religion in a Siberian Collective Farm*
    CAROLINE HUMPHREY
41 Ecology and Exchange in the Andes
    edited by DAVID LEHMANN
42 Traders without Trade: Responses to Trade in two Dyula Communities
    ROBERT LAUNAY
43 The Political Economy of West African Agriculture*
    KEITH HART
44 Nomads and the Outside World
    A. M. KHAZANOV, translated by Julia Crookenden
45 Actions, Norms and Representations: Foundations of Anthropological Inquiry*
    LADISLAV HOLY and MILAN STUCHLIK
46 Structural Models in Anthropology*
    PER HAGE and FRANK HARARY
47 Servants of the Goddess; The priests of a South Indian Temple
    C. J. FULLER
48 Oedipus and Job in West African Religion*
    MEYER FORTES

49 The Buddhist saints of the Forest and the Cult of Amulets: A Study in Charisma, Hagiography, Sectarianism, and Millennial Buddhism*
  S. J. TAMBIAH
50 Kinship and Marriage: An Anthropological Perspective (available in paperback/in the USA only)
  ROBIN FOX
51 Individual and Society in Guiana: A Comparative Study of Amerindian Social Organization*
  PETER RIVIERE
52 People and the State: An Anthropology of Planned Development*
  A. F. ROBERTSON
53 Inequality among Brothers; Class and Kinship in South China
  RUBIE S. WATSON
54 On Anthropological Knowledge*
  DAN SPERBER
55 Tales of the Yanomami: Daily Life in the Venezuelan Forest*
  JACQUES LIZOT, translated by Ernest Simon
56 The Making of Great Men: Male Domination and Power among the New Guinea Baruya*
  MAURICE GODELIER, translated by Rupert Swyer
57 Age Class Systems: Social Institutions and Polities Based on Age*
  BERNARDO BERNARDI, translated by David I. Kertzer
58 Strategies and Norms in a Changing Matrilineal Society: Descent, Succession and Inheritance among the Toka of Zambia
  LADISLAV HOLY
59 Native Lords of Quita in the Age of the Incas: The Political Economy of North-Andean Chiefdoms
  FRANK SALOMON
60 Culture and Class in Anthropology and History: A Newfoundland Illustration
  GERALD SIDER
61 From Blessing to Violence: History and Ideology in the Circumcision Ritual of the Merina of Madagascar*
  MAURICE BLOCH
62 The Huli Response to Illness
  STEPHEN FRANKEL
63 Social Inequality in a Northern Portuguese Hamlet: Land, Late Marriage, and Bastardy, 1870–1978
  BRIAN JUAN O'NEILL
64 Cosmologies in the Making: A Generative Approach to Cultural Variation in Inner New Guinea*
  FREDRIK BARTH
65 Kinship and Class in the West Indies: A Genealogical Study of Jamaica and Guyana
  RAYMOND T. SMITH
66 The Making of a Basque Nation
  MARIANNE HEIBERG
67 Cut of Time: History and Evolution in Anthropological Discourse
  NICHOLAS THOMAS
68 Tradition as Truth and Communication
  PASCAL BOYER
69 The Abandoned Narcotic: Kava and Cultural Instability in Malanesia
  RON BRUNTON
70 The Anthropology of Numbers
  THOMAS CRUMP
71 Stealing People's Names: History and Politics in a Sepik River Cosmology
  SIMON J. HARRISON

*Available in paperback